P9-DWE-727

ROADSIDE HISTORY OF
UTAH

ROADSIDE HISTORY OF
UTAH

Cynthia Larsen Bennett

MOUNTAIN PRESS PUBLISHING COMPANY
Missoula, Montana
1999

© 1999 Cynthia Larsen Bennett

Cover painting "Chief Tuba and Jacob Hamblin Near the Crossing of the Fathers on Route to Salt Lake City" by John Jarvis. Copyright The Church of Jesus Christ of Latter-day Saints. Courtesy Museum of Church History and Art, Salt Lake City. Used by permission.

Photographs not otherwise credited are by the author.

Maps by William L. Nelson.

PRINTED IN THE UNITED STATES OF AMERICA

Library of Congress Cataloging-in-Publication Data
Bennett, Cynthia Larsen, 1957–
        Roadside history of Utah / Cynthia Larsen Bennett.
            p.   cm. — (Roadside history)
        Includes bibliographical references (p.   ) and index.
        ISBN 0-87842-383-4 (alk. paper). — ISBN 0-87842-384-2
(pbk.: alk. paper)
            1. Utah—History, Local. 2. Historic sites—Utah—Guide-
books. 3. Utah—Guidebooks. 4. Automobile travel—Utah—
Guidebooks.
        I. Title. II. Series.
        F826.B45 1999
        979.2—dc21   99–10612
                                                                          CIP

Mountain Press Publishing Company
P. O. Box 2399 • Missoula, MT 59806

To my companions in this great adventure:
Keith, Avrina, Nisha, and Alex;
and to my father, Dr. R. Paul Larsen,
who taught me to love the "old roads"

The Great Seal of the State of Utah contains references to Utah's loyalty to the union (the eagle and U.S. flag), as well as references to its early history, e.g., 1847, the year Utah was founded, and the beehive symbol, representing the Mormon credo of industry. —UTAH STATE HISTORICAL SOCIETY

Contents

Acknowledgments

It is impossible to compile a history of Utah without acknowledging the works of previous authors. John W. Van Cott's excellent work *Utah Place Names* was extremely helpful in my initial research of the names of Utah's villages and towns. Upon further research I found many of Van Cott's sources in the county histories published by the Daughters of the Utah Pioneers. Another excellent aid in my initial research, *Utah's History*, edited by Richard D. Poll, Thomas G. Alexander, Eugene E. Campbell, and David E. Miller, provided me with much-needed information on the history of the state. The *Utah History Encyclopedia*, edited by Allan Kent Powell, was irreplaceable during the final editing of my work.

While the excellent books available on Utah history were vital to my research, other sources greatly enhanced the work. The Utah State Historical Society offered a wealth of information in a number of different media, as did the Daughters of the Utah Pioneers in their unpublished histories submitted over the years by their members. The archives of the LDS Church and Utah State University libraries were also very helpful.

The people of Utah, always friendly and helpful, were another great resource. Never was a phone call placed to a remote county without questions answered and names of other knowledgeable people given. Roger Holland in Kanab was especially helpful in providing the photo of the first all-female town council.

I must thank those who took the time to critically read this work, particularly Dr. Stanford Cazier, president emeritus of Utah State University, and A. Dean Larsen at Brigham Youn University. I must expressly thank my father, Dr. R. Paul Larsen, who contributed materially to this book through his input on the trappers and railroads, and through his editing.

Most of all, I must acknowledge the vast richness of this marvelous state, which was a magical destination for me as a child, and again as an adult has drawn me to discover its every backway and village. The beauty of the land and the heroic history of the remarkable people who have created the Utah of today could not be reproduced anywhere in the world.

In discovering this incomparable place, I must finally acknowledge the untiring companionship, first of my husband, Keith, then of my children Avrina, Nisha, and Alex as we have gone on countless adventures over innumerable dirt roads, flying over cattle guards, and experiencing flat tires in the most inconvenient locales. It has all been a fantastic adventure.

Utah Chronology

25,000 B.C. Ancient Lake Bonneville covers much of Utah

15,000 B.C. Lake Bonneville breaks through Red Rock Pass in southern Idaho

10,000 B.C. Ancient desert tribes inhabit Utah

A.D. 400–
A.D. 1300 Fremont and Anasazi groups take over most of Utah

A.D. 1400 Numic-speaking tribes (Shoshone, Utes, Paiutes) infiltrate Utah

1776 Dominguez-Escalante expedition, the first well-documented European exploration of Utah, takes place

1805 December 23—Joseph Smith, founder of the Mormon Church, born in Sharon, Vermont

1820s Fur trade begins in Utah

1830 Mormon Church organized in Fayette, New York

1838 Mormons expelled from Missouri

1839 Mormons establish city in Nauvoo, Illinois

1843 John C. Frémont begins exploration of what would become Utah Territory

1844 June 27—Joseph Smith and his brother Hyrum murdered in Carthage, Illinois; Brigham Young takes over as head of Mormon Church

1846 February—Mormons driven out of Nauvoo

Several migrant parties (including Donner party) cross Utah

1847 July—first Mormon pioneers arrive in Salt Lake Valley

1849 First gold-rush prospectors pass through Utah

1849–50 Parley P. Pratt leads exploration of southern Utah

1850 Utah becomes a territory

1852 Polygamy publicly acknowledged by Mormon Church

1856	Migrating Mormons begin using handcarts
1857	James Buchanan sends U.S. Army to take control of Utah
1861	Brigham Young calls for settlement of Dixie Abraham Lincoln sets aside Uinta Basin as an Indian reservation
1865	Ute subchief Black Hawk declares war on Mormons
1867	Black Hawk declares a truce, though fighting continues until 1872
1869	May 10—Golden Spike ceremony completing the first trans- continental railroad takes place at Promontory Summit
1870	February—Utah women become first in the nation to vote
1880s	U.S. Congress declares "war" on polygamy through legislation
1890	The Wilford Woodruff Manifesto ends polygamy
1893	Salt Lake Temple completed
1896	Utah becomes forty-fifth U.S. state
1904	World's first open-pit copper mine established in Bingham
1905	Indian lands in Uinta Basin opened to homesteading
1911	Nation's first all-female town council elected in Kanab
1919	Zion National Park created
1928	Bryce Canyon National Park created
1950s	Uranium boom in southeastern Utah
1964	Canyonlands National Park created
1971	Arches National Park created Capitol Reef National Park created
1996	Grand Staircase–Escalante National Monument created
2002	Salt Lake City to host Winter Olympic Games

Utah Facts

Founded: 1847

Statehood: January 4, 1896 (forty-fifth)

Named for: Ute Indians

Capital: Salt Lake City

Area: 84,990 square miles

Highest point: King's Peak, Duchesne County: 13,528 feet

Lowest point: Beaver Wash Dam, Utah-Arizona border: 2,200 feet

Population: 2,048,753 (estimated 1997 population)

Climate: Utah has, for the most part, a desert climate. The average annual precipitation is 11.6 inches, most of it snow. The dry eastern valleys receive the least precipitation, with Green River at 6.11 inches per year. The Wasatch Mountains receive the most, with Brighton, Salt Lake County, averaging 43.81 inches. Salt Lake City averages 13.9 inches of precipitation. Temperatures range from 50 degrees below zero in the colder valleys of northeastern Utah to well over 100 degrees in the desert. Salt Lake City has recorded temperatures from 20 degrees below zero to 106 degrees above.

Great Salt Lake: Covers about 1,500 square miles; largest natural lake in western United States

State symbol: Beehive (for industry)

State flower: Sego lily

State grass: Indian ricegrass

State bird: California gull

State tree: Blue spruce

State animal: Rocky Mountain elk

State fish:	Rainbow trout
State fossil:	Allosaurus
State gem:	Topaz
National parks:	Arches National Park
	Bryce Canyon National Park
	Canyonlands National Park
	Capitol Reef National Park
	Zion National Park

National monuments:
        Cedar Breaks National Monument
        Dinosaur National Monument
        Golden Spike National Monument
        Grand Staircase–Escalante National Monument
        Hovenweep National Monument
        Natural Bridges National Monument
        Rainbow Bridge National Monument
        Timpanogos Cave National Monument

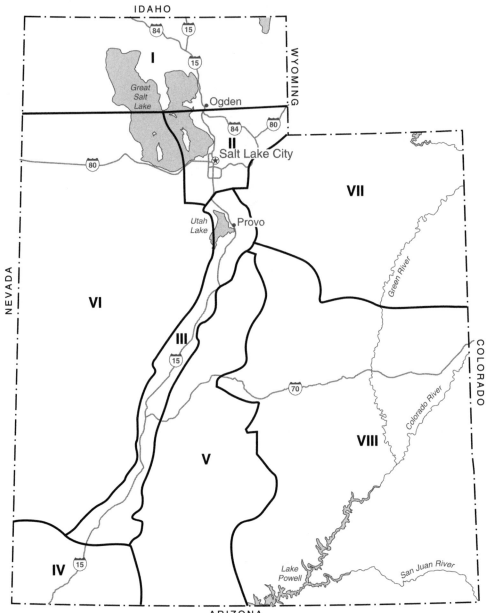

Introduction

Utah is one of the nation's most diverse states—in climate, geography, agricultural diversity, and population density. Its lands are separated by a backbone of interconnected mountain ranges and high plateaus that run southward for over 400 miles, from its Idaho border to the Vermillion Cliffs of the Arizona Strip. The mountain peaks and high countries of this backbone reach elevations of over 12,000 feet and form the geographical features that allow much of the state's heavy snow accumulation, which provides water for farms, families, and factories. These highlands are places of vast forests and summer grazing lands, where great herds of deer, elk, and other wildlife roam. They also provide summer and winter playgrounds for people from all parts of the world.

The Uinta range of northeastern Utah extends like a muscular shoulder from the central spine of the Wasatch Mountains eastward to the Green River gorge near the Wyoming-Colorado border. The Uinta Mountains are the highest in Utah, with several peaks that rise above 13,000 feet. King's Peak, at 13,528 feet, is Utah's highest mountain. Utah's major rivers all rise in the Uinta Mountains. These include the Bear, Weber, and Provo Rivers, which eventually find their way into the Great Salt Lake, and the Strawberry, Duchesne, and Uinta Rivers, which flow into the Green River system.

Northwestern Utah consists of small valleys and lonely mountain clusters interspersed with vast expanses of desert and salt beds around the Great Salt Lake. West-central and southwestern Utah contain mountains, desert valleys, volcanic flows, and red-rock canyons. Southeastern Utah, a mostly inaccessible region of high mountains, deep canyons, and wide deserts known as the Colorado Plateau, includes the mighty gorges of the Green, San Juan, and Colorado Rivers, all of which are captured by Lake

1

Powell before the Colorado continues its journey into the Grand Canyon of Arizona.

Just as the mountain ranges and their adjoining high plateaus have defined the geographical character of the state, agriculture helped build its economic strength for at least the first 100 years following settlement. The first act of the Mormon pioneers upon arriving in the Salt Lake Valley in July 1847 was to divert water from what became known as City Creek onto the parched lands, to soften them for planting cereal grains and potatoes. As the Mormon settlements spread north and south from Salt Lake, people struggled for existence by combatting drought and crickets and preparing the land for the plow. U. P. Hedrick, one of America's foremost horticulturists, wrote in *A History of Horticulture in America to 1860* that

> it is doubtful that in any other state in the Union the growing of fruits, vegetables and flowers made so rapid a progress in so short a time. They were found in every valley from the northern to the southern boundary. When it is remembered that the land is a desert in which the earth yielded nothing without artificial help, one must pay tribute to Brigham Young and those who helped him settle Utah as notable horticultural pioneers.

Water is one of the most important elements in the story of Utah. The Native Americans lived close to the best sources of water, and the Mormons made their settlements at the same waterways. Controlling and taming the water caused the greatest hardship, and lack of water meant starvation. Water was a partial cause for the Indians' resentment of and finally war on the intrusive white man. Water brought sickness, from cholera and dysentery to the debilitating malaria experienced by the early settlers in southwestern Utah. Water was also the mother of some of Utah's most beautiful canyon country, from Flaming Gorge and the canyons of the Green River in the north to the red-rock chasms of the San Juan and Colorado Rivers in the south.

The development of irrigation brought the necessary lifeblood for agricultural expansion and even survival in Utah. Without the digging of canals to move water to land and the building of reservoirs to store melting snow for use during the dry summers, valleys would have remained deserts. Cities and towns would not have progressed without these sources of water, originally developed for farms. The pioneer people had to contol water, their single greatest need, before they could make progress. They jealously sought it and tenaciously held onto it. Some old-timers used to say that far more men were killed over water than over women.

ORGANIZATION OF
ROADSIDE HISTORY OF UTAH

This book has been divided into eight sections that tell the story of Utah's settlement: the North Country; the Salt Lake Area; the Mormon Corridor; Dixie; the Farm Belt; the West Desert; the Uinta Basin; and Canyon Country.

Part One centers primarily on the area north of Salt Lake City where the mountain men trapped, explored, and caroused during the first half of the nineteenth century. They were succeeded by the initial colonization of Mormon and non-Mormon settlers. Then came the railroads: with the meeting of the Central Pacific and Union Pacific at Promontory Summit, north of the Great Salt Lake, they tied the nation together, ending the isolation of the desert kingdom.

Part Two covers the routes the first immigrant parties took into the Salt Lake Valley and the subsequent explorations and settlement of the Salt Lake and Ogden areas by the Mormons and miners.

Part Three explores the "Mormon Corridor," which extends from Salt Lake Valley down the west side of the Wasatch Mountains. Along this route, towns and villages were located approximately one day's journey apart for nearly 300 miles to present-day Dixie. The string of settlements and way stations ensured a safe journey for Mormon travelers between Salt Lake City and California.

Part Four, Dixie, surveys the beautiful southwestern area of Utah with its red rock canyons, its lasting pioneer heritage, and its rapidly expanding retirement communities. The call to settle Dixie—the portion of Utah that comprises present-day Washington County and parts of Kane and Garfield Counties—came from Brigham Young in 1861. The urgent need to spread Mormon settlements farther south into Utah was inspired by many things: Young's insistence that Mormons be self-reliant and not dependent on the rest of the world for their needs, a desire to convert the Indian population to Mormonism, and the anti-Mormon sentiment that prevailed throughout the nation. The larger the Mormon nation, the greater its chances for survival. Young hoped a thriving cotton enterprise would fulfill many of the requirements for self-reliance he felt were so important. Cotton would produce clothing for his people as well as cash crops. Taming Dixie, however, proved to be a hazardous endeavor, filled with hardships and catastrophes not experienced in other areas of Mormon settlement.

Part Five highlights the Forgotten Corridor, the central valleys from Provo Canyon to the Arizona border. Blessed with mountain streams and good soil, farming settlements sprang up and flourished here in Utah's early pioneer history, only to be stifled later by economic depression and lack of modern transportation: the rail and highway systems that developed bypassed the central valley communities. This section follows the old highway US 89, which links a series of small towns, farms, and ranch villages, flanked on both sides by mountain ranges. These connected valleys extend from Thistle in southern Utah County to the Arizona border near Kanab.

Part Six, the West Desert, is laden with tales of pioneers attempting to cross the Great Salt Lake Desert in western Utah. The huge stretch of sand and salt flats challenged all those who wanted a quicker, shorter route to California gold; many of them lost their lives in this barren, unexplored territory. Home to the Pony Express and the Overland Stage Trail, this section of Utah fascinates those who dream of the Wild West. The disconnected West Desert region extends from the salt flats of the Great Salt Lake south for 300 miles to the Pine Valley Mountain country of southern Utah. No major north-south road traverses this wasteland, and only a few east-west roads connect it to the backbone of the state. In spite of its remoteness, its history of ranching, mining, railroading, and military activity (including nuclear testing in the post–World War II era) could fill many volumes.

The great Uinta Basin, described in Part Seven, traverses three states and includes the Uinta Mountains in northeastern Utah. An isolated area rich in dinosaur bones, the basin was separated from the rest of Utah for years by the mountain ranges that bordered it to the north, south, and west. Butch Cassidy and Etta Place hid out at Brown's Park in the far northeastern corner near Dinosaur National Monument and Flaming Gorge National Recreation Area. The history of the basin includes the formation of the Uintah and Ouray Indian Reservation and the negotiations of the great Ute chief Ouray, who traveled to Washington D.C. to speak for his people. Just south of the reservation, oil also played a part in the basin's history, and the industry is still a major employer in the area today. US 40 traverses the Uinta Basin near the ski slopes of Park City. The basin then extends eastward through some of the finest valley and mountain country in Utah.

Part Eight, Canyon Country, explores the large, remote section of southeastern Utah once inhabited by outlaws. More commonly known today for its amazing canyons and its coal, its major points of entry are US 6 from Spanish Fork in Utah County or I-70 from Salina. These highways join and enter Colorado together west of Grand Junction. North-south highways in this area lead to many scenic spots, including Goblin

Valley, Lake Powell National Recreation Area, Natural Bridges National Monument, Dead Horse Point, Arches National Park, Canyonlands National Park, and the new Grand Staircase–Escalante National Monument. This is the land of deep canyons, roaring rivers, and desert spires that reach to the sky. From the long, lazy Green River to the sacred Four Corners, Canyon Country attracts bikers, backpackers, and tourists from all over the world.

An Overview
of Utah's History

The story of human life in Utah begins with the Native Americans who lived here, struggling against the elements for many centuries before their lives were turned upside down by the unstoppable advance of white society. Many millennia before the arrival of the white race, ancient desert tribes roamed much of Utah, gathering nuts, grasses, and insects, and hunting game for survival. Many dwelt in caves around the ancient lake beds.

Fremont Indians displaced the ancient Desert Culture around A.D. 1000. They roamed the mountains and valleys of northern and central Utah, spreading as far west as Nevada and east into Colorado. Fremont tribes often farmed to supplement their gleanings from the land. The Anasazi, or Ancient Ones in the Navajo language, lived in the Four Corners area and the San Juan drainage basin from about the time of Christ to approximately A.D. 1300. (This is the same group that built the ancient cliff dwellings at Hovenweep in San Juan County and at Mesa Verde in Colorado.) The Fremont Indians lived in the area to the north and northwest of the Anasazi from about A.D. 400—1300. Fremont and Anasazi groups were pushed out of the region by Numic-speaking peoples around A.D. 1400–1500. They were followed by the Ute, Goshute, Paiute, Shoshone, and later, the Navajo. Very few Navajos lived in Utah at the time of the pioneers' arrival.

As the Spanish moved north from Mexico, some traveled as far as Colorado and Utah. The best-documented European exploration of Utah was the Dominguez-Escalante expedition: a group of Franciscan monks who, in 1776, searched for an overland route from Santa Fe, New Mexico, to their new missions in Alta, California. Athanasio Dominguez was the group's leader, but Silvestre Velez de Escalante kept the journal, so his name is more familiar in modern-day Utah.

6

The party originally planned to set out on July 4, 1776, but was delayed several weeks by illness and other hardships. They traveled north from Santa Fe, keeping mainly in Colorado until they entered Utah, crossing the Green River near the present site of Jensen in Uintah County. They journeyed west along the Duchesne River and then down Spanish Fork Canyon into Utah Valley. Heading south, the weary group searched for a likely place to turn west to California. Unsuccessful, they veered southwest until they reached a point south of St. George where they turned east and returned to New Mexico. Anxious to reach home before winter, Dominguez and his assortment of monks and Indian guides traveled through the rugged slickrock country of southern Utah in search of a suitable spot to cross the Colorado River. Finally, in October 1776, the group of travel-worn Spanish monks carved steps in the canyon wall of the Colorado River at a point about three miles north of the present Utah-Arizona border. The site, known as "The Crossing of the Fathers," is now buried under the waters of Padre Bay in Lake Powell.

The Spanish monks of the eighteenth century sought converts for Christ. The next group of nonnatives sought something more basic: wealth. Trappers started working the mountain streams of Utah in the years 1824–25. The fur traders were the first to explore the mountain passes and paths leading into Utah's valleys. Some later served as guides for the permanent settlers.

By the early 1840s the beaver was nearly extinct and silk had replaced beaver as the fashionable fabric for men's hats. When the Mormon pioneers arrived, the only remaining trappers' outposts were Fort Bridger in Wyoming and Fort Buenaventura at the site of present-day Ogden.

In the 1830s and 1840s, government surveyors started exploring the country around the Great Salt Lake. They made valuable maps and guides that would prove indispensable as tools for coming home seekers. The Bonneville expedition of 1833 was responsible for the initial mapping of the Great Salt Lake. Captain B. L. E. Bonneville traveled north while some of his men went to document the lake; still, he gave his name to the great salty body of water he had never seen. The name was changed, but Bonneville is still familiar to Utahans as the name of an ancient, now-extinct lake that preceded the Great Salt Lake and covered much of Utah west of the Wasatch Mountains.

Ancient Lake Bonneville, the ancestor of the Great Salt Lake, made a prominent and lasting mark on much of Utah's landscape. At its height, Lake Bonneville covered approximately 19,750 square miles. Great basins, some still containing water, are remnants of the old lake bed. The shorelines of the extinct lake are evident in the foothills all along the mountains surrounding its vast basin. After the lake broke through Red Rock Canyon in southern Idaho and flowed into the Snake River, it gradually receded to its current level.

The Great Salt Lake covers about 1,500 square miles and is the largest natural lake in the western United States. John C. Frémont, who made several trips to the area, gave the name Great Basin to the Great Salt Lake's drainage area. Frémont was instrumental in mapping out a good deal of the West so permanent settlers would have detailed maps to follow in their westward treks.

In September 1843, Frémont and his men tried to approach the Great Salt Lake from the marshy mouth of the Bear River but couldn't get a good view because of the abundance of willows and reeds. They did enjoy the wildfowl they were able to harvest.

The great explorer received his first good view of the Great Salt Lake on September 5, 1843, from a point on Little Mountain. Frémont, quoted below in *Utah's History*, was awed by the sight.

> Immediately unfolding at our feet beheld the object of our anxious search—the waters of the Inland Sea, stretching in still and solitary grandeur far beyond the limit of our vision. . . . It was one of the great points of the exploration. . . . I am doubtful if the followers of Balboa felt more enthusiasm when . . . they saw for the first time the great Western Ocean.

Frémont was the first person to analyze the salt content of the Great Salt Lake. He boiled five gallons of water over his fire to make fourteen

John C. Frémont.
—UTAH STATE
HISTORICAL SOCIETY

pints of fine salt. He was also the first to calculate altitude in the area, figuring the Great Salt Lake to be 4,200 feet above sea level. This calculation has proven to be accurate.

Close on the heels of the explorers came immigrant parties eager to claim newly discovered territories. With their eyes fixed on the West Coast, these early groups were not interested in Utah. But to get there they had to cross Utah's desert. The Bartleson-Bidwell company were the first known to have crossed Utah. Having split with the rest of their group in 1841 at Soda Springs, Idaho, they traveled through Cache Valley, followed the Bear River to the Great Salt Lake, skirted the lake to the north, and entered Nevada about halfway between present-day Lucin and Wendover. The company included one woman and her infant daughter, believed to be the first white females to cross Nevada and Utah. In 1846, other migrating parties, among them the Donner party, traversed the Great Salt Lake Desert.

THE MORMONS

No story of Utah is complete without an understanding of Mormon history and the Mormons' quest to settle Zion—their promised land. It was the Mormons who most affected Utah's population and left a permanent mark on its valleys, rivers, and canyons. The group-oriented Mormons, because of conflicts with neighbors who did not approve of their religion or their lifestyle, were forced to move farther and farther west—from New York to Ohio and Missouri, then to Nauvoo, Illinois, which they left in 1846. After a one-year sojourn in the Missouri River valley, their search for peace and security continued. On July 24, 1847, a vanguard of Mormons led by Brigham Young entered the Salt Lake Valley. In the years to come, thousands would follow along the Mormon Trail in a hard-fought migration that eventually populated and settled Utah as the state we know today.

The Origin of the Church
Joseph Smith

Joseph Smith Jr. never lived in Utah, though he did envision a place in the mountain west where his people would be free from the persecution that culminated in his own martyrdom. Born on December 23, 1805, in Sharon, Vermont, Smith was the third of nine children born to Joseph and Lucy Mack Smith. When Smith was a young boy, his father moved the family west to Palmyra, New York, where they continued struggling with the difficulties of farm life.

Joseph Smith.
—UTAH STATE
HISTORICAL SOCIETY

Because of the relative poverty of his family and the need for as much help on the farm as possible, Smith received little formal schooling. Nevertheless, he was a deep-thinking young man who sought religious understanding by studying the Bible and attending various churches in his area. At age fourteen, while continuing his search for the "true church," Smith reported to the people in his village that he had seen a vision. In answer to his prayers, God the Father and His son Jesus Christ had visited him and told him not to join any church. Smith immediately became the butt of many jokes. When, three years later, he announced that he had been visited by an angel who revealed the location of ancient records written on gold plates, the persecution became more severe.

Smith moved for a time to Pennsylvania, where he met and married Emma Hale. Still persecuted, he and his bride were forced to move between New York and Pennsylvania a number of times while he translated the writings on the gold plates into the Book of Mormon. In 1830 Smith and five other men established the Church of Christ at Fayette, New York, based on Christian principles and continuing revelation from God. (At the time of its organization, the Mormon Church was known as the Church of Christ. For a number of years thereafter it was alternately known by that name, the Church of Jesus Christ, and the Church of the Latter-day Saints. In 1838 the name officially became the Church of Jesus Christ of Latter-day Saints and has remained so. The term *Mormon* comes from the Book of Mormon, considered scripture by members of the church. Hereafter in this book the church may be referred to as the LDS Church, the Mormon Church, or simply the church.)

When persecution toward the rapidly growing church became extreme, Smith and his followers moved from New York to Ohio then to Missouri. After many moves within Missouri and finally an expulsion order from Missouri governor Liliburn Boggs, the destitute group fled east across the Mississippi River to Illinois during the winter of 1838–39. In Illinois they found peace for a time, building their shining city by the river, "Nauvoo the Beautiful."

The respite in Illinois was brief, however. Hatred of the clannish Mormons, and particularly for their prophet, increased until Smith's final incarceration in Carthage, Illinois, in 1844. On June 27 a mob attacked the jail, murdering Joseph Smith and his brother Hyrum, and seriously wounding future church president John Taylor.

Though the church's opponents hoped his death would end the teachings of the prophet, it immortalized them. Among the philosophies that endured and flourished after the Mormons arrived in Utah were the importance of the temple, plural marriage, and a church government based on a prophet and twelve apostles. Smith's idea for centralized city planning—small city lots where all could live close together and farm outside of town—has clearly left its stamp on the small communities of Utah. Smith also initiated the great missionary efforts of church members, a practice that continues today throughout the world.

Though Smith died more than two years before any of his followers entered the Great Salt Lake Valley, they carried his teachings with them. Smith's doctrines continue to influence the lives of Mormons today, but it was Brigham Young who proved to be the most influential figure in the history of Utah and Mormonism.

Brigham Young

Upon Smith's death, Brigham Young, president of the Quorum of the Twelve Apostles, the church's highest governing body, became the leader of the LDS Church. Young, one of the most powerful men ever to lead a migration, and, indeed, one of the most significant in the history of the United States, did not come from an important, rich, or even well-educated family.

Young came into the world on June 1, 1801, in Whitingham, Vermont, the ninth child of John and Abigail Young. Like Joseph Smith, Young was born to parents of little means. In 1832 Young was baptized into the Church of Jesus Christ.

*Brigham Young
circa 1850.*
—UTAH STATE
HISTORICAL SOCIETY

Young was particularly faithful and devoted to the doctrines and principles of his new religion. Even while working as a carpenter and taking care of a wife dying of tuberculosis, he dedicated himself to the work of the church. He was appointed to the Quorum of the Twelve Apostles in 1835. When many other church leaders fell away either temporarily or permanently, Young remained faithful and extremely loyal and obedient to Joseph Smith. In 1844, after the martyrdom of the prophet, he assumed the role of leader of the church.

Because of persistent and overwhelming persecution, the Mormons were forced to leave Nauvoo, Illinois, in 1846. In 1847 Brigham Young led the Mormon exodus to the valley of the Great Salt Lake.

Young continued to direct and advise all Utah's Mormon settlements throughout his life. Few decisions were made without his approval. Most counties and towns in Utah were established under his guidance. Parts of Idaho, Arizona, and Nevada were also settled as Mormon communities under the direction of Brigham Young.

Much has been made of Young's polygamy. He married fifty-five women and fathered a total of fifty-seven children with sixteen of them. Most of his wives were wives in name only and believed they were bound eternally to Young whether they lived with him or not.

Cartoon from Puck *in September 1877, after the death of Brigham Young.* —UTAH STATE HISTORICAL SOCIETY

Young died in Salt Lake City on August 29, 1877, at the age of seventy-six.

The Great Exodus

After Joseph Smith was killed, church members hurried to finish their temple in Nauvoo. They knew the time was approaching when they must flee or perish, but were desperate to fulfill a spiritual commitment to complete vital work on the temple. The temple was ready for use in December 1845. Three months later, mobs forced the Saints—as Mormons sometimes call themselves—to abandon Nauvoo. In February 1846, 3,000 miserably poor, faithful Mormons fled Nauvoo in search of a refuge in the West. Other thousands would follow in subsequent months. Temperatures were so bitterly cold that some groups were able to cross the Mississippi on ice. With horses and oxen pulling wagons loaded with all their provisions and possessions, the pioneers slogged through the mud, snows, and rains of Iowa. By late spring, much of the group had reached Nebraska, where they set up camp near Council Bluffs. This first portion of the trek took longer to complete than the subsequent push to Utah: 131 days to cross Iowa versus 111 to travel from Winter Quarters, Nebraska, to the valley of the Great Salt Lake.

While the Mormons mucked their way across Iowa, tensions between the United States and Mexico built until war erupted in May 1846. President James K. Polk, who had previously ignored all Mormon requests for aid, now decided to enlist Mormons as a way to benefit both himself and them. Brigham Young also viewed induction as an opportunity to gain the funds he so desperately needed for the pilgrimage west. With the president's promise that Mormons would be able to camp on government land for the next year, Young enlisted 549 of his men to fight in the Mexican War. Some eighty women and children accompanied the men, most of the women serving as laundresses for the company. The Mormon Battalion, as it came to be known, departed from Winter Quarters in July 1846. Though this large group had been important in the initial pioneer trek, the $21,000 the church received in advance pay for the battalion was even more valuable. The church eventually received well over $50,000 for the service—funds used to purchase provisions for the westward move.

Part of the Mormon Battalion became ill on the march to California. Along with most of the women and children traveling with them, the sick soldiers wintered in Pueblo, Colorado, then joined the Mormon immigrants the next year in the Salt Lake Valley. The rest went on to California, where they served as occupation troops. Most of this contingent

A group of Utah-bound emigrants along the Mormon Trail in the 1860s.
—UTAH STATE HISTORICAL SOCIETY

William Clayton was an instrumental member of the vanguard company of pioneers to enter the Salt Lake Valley.
—UTAH STATE HISTORICAL SOCIETY

traveled to Utah in October and November 1847 while some stayed in California to work for the winter. Six troops participated in an event that shook the nation: the discovery of gold on January 24, 1848.

Those who stayed behind on the plains of Nebraska endured a long year of preparation filled with cold, hunger, sickness, and, for some, death. By spring many were anxious to depart. The first company of Mormon emigrants bound for the Great Basin left Winter Quarters on April 5, 1847. Among this group was William Clayton, a close associate of Joseph Smith. Clayton helped invent the roadometer that measured distance along the trail and later wrote the widely utilized *The Latter-day Saint's Emigrants' Guide*. Clayton also penned the words to "Come, Come, Ye Saints," the most famous of all Mormon hymns.

Though long and difficult, the journey went fairly well for the group until it reached the Bear River in Wyoming, where Brigham Young fell ill with Rocky Mountain spotted fever. Unable to move, he sent an advance party to find the best route into the Salt Lake Valley. Members of the party investigated Weber Canyon but rejected it. They located the trail cleared by the Donner party the previous year and followed it to the top of Big Mountain. On July 21, Orson Pratt and Erastus Snow entered the Salt Lake Valley and explored parts of it before returning that night to camp. The first wagons moved into the valley on July 22, using the

Donner trail. To avoid the section that crested Donner Hill, the group cut a new route around the north end of the rise. This one-mile section was the only new trail the Mormons had to build. The main party, including Young, entered the valley on July 24, 1847.

Several other companies of Mormons arrived in the valley that fall, bringing the number of pioneers that wintered there to about 4,000. Estimates put the number of Mormons immigrating to Utah over the next forty years at 80,000, including 6,000 who died along the way.

Because of the great expense of purchasing teams and wagons, the migrants began to use handcarts in 1856. Most of the handcart companies traveled from Iowa to Utah between 1856 and 1860. During this period, nearly 3,000 people made the long walk pulling their belongings in wooden carts.

Hosea Stout, an early pioneer and diarist, recorded the arrival of the first groups of handcart companies in the Salt Lake Valley on September 26, 1856:

> To day the Hand Cart Company of saints arrived under the direction of E. Ellsworth and D.D. Mc Arthur The company was escorted in by Prest Young and a large concourse of Saints who met them in

A reenactment of the handcart exodus from Omaha, Nebraska, to Salt Lake City was staged in 1997 for the sesquicentennial of the settlement of the Salt Lake Valley. Here modern handcart pioneers are shown with their burdens near I-80 soon after entering Utah.

Emmigration Kanyon with a treat of melons, fruits vegtables They marched in good order & fine Spirits and seemed to be happy and in excellent health They have drawn their Carts from Iowa City a distance of 1300 miles. Thus men women & children young & old have been their own teams and performed this long journey far out travelling ox trains without incurring the expense for an outfit which would have taken them years of harder labor to procure than thus coming in Carts. This is a new and improved method of crossing the plains.

All went fine for the first handcart companies, but those who left too late in the summer season didn't fare as well. The Martin Handcart Company is the best known of the later groups. Departing Iowa City on July 26, 1856, they were slowed by repairs in Nebraska. With inadequate clothing and their food running short, they got caught in early winter snowstorms in Wyoming. Many in the company froze or starved to death before rescue parties could reach them. About 150 of the original 576 people died on the way to Salt Lake City. This was the gravest tragedy of the Utah pioneer period.

Starting in 1861, the church sent teams of oxen and cattle east every spring to meet migrating settlers heading west. Through the end of 1868,

"Down and Back" wagon train in Echo Canyon, circa 1866.
—UTAH STATE HISTORICAL SOCIETY

nearly 2,000 wagons journeyed east to intercept the westbound pioneers. These later pioneer groups, combined with others who immigrated to Utah, made up a large European population. Most of the foreign converts who moved to Utah were British. A smaller number came from Denmark, Sweden, and Norway, and a few emigrated from France, Italy, and Germany. The last known living pioneer, Hilda Anderson Erickson, who crossed the plains before 1869, died in 1968 at age 108, ending a long era of pioneers.

Organization of the Mormon Church

A Mormon congregation is called a ward and is made up of approximately 250 to 600 people headed by a bishop. Wards were extremely important in Mormon life, and continue to be so. Active church members refer to their ward almost as often as they do to their family. The ward is often the spiritual and social center of Mormon lives. A stake, another ecclesiastical unit of the church, includes about five to eight wards. Stake presidents were extremely powerful in Utah's early history. Their decisions directly affected where and how Utah was settled. They assigned pioneers to regions, named towns, and directed industry.

The Polygamy Controversy

Mormons faced many challenges in Utah—among them making a living in a desert land and contending with often-hostile native peoples—but one of their greatest challenges came from reactions to the church doctrine of polygamy. Polygamy was not the most important doctrine of Mormonism, but it was certainly the one that garnered the church the most negative attention during its first half century.

Though polygamy was first practiced by church leaders in Nauvoo, Illinois, before 1844, it was not publicly proclaimed until August 1852 when Joseph Smith's revelation was read in Salt Lake City at a general conference. Hosea Stout, a prominent pioneer and diarist, recorded the events on Sunday, August 29, 1852:

> In the after noon the Revelation on [polygamy] given to Joseph on the 12th of July 1843 was publicly read for the first time to the great joy of the Saints who have looked forward so long and so anxiously for the time to come when we could publicly declare the true and greatest principles of our holy religion and the great things which God has for his people to do in this dispensation.

Three years later, Stout recorded in his diary the marriage of some acquaintances in Utah County. In this instance he seems to feel the benefit was on the woman's side:

> I had the satisfaction to witness the triumph of Mormonism over the traditions of our fathers for George A. sealed Arza Adams to an old maid aged 48 as withered and forbidding as 4 Doz. years of celibacy might natturally be supposed to indicate. She joyfully took his hand and consented to be part of himself as number two. Thus entering into a respectible state of matrimony under auspicious circumstances when nothing except the privileges of Mormonism would have permitted.

Mormons saw polygamy as a religious duty. A man had to meet several requirements before he could take plural wives. He had to obtain the permission of his first wife, then that of church leaders who would determine whether or not he was worthy to live the "higher law" of marriage. If financial and other circumstances were favorable, he could take another wife. It is difficult to say how many Mormon men participated, but estimates range from 10 to 20 percent. The highest numbers of such marriages were performed when government opposition was the strongest. In Kaye C. Watson's *Life under the Horseshoe: A History of Spring City*, a man from Spring City expresses his feelings about plural marriage:

> I wish to insist that in marrying my plural wives it was perfectly agreeable with my first wife and with all parties concerned, and while I married from a motive of love, it was also from a sense of duty to the law of God as understood by us all, and with the purest motive and I always honor virtue more sacred than life.

Non-Mormons often viewed polygamy as an abomination. Elizabeth Kane, who traveled through Utah with her family in 1872, arrived with preconceived notions about polygamy. Though she never lost her abhorrence of the practice, Kane grew to respect those women who entered into the covenant. She was surprised to find the Mormon polygamous wives she visited happy, productive, intelligent women. She wrote in a letter, later included in a book entitled *Twelve Mormon Homes*, that in her estimation Mormon women embodied

> a religious faith that animates the whole being, enabling a woman to be cheerful in spite of adverse circumstances, industrious in spite of sickness, loving God and her neighbor; and showing it by charity in word and deed; this faith above doctrine I have found quite as often among Mormon as among other Christian women.

Kane also commented on Mormon parents' attitudes toward their children:

> I think [children] are very kindly, as well as carefully nurtured. They are admitted very freely to their parents' society, and are not always "snubbed" when they proffer their small contributions to the conversation going on among their elders. Generally, too, they are well-behaved. I think the tie between mother and children is closer than that between

them and the father. Whether the fathers can love each one of so many children, as much as they could if there were six or seven—or *say fifteen*—less, I will not pretend to say.

I have seen a Mormon father pet and humor a spoiled *thirty-fifth* child (a red-headed one, too!) with as unreasonable fondness as the youngest papa could show his firstborn.

Women wishing to escape from plural marriages could usually do so. It was very difficult for men to obtain a divorce, and most male petitioners were denied. However, a woman who requested a divorce usually received it. Church leaders emphasized the importance of affection in a marriage, and felt it unnecessary and even a sin for two people to produce children when they felt no affection for each other. Though Brigham Young urged his people to accept their situations and "not to expect heaven on earth but to prepare for it in due time," more than 1,600 divorces were granted—mostly to women—before polygamy was discontinued. Although the church no longer performed plural marriages after 1890, the family relationships that resulted from the practice endured for years afterward.

The Utah War

Political activists of the 1854 and 1856 national elections tied slavery and polygamy together and referred to them as the "twin relics of barbarism." Both the Democratic Party and Republican Party soundly denounced plural marriage as an abomination. When the new Democratic president, James Buchanan, took office in 1857 he felt bound to show his authority over the Mormons by forcibly replacing Brigham Young as governor of the Utah Territory. Buchanan appointed Alfred Cumming of Georgia as governor, and ordered 2,500 troops to make sure he held office.

On July 24, 1857, a large group of Mormons gathered in Big Cottonwood Canyon to celebrate the tenth anniversary of their arrival in Utah. A messenger raced up the mountain canyon to announce that an army 2,500 strong commanded by General Albert Sidney Johnston from the United States government was marching toward Utah. The celebration ended, and preparations to defend Utah were begun. Brigham Young called up the Mormon militia unit—the "Nauvoo Legion"—and started building fortifications in the mountain canyons in order to repel the onslaught of the government troops. The Nauvoo Legion had originally been organized in Nauvoo in 1840, and it continued to function in Utah until 1887.

The Mormon army was under strict orders not to shed any blood, but they did wreak havoc on the advancing army, burning three supply trains, turning livestock loose, and reportedly causing one U.S. soldier to die of fright. The U.S. troops were forced to spend a miserable winter at the burned-out remains of Fort Bridger and Fort Supply in Wyoming.

Rumors of the Mormons' intentions spread rapidly through the nation. In a time rife with political unrest and insecurity in the East, people welcomed news that there were troubles elsewhere; the Utah War distracted them from the disputes between the North and the South. Some people said the Mormons would fight. Others believed Brigham Young, who had already led the Mormons from New York, Ohio, Missouri, and Illinois on to Utah, would move his people once again. Some said they might go to Mexico, others thought they were planning to relocate to Alaska. Though Young did recall settlers from far-flung areas of California and Nevada, he was calling in reinforcements, not preparing for a mass exodus.

Young did intend to find a safe haven for his people if they should have to evacuate their Wasatch Front settlements. In 1858 he began looking at unexplored territory overlapping today's Utah-Nevada border. He hoped the region southwest of Fillmore known as the White Mountain area might serve as a safe haven for the Mormons. Young outlined his plan in a letter to Lewis Brunson, quoted in Clifford L. Stott's *Search for Sanctuary*:

> It is our intention to . . . find places where we can raise grain and hide up our families and stock in case of necessity. It is our wish to have the brethren go prepared with teams, seeds of various kinds and farming utensils so as to have grain raised at these places the present season. . . . Send out a party of fifteen or twenty men to search out and make a selection of and location at such place or places as may be suitable for the purposes above mentioned.

The White Mountain expedition explored the western valleys of Utah but found no place with sufficient water and suitable soil for agricultural purposes. They moved on to the central valleys of what is now Nevada, in particular noting the possibility of settlements at Ely (though it was considered too cold for reliable crops) and points farther south.

While continuing his search for places of refuge, Brigham Young ordered the people in the northern settlements to evacuate after making preparations to burn everything if necessary. Young's greatest desire was to keep peace and avoid property damage if at all possible. After misunderstandings on both sides and, finally, negotiations, Governor Cumming was peacefully installed as governor and a truce was declared on June 12, 1858. General Johnston's army marched quietly through the silent, empty streets of Salt Lake City on June 26 and the war was over. Within a few months the inhabitants of Salt Lake City and other northern settlements returned to their homes.

Still under Johnston's command, the army remained at Camp Floyd for more than two years. General Johnston continually requested to be replaced at his command. He felt too restricted and had to spend most of the time trying to prevent his men from ruining themselves with women and alcohol. Finally, on March 1, 1860, he left for a new command in California. The following year the troops were needed to fight in the Civil War, and they were withdrawn. Local citizens benefitted from the sale of U.S. property at greatly reduced prices. Some, the Walker brothers in particular, purchased so much merchandise they were able to make their fortunes on its resale. General Johnston went on to serve the Confederacy in the Civil War and was killed at the Battle of Shiloh.

Antipolygamy Legislation

Troubles with the government didn't end with the Utah War. After the Civil War ended, the eyes of government officials once more turned west. Many felt something must be done about the Mormons. Congress passed a number of laws intended to stop the practice of plural marriage. One of the most restrictive, the Edmunds Act of 1882, resulted in the imprisonment of hundreds of Mormon men and a few women. The terms were hard: up to five years in prison and large fines. Many polygamists went underground by hiding, going on overseas missions, and communicating through secret code via telegraph.

From 1884 to 1889 the federal government conducted extensive raids throughout Utah, in the large population centers of the Wasatch Front as well as in more isolated rural locations—wherever U.S. marshalls suspected a culprit might be hiding. The antipolygamy raids devastated families and whole neighborhoods. Strange men entered houses unannounced in the middle of the night, searching under beds and ripping up carpets to find hidden passages. Children became frightened of any outsider who passed through the neighborhood.

Raids also took place during family gatherings such as weddings and funerals. LDS Church president John Taylor was not able to attend his daughter's wedding reception because he was warned of deputies who hoped to catch him there. Deputies searched businesses. One marshall found a man hiding in the cellar of a Zions Cooperative Mercantile Institution (ZCMI) building. Church meetings became common hunting grounds. Sometimes the men escaped through tunnels dug under houses. In Richfield, Utah, a tunnel was discovered in the 1960s that had hidden the Mormon fugitives from the law.

Many searches and arrests were made without a warrant. The *Deseret News* reported on January 20, 1886:

Men imprisoned for illegal cohabitation, Sugarhouse. Prisoner in center holding flowers is LDS apostle George Q. Cannon. —UTAH STATE HISTORICAL SOCIETY

The deputy U.S. Marshals first appeared at the residence of Mr. Goff, on the east side of the river. Mrs. Goff met them at the door, and to their queries replied that her husband was not at home. They then demanded admittance to the house, and Mrs. Goff inquired whether they were authorized to do so. To this Deputy J.W. Franks replied insolently that the only search warrant he needed was an axe with which to break in the door. The deputies then searched the house.

Federal marshalls were given incentives for arresting polygamists—$2 for serving a warrant and $20 for each arrest, pretty hefty sums considering their $200 annual salary. Many deputies paid informers to help them in their quest.

The U.S. government's pressure on polygamists was bankrupting both the LDS Church and its members. But Mormons refused to change their marriage customs until the order came from God. After reportedly pleading with the Lord for many agonizing months, Mormon president and prophet Wilford Woodruff announced God's will on September 24, 1890, ending the practice condemned by the rest of the nation.

Splinter groups still practice polygamy, but the church does not condone plural marriage, and anyone who enters into a polygamous union is excommunicated.

Women in Utah

Mormon women were among the first white women in Utah. The prevalent view of early Mormon women may have been one of meek, submissive creatures totally dominated by their husbands, but women in Utah had to be tough, strong willed, and independent. As polygamous wives, they were often left alone with farms and small children for long periods of time. They were responsible for raising food, butchering animals, and meeting every family crisis.

In pioneer times, church leaders recognized the strength, abilities, and intelligence of women. Unlike women in other parts of the United States, Mormon women were allowed to hold property, independent of their husbands. And, in addition to their domestic responsibilities, women were often given professional training in education, law, and medicine. Brigham Young issued the call for women to come forward and obtain medical training, and a number of them traveled east to attend school. Romania Bunnell Pratt, Ellis Reynolds Shipp, and Margaret Curtis Shipp Roberts studied at Women's Medical College in Philadelphia, Pennsylvania. Ellen Brooke Ferguson, Jane Wilkie Manning Skofield (Utah's first woman surgeon), and Martha Hughes Cannon also studied medicine and returned to practice in Utah. Martha Hughes Cannon not only distinguished herself in the medical field, she was also a very influential early politician in Utah. After successfully lobbying for women's suffrage at the state constitutional convention, she defeated her husband in a race for the

Dr. Ellis R. Shipp.
—UTAH STATE
HISTORICAL SOCIETY

Utah State Senate on November 3, 1896, becoming the first woman in the United States elected to that office.

Church leader George Q. Cannon, quoted in Thomas Alexander's *Utah: The Right Place*, summed up the early church's attitude toward women:

> With women to aid in the great cause of reform, what wonderful changes can be effected. Give her responsibility, and she will prove that she is capable of great things; . . . make a doll of her . . . and instead of being a help meet to man, as originally intended, she becomes a drag and an encumbrance. Such women may answer in other places and among other people; they would be out of place here.

In accordance with their freedom and independence, some well-educated and powerful women in Salt Lake City determined it was their time to stand up and vote. They demanded this right, and the men in power agreed. In February 1870, the Utah territorial legislature granted women the vote. In a municipal election two days later Seraph Young, a niece of Brigham Young, cast the first vote. Though Wyoming had passed women's suffrage in December 1869, they had not yet held elections, so women in Utah were the first in the nation to vote.

Non-Mormons hoped the vote would give Mormon women the power to throw over polygamy; they believed Mormon women would outlaw the practice if they had their say. They were wrong. The women overwhelmingly supported their church leaders, giving the church even more power in Utah politics. With increased numbers of Mormon voters,

Martha Hughes Cannon was the first woman state senator in the United States.
—UTAH STATE HISTORICAL SOCIETY

non-Mormon women in Utah felt female suffrage only put the antipolygamy cause at more of a disadvantage, and they lobbied against it throughout the 1870s and 1880s. In their efforts to stifle Mormon political rights, Congress repealed the women's vote in the 1887 Edmunds-Tucker Act.

State politics, however, continued to champion women's rights. In the summer of 1895, a body of men assembled on the third floor of the newly completed Salt Lake City and County Building to write the new state constitution. At first, suffrage for women seemed assured. The female vote had already been a part of life in Utah, and there was no reason it should not be a part of the constitution. However, Utah had suffered for years because of its unusual institutions. Some legislators, including B. H. Roberts, a prominent Mormon leader, felt that if women's suffrage was included in the Utah constitution, the U.S. Congress might find a way to reject Utah's petition for statehood. The body argued women's suffrage for a number of weeks and came close to rejecting it. Finally, though, the men voted in favor of the female vote, and Utah was again a national leader in supporting suffrage.

The Black Hawk War

By 1865, Mormons had lived in the Utah Territory for eighteen years. At first, the native tribes welcomed the Mormons as trading partners, but soon large numbers of Mormon families filled the more desirable valleys, pushing Utes and Paiutes from their traditional hunting, gathering, and farming grounds. The Indians faced a slow starvation. Relations between Utah settlers and native groups reached their low point during the Black Hawk War of 1865–72 (not to be confused with the 1832 Black Hawk War in the Midwest, led by a Sauk chief also called Black Hawk).

An 1865 treaty between Utah superintendent of Indian affairs Oliver H. Irish and the Ute chiefs promised the tribes money, shelter, food, goods, and agricultural training in return for their moving to the Uinta Basin. The Indians moved to the basin, but the federal government did not back the treaty, leaving the destitute Indian families to starve in the barren land.

Fed up with empty promises and hoping to drive the white settlers out, Ute subchief Black Hawk declared war against the Mormons. He was joined by angry warriors from the Paiute and Navajo tribes. The warriors raided cattle and horses and harassed settlers in central and southern Utah.

Sanpete, Sevier, and Paiute Counties were hardest hit, though all of Utah felt the effects of the Black Hawk War. Small white settlements banded together in forts. Travelers took extra precautions, staying in large groups and camping only in established communities. Some towns became overcrowded with refugees from abandoned settlements.

To the white settlers, losses during the war were devastating. Thousands of head of cattle were stolen in raids. Human deaths were estimated at about seventy. The bloodiest incident of the war occurred on a road in Sevier County, when Ute warriors ambushed a Richfield family who were traveling to a store in Glenwood, scalping and mutilating three people. This event sparked an exodus in Sevier and Paiute Counties, as well as the abandonment of newly formed settlements in Panguitch and Long Valley.

Though his comrades continued their raids sporadically through 1872, Black Hawk declared a truce in 1867. He signed a peace treaty and even traveled to central Utah congregations asking for forgiveness and imploring the settlers to understand the plight of his people. Some forgave and sought peace; others refused to forget their losses.

Black Hawk died in 1870 of tuberculosis.

The Coming of the Railroads

Legislation passed by the U.S. Congress encouraged the settling of the West and the building of railroads. In July 1865, after the end of the Civil War, track laying commenced; the great race was on between the Central Pacific (CP)—building eastward from California—and the Union Pacific (UP)—laying tracks westward from Omaha—to see which railroad could build the most miles. Railroads were also pressing hard to reach the "Mormon Kingdom" in Utah first, in order to dominate the freight business of that growing territory. Railroad building across the high prairies of Nebraska was relatively rapid, but from Cheyenne west, the mountain ranges, canyons, and high deserts made the work much more difficult. The UP construction gang moved forward at breakaway speed with 1,000 mostly Irish workers on the line and 500 teams of horses and mules to support them. They reached the Utah territorial line at the end of 1868.

While the UP raced across the prairies of Nebraska and eastern Wyoming, the CP fought its way through the granite mountains and frozen ground of the Sierra Nevada. By June of 1868, the Sierra Nevada tracks of the CP joined those that had been laid up the eastern slope from the Nevada line. The crews were now out on the desert and could move hell-bent at a mile or more a day, racing to beat the UP to the center point of the Utah Territory some 500 miles away.

Both railroads needed help, and they turned to Brigham Young. In May 1868 Young contracted with the UP to do all the grading, tunneling, and bridge work on the UP line for over 100 miles from the head of Echo

Canyon to the shores of the Great Salt Lake. The work was expected to require 5,000 men and several hundred teams, at a cost of $2,125,000. The UP agreed to transport, free, some European immigrants from Omaha to the railhead at Laramie during the summer of 1868 to assist in the project.

Financial difficulties plagued both railroads, and their unhonored debts led to serious economic worries in Salt Lake City. Despite money problems, the two railroads continued their race to Ogden unabated during the late winter and early spring of 1869. By March 8 the UP had reached Ogden and the CP was racing across the desert near the Utah line. Both were determined to build as far as possible, even if they had to pass each other, which they did. But on April 10, 1869, Congress fixed a meeting point at Promontory Summit, a barren spot north of the Great Salt Lake.

At 11:00 A.M. on May 10, 1869, a Central Pacific train from the West and a Union Pacific train from the East, both with highly decorated engines and with whistles blowing, came nose to nose. A polished piece of California laurel served as the connecting tie and a solid-gold spike was the ceremonial last spike. Thus, with much fanfare and many political speeches, the rails were joined, tying the United States together from the Atlantic to the Pacific.

Meanwhile, Brigham Young was determined to have a railroad to connect Ogden and Salt Lake. As part of the settlement owed him by the UP, he obtained trackage, engines, and cars and quickly went to work on his own railroad. The Utah Central, some thirty-seven miles long, was completed in January 1870. Soon Young and his sons wanted to build more rails in Utah. The UP still owed Young money and goods, which they repaid with construction materials, locomotives, and cars. From this beginning, Brigham Young, his family, and his associates oversaw the expansion of Utah Central rail lines into many parts of the state.

The coming of the railroads to Utah was of great concern to many of the Latter-day Saints. They had been beset in the past by persecution and did not look forward to an influx of "gentiles" (non-Mormons) who might, again, disrupt their isolated way of life. But Brigham Young was reported to have said he wouldn't give much for a religion that could not withstand the coming of a railroad.

There is little doubt that Utah was changed forever by the coming of the railroads—and the influx of gentiles. In one decade after 1869, the non-Mormon population more than tripled. By 1880 the Utah Territory population had grown to 144,000, of which 32,000 were non-Mormons. From an economic standpoint, things improved: the 1880 census also recorded that Utah had 640 manufacturing establishments and that ten carloads of agricultural produce were leaving Ogden daily for eastern points. One merchandising firm had shipped 250 carloads of flour to Montana. The population of Salt Lake City had increased from 27,000 to 40,000 in just a three-year period, and real estate prices had risen between 50 and 200 percent. Even skeptical Mormons finally found an occasional kind word to say about that fateful creature known as the Iron Horse.

The Struggle for Statehood

After their arrival in Utah, Mormon leaders quickly saw the importance of pursuing statehood. Though the territory first belonged to Mexico, the 1848 Treaty of Guadalupe-Hidalgo had turned the region over to the United States. Utah leaders petitioned for statehood in 1849. They chose "Deseret" as the state name, a term for honeybee found in the Book of Mormon. (In Mormon culture, the bee is a symbol of hard work.) The boundaries of the proposed state included not only present-day Utah, but all of Nevada and parts of Idaho, Oregon, California, Arizona, New Mexico, Colorado, and Wyoming. The appeal for statehood was promptly dismissed. The population was too small, and those in Congress felt Utah did not have the power to merit statehood. Instead Utah was made a territory that included its present area as well as Nevada, a corner of Wyoming, and western Colorado.

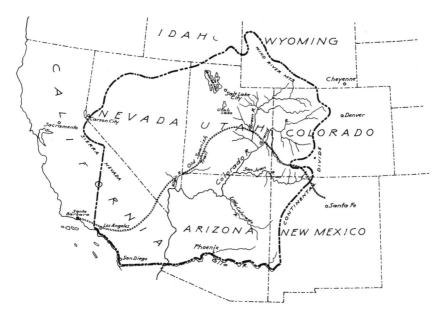

The State of Deseret as envisioned by Mormon leaders.
—LDS CHURCH HISTORICAL DEPARTMENT

Territorial leaders prepared six more petitions for statehood, all of them doomed because of the growing conflict over polygamy. Finally in 1890, church president Wilford Woodruff issued his Manifesto, discontinuing the solemnizing of new plural marriages. Another attempt for statehood made in 1894 was more successful. In July of that year Congress passed the Enabling Act, permitting any eligible territory such as Utah to become a state. On January 4, 1896, U.S. President Grover Cleveland signed legislation making Utah the forty-fifth state.

Utah's growth has continued unabated since statehood. During World War II, massive amounts of military spending boosted the state's economy; since then, Utah's emphasis has shifted from an agrarian to an industrial economy. In recent years, the state has added technology to its holdings, with many software companies starting up in and moving to the state. Utah's advantageous climate and ready supply of well-educated labor have attracted other large businesses as well. The Wasatch Front is particularly popular with companies and people from other states seeking better business and living conditions.

Along with the benefits, Utah is encountering all the problems of growth: school overcrowding, heavy traffic, and loss of green space and the agricultural occupations. Lawmakers scramble to adjust school schedules, allocate funds for new buildings, widen highways, and adapt zoning laws. Utahans' natural tendency to welcome new residents and jobs has been tempered by the fear of seeing their mountain paradise become increasingly urban.

Statehood celebration, January 1896, in front of Dinwoody's furniture store at 100 South Street, Salt Lake City. —UTAH STATE HISTORICAL SOCIETY

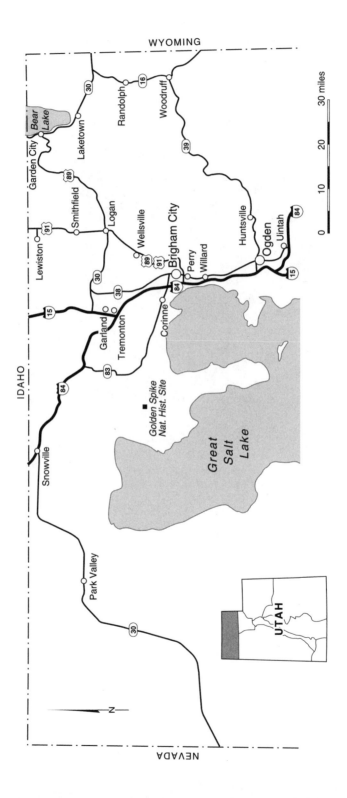

PART I

The North Country

The northern part of Utah was familiar territory to the ancient Fremont Indians and people of the Desert Culture and more recently to the western Shoshones. Beginning in the early nineteenth century, mountain men found the region northeast of the Great Salt Lake to their liking. In 1845, at the tail end of the mountain man era, Miles Goodyear established the first "town" along the Wasatch Front, Fort Buenaventura. But when the Mormons arrived in 1847, Goodyear moved on.

The railroad people, however, were not intimidated by the power of the Mormons. They ignored Salt Lake City and ran their line through Ogden and north of the Great Salt Lake, creating wild boomtowns quite foreign to the sober Mormon territory. The towns later either died or were taken over by Mormons, but their shadows survive to whisper of the wild days when the rails ruled northern Utah.

The Trappers

Trappers' gunshots were the first sounds made by white men in northern Utah. For nearly forty years following the Lewis and Clark expedition (1804–6), trappers and fur traders explored the West and established the routes of travel and avenues of commerce from the Mississippi River to the Pacific Ocean. By the time the Mormon pioneers arrived in the Salt Lake Valley, most of the mountain ranges, rivers, lakes, and other waterways in the Great Basin had been thoroughly explored, hunted, and trapped by the fearless mountain men.

For many years the fur trade was the leading branch of commerce in the western world. Such outfits as the American Fur Company and Hudson's Bay Company dominated the fur trade in the West. Most of Utah's famous mountain men were involved in the Rocky Mountain Fur

Company established by William H. Ashley. A remarkable group of 100 young men led by Andrew Henry, the company left St. Louis in 1822 and included Jedediah Smith, seventeen-year-old Jim Bridger, David E. Jackson, William L. Sublette and his brother Milton, Robert Campbell, Thomas Fitzpatrick, and many others. They made history as the first white men to spend a winter trapping in Utah. They established a fur cache in present-day Cache Valley.

Jim Bridger was generally considered the most able hunter and mountaineer guide of the West. Along with Jedediah Smith and other explorers who discovered South Pass, he helped open trade to the Great Salt Lake and Green River valleys. In the autumn of 1824 Bridger traveled down the Bear River from Cache Valley and came upon a body of extremely salty water. He believed it to be an arm of the Pacific Ocean, but it turned out to be the Great Salt Lake. Bridger may or may not have been the first white man to discover the Great Salt Lake, but he was the first to give an eyewitness report of it. Apparently Bridger spent little time in Utah after 1830, but he had substantial contact with the Mormons and other westward movements from his headquarters at Fort Bridger on the Blacks Fork of the Green River. He later served as an army guide on western expeditions and during conflicts with the Indians. In 1866 he moved back to Missouri and continued army guiding in Wyoming and Montana. He died on his Missouri farm in 1881.

Jedediah Smith, one of the most remarkable men ever engaged in the American fur trade, led the expedition that found a natural gateway to the west (South Pass). He was the first traveler to reach California overland, going from Cache Valley through the full length of current-day Utah to the Colorado River and into the Los Angeles Basin. On his return trip from California to Cache Valley, he was the first white person to cross the Sierra Nevada; he was also the first to traverse the Great Basin on its most direct desert route. Smith was one of a few mountain men who were ardent Christians. He possessed undaunted courage and untiring energy. He was killed at an early age on the Cimarron River by Indians while leading a wagon train from St. Louis to Santa Fe.

Other important groups of trappers and mountain men explored and trapped across Utah. These included various contingents from New Mexico, often known as Taos Trappers, the most prominent led by Etienne Provost, Kit Carson (who later achieved fame as John C. Frémont's western guide), and Antoine Robidoux.

The arrival of the Mormons roughly corresponded with the decline of the fur trade, and soon northern Utah was dominated by Mormon settlements and, some twenty years later, railroad towns.

US 89
Idaho State Line–Ogden
65 miles

US 89 is one of the major north-south highways in the western United States. It runs from Montana to Mexico, via Arizona, and covers some fantastic territory. The Utah portion of US 89 extends from the Bear Lake Valley south into Arizona, traversing several mountain passes and all the state's major population centers.

In 1863 Brigham Young sent a group of Mormons with LDS apostle Charles C. Rich to settle the Bear Lake Valley (named earlier by trappers for the abundance of bears in the region). This group went north by way of Franklin, Idaho, in Cache Valley up to Mink Creek, Idaho, and northeast through a pass in the mountains. The first settlements of 1863 were actually all north of the present Utah-Idaho border. Later that same year, other exploration parties entered the Round Valley (south of Bear Lake) from the Blacksmith Fork of Cache Valley. As Indians had already claimed the southern part of Bear Lake, the Mormons decided it was best to leave that area unsettled and free for the native inhabitants' use. This resolve did not last long, though, and whites had moved into the area by the end of the 1860s.

The people brave enough to face the severe winters and isolation of northeastern Utah also had to be tough and self-reliant. Most were ranchers, as few food crops could mature in the short growing season. The descendants of these hardy pioneers continue to battle the elements. They are, for the most part, still ranchers. No large industry or mining has ever been established in the region. Some tourism-related industry exists, but people still rely on the land to support their families.

Bear Lake

Bear Lake, though practically devoid of surrounding trees, never fails to inspire the motorist with its vivid and changeable colors. American geologist F. V. Hayden remarked in 1871 that the lake was "set like an emerald among the mountains. . . . Not even the waters of Yellowstone Lake present such vivid coloring." Early settler Joseph Rich, after exploring the Bear Lake country, exclaimed:

> Only men with plenty of hair on 'em are tough enough to stand the climate of Bear Lake, but what a country! Streams full of fish; the most beautiful lake on earth; wild game; grass up to a horse's belly; timber in the mountains; fine locations for townsites; everything.

The Bear Lake Monster

Early in the history of Bear Lake Valley settlement, a monster scare took place. The story of the Bear Lake Monster was spread by Joseph Rich in 1868, who hoped to bring attention and settlers to that corner of Utah. Some people did claim to have seen a monster in the lake, though Rich didn't really believe it when he began writing about the beast in the *Deseret News* (a Salt Lake City newspaper that is still published daily) as if it were real. Several people reported seeing an enormous seventy-five-foot lizardlike monster, which terrified swimmers. Guns boomed into the lake, blasting the imagined monster, and some people even moved away.

One explanation for the monster was given by Lt. Samuel Tillman, a member of a U.S. Geological Survey team. In 1877 the group of men was camped near Bear Lake, and, having been warned of a monster, they were curious to verify or disprove the tale. Early in the morning, they discovered a number of mules missing, and Lieutenant Tillman set out to find them. The lake was overlaid with fog a few feet thick, making it impossible to see the water. Soon Tillman heard noises that seemed to be coming from some sort of animal, and he saw water spraying into the air. Feeling he was about to discover the monster, he went closer to investigate. Soon he located two bulls standing in the water, charging each other. They struck their horns together with lowered heads, and when their nostrils filled with water, they lifted their noses and blew water into the air. The sounds of spraying water came not from some mysterious monster, but from the local cattle.

In spite of monster scares, Bear Lake became a popular resort spot for local residents from the time the white settlers started inhabiting the region. As automobiles became more popular, so did the lake. However, it wasn't until the 1970s that large resorts started appearing on the lake's beaches.

Garden City

Five miles south of the Idaho border at the junction of UT 30 and US 89, Garden City is more a place of beaches, summer homes, and lake views than it is a garden spot. But when the residents applied for a post office they were refused under the name of Belleview, so they changed it to Garden City. In 1910 Theodore Hildt introduced raspberries to Garden City, and the berries became known as the specialty of the small town. During raspberry season, fresh fruit, raspberry pies, ice cream, and milkshakes are sold in abundance throughout the city.

The area around Garden City was known as Little Valley before it was settled. Towns were already established in Round Valley, and farther southeast at Randolph and Woodruff, when Phineas Cook built a canal in 1877 to water Little Valley. His idea was to sell shares in the new irrigation company and lure farmers into the area who would need to grind their wheat at his Swan Creek grist mill. The idea worked. Several families moved their log cabins the twenty-seven miles from Randolph to the comparably balmy new locale.

Road to Logan

The portion of US 89 between Garden City and Logan is one of Utah's most accessible mountain areas. Just before climbing out of the Bear Lake Valley, look for a scenic turnout with a spectacular view of Bear Lake, the Uinta Mountains, and Wyoming's Star Valley. Farther down the road is a series of deep, sagebrush-covered hollows. One of these spots, Peter's Sink, has the dubious distinction of recording one of the lowest temperatures in North America. In the upper reaches of Logan Canyon are several resorts, including the Beaver Mountain ski area and a beautiful glacial lake, Tony Grove Lake.

From the Tony Grove Lake road west, US 89 follows the Logan River. This long, winding canyon road has been the subject of controversy for many years. As the main route between Cache Valley and points north and east, the highway carries a lot of traffic. Bridges are getting old, and extra lanes would help facilitate the traffic flow. On the other hand, the

The Bear Lake Valley has earned a reputation for wonderful raspberries.

scenery in this canyon is dramatic and, for the most part, unblemished—environmentalists are concerned that widening the road would destroy the scenery. Numerous proposals have been put forth for highway improvements, but thus far they have all been halted in the courts.

CACHE VALLEY

From Logan Canyon, US 89 drops quickly into Cache Valley. The valley is blessed with summers that are generally cooler than in the rest of the state, but its winters are considerably colder than those of the Wasatch Front valleys.

Bartleson-Bidwell Party

The first group of California-bound migrants to cross Utah wandered through Cache Valley in 1841. The Bartleson-Bidwell party were unable to find a guide at Fort Hall, Idaho, so they picked their way through the mountain valleys, climbing hills and wandering to find the best route west. They descended into Cache Valley near Cornish and veered southwest. The group feasted on the "very large and exquisitely delicious" chokecherries they found along the way. On August 17 they crossed the hills west of today's Newton and skirted the north end of the Great Salt Lake along portions of the future railroad site until they steered northwest to the Raft River Mountains looking for water. From the approximate location of Cedar Creek at the eastern tip of the Raft River Mountains, the wanderers headed southwest until they found water again in the Grouse Creek Mountains. They moved down along the Pilot range and found their next water source near the spot where the Donner party would revive themselves five years later after their ordeal in the salt desert. Then they passed into Nevada.

Exploration of Cache Valley

In 1849 Captain Howard Stansbury of the U.S. Corps of Topographical Engineers surveyed Cache Valley to ascertain whether it would be suitable for a military post. Captain Stansbury was impressed with the plentiful water, excellent soil, and lush grasses in the valley. As a result of his findings, the army wintered all the cattle and mules from Fort Hall in the valley. Unfortunately, that winter proved an exceptionally hard one and more than half the livestock perished. The military decided against establishing a permanent post in Utah.

The Mormons didn't turn their attention north to Cache Valley until the 1850s. In August 1847 a Mormon exploration party visited the area and brought back glowing reports of the abundant timber in the lush valley. However, Brigham Young had heard other reports that the northern regions were too cold to sustain a permanent population, so he concentrated the colonizing efforts to the south. In 1855, as other valleys began to fill, he decided to try Cache Valley for settlement.

Young sent several men to Cache Valley with his cattle, where he hoped they could graze through the winter. The men built the Elk Horn Ranch near Providence, south of Logan. Several other ranchers also herded their cattle into the valley. The winter of 1855–56 was another exceptionally hard one. After the first big snowfall early in November it became apparent that winter would be severe, and the settlers moved many of the livestock through Sardine Canyon back to the Salt Lake Valley. Those people and animals left behind struggled through the winter, and many of the cattle perished in the cold.

Despite the difficult winters, the land was valuable and well watered, and some families were willing to brave the frigid temperatures and deep snows. Permanent settlers moved into the southwestern section of Cache Valley in the summer of 1856.

Reports in the *Deseret News* in 1859 described Cache Valley as a farming paradise. As a result, many people in settlements to the south, where valleys were already becoming crowded, and newly arrived immigrants from Europe flocked to the remote settlements in the north.

Since these first pioneer experiments in Cache Valley, the area has remained an important contributor to the state's economy. It leads the state in dairy production, and Cache Valley cheeses are widely known and marketed.

Logan

US 89 travels from the bench occupied by Utah State University into the central business district of Logan. With a population of about 40,000, Logan is the major city of northeastern Utah. It is the business center of three counties and the Cache County seat.

In June 1859 four men found a good farming site on "the Island"— the low part of the town where the Logan River flows. Here they plowed and planted three acres of wheat. Other settlers built cabins in two rows facing each other along what is now Center Street. By winter Logan had become an important settlement with more than thirty-six families.

In *Sinners and Saints*, Phil Robinson gives a view of how Logan must have appeared to gentiles (what Mormons call anyone not of their religion) in its early days.

> The Gentile does not take very kindly to Logan. There are no saloons, there are no public animosities to give it what they call 'Spirit';

Brigham Young, 1876.
—UTAH STATE HISTORICAL SOCIETY

everybody knows his neighbor, and the sightseeing fiend is unknown. The one and only newspaper hums . . . on like some self-satisfied bumble bee; Everything is Mormon. The biggest shop is the Cooperative Store; the biggest place of worship the Tabernacle, the biggest man the President of the Stake. Everybody that meets, 'Brothers' and 'Sisters' each other in the streets, and after nightfall the only man in the streets is the policeman, who as a rule retires early himself. It is a well-fed, neighborly, primitive life among orchards and cornfields . . . with every bee bumbling along its own busy way, but all taking their honey back to the same hive.

Today's citizenry would struggle with the laws of early Logan. In 1883 the first punishment for profanity was issued to a man who pleaded guilty and was fined $5. Another man, convicted of selling alcohol, was fined $85 and sentenced to ninety days in jail.

A dominant feature in the city of Logan is the Mormon temple on the hill east of the city center. Though the idea was mentioned as early as 1867, the church's official announcement of plans to build a temple in Logan came in 1876. The following May, Brigham Young chose the site for the temple and ground was broken. Lumber for the temple was milled in Logan Canyon and its stone was quarried in Green Canyon. The temple was dedicated in May 1884, the second Mormon temple in Utah to be completed (the first was the St. George Temple). Though extensively remodeled in the 1970s, the temple continues to function as an important house of worship for Mormons in northern Utah, southern Idaho, and Wyoming.

On Main Street, the Logan Tabernacle is another imposing city structure. It was constructed during the years 1865–78. Work was slow because of a plan to increase the size halfway through the project. The tabernacle is used for both church and public meetings. It is sometimes open for tours.

Before his death in 1877, Brigham Young set up an endowment for a college in Logan. Started the next year, Brigham Young College was open from 1878 to 1926, when it was taken over by the board of education for use as a high school.

Utah State University

Before you reach downtown Logan on US 89, you'll pass over the bench occupied by Utah State University (USU). In 1888 the Utah Land Act provided funding for Utah's land-grant agricultural college. The Morrill Act of 1862, signed by President Lincoln, had provided for such colleges in each state and territory. Logan was chosen as the site of the land-grant institution in Utah. In 1890 the college started classes with eight students. It was later called Utah State Agricultural College and finally Utah State University. The university has shouldered a statewide responsibility for education and research pertaining to agriculture, homes and families, and business and mechanical industries.

Old Main building,
Utah State University.
—UTAH STATE
HISTORICAL SOCIETY

Utah State University currently enrolls 22,000 students in nine colleges, including agriculture, and maintains extension and research programs in all parts of Utah and in many foreign countries. It is the largest employer in the area.

Wellsville

On US 89 southwest of Logan, several major dairy operations dot the landscape, including the experimental farms of Utah State University located approximately halfway between Logan and Wellsville. The first commercial creamery and cheese factory in Cache Valley was established at Wellsville in 1889. Wellsville, the last town before US 89 descends into Sardine Canyon, was the first permanent settlement in Cache Valley. In September 1856, settlers fled drought, poor soil, grasshoppers, and other problems in Tooele (pronounced too-WIL-ah) County and, led by Peter Maughan, moved to Cache Valley. They called the settlement Maughan's Fort until the name was changed to honor Daniel H. Wells, a counselor to Brigham Young. Despite the very difficult winter, families survived to raise a successful crop in 1857. Soon other hopeful pioneers moved to Wellsville, and it grew to nearly 600 people by 1860.

The Wellsville Tabernacle, constructed by the LDS Church in the years 1902–8, dominates the landscape of Wellsville and the surrounding

Utah State Agricultural College Extension Service demonstration, spraying arsenic to control alfalfa weevil, 1921. —UTAH STATE UNIVERSITY

fields. Near Wellsville on US 89 is the Jensen Historical Farm, a living museum operated by Utah State University. This unusual museum depicts life shortly after the turn of the century and is open to the public. Each August the university holds the Festival of the American West here. The weeklong celebration of frontier settlement includes cooking demonstrations, quilt displays, cowboy poetry, old-time singing, Native American dancing, and a pageant depicting the history of the West.

Mantua

Climbing down from the mountain pass through Sardine Canyon, US 89 enters into a small valley with a tranquil man-made lake. In 1863 Lorenzo Snow called several families to this little valley east of Brigham City to raise flax for linen cloth. Most of these people were Danish Mormon converts, and they named their town for Mantua, Ohio, Snow's birthplace.

In the late 1950s a reservoir was constructed in the little valley, inundating a lot of farmland but making a very pretty lake and providing needed irrigation water.

Brigham City

From Mantua, US 89 winds through a short canyon before the shining waters of the Great Salt Lake come into view. The Mormons were the first permanent white settlers of this region, and Brigham City is the principal town of Box Elder County, as the area was called. It is a pleasant little pioneer town set in the foothills of the Wellsville Mountains and presided over by an impressive tabernacle constructed between 1865 and 1890.

In 1851, the first settlers arrived in Box Elder, as Brigham City was called at the time. They built a row of log rooms in the area of present-day 700 North and 600 West Streets. In 1853 all the families in the area joined together in a fort to protect themselves from Indian attacks. Lorenzo Snow was called to take fifty additional families to Box Elder in the fall of 1853. He became the father of Brigham City and Box Elder County, the spiritual leader of northern Utah, and, later became the fifth president of the LDS Church.

The area proved to have excellent agricultural land. Crops matured well, and in 1856 Mormon settlers planted the first peaches in Brigham City. Within a few years trees had grown and produced fruit, and the county became widely known for its peaches.

From the beginning, residents of Brigham City cooperated with one another. They joined together in burning sagebrush to make ashes for lye and they harvested their crops together. Because of this cooperative spirit, Brigham City was an ideal place to practice the United Order of Enoch. Lorenzo Snow offered the leadership for this movement in which the Mormon community owned businesses cooperatively and shared in the profits or losses. The United Order was practiced by the Latter-day Saints as early as 1831, long before the westward trek began. It was again attempted by various settlements in Utah in the 1850s, but the largest push for the United Order came in the 1870s, when Brigham Young urged settlements throughout Utah to join.

The principle upon which the United Order was founded is stated by Joseph Smith as follows:

> All people are literally sons and daughters of God. The earth is His and all that it contains. He created it and its fullness especially for the benefit of his children, and all, provided they keep his commandments, are entitled to the blessings of the earth. With proper regulation there is enough and to spare for all. Every person is simply a steward and not the owner of property that he is in charge, and he is obliged to use it and his time, strength, and talents for the good of all.

By the 1870s all the businesses in the town were owned cooperatively, and the people of Brigham City produced everything they needed, making it a nearly self-sufficient community. Because it was self-contained, Brigham City was able to avoid the suffering from economic depressions that affected other Utah settlements. Brigham City's was the most successful cooperative organization in all of Utah until the late 1870s, when some financial difficulties developed partly because of federal antipolygamy legislation. Gradually, various businesses were sold to private owners, and by 1895 the entire order had been dissolved.

World War II introduced change into the quiet farming town. In 1942 the U.S. government constructed Bushnell Hospital for treatment of men wounded in the war. Sixty buildings stood on a 235-acre site at the south end of town near US 89. The hospital provided not only employment, but also a ready market for farmers' produce. After the war the hospital closed, but the buildings did not stand vacant long. They were converted to an Indian school, where students from reservations boarded. The school closed in 1984; some of the buildings were torn down, but many are now used by the city or private enterprise, and a golf course has been constructed on part of the site. In the distance, a fading letter *I* on the mountainside stands for Intermountain Indian School.

Agriculture remained a major source of income in this part of Utah for more than a century, but manufacturing has gradually taken its place. The Morton-Thiokol company began building missiles and other defense-

Rocket display at Morton-Thiokol.

The Box Elder Stake Tabernacle in Brigham City. Today the building is used for various church and community meetings.

related apparatus in 1957. The plant also constructs booster rockets that launch space shuttles. Morton-Thiokol has been a major employer in Box Elder County, with as many as 5,000 people working for the company at a time.

Entering Brigham City is like driving back through time. The trees along the wide main street shade businesses with storefronts that look like they came straight from an old *Andy Griffith Show* set. Open irrigation ditches run through the streets downtown, where children can wade and float their boats. Old buildings add a sense of history few other small towns maintain. Look for the three-story 1891 Brigham City Co-op Mercantile Store (now owned by First Security Bank). Also of interest are the Brigham City Fire Station, built in 1909; the flour mill from 1855; and a host of old pioneer homes. Especially notable is the Box Elder Stake Tabernacle, which dominates the little town. Originally constructed between 1865 and 1890 and expanded in 1910, the building has been extensively restored and is open for tours.

Perry

US 89 turns south from Brigham City and runs nearly parallel with I-15 for about ten miles. In 1850 Orrin Porter Rockwell and his brother Merritt settled for a time at Porter Springs near Perry.

Porter Rockwell is among the more colorful characters in Mormon history. An early convert to Mormonism, Rockwell was a zealous defender of Joseph Smith, and he put the prophet above the law. After Smith was

Orrin Porter Rockwell.
—UTAH STATE
HISTORICAL SOCIETY

killed, Rockwell continued his exploits in Utah, where he became famous as Brigham Young's bodyguard. In 1843 Joseph Smith had told Rockwell that if he never cut his hair he would never be killed by "bullet or blade." He didn't, and he died of natural causes in 1878.

Rockwell and his brother stayed in the Perry area only about one year. In 1853 other families moved to this remote little spot, among them Gustaves Perry, for whom the town was named, and his three sons. The original settlement was on a favorite Shoshone camping ground. Rather than fighting the Indians, the townspeople made friends with them, trading them bread for wild game.

For years prior to the completion of I-15, motorists were forced to take US 89 through Perry. The road was lined with fruit stands and farmers hawking their local produce to passing drivers. In the 1970s the completed freeway allowed travelers to bypass US 89 through Perry. In spite of the lessened traffic, many of the fruit stands remain and the fame of the strip has endured well enough to lure people for miles around to Box Elder County to purchase fruit in season.

Willard

Willard is sandwiched between Willard Bay and rugged Willard Peak. In 1964, the diking of the Great Salt Lake created Willard Bay, a freshwater arm that affords fishing and boating opportunities not available on the rest of the lake. Called North Willow Creek by the early settlers, Willard in 1851 was the first settlement in Box Elder County. In 1853 the settlers constructed a fort because of the Walker War in Utah County. In 1857 the residents voted to change the name of their town to honor LDS apostle Willard Richards.

Willard is sheltered by rugged mountain peaks that provided the rock for many of the town's old structures. These stone homes continue to give a rustic character to the town. A Welsh stone mason, Shadrach Jones, built many of Willard's homes and outbuildings using the native stone, giving the town the feel of an old Welsh village.

Settlers traveled up the canyon, where they harvested timber, quarried stone, and diverted the stream to irrigate their crops. One year in the 1920s, the stream ran so high during spring runoff that it washed 189 bodies from the old pioneer graveyard and left only seven gravestones standing. For a while, bodies lay strewn in the fields until they were all buried in one mass grave.

As with surrounding towns, Willard residents soon discovered they had an excellent location for growing fruit. Orchards still decorate the landscape, and many fruit stands sell the fruit of the season along US 89.

Bear River National Migratory Bird Refuge

Road signs on I-15 and in Brigham City direct travelers west over a sometimes very rough dirt road to the Bear River National Bird Refuge. John C. Frémont first explored the mouth of the Bear River in 1843 and was amazed by the number of waterfowl in the area. As the northeastern section of the territory became more heavily farmed, and local farmers took more and more water out of the Bear River for irrigation, the delta area began to dry up. Then two large avian botulism epidemics (caused in large part by decreased water flow and stagnant pools) destroyed thousands of waterfowl in 1910 and 1920. These events combined to cause serious concern to bird lovers, who lobbied for the birds' protection. In 1928 Congress passed an act creating the national wildlife refuge at the mouth of the Bear River.

Over the years a series of dikes and other structures were built in the refuge, enlarging the freshwater nesting and feeding areas for the waterfowl. In 1982 and 1983 Utah experienced its wettest winters and springs on record. Extensive flooding in the Bear River and surrounding streams destroyed the dikes and all the buildings at the refuge. Salt water flooded the freshwater oasis, and the refuge was closed to motor vehicles for a few years.

By 1989 dikes had been rebuilt, and habitats for migratory birds were once more being restored. Refuge buildings have also been reconstructed. Birds commonly viewed are white pelicans, Canada geese, ducks, avocets, stilts, grebes, tundra swans, ravens, hawks, falcons, and occasionally bald eagles in the winter.

Ogden

Ogden was really settled before Salt Lake City, though not by the Mormons. The confluence of the Weber and Ogden Rivers, on the west side of present-day Ogden, was a favorite camping spot for Indians and mountain men. In *Journal of a Trapper*, Osborne Russell recorded the events of Christmas 1839, which he spent in an encampment of Snake Indians near the present site of Ogden. Russell was lodging with a Frenchman and his Flathead Indian wife and child. The neighboring lodges housed a mixture of Indians of various tribes, and an additional fifteen lodges belonged to Snake Indians. Russell described the Christmas dinner they all ate together:

> The first dish was a large tin pan, 18 inches in diameter, rounded full of stewed elk meat. The next dish was similar, heaped with boiled deer meat. The third and fourth dishes were equal in size and contained boiled flour pudding, prepared with dried fruit, accompanied by four

quarts of sauce made of the juice of sour berries and sugar. Then came cakes followed by about six gallons of strong coffee already sweetened.

Russell refers to after-dinner discussions concerning political activities, the state of governments among the different tribes, and the characteristics of distinguished warrior chiefs. "Dinner being over," he recorded, "the tobacco pipes were filled and lighted while the squaws and children cleared away the remains of the feast to one side of the lodge where they held a sociable tit-a-tit over the fragments."

Before Brigham Young's arrival in the Great Basin, when he was planning where the Saints should settle, he considered the valley where the Weber River empties into the Great Salt Lake. However, an obstacle existed: Miles Goodyear, a mountain man and trapper, had built a trading post and small fort—Fort Buenaventura—at the current site of Ogden.

Goodyear was born in Hamden, Connecticut, in 1817. He worked as an indentured servant for a time and was happy to escape to the great freedom of Rocky Mountain country. When Goodyear moved west he married a Ute princess, Pomona. They had two children. Because of his occupancy, the Mormons set their sights south. After the severe persecution they had faced, they wished to be left alone for a very long time.

Before Goodyear set up his home in about 1845, the valley that would make up the greater part of Weber County was uninhabited. Several explorers and trappers had passed through on their journeys, including Peter Skene Ogden. Ogden was a fur trapper from Quebec who worked for the Hudson's Bay Company. He came west in 1818, but didn't explore the Great Salt Lake area until 1828. Though Ogden gave his name to one of Utah's largest towns, he didn't stay, nor did any of the other explorers who followed him.

Miles Goodyear was the only trapper or explorer who thought the valley made a good home site. The winter climate was milder than in the higher mountain valleys. The area was graced with numerous streams, pasture for livestock, and plenty of wild game. For a mountain man who sought the solitude of the mountain west, it was an isolated paradise. Goodyear's cabin, built before he established Fort Buenaventura, now sits on the Ogden LDS temple grounds. The Mormons' arrival in Utah meant the end of the trapper's isolation. Captain James Brown of the Mormon Battalion used his and other officers' military pay to buy Goodyear out for $1,950 in November 1847. The purchase netted the Mormons Goodyear's fort, livestock, and most of Weber County.

Subsequently, Brigham Young sent Captain Brown to start a permanent settlement. The place, called Brown's Fort until 1851, when the name was changed to Ogden, was near what is now Twenty-eighth Street west

Lorin Farr, president of the Weber Stake and first mayor of Ogden, exercised more power than any other man north of Salt Lake City. —UTAH STATE HISTORICAL SOCIETY

of Pacific Avenue. Brown built a number of toll bridges over the Weber and Ogden Rivers. Brown generously shared the fruits of his gardens, but Young reprimanded him for charging excessive tolls on his bridges.

In 1850, Young sent Lorin Farr to supervise Weber County. He was Ogden's first mayor, and the first president of the Weber Stake, established in 1851. As stake president, he wielded a great deal of power in Weber County's decision making. Settlers took counsel with Farr on many matters of both public and private life.

Ogden and the Railroad

The joining of the Union Pacific and Central Pacific Railroads in the desert in May 1869 marked a new era for northern Utah and indeed for the entire nation. Advance railroad camps arrived in Ogden in 1868, and in 1869 Ogden was made the main terminus of the transcontinental railroad line. Suddenly all roads led to Ogden. Many freight companies set up business transporting goods and people to and from locations not connected by rail. Hotels, saloons, and restaurants opened—everything a traveling populous required. Mills were built. By the 1880s, the railroads' shops were all in Ogden. At the beginning of the twentieth century, the Southern Pacific Railroad was the city's leading employer, and the Union Pacific had its major shops west of Omaha in Ogden. Ogden became a major freighting and passenger center.

Along with the growth of the railroads, the city continued to expand its business base. In 1906 the Ogden Packing Company was established and within ten years became the largest meatpacking company west of Omaha. In 1915 the Ogden Chamber of Commerce boasted of a city with 35,000 inhabitants growing at a rate of 1,000 per year. Ogden had factories of every description, including automobile plants, bakeries, bottling works, canneries, coal companies, construction-related industries, and sugar factories. The railroads alone employed 3,300 people in 1915.

The Ogden depot felt the pulse of the nation, possibly more than anywhere else in Utah. In 1894 the United States was in the depths of a serious economic depression. Jacob Coxey of Ohio rallied unemployed laborers from across the nation to form "industrial armies" and converge in Washington D.C. to demand that the government solve their problems. A number of the men who responded to the call rode cattle cars to Ogden, hoping to transfer there to the Union Pacific and travel east. But the railroad denied them passage. The National Guard was called in to contain the angry men, who were held for a few days. Upon their release they walked to Uintah (near the mouth of Weber Canyon), where they boarded eastbound freight cars. Other groups converged on Ogden during the same period, seizing trains and causing general havoc.

The same year (1894), striking railroad workers halted trains and allegedly set fires in Ogden that destroyed $135,000 worth of property.

In the early days of Ogden railroading, a sad jumble of shacks and saloons surrounded the bright red wooden clapboard depot. People traveling through saw all that was raunchy in Utah, and none of the good. One railroad passenger noted that

> the railroad traveller gets a very wrong impression of Ogden. He sees nothing but the Gentile part of the town, the stations of the U.P. and C.P. railroads, their offices and engine houses, and a dozen or two shanties occupied as restaurants, grog shops and gambling-houses.... [Away from the depot] Ogden is a pretty quiet town, somewhat larger than Brigham City.

In the late 1880s, after years of complaints over the ramshackle state of the Ogden depot, the railroads constructed a new station.

When the depot was completed in 1889, it thrilled the people of Ogden. But in 1923, when a fired gutted it, Ogdenites did not view the fire as a great tragedy. They felt the old depot had become outdated and unsafe, and they were ready for a new one. Though railroad officials initially declared their intention to repair the old depot, the outraged cries of the citizens convinced them to build a new station. Los Angeles architects John and Donald Parkinson designed an Italian

Renaissance–style building. Erected in 1924 at a cost of $400,000, it was called Union Station.

Rail traffic continued to increase through the 1920s. The 1930s saw a downturn in all business, but World War II brought a new prosperity to the great railroad junction. During the war years, up to 120 trains a day passed through Ogden's Union Station.

The 1950s marked the beginning of the decline of passenger trains. By the late 1960s, few remained. In the 1970s Ogdenites realized Union Station was worth preserving, and in 1978 they rededicated it as an Amtrak stop and historical museum. The station continues to serve as a depot as well as housing a number of restaurants and meeting halls.

Ogden during World War II

World War II provided the greatest stimulus to employment and structural change of any event in Ogden's history. Because of its location— about equidistant from the major Pacific Coast ports of Seattle and San Diego—and its railroad advantage, the Ogden area was selected for four major military establishments.

The Ogden Arsenal was one of the nation's major ordnance supply depots, storing and shipping munitions of all types to all the Pacific ports and employing over 6,000 people. A major military base was constructed at Clearfield, which became Hill Air Force Base. The Utah General Depot was also built near Ogden and was the largest quartermaster depot in the United States. It shipped all nonweapon supplies to the West Coast for

Peery's Egyptian Theatre, Washington Boulevard, Ogden.

transportation to overseas locations. The depot employed 4,000 civilians and 5,000 Italian and German prisoners of war. Suddenly, government jobs were abundant, and along with those jobs came the need for new communities, more housing, and goods and services for the people who would live there.

After the war, military activity slowed considerably. Though for the most part the installations remained active, they were scaled back.

Weber State University

In 1889 the LDS Church started Weber Stake Academy in Ogden, providing basic education and religious training to Mormon students in Weber County. In 1918 the school's name was changed to Weber Normal College, and teacher training became its primary emphasis. The church signed the school over to the state in 1933, and it changed its name again to Weber State College. The school became a four-year institution in 1962 and a university in 1991. It maintains a student body of approximately 15,000.

The Bigelow Hotel

Though Ogden has changed a bit since the glory days of the railroad era, some fine landmarks remain from former prosperous times. On the southeast corner of Washington Boulevard and Twenty-fifth Street is the grand old Bigelow Hotel (now the Radisson Hotel). Constructed in 1927, this fine hotel was one of a trio of great Utah hotels. The other two were in Salt Lake City: the Newhouse (now demolished) and the Hotel Utah (now the Joseph Smith Memorial Building, belonging to the LDS Church).

The Bigelow, designed by the Salt Lake architectural firm of Hodgson and McClenahan, matches the Italian Renaissance style of Union Station. A number of the Bigelow's interior rooms paid tribute to other European countries: an Arabian coffee shop, a businessman's meeting room in the atmosphere of old Spain, an English room paneled to look like Bromley Castle, and, returning to Italy, a Florentine ballroom. Unfortunately, much of the character of these grand old rooms has been lost through years of remodeling.

Peery's Egyptian Theatre

A major landmark on Washington Boulevard, Peery's Egyptian Theatre has recently been restored by a consortium of private and public groups. The historic structure was built by the Peery brothers in 1924 on the site of their father's 1866 adobe home. It was condemned in 1984. A number of Ogden businesspeople joined together to buy the building soon after. To raise funds for the purchase, local attorney Bernard Allen

Reconstructed Fort Buenaventura, Ogden.

sold Egyptian Theatre T-shirts from the trunk of his car. Eventually, through the efforts of many contributors, funds were accumulated to restore the structure. The building reopened in January 1997, along with an adjacent conference center. The theater is used today for ballet and symphony performances and other cultural and civic events.

Fort Buenaventura

Located at 2450 A Avenue, the site of Miles Goodyear's original homestead in Ogden has been set aside as a state park. Guides dressed as mountain men help visitors understand the lifestyle of the period. The park also has camping and picnic facilities.

UT 16 and UT 30
Wyoming State Line–Garden City
53 miles

This section of Utah is characterized by wide-open high-altitude sagebrush deserts dominated by the rounded Monte Cristo Mountains. In this often wintry section of Utah, only rugged individuals willing to work the hard ranch life can make a living.

UT 16 traverses Rich County, a region known by most people for its extremely cold winter temperatures. Randolph and Woodruff vie for the coldest winter lows in the state, and often in the United States, with tem-

Rendezvous Beach, at the south end of Bear Lake.

peratures dropping to sixty degrees below zero. Summers are characterized by pleasantly warm days and cool nights. In the valleys around
Randolph and Woodruff, frosts in July and August are fairly common. J.
Golden Kimball, a colorful early Mormon church leader, summed it up
the best when he said Rich County had nine months of winter and three
months of late fall.

Despite its reputation, this section of Utah has much more to offer
than frigid temperatures. Beautiful blue Bear Lake, one of the best places
to swim and boat in Utah (though the water is never very warm), straddles
the Utah-Idaho border. With its gently sloping sandy beaches, Bear Lake
is ideal for adults and children alike. Ice fishing during the winter is also
very popular on Bear Lake.

Woodruff

Woodruff is a lonely outpost at the junction of the Monte Cristo road
(UT 39) and UT 16, which heads north to Randolph. The Mormons were
not the first white settlers in Woodruff. Ranchers with large cattle herds
came shortly before the Mormons, and, having far more money and power,
they were able to claim more land. Mormon ranchers came in 1870 and
1871 from Bountiful in search of new territory. Attracted by the lush grasses

Wilford Woodruff home, Woodruff.

and plentiful water for their cattle, they made this their home. They named the place for LDS apostle Wilford Woodruff, who lived in the town. The apostle Woodruff later became fourth president of the church.

Woodruff struggled as a town for a number of different reasons. Settlers wanted to live on their lands, not in town as was the Mormon custom, which made cooperative efforts difficult. Also, large cattle operations from Wyoming bought up sizable blocks of land. Publicly held lands were cheap, but much of the land around Woodruff had been deeded to the Union Pacific Railroad by the U.S. government during construction of the transcontinental railroad. These lands were now being sold for a high price—too high for Mormon settlers to pay. Wyoming ranchers came in and purchased these blocks of land.

Though non-Mormons were the first ranchers in the area, the Mormons managed to outlast them. The Mormons had the religious faith to stay through the cold and drought. They persevered through hard times, outlasting most of the non-Mormon ranchers. Woodruff is still basically a ranching community today.

One of Woodruff's native sons, David Kennedy, was secretary of the treasury in the Nixon administration, following an illustrious banking career in Chicago. He was also a prominent LDS Church leader.

Randolph

Ten miles north of Woodruff is Randolph (elevation 6,442 feet), the Rich County seat and a place famous for its freezing air. How cold is it? Randolph is so cold that one early resident was told that only a Mormon could live in such a frigid place. On January 14, 1888, Randolph's temperature supposedly plummeted to the coldest ever recorded in Utah history, sixty-five degrees below zero.

Randolph was established by Mormons in 1870. When they arrived, large herds of antelope roamed the range. As sheep ranching became prevalent, the antelope disappeared. Fur trading was another important source of income for early Randolph citizens. People didn't like the extreme cold temperatures in the region, but the cold produced thick coats on mink, muskrat, marten, otter, beaver, fox, coyote, and wolf, and each pelt brought a good price. As the antelope and deer herds dwindled, and other furbearing animals became scarce, wolves got aggressive and the coyote population soared. Ranchers began an assault on the predators to defend their livestock. By about 1920 the wolves were gone and coyotes had all but disappeared.

The severe winter cold and the frosts the rest of the year were hard for Randolph residents to endure. In 1872 ninety families lived in Randolph; five years later just fifty-one remained. Those who survived realized they could not grow gardens or field crops. Livestock would have to be their main source of income.

In 1883 the Oregon Shortline Railroad was completed to Sage Creek Junction, giving Rich County ranchers easier access to markets. The area became more desirable and Randolph's population nearly doubled between 1877 and 1897.

Only one legal execution ever took place in Rich County, the result of a stolen case of raspberries. In 1896 two young men, Patrick Coughlin, age twenty-one, and Fred George, age nineteen, stole some raspberries from a peddler near Salt Lake City. They were jailed, but soon escaped and stole two horses to make their getaway. They shot their way past several posses, wounding a Summit County sheriff in the process. The fugitives ended up at a ranch near Randolph. Another gunfight ensued, and two lawmen were killed. Coughlin and George escaped, but they were finally recaptured. Though Coughlin insisted he had only fired in self-defense and took his case all the way to the U.S. Supreme Court, he was executed by a firing squad. George served a prison term and was later released. He lived out his life peacefully in Park City.

The most prominent building in Randolph is the Randolph Tabernacle, constructed between 1898 and 1914 for the Randolph Ward. The ward's

Randolph Tabernacle.

leader, or bishop, John C. Gray, who served in that capacity for twenty years, was the architect and general contractor of the project. The work progressed slowly because of the size of the project and the limited funding provided by the approximately 100 families who contributed to its costs. In 1984–85 a well-designed addition was made to the tabernacle, and the original building was remodeled.

Laketown

UT 30 climbs through some hills and then travels down into Bear Lake Valley. If you had traveled to the southern end of Bear Lake before the establishment of white society, you would have found hundreds of tepees belonging to the Ute, Sioux, and Shoshone Indians, who made their summer camps on its shores. In the summers of 1827 and 1828, mountain men added their numbers to the native inhabitants in this part of the valley. Shoshone and Bannock Indians had been using the area to meet and trade long before they ever saw any white people.

Despite the established domain of the natives, Mormon settlers moved to the south end of Bear Lake in 1864 and built a fort there in 1867. Because of the determination on both white and native sides to keep peace, no serious conflicts occurred. The white population tried to cooperate with the Indians, and Shoshone Chief Washakie, despite the Mormons breaking a treaty giving his tribe the southern half of the lake, made sure the Indians avoided fights with the settlers. However, because of the whites' continued intrusions on Indian hunting and fishing grounds, tensions mounted, and in 1870 Mormon Church officials and Indian tribal leaders held a crucial conference. After the meeting, the natives relinquished their territorial claim and moved to Wyoming's Wind River Mountains.

UT 39
Woodruff–Ogden
62 miles

UT 39 between Woodruff and Ogden traverses Monte Cristo Pass, one of the prettiest passes in the state. The Monte Cristo road is a wonderful place to leave the hustle and bustle behind and enjoy wide-open views. UT 39 begins in Woodruff and climbs quickly through ranch country to scenic alpine heights. You can see five counties from the top of Monte Cristo Pass and east into Wyoming. The highway then curves down to Huntsville and past the Pineview Reservoir to Ogden.

Abbey of Our Lady of the Holy Trinity

Southeast of Huntsville, against the foothills of the sheltering mountains, the Order of Cistercians of the Strict Observance (Trappists) operates a monastery with a farm, chapel, and small gift store.

The Trappist order originated in France in the 1100s. The order has ninety monasteries and fifty-nine convents worldwide. Operating in the

The Abbey of Our Lady of the Holy Trinity, near Huntsville.

United States since 1848, they now have seventeen abbeys throughout the country. The Trappists seek seclusion and beauty through prayer, manual labor, and meditation.

The Abbey of Our Lady of the Holy Trinity was built in 1947. The monks attend worship services seven times a day and work on the farm, which produces honey, poultry and beef products, and baked goods. Visitors to the monastery are welcome in the chapel and gift shop, but tours are not conducted and large groups are urged to call ahead. Men over twenty who seek a day or two of meditation are welcome at the abbey, regardless of religious affiliation.

Huntsville

Captain Howard Stansbury, who was in charge of an exploratory and mapping expedition for the Army Corps of Topographical Engineers, visited the Ogden mountain valley where Huntsville now sits in 1849. In his journal, Stansbury called Ogden Valley "the most interesting and delightful spot" of his entire journey.

Weber County residents began using this beautiful valley as summer range for their cattle in 1856. In the fall of 1860 the Hunt family came here to cut hay and build homes. With the help of additional families, they built a fort and faced the deep snows of a long winter. By 1861 a number of new families had arrived and a small town came into being.

Huntsville, besides being a beautiful town, is perhaps best known as the childhood home of LDS Church president David O. McKay. McKay, best remembered as the kindly white-haired gentleman who headed the church from 1951 to 1970, was born in Huntsville in 1873. As an adult he became a popular and effective educator. In 1906 McKay was called to the church's Quorum of the Twelve Apostles but continued to serve in various aspects of education. Built in 1871, McKay's boyhood home at 7600 East between First and Second Streets is owned by the descendants of the family and is open to visitors on Saturdays during the summer months.

Huntsville today remains a pleasant farming town, though tourism is also an important part of the local economy. The town boasts the oldest continually operating saloon in Utah, located at 200 South Street.

Eden and Liberty

North of UT 39 on UT 158, two little towns tucked into the north end of Ogden Valley vie for the honor of being the most picturesque hamlets in Utah. They are Eden and Liberty. Settled in the 1860s, the whole Ogden Valley served as rangeland for the residents of Weber County. Even after some families started making homes in the higher valley, cattle herds still grazed in the area.

Both Eden and Liberty were first used as a grazing area. A cattle herder built his cabin at Eden in 1857. In 1859 permanent settlers came to live. Soon these people were ready for a town site, so they sent for Washington Jenkins to survey the town. He said it was the most beautiful place he had ever surveyed and told the settlers they ought to call it Eden. They agreed.

The residents of Eden lived on their farms until 1865, when the Black Hawk War broke out in central Utah. Because Indians all over the territory became more hostile, the settlers banded together in a fort. They remained together until the late 1860s, when life became safer in northern Utah's remote areas.

Eden remains a beautiful mountain-valley town. Much of its farmland was obliterated in the 1930s by the waters of Pineview Reservoir, but jobs relating to tourism have replaced the farm income. The huge reservoir attracts many water recreationists during warm weather. Nordic Valley ski resort is also close to Eden, so the town's motels and inns see business year-round.

US 91
Idaho State Line–Logan
17 miles

US 91 runs north and south through the verdant farmland of northern Cache Valley. Small towns dot the countryside and beautiful mountains frame the valley.

Richmond

Follow US 91 south through peaceful farm country to the northern agricultural town of Richmond. For many years a large part of Richmond's economy has been based on the dairy industry and its black-and-white Holstein cows. Black and White Days is the annual celebration held every May in Richmond.

Richmond was settled in 1859. Despite snow depths of two and a half feet and severe cold, seventeen families wintered here in 1859–60. In 1904 Utah's first evaporated-milk factory, the Sego Milk Company, was built in Richmond. Another dairy-products company in Richmond is Casco, maker of the Fat Boy ice cream sandwich and the Casco ice cream bar. The Casco bar, a chocolate- and nut-covered ice cream bar, was born when Casper Merrill decided to sell nut sundaes to the crowds at Richmond's

Richmond celebrates its Black and White Days each May to honor the Holstein cows—such as this mother and new calf—that employ a large part of the population.

Fourth of July celebration in 1925. The operation was so successful that Merrill expanded his line of ice cream treats, which are now marketed throughout much of the nation. Also in Richmond, Pepperidge Farms manufactures their famous baked goods.

Smithfield

The landscape changes little in the ancient lake bottom of Cache Valley between Richmond and Smithfield. Summit Creek, Smithfield's main water source, first attracted settlers in 1859. Eleven families wintered there in 1859–60. Smithfield was named for John Glover Smith, the first bishop of the area's LDS ward. It has long been an agricultural community. However, a lot of the farms are being developed into housing projects, and Smithfield has become a bedroom community to Logan.

Main Street in Smithfield is a lovely, tree-lined avenue. At 100 Main Street sits an impressive old white rock-and-brick structure, the Douglas General Mercantile. Built in 1883, it was a major business establishment for this small farming town and remains the oldest commercial building in Smithfield. In 1964 the building was converted to an American Legion post.

UT 83
Brigham City–Promontory
25 miles

Corinne

By 1868 it was clear that the land around present-day Corinne would be right in the path of the transcontinental railroad. Mark Gilmore purchased 160 acres that year and built a house in anticipation of a land boom. Others joined him, intending to establish the biggest city in Utah. They laid out a large town, even setting aside a university block, and by the end of March 1869, 1,500 people lived in this newly formed railroad town.

The town thrived with all the industries related to railroad freighting, and many other businesses and entertainment centers sprang up as well. All the California-bound trains stopped at Corinne, and such notables as Tom Thumb and Maude Adams performed at Corinne's opera house. Montana mines were booming, and much of the ore came through Corinne. The railroad was not the only form of transportation in and out of Corinne. The city was close enough to the Great Salt Lake to serve as a port on the Bear River. The boat *The City of Corinne* transported ore and passengers back and forth between Corinne and Tooele County.

Corinne was the first non-Mormon town in Utah. Mormon leaders abhorred it, not just for its strong anti-Mormon attitude, but for the sinful episodes that occurred there. Twenty-eight saloons and over eighty prostitutes served the miners who worked in town, as well as those traveling through. Quick divorces became a specialty in Corinne. Couples could pay $2.50 in gold and turn the crank on a machine that produced a form signed by the Corinne city judge. The applicants simply filled in their names and they were divorced. The process was so successful that the city soon provided the service mail-order. Unfortunately it proved

Corinne, circa 1869. —UTAH STATE HISTORICAL SOCIETY

illegal, and the mess of over 2,000 illegally dissolved marriages had to be cleared through the courts.

Corinne quickly became the political and social center for Utah's non-Mormons. They organized the American Liberal Party of Utah in Corinne in 1870. The strong anti-Mormon contingent of this party tried unsuccessfully to move the territorial capital from Salt Lake City to Corinne. The first Methodist-Episcopal church in Utah was dedicated in 1870 in Corinne. Because of the largely non-Mormon population, raising money for the structure was not difficult. Over $1,500 was raised within just two days of the project's announcement.

When LDS Church leaders began construction on the Utah Northern Railroad in 1871, they intended to divert Corinne's Montana trade to other Mormon settlements in northern Utah. Their plan largely succeeded, and, within just a few years, much of the freight traffic bypassed Corinne. By the end of the 1870s, many of Corinne's businesses had closed. The boom was over, and most of the non-Mormons had left. Train service to Corinne became less needed, and in 1903–4 the Southern Pacific Railroad built a trestle (Lucin Cutoff) across the Great Salt Lake, bypassing Corinne altogether. Non-Mormons sold their property cheaply to Mormons, who moved in and changed the town into a Utah Mormon agricultural settlement. However, this small town never lost its old buildings and town center.

Though dilapidated and partly abandoned, Corinne still has the air of an Old West boomtown that has gone to sleep and dreams of the fun and wickedness of days long ago—and of the time when others shared the aspiration that Corinne would someday be the Queen of Utah.

Promontory

About twenty miles west of Corinne a road turns off UT 83 to the west. Due west a few miles is a state park commemorating the joining of the railroads at Promontory Summit in 1869. Promontory Point itself is actually south of here, but it's not developed for tourists. Although Promontory is one of the most significant locations in the history of the United States, the place is now practically deserted except for a museum and a couple of railroad engines. At this lonely desert site on May 10, 1869, officials drove the last spike to connect the Central Pacific and the Union Pacific Railroads, uniting the country from coast to coast with the iron road. The Central Pacific's engine Jupiter and the Union Pacific's No. 119 bumped noses here and changed the West forever.

The ceremony was supposed to take place a few days earlier, but torrential rains caused flooding all along the Wasatch Front, delaying the last stages of the work. Those awaiting the ceremonies didn't hold off on the festivities. Though nine miles from the nearest water source, Promontory was not a "dry" town. It had more than its share of saloons, and those waiting for the final ceremony kept themselves occupied in the camp's watering places. Quoted in Stephen Carr's *Historical Guide to Utah Ghost Towns*, the editor of the *Utah Reporter* described Promontory as "4,900 feet above sea level, but it ought to be 49,000 feet below it, for its size, morally nearer to hell than any town on the road!"

Promontory's wickedness, however, was short-lived. After the joining of the rails, there was little need for the town. The main terminus moved to Ogden, leaving no reason for anyone to live so far out in the desert. After Lucin Cutoff was completed in 1904, the rail traffic passed far to the south.

On September 8, 1942, a significant quasireenactment of the driving of the Golden Spike took place at Promontory. Though two locomotives faced each other, and dignitaries and a crowd of 200 people attended, this ceremony differed from the original in one important way: this time the spike was lifted up rather than hammered down. The old rail line north of the lake had become obsolete, and the steel of the rails was necessary to the war effort. Crews worked through the summer pulling up 123 miles

Joining the rails at 11:00 A.M. on May 10, 1869, Promontory, Utah.
—UTAH STATE HISTORICAL SOCIETY

of track. One observer at the 1942 ceremony had also attended the 1869 event. Her name was Mary Opsen, and she had worked as a waitress on the Promontory Mountain line crew's dining car in 1869.

Promontory was declared a national historic site in 1957. Here, replicas of the Jupiter and No. 119 engines chug along the tracks several times a day in minireenactments of the great moment in 1869. A museum displays artifacts from the railroad construction.

I-15
Idaho State Line–Tremonton
22 miles

I-15 crosses from Idaho into Utah in Box Elder County, traveling past productive farm country and bypassing many almost-forgotten towns.

Garland

One of the many towns east of I-15, Garland is another quiet place. Davis County settlers moved here in 1892 to start dry farming. They called their town Sunset for a time because of the beautiful sunsets to the west. After they built their canal, locals changed the name to honor its builder, William Garland.

The old sugar factory in Garland.

Sugar beets have long been a very successful crop in Garland. When the Utah Idaho Sugar Company built a sugar plant at Garland in 1903, the town boomed. It knew a long period of prosperity until 1978 when the plant closed. The population remains fairly steady, even without the work from the plant. Many people maintain their farms and others work at the Morton-Thiokol company in Brigham City.

Tremonton

Tremonton, south of Garland, is the largest Utah town north of Brigham City. Farmers moved to this area in the late 1880s, and in 1903 they laid out a town. A number of businesses moved here, and the place bustled for several years. Previous to the 1900–1901 town survey, a German colony settled to the west of what is now Tremonton and organized the Christian Apostolic Church.

Tremonton is the trade and banking center for northern Box Elder County's extensive farms, and is home for many employees of Morton-Thiokol.

I-84
Idaho State Line–Tremonton
48 miles

Rounding the bend and meandering through the mountains that separate this section of Utah from Idaho, I-15 passes the sleepy little town of Snowville.

Snowville

The Curlew Valley, so named for the numerous curlew snipes that nest around Snowville, was frequented by trappers long before Mormons came. In 1848 some members of the Mormon Battalion traveling to Salt Lake City from California camped in a cave near Snowville.

In 1871 settlers from Malad, Idaho, moved south to build cattle ranches in this area. The place attracted them with its lush, deep grasses and good water source. The town was named Snowville in honor of Lorenzo Snow, who called families to settle this valley.

The first town travelers usually pass when driving into Utah from Idaho is Snowville. The place is small, but when a car breaks down on the lonely stretch of I-84, it is heaven-sent.

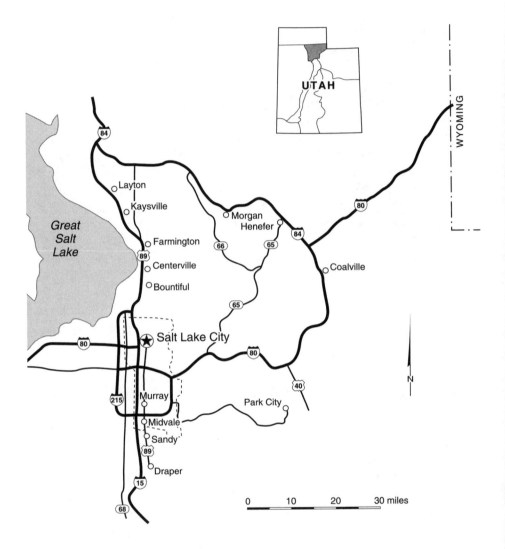

UTAH

WYOMING

Great
Salt
Lake

○Layton

Kaysville

Morgan
Henefer

○Farmington

Centerville

○Bountiful

Coalville

⭐ Salt Lake City

Murray

Midvale
Sandy

Draper

Park City

0   10   20   30 miles

N

PART II
The Salt Lake Area

Although the Mormon pioneers were not the first group of people to enter Utah, they made the strongest impact. In ancient times, the Fremont Indians roamed the mountains and valleys of northern and central Utah. By the time the Spanish started pushing north from New Mexico in the 1700s, the land was inhabited by Ute Indian bands. The Spanish explorers stayed in the region south of the Great Salt Lake, probably never even glimpsing its briny expanses. During the first half of the nineteenth century, trappers came and went and, though depleting the mountain streams of their beaver populations, they left without creating settlements in the area.

In the 1840s a few parties bound for California had the courage (or misjudgment) to attempt crossing the Great Salt Desert of Utah. A few of the migrants of 1846 considered settling in the Salt Lake Valley, but, unwilling try it all by themselves, they continued west with their comrades. Thus the arid valleys of Utah were left waiting and available for the Mormon pioneers.

It was in 1847 that a group of Mormons determined to make a permanent settlement left Fort Bridger in Wyoming, bound for the valley of the Great Salt Lake. In a land that had previously been only a crossing ground, never inhabited even by the native tribes for more than a few months at a time, theirs was destined to be the first lasting white settlement.

THE GREAT SALT LAKE

The valley, the county, and the city all receive their name from the enormous body of water in the northwest corner of the valley. The Great Salt Lake is one of Utah's most remarkable geographical features. The average salinity of the lake is eight times as high as that of the ocean, ranging from 11.4 percent at the lake's south end to 22 percent at its north end, and sometimes reaching 26 percent in years of extreme drought. Its depth is usually about thirty-five feet at the deepest point, and much of that is composed of a lower layer of thick, gooey sediment. Because of the extreme lack of visibility for divers and the inability of magnetometers to locate wreckage in the mineral-rich water, a number of downed planes have never been found. The lake covers about 1,500 square miles, depending on level variations due to rainfall.

In addition to being a wonder of nature, the lake provides some natural product resources. From its waters are harvested brine shrimp and eggs for use in fish hatcheries and fish food. Salt, potash, and magnesium are also mined from the lake. Gunnison and Hat Islands, favorite gull, pelican, and heron nesting grounds, were once also mined for their rich fertilizer. For a few years in the late 1890s, men dug and sifted the bird droppings and sold them to farmers. Though agriculturally successful, the product was not a huge financial success, and the guano industry lasted only a few years.

Above all, however, is the Great Salt Lake's role in the area's tourism industry. Water recreation abounds here. By the way, it is true that swimmers float quite readily in the briny waters, but be careful not to get any in your eyes!

I-80
Wyoming State Line–Salt Lake City
81 miles

I-80 is one of the country's major arteries, stretching west from New York City all the way to San Francisco. The Utah section of this freeway follows part of the Mormon Trail. After departing Evanston, Wyoming, I-80 descends into Echo Canyon.

ECHO CANYON

The first advance company of Mormon pioneers reached what they named Echo Canyon on July 13, 1847. The echoes reverberated off the steep red rock of the canyon walls, causing distinctive amplifications of all the sounds below. William Clayton, an early pioneer and author of the well-known Mormon hymn "Come, Come Ye Saints," said the wagons rattling through the canyon sounded like someone hammering.

Ten years after the first group of Mormons rumbled down Echo Canyon, word came that General Johnston's army, sent by the U.S. government, was approaching Utah with the aim of obliterating the

Pioneers nearing the end of their journey. —UTAH STATE HISTORICAL SOCIETY

Mormons (at least, that was the way the pioneers understood it). Over 1,200 men worked to dig breastworks and fortifications in Echo Canyon. The area was manned for several months in 1857, but in December the men were sent back to Salt Lake City for the winter. Some of the breastworks still exist in the canyon. No shots were fired from the fortifications, but they delayed the advance of the army, allowing time for peace talks before the army finally entered Utah the following summer, thus preventing a war.

The hooves of the Pony Express thundered down Echo Canyon for eighteen short months from April 1860 to October 1861. The swaying Overland stagecoaches also rushed headlong down to the lower valleys.

Mark Twain traveled through Echo Canyon via stagecoach during the Pony Express era. In *Roughing It* Twain describes his impressions:

> Echo Canyon is twenty miles long. It was like a long, smooth, narrow street, with a gradual descending grade, and shut in by enormous perpendicular walls of coarse conglomerate, four hundred feet high in many places, and turreted like medieval castles. This was the most faultless piece of road in the mountains, and the driver said he would "let his team out." He did, and if the Pacific express-trains whiz through there now any faster than we did then in the stage-coach, I envy the passengers the exhilaration of it. We fairly seemed to pick up our wheels and fly.

A 1997 reenactment of the pioneer trek through Echo Canyon.

A few years later, a major link with the outside world was established when the telegraph was built down Echo Canyon. The tall trees for its poles were cut in the mountains of Summit County. Brigham Young sent the first message over the new telegraph line on October 18, 1861. Part of the message read, "Utah has not seceded but is firm for the Constitution and laws of our once happy country."

In 1868 the Union Pacific Railroad built its iron way down Echo Canyon, forever joining Utah with the rest of the world. From there the railway continued northwest through Weber Canyon.

Castle Rock

Today on a Utah highway map, three dots appear in Echo Canyon going southwest on I-80: Wahsatch, Emory, and Castle Rock. They are all basically uninhabited railroad sidings now, but Castle Rock was the scene of a suspicious incident in the 1860s. A French trapper purchased an old Pony Express station there and moved it about one mile away. He disappeared and another man claimed to have bought the station from him, but several years later the Frenchman's body was discovered in a nearby canyon.

Castle Rock was the site of a Union Pacific Railroad stop for a time after the tracks were laid in 1868. A small town grew up, consisting mostly

The Thousand Mile Tree, near the junction of Echo and Weber Canyons, was an important landmark near the end of the Mormon Trail. This excursion party made the trip back to the tree after rail transportation had made travel much easier. With construction of highways, the tree no longer exists.
—UTAH STATE HISTORICAL SOCIETY

of ranchers. Gradually, though, it faded, and most of the buildings were moved or burned.

The Thousand Mile Tree

At the town of Echo, I-80 meets I-84. The latter heads into Weber Canyon while I-80 continues south and west through Parley's Canyon. The Thousand Mile Tree grew near the junction of I-80 and I-84. A major milestone on the Mormon Trail, the tree marked 1,000 miles from the start of the trail in Winter Quarters (Omaha), Nebraska. From this point the Mormon Trail heads north a few miles to circle into Emigration Canyon.

PARLEY'S CANYON ROAD

The pioneer route to Salt Lake through Emigration Canyon, pioneered by the Donner party and later the Mormons, was grueling. Climbing the two steep mountains exhausted people and animals alike, and rattling along winding, narrow canyon bottoms took a great toll on wagons. The route crossed streams some forty-four times after passing Henefer. In short, a better route was needed.

Parley P. Pratt, an apostle of the Mormon Church, set out one summer day in 1848 to look for a better way into the valley. After some preliminary investigation, he reported back to the city fathers that a route might

Parley P. Pratt.
—LDS CHURCH
HISTORICAL
DEPARTMENT

be feasible through what they called the Kanyon of Big Canyon Creek. Two men, John Van Cott and Daniel Spencer, were recruited to accompany Pratt on a further investigation. The three came up with an even better possible route, which would turn southwest after Echo Canyon and follow the approximate course of the present I-80. Workers immediately began constructing the road in the hope that it would accommodate immigrants by August. Unfortunately, work was slow, and the project had to be abandoned for the winter that November.

The following spring, Pratt decided to complete the road himself. His crops had failed that year and he had some time on his hands, so he went to work in the canyon (most likely hiring help). But in the winter of 1849–50 Brigham Young called Pratt to head an exploratory party into southern Utah, which delayed road building until the next summer. Upon returning north, Pratt resumed his labors, and he was able to open his "Golden Pass Road" in July 1850 as a toll road. As reprinted in *West from Fort Bridger*, edited by J. Roderic Korns and Dale L. Morgan, advertisements in the *Deseret News* posted the cost of the tolls:

> 50 cents per conveyance drawn by one animal.
> 75 cents per conveyance drawn by two animals.
> 10 cents per each additional draught, pack, or saddle animal.
> 5 cents per head for loose stock.
> 1 cent per head for sheep.

Then it added:

> If a road worked by the most persevering industry, and open country, good feed and fuel, beautifully romantic and sublime scenery, are any inducement, take the new road, and thus encourage public improvement.
>
> —G.S.L. City. June 22, 1850
> P. P. Pratt, Proprietor

Pratt's new road was a success. He took in $1,500 that season and felt he had eased the immigrants' journey into the Salt Lake Valley. Unfortunately, when Pratt was called as a mission president to South America and the Pacific Islands, the road lay nearly idle for a time. In order to fund his mission, he sold his interest in the road. Soon the Golden Pass Road fell into disrepair, with only occasional travelers using it.

The road returned to popularity in 1862 when the Overland Stage chose Pratt's road for its route, and subsequent migration was almost entirely diverted from the old Emigration Canyon way.

Coalville

The site of Coalville, south of Echo off I-80, became a popular camping spot on the Mormon Trail after Parley Pratt blasted his road through Parley's Canyon. In the fall of 1858, William Henderson Smith found ripened wheat growing in the Chalk Creek campground. Someone had spilled the wheat and it sprouted. He felt if wheat would ripen there, then it was a good place for a settlement. The following spring several families from Sugar House moved to Chalk Creek to make a permanent home. Soon thereafter, hunters discovered coal.

A number of mines opened at Coalville, bringing much needed revenues to the district. Several mines continued operating in Coalville until the 1950s or 1960s, but none are operating currently. The town was named for miners who came from Coalville, England.

The Summit County Courthouse

The Summit County Courthouse established Coalville as the most important town in the county when it was built in in 1871. A more permanent structure replaced the courthouse in 1903, built in the Romanesque Revival style of locally kilned brick. The fortresslike courthouse dominates Coalville's main street.

Hoytsville

The highway follows the Weber River south about three miles to Hoytsville, an old wayside town. A ferry operated at Hoytsville to move all the travelers across the Weber River. The Bradburys, the first people to make a permanent home here, came in the fall of 1859. The early residents scraped out a meager living from whatever they could grow, selling any surplus to passing travelers.

In 1861 Brigham Young called Samuel P. Hoyt, an expert miller from Fillmore, to go to what is now Hoytsville. Until 1862, when Hoyt completed his mill, everyone in Summit County had to travel to Salt Lake City to have their wheat ground into flour. The mill closed in 1867 because of water problems.

Hoytsville received a needed boost in 1864 when a coal mine was opened. It was mined intermittently for many years.

Wanship

Round a bend in the interstate the little town of Wanship straddles the freeway. Settled in 1859 by a family from Provo, Wanship was named for Shoshone Chief Wanship, which means "good man."

About 1870 Park City and Coalville competed for the Summit County seat. Though Wanship was Summit's first county seat, residents knew they didn't have enough power to hang on to control. Not wanting the gentile Park City to get the title, they threw their support behind Coalville. Coalville became county seat, a distinction it still retains.

From Wanship I-80 squeezes through a brief narrow canyon and emerges into a conglomeration of Summit County bedroom communities that are some of the fastest growing towns in Utah: Jeremy Ranch,

Park City's Ontario Mine. —UTAH STATE HISTORICAL SOCIETY

Snyderville, Silver Springs, Kimball Junction, Summit Park, Pinebrook. This high ranch country first served Mormon settlers as grazing land, and Snyderville was the first town in Summit County. Parley P. Pratt discovered this beautiful area in 1848. In 1849 Samuel C. Snyder, a pioneer from New York, bought Pratt's rights to the area and helped build a road up the canyon (called Big Canyon at that time). He moved to Snyderville in 1850. The town was not named for Samuel Snyder, however, but for his younger brother, G. G. Snyder, a probate judge.

The area was heavily timbered, and milling of lumber became an important early occupation. The sawmill helped supply the lumber for the big building boom that occurred in Park City in the latter 1800s. Cattle also proved a good source of income, providing a living to many families that came to Snyderville and built their cabins.

Gradually all the small farms in Snyderville were bought up and joined to make larger ranches. The town disappeared for many years, with little evidence that a community once thrived there.

Park City

Though not originally a bedroom community, Park City, five miles south of I-80 on UT 224, is becoming increasingly crowded with escapees from the cities of the Wasatch Front.

Soon after the railroad came, rich ore was discovered at Park City. A mining boom changed Summit County from a ranch-based society to a gold- and silver-based one. Prospectors discovered silver and lead ore in Park City in 1868 and 1869, and a number of mines opened. Gen. Patrick Connor's soldiers were the first to discover ore in the Flagstaff Mine. In the beginning, more lead than silver was produced. In 1872 silver was struck in the Ontario Mine, which for many years was felt to be the greatest silver mine in the world. George Hearst, owner of the *San Francisco Examiner*, bought the Ontario Mine for $27,000, giving the Hearst fortunes a big boost. With the Ontario Mine, the big boom started in Park City. The Silver King Mine was discovered in 1892. Mining magnates Thomas Kearns and David Keith both made their fortunes from the Park City mines.

Unlike in some mining communities, families moved to Park City and set up businesses. Though Park City had twenty-three saloons and plenty of prostitutes, shootings, and rabble-rousing, it was generally a quieter and more respectable place than the other mining towns of the period. Mine owners did not control all the businesses, which made Park City more balanced than other mining towns. Many miners had families, and the city operated a decent water system and a well-controlled government.

Park City, October 23, 1912. —UTAH STATE HISTORICAL SOCIETY

After the town was incorporated in 1880, the local government assessed an annual $1,200 licensing fee on saloons, and those saloons able to pay stayed open. They were not allowed to sell alcohol to a man whose family was in need or to one who had drunk too much already. The town government also regulated prostitution, which stayed legal well into the twentieth century, even through Prohibition.

A number of different religions were practiced in Park City, but Mormonism was greatly discouraged. Mormons had to meet in secret in a cellar. A Loyalty League was established in the town with the sole purpose of wiping out Mormonism by lawful and peaceable means.

The town had fires in 1882, 1889, and 1898. The 1898 fire started in a boardinghouse near the center of town and quickly spread until the flames had consumed 260 homes and businesses and two churches. The city sustained more than a million dollars in losses. Some felt Park City would never recover, but people from all over the nation and all local denominations, including the Mormons, contributed to rebuilding it. This united effort went a long way toward mending differences between the religions.

Mining in Park City lasted well into the 1940s—much longer than it did in most other Utah mining towns. By the 1950s most of the mines had shut down. The place was becoming a ghost town until the ski industry recognized it as a ski haven. Lifts were built at Park City in the 1960s, and it has been on the rise ever since. The local economy relies on money brought in by skiers, tourists, and part-time residents. The main street was recognized as a National Historic District in 1976.

Park City is now one of the fastest growing cities in Utah. Growth has been so rapid that the city and county have had to experiment with building moratoriums and fees to try to control the area's overwhelming increase in population and building.

The little valley that encircles the town of Park City was once filled with trees. When the first settlers came, they chopped down the trees so they could get their wagons through. This parklike setting, as well as nearby Parley's Park (where Parley P. Pratt owned ranching property), gave the town the name Parley's Park City. It was eventually shortened to Park City.

Kimball Art Center and Park City Museum

The Kimball Art Center at Park and Heber Avenues displays local and national artists and features musical performances. The museum also has a gift shop.

The Park City Museum, 528 Main Street, is in the old Territorial Jail. It offers changing exhibits and guided tours of the old historic district.

SALT LAKE VALLEY

I-80 drops steeply along walls of Jurassic nugget sandstone into the Salt Lake Valley, a broad, flat, ancient lake bed about twenty miles long by fifteen miles wide. Public perceptions of the Salt Lake area vary greatly. To some it is Zion, to others, a marvelous ski destination. Still others may think of it as the home of the Mormons and their mysterious ways. The lake itself has an almost mythical image for many. Whatever your perception of Salt Lake, this valley has been Utah's center of activity for over 150 years.

When Brigham Young led his people to the Salt Lake Valley in 1847, he sent Parley P. Pratt and Erastus Snow ahead to scout out the best way down to their new desert home. The two first saw the valley of the Great Salt Lake on July 19, 1847, and, sharing a horse, entered it on July 21. The next day the first wagons rumbled down the steep, brush-covered slopes into the valley. On July 23, Pratt led the group to the place he felt most suitable for farming, near present-day 400 South and Main Streets. Young, after recovering from a bout of Rocky Mountain spotted fever, arrived in the valley on July 24, the date Utahans officially celebrate Pioneer Day.

Towns grew up fairly quickly in the valley. Salt Lake was the first city, but within less than two years families had formed communities throughout the valley.

The Salt Lake Cutoff

Settlers traveling to Oregon and California before 1846 had only one route available to them. It ran north of Utah through Fort Hall, Idaho, then on west. A few ill-advised groups took the Hastings Cutoff across the Great Salt Desert, and they didn't fare well.

After the Mormons built their rough wagon road from Fort Bridger to Salt Lake City, they encouraged other westbound migrants to follow the new route, since they could rest and buy supplies in Salt Lake City, then continue north to Fort Hall. Some historians estimate that as many as one-third of the migrating pioneers took advantage of this opportunity in the period between 1849 and 1857. The Utah War interrupted the cutoff's use in 1857 and 1858, but afterward travelers again utilized the trail until 1869. Among the towns along the route that benefited from the increased traffic were Bountiful, Centerville, Farmington, Kaysville, Layton, Ogden, Willard, Perry, Brigham City, Honeyville, Tremonton, Deweyville, Colinston, Fielding, and Plymouth.

Salt Lake City

The season was growing late when the Mormons finally reached Utah. A long, hungry winter loomed ahead, so the pioneers had to plant crops as quickly as possible. New settlers diverted water from City Creek to soften the hard desert land so it could be tilled, and even before Brigham Young entered the valley, plots of land had been plowed and planted. Within eight days of planting, three acres of corn emerged from the ground and the potatoes and beans had also started to grow.

As soon as the first company of pioneers settled in the valley, they divided into work committees. One group was assigned to farming, another to surveying the city into 135 ten-acre blocks—with the temple at the center—and still another to erecting buildings. Other groups made bricks, harvested timber, hunted, or built roads, among other things.

As members began to shape their new community, one of their first orders of business was to build a fort. They chose a site at present-day Pioneer Park, at 300 West and 300 South Streets (the block became a park in 1898). The first school was started in the fort in October 1847, and during that first winter, over 2,000 people took shelter within the walls of the fort.

The first winter was very mild. Winter wheat did well and livestock thrived. Though March proved miserable and wet for the families in their

Monument in Temple Square, Salt Lake City, commemorating the Miracle of the Seagulls. The Tabernacle is in the background.

crude homes, crops sprouted up nicely. All signs pointed to a bountiful harvest, but a late spring frost on May 29 froze a lot of crops. Then the crickets descended. For two weeks the desperate homesteaders fought the insects, which devoured hundreds of acres of young plants. Finally seagulls came and ate a good percentage of the crickets, an incident later considered a miracle. In spite of the problems, Parley P. Pratt said the Mormons harvested 10,000 to 20,000 more bushels of grain than they had originally expected.

The second winter, 1848–49, was much more of a trial than the first. Thousands of new immigrants had arrived during the summer, and food had to be rationed by the bishops of the nineteen wards to those in need. The pioneers ate a lot of fleshy thistle roots and rawhide that winter. They also ate the small bulbs of the sego lily. They generally cooked the bulbs before eating them, and although no one found them particularly good, their mild flavor was not offensive.

Growth and Prosperity

In the spring of 1849 the news of gold discovered in California lured a few dissatisfied settlers away, but their numbers were small because of

Brigham Young's counsel against seeking worldly riches. Gold seekers from the East, however, would make a big impact on Salt Lake's economy.

One-third of the gold rushers on the trail to California turned toward Salt Lake City after reaching Fort Bridger in Wyoming. Fortune seekers procured fresh animals and vegetables from the pioneers, and Mormons obtained fabric, tea, coffee, and scrap iron from the visitors. Though a few of the miners who stayed for the winter publicized negative experiences with the Mormons, the majority reported in their journals that they were favorably impressed with the desert city. Many trail-weary gold seekers were thrilled to eat home-cooked meals in pioneer homes after months of salt pork, dry beans, and hard bread.

The Pony Express arrived in Utah in 1860. It traveled through Salt Lake City, then south to Utah County. The Pony Express station in Salt Lake City was located between 100 and 200 South on the east side of Main Street. A historic monument marks the spot of the old station.

The Pony Express was not the only outside contact Salt Lake City had with the rest of the United States in the mid-nineteenth century. Salt Lake City was the most important transportation and freighting center between Missouri and California from 1850 to 1870. The Overland Mail & Stagecoach and the Wells, Fargo & Company wagons all passed through the Mormon city heading east or west. The U.S. government contracted with various mail carriers to take parcels from Independence, Missouri, and exchange them in Salt Lake City, with carriers coming from and

Salt Lake street scene, 1869. —UTAH STATE HISTORICAL SOCIETY

heading to California. Deliveries were made year-round, in horrible weather in many instances. Sometimes horses were lost and men carrying mail had to struggle on foot through storms and snow. Indian attacks were equally devastating. Many carriers lost horses, and some were killed in the raids.

Salt Lake City was the subject of great curiosity to the rest of the nation in pioneer times. Mark Twain visited the City of the Saints in 1860 while traveling by stagecoach to Nevada. He later described his experience in *Roughing It*.

> We strolled about everywhere through the broad, straight, level streets, and enjoyed the pleasant strangeness of a city of fifteen thousand inhabitants with no loafers perceptible in it; and no visible drunkards or noisy people; a limpid stream rippling and dancing through every street in place of a filthy gutter . . . branches from the street stream winding and sparkling among the garden-beds and fruit trees—and a grand general air of neatness, repair, thrift, and comfort, around and about and over the whole.
>
> There was fascination in surreptitiously staring at every creature we took to be a Mormon. . . . We felt a curiosity to ask every child how many mothers it had, and if it could tell them apart; and we experienced a thrill every time a dwelling-house door opened and shut as we passed, disclosing a glimpse of human heads and backs and shoulders—for we so longed to have a good satisfying look at a Mormon family in all its comprehensive ampleness.

Patrick Edward Connor in Salt Lake

Mark Twain looked on polygamy as a source of curiosity and humor. Many others in the nation viewed the institution as an abomination that must be abolished.

Because the U.S. government viewed the Mormons as disloyal to the union, and because of continual Indian problems in Utah, a regiment of California volunteers, commanded by Colonel Patrick Connor, was sent to Salt Lake City in 1862, not long after the Civil War began.

The U.S. Army established Camp Douglas that year on the bench overlooking the Salt Lake Valley. Connor reported that the Mormons were "a community of traitors, murderers, fanatics, and whores." He knew the only way to unbalance Brigham Young's power was to bring a lot of non-Mormons into Utah. He urged non-Mormon prospectors, including his soldiers, to exploit the minerals available in the area in order to lure outsiders into the territory.

Connor fulfilled his wish. With the coming of the soldiers to Utah, the Mormons' isolation from the gentile world ended. When mining of precious metals began in earnest, gentiles crowded into Salt Lake City, and soon it was no longer a Mormon town.

Patrick Edward Connor.
—UTAH STATE
HISTORICAL SOCIETY

Connor, later promoted to general, was discharged from the army in 1866, after which time he devoted all of his efforts to mining and politics. He managed to start the Liberal Party in Utah, the only opposition the Mormons ever encountered in their aim at total political dominance of the territory. Connor had some success in mining but his interests were fickle, and by the time of the general's death in 1891, he had little personal wealth.

Salt Lake City in the Late 1800s

Streetcars hit the thoroughfares of Salt Lake City in 1872. At first they were pulled by mules, but after 1889 electricity powered public transportation. As the system grew, people wanted to go farther, and transfers allowing them to change from streetcar to streetcar came into being. To prevent people from giving away their transfers to friends for free rides, conductors were asked to identify the rightful owner of the ticket by punching an appropriately identifying drawing on the pass. They could choose between five different men with various amounts of facial hair, ranging from clean shaven to full beard. Apparently, fewer women rode the streetcars—there were only two choices for the ladies: a sailor hat on a younger woman and a bonnet on an elder. The conductor either insulted or complimented the passenger depending on which picture he

View of Salt Lake City taken in 1882 from Arsenal Hill.
—UTAH STATE HISTORICAL SOCIETY

punched. Neither the company employees nor its customers were happy with the transfers, and they abandoned the system after a short time.

In 1894 General William Booth, founder of the Salvation Army, paid a brief visit to Salt Lake City and spoke to a large crowd. Though he thought the audience one of the most restless he had ever addressed, the warm welcome he received highly impressed him. He was even more taken with the Mormons' prosperous circumstances. In *The History Blazer*, Booth recommended that the British learn a lesson from them. "Get hold of the men who have some fitness for the business, and give them seed to sow and implements with which to cultivate the land, as well as a horse; and let them pay you back again what you have expended on them. That is the principle of the Mormons."

Salt Lake City received the first announcement of Utah's statehood on January 4, 1896. At 9:13 A.M. Western Union received the telegram telling the citizens of their new status. The superintendent fired a signal from his shotgun, and the celebration was on. Two days later, when everything was fully organized, the people of the city came together to dance in the streets and make noise. The big celebration in the Tabernacle was presided over by a 160-by-78-foot United States flag hung from the ceiling.

Salt Lake City in the Twentieth Century

By World War I, Salt Lake was truly a city. Its population had surpassed 100,000, and fewer farms could be found in the city limits. Highrise buildings lined Main Street and streetcars hurried up and down the busy thoroughfares. The world-class Hotel Utah had been built, as well as the Cathedral of Madeleine and the Salt Lake Mormon Temple, and a new capitol building looked out over the city.

In the spring of 1918 a devastating influenza epidemic traveled around the world, killing more than 21 million people before it ended in late 1919. Utah was struck hard by the disease. By October 30 Salt Lake City alone had recorded 2,300 cases and 117 deaths. Schools were closed and public gatherings banned. On November 11, when the war ended, people took a break from the isolation brought on by the flu—streets filled with wildly celebrating crowds. But the joy ended in a few days when the revelers paid for their moments of joy. The epidemic renewed itself; within days hundreds more fell sick.

The death toll was so severe and the danger so intense that funerals were either brief graveside affairs or forbidden entirely. By the end of the winter of 1919–20, the horror had finally passed and life returned to normal.

Winter Olympics, 2002

On June 16, 1995, International Olympic Committee (IOC) president Juan Antonio Samaranch announced in Budapest, Hungary, that Salt Lake City would host the 2002 Winter Olympics. A deafening cheer went up from a crowd waiting anxiously for the announcement at Washington Square at 400 South State Street in Salt Lake City and from many television viewers throughout the state. Other Utahans were disappointed, having campaigned against the Olympics because of environmental concerns, worries about higher taxes, and fears that the quickly growing local population would become even more uncontrollable.

In 1998, a worldwide scandal broke when it was discovered that during the bidding process IOC members had received huge gifts and payments from both Salt Lake Olympic Committee members and those from competing cities. As a result, a major effort began to clean the entire Olympic house, changing the bidding process for all future Olympic sites.

The Salt Lake City games are scheduled for February 8–24, 2002, and will take place in various locations in northern Utah.

Historic Buildings and Sites of Salt Lake City

Salt Lake City has a number of historic buildings, some dating from pioneer times. Following are descriptions of a few.

Council Hall. Located on State Street, south of the state capitol, the old Council Hall is an excellent place to start a tour of Salt Lake City and Utah. This historic structure was originally built at the corner of First South and State Streets between 1864 and 1866. It was Salt Lake's original municipal government building and its territorial capitol building until 1894. The Council Hall began housing Salt Lake City police in the 1890s, and the municipal board of health in 1915.

In 1948 the LDS Church appropriated $300,000 for the removal of the old Council Hall to its present location. The work of dismantling and restoration took place between 1961 and 1962. The addition of a small basement and a sandstone apron around its exterior were the only changes.

State Capitol. The Utah State Capitol dominates the skyline in Salt Lake City. Built between 1912 and 1916, the structure more closely resembles the nation's Capitol than any other state's. The territory of Utah fought long and hard for statehood, and when it finally came in 1896, a desire to show conformity and allegiance to the country inspired the design of the capitol building.

The building is Corinthian in design, and was made mostly with materials found in Utah, including bird's-eye marble, Tooele onyx and travertine, granite from Little Cottonwood Canyon, and the roof's copper. The marble on the main floor is from Georgia.

Historical paintings in the dome and interior depict scenes from Utah's history. Brigham Young's dream of the settlement of the Salt Lake Valley is shown on the east end, and another mural on the west end is entitled *Reclaiming the Desert by Irrigation.* In the House chamber is a painting depicting Jim Bridger discovering the Great Salt Lake. The painting in the Senate chamber offers a view of Utah Lake.

Looming over State Street at South Temple is Eagle Gate, which marked the entrance to Brigham Young's property. The original eagle at the gate commemorated an eagle killed in City Creek Canyon soon after the pioneers' arrival. The bird measured eleven feet from wing tip to wing tip. Young's farm included much of City Creek Canyon and the area now known as "the Avenues." The original eagle from the gate is on display in the Daughters of the Utah Pioneers Museum on North Main Street. The one that now tops the arch is a replica.

Salt Lake Mormon Temple. This temple is a symbol throughout the world of the Church of Jesus Christ of Latter-day Saints. Construction on the temple, located at the northeast corner of Temple Square, was begun soon after the Mormons arrived in the Salt Lake Valley. During the Utah War, when Johnston's army threatened Salt Lake in 1857–58, work on the temple ceased, and the entire foundation was buried in the spring of 1858 so the temple block would look like a newly plowed field. When the foundation was later reexcavated, cracks were discovered, so work was started anew. After years of struggle and sacrifice, the temple was completed in 1893. The temple is open only to active members of the LDS Church. Rites sacred to church members are performed in the temple, such as marriages, uniting of families, and other promises and covenants made by church members.

Temple Square. All the buildings on Temple Square except the temple itself are open to the public. The Tabernacle, constructed between 1864 and 1867, is the home of the Mormon Tabernacle Choir. The choir had its beginnings in 1849 when a group of Welsh converts arrived in Utah. The singing has never stopped. Membership in the choir is highly competitive and is a great honor. Great musical ability is a prerequisite, as well as honorable religious standing. The 320 unpaid members of the choir perform on the oldest continuing network radio broadcast in the nation, *Music and the Spoken Word.* The Tabernacle is open to the public for tours, organ recitals (every day at noon), and other performances. During the first weekend of April and October, the Church of Jesus Christ of Latter-day Saints holds their semiannual conferences in the Tabernacle. These conferences are open to the public, but the huge turnouts mean long waits in lines.

Salt Lake Mormon Temple.

The Assembly Hall, built between 1877 and 1882, was restored extensively in the early 1980s. It is now primarily used for free public concerts and as overflow space for the Tabernacle. Those wishing to attend conferences, and unable to get a seat in the Tabernacle, may be seated in the Assembly Hall, where they will view the conferences on a screen. Two visitor centers on the square are also open to the public. Missionaries provide free tours and information regarding the Mormon Church and Temple Square.

In addition to the buildings, the gardens on Temple Square attract many visitors every year. They are immaculately maintained, and something is always blooming from late March until October, when the beds are prepared for winter. In December, Temple Square comes to life with 300,000 lights celebrating Christmas. A life-sized nativity with accompanying music depicts the story of the birth of Jesus.

Hotel Utah/Joseph Smith Memorial Building. The Hotel Utah on South Temple and Main Streets was a magnificent hotel from its construction in 1909–11 until 1987, when its owner, the Mormon Church, converted it into an office building. Though enormous protests went up from the community at large, the church stuck to its plan, and in 1993 the structure reopened as the Joseph Smith Memorial Building. It currently houses facilities for genealogical research (open to the public), offices, restaurants, and a theatre featuring the film *Legacy*. *Legacy* depicts the beginnings of the Mormon Church and the westward trek. It is free to the public.

Headquarters for the Church of Jesus Christ of Latter-day Saints. The government of the 10-million-member Church of Jesus Christ of Latter-day Saints is located on the block between State and Main Streets and North and South Temple Streets. Visitors are welcome to ask questions of the information specialists on the main floor of the high-rise office building on the north side of the block. The neoclassical structure on the south side of the block houses the offices of the First Presidency of the Church and other church leaders.

Lion House/Beehive House. These two old mansion houses on South Temple and State Streets were just two of Brigham Young's residences in Utah. The Beehive House (named for the Mormon beehive or "deseret" symbol, representing the industry of the honeybee) was constructed in 1854 and the Lion House in 1856. Young's office was in an annex between the two houses. The Beehive House offers free tours to the public. The Lion House is mainly a reception center but has excellent cafeteria facilities in the basement (enter through the west door).

Plum Alley. On an entirely different track from the previous buildings are the ones on Regent Street, known in earlier times as Plum Alley.

Salt Lake City looking east. The structure with ten small gables facing the camera is Brigham Young's Lion House. The Gardo House (no longer existing) is across the street to the south. Date of photo is unknown. —UTAH STATE HISTORICAL SOCIETY

These buildings, not open to the public, played a part in Salt Lake City's colorful history. Regent Street was the red-light district of the city from about 1880 through the late 1930s. The upper floors of the old Felt Electric Building and Tampico's Restaurant (replaced by another building a few years ago) were brothels. Legitimate businesses occupied the lower floors.

John Held, quoted in the *Utah Historical Quarterly*, remembers the district from firsthand experience:

> Within the street were saloons, cafes and parlor houses, with cribs that were rented nightly to the itinerate "Ladies of the Calling." Soliciting was taboo, so these ladies sat at the top of the stairs and called their invitation to "come on up, kid." The parlor houses allowed no such publicity. There was no outward display to gain entran[ce] to a parlor house. One pushed an electric bell and was admitted by a uniformed maid or an attendant. The luxury of these houses always included a "professor" at the piano. . . . One of the madams called herself Miss Ada Wilson. Hers was a lavish house on Commercial Street. Another gave her name as a Miss Helen Blazes. Her establishment catered to the big money, and in it only wine was served. In other houses, beer was the popular refreshment, at one dollar a bottle, served to the guests in small whiskey glasses.

After living with prostitution in the downtown business district for more than three decades, merchants started to complain that their shady neighbors kept away customers. Feeling that prostitution would always be a part of the community, Salt Lake City mayor John Bransford (a non-Mormon) and some other prominent men organized the construction of a "stockade," buildings to accomodate the ladies and their clientele. The chosen site, between 500 and 600 West and 100 and 200 South Streets, was farther away from the central business district and was felt to be less desirable because it was near the railroad tracks. Of course, it didn't hurt that the mayor owned property just across the street, which benefited from the increased traffic in the district. The newly built complex of "cribs" (small rooms that held just a bed and a chair), as well as some larger, parlor-type establishments, were sold to one of Salt Lake's most notorious madams, Belle London, who then rented out quarters to other madams and their girls. The red-light district moved to the new facilities in 1908.

Though prostitution was illegal, the various raids staged by the police were mostly unsuccessful because the authorities warned the women ahead of time. Those who were arrested paid fines and were set free.

In 1911, the stockade closed for some unexplained reason, and the women began to ply their trade wherever they chose—though West Second South remained a prime location for such activities until the late 1970s.

Photo of the Salt Lake City "stockade," West Second South, dated September 21, 1908. —UTAH STATE HISTORICAL SOCIETY

In the latter part of the nineteenth century, Plum Alley was home to Salt Lake City's Chinese community. The Chinese population in Utah swelled when work on the transcontinental railroad began. At first, Chinese immigrants congregated in groups near the railroad, but they gradually moved into the cities. Such cities as Corinne, Ogden, Salt Lake, and Silver Reef (in southwestern Utah) had Chinese communities. The largest of these was centered around Plum Alley, where 400 Chinese people, mostly men, lived in flats above their stores and restaurants. The section was particularly popular among white Salt Lakers during the Chinese New Year when food, wine, parades, and fireworks were abundant.

Initially, most of the white population was happy to have the Chinese. While Irish, Italian, and other ethnic laboring groups felt threatened by the Chinese, the *Deseret News* expressed the feeling of the majority in a May 1869 article that described the Chinese as skillful, hardworking, and intelligent. However, as time passed, many whites became distrustful of the close-knit Chinese communities, where they felt gambling, prostitution, and opium dens flourished. The Chinese accepted these as forms of recreation, but Victorian America viewed them as corrupt. In addition, white workers who competed directly with Chinese workers for jobs resented the Chinese workers' willingness to accept lower pay and poorer living conditions.

All this bitterness made conditions very difficult for the Chinese. They met increasingly with open ridicule and sometimes assault on their property and persons. In Ogden the Knights of Labor organized a boycott of Chinese vegetable growers. The Chinese, however, refused to be moved, and their sales increased. Chinese immigrants became especially successful in the laundry business. Many non-Mormons refused to patronize Mormons, so they took their clothing to the Chinese. As a result, Mormon women lost business, which added to their resentment.

Increasing local and national indignation against the Chinese resulted in a number of laws being passed at both state and federal levels. The new laws drastically reduced the Chinese people's freedoms and immigration into the United States. Gradually Chinese returned to their homeland or grew old and died. Because few men had families, no new generation took their place. The last Chinese left Plum Alley in 1940. The last Chinese building was torn down in 1952 to make way for a parking structure.

Fort Douglas. The fort, located at 400 South and 2100 East, was named for Senator Stephen A. Douglas of Illinois. Construction began on Fort Douglas in 1862 when Colonel Patrick Connor and his troops were ordered to Utah to protect western mail routes. Many of the buildings at the fort were erected soon after the troops camped in Salt Lake

City. The majority of the structures were built between 1873 and the early 1900s. Ownership of most of the fort has been transferred to the University of Utah.

Salt Lake City/County Building. The block now known as Washington Square—between 400 and 500 South Street and State Street and 200 East Street—was first called Emigration Square, commemorating the spot where immigrants entering the valley stopped temporarily before they were given a permanent assignment. Later, part of the block was used as a racecourse and baseball diamond; however, because of complaints about the players' profanity, baseball was no longer allowed. When the need for a large city-county complex arose, the square was the obvious choice. The architectural firm of Henry Monheim, George Washington Bird, and William T. Proudfoot designed the building in the Richardsonian Romanesque style. The structure cost $900,000. At the time of the building's construction, Utah was in a slump with an unemployment rate of 36 percent. Seven hundred and fifty men applied to work on the building. Only sixty-three were hired—all married men. The workers were allowed to labor for a week on the project, then a new crew came on. Frendman Linde, the chief sculptor, carved his face on the north side of the building between the words *city* and *hall*.

The impressive structure was originally completed in 1894. During the summer of 1895 a state constitutional convention was held on the third floor of the new building. Though the space was hot and crowded, the convention was free of charge, so the 107 delegates endured it. The sign on the door of the room—Criminal Court Room—became the seed for numerous jokes about the character of the men in the meetings.

In 1984 work began on a complete renovation of the building. It was restored from its highest tip to its foundations, which were placed on isolation pads that act like big shock absorbers during an earthquake. The interior of the building was also restored; old fireplaces were uncovered and the offices were repainted in their original colors. Work was completed in 1989.

Cathedral of the Madeleine. The magnificent gothic-style Cathedral of the Madeleine (dedicated 1909) dominates east South Temple Street. The cathedral represents years of work by Bishop Lawrence Scanlon (1843–1915), who once presided over all of Utah and eastern Nevada—the largest catholic diocese in the United States. The cathedral was completely restored in 1993.

Daughters of the Utah Pioneers Museum. The museum, at 300 North Main, houses thousands of pioneer artifacts from 1847 to 1869.

Church History Museum and Family History Center. The Church of Jesus Christ of Latter-day Saints constructed a museum and family-history research library complex on West Temple between North and South Temple Streets (just west of Temple Square). These facilities are free and open to the public. The museum features permanent and changing exhibits dealing with the pioneer period, as well as historic church artwork.

The world-famous Family History Center is a destination for many genealogy buffs from around the world. Trained staff are available to answer questions in this building and in the Joseph Smith Memorial Building on the corner of Main and South Temple Streets.

Hansen Planetarium. Located at 15 South State Street, what is now the planetarium was built in 1905 as the Salt Lake City Library. In 1965 a new library was constructed and the old building became the Hansen Planetarium.

Utah State Historical Society. The terminal for the old Rio Grande Railroad, at 300 South Rio Grande, now houses the Utah State Historical Society. The main waiting area of the station features pioneer memorabilia and other displays relating to Utah history. An accompanying bookstore carries books related to Utah and the West.

University of Utah. Salt Lake City is home to the University of Utah. Originally founded in 1850 by the LDS Church as the University of Deseret, the school is the oldest state university west of the Missouri River.

Aerial view of the University of Utah, circa 1925.
—UTAH STATE HISTORICAL SOCIETY

The university has developed into an excellent institution with a medical school, a law school, and a number of graduate schools. The university also has an excellent engineering program. Approximately 24,000 students enroll at the University of Utah annually. The university features an art museum and a natural history museum with wildlife and dinosaur exhibits.

The Avenues. On the northeast bench of Salt Lake City is a unique suburban community. "The Avenues" was developed in the late 1900s as a commuter section for families whose wage earners worked in the city. The lots were smaller than those in the main part of the city because they were not designed for farming. The Avenues represents a wide variety of house styles that reflect the period of their construction, from the late pioneer homes to the bungalows and period revivals of the early twentieth century. The area became run-down for many years, but in the past three decades the Avenues has once again become popular and people are restoring its old homes. The entire district is on the National Historic Register.

Liberty Park. Liberty Park is a good-sized municipal park between 500 and 700 East Streets and 900 and 1300 South Streets. On the last weekend in August, the park hosts the Salt Lake Belly Dance Festival, the largest of its kind in the United States. During that weekend, the neighborhood reverberates with exotic music and the beating of drums. Vendors sell clothing, jewelry, and musical items associated with this ancient art.

Sugar House. Sugar House is a business and residential area around 2100 South and 1100 East Streets in Salt Lake City. In 1852 farmers began growing sugar beets in Utah. John Taylor imported sugar-manufacturing equipment from England. It was first set up in Provo, then moved

The old Utah Territorial Prison, at the spot now occupied by Sugar House Park at approximately 1300 East and 2400 South. —UTAH STATE HISTORICAL SOCIETY

temporarily to Temple Square, and finally settled four miles south of Salt Lake in what became known as Sugar House.

In 1855 a three-story adobe factory was completed and sugar beet processing began. More than 22,000 bushels of the beets were made into molasses in less than two months. The molasses was bad, though, and after grasshoppers devoured the sugar beet crop in 1855–56, the sugar project was abandoned.

The Utah Territorial Prison stood in Sugar House on 1300 East (the present location of Sugar House Park) for many years. This prison did not hold only hardened criminals; during the 1870s and 1880s, large numbers of Mormon polygamist men were imprisoned as punishment for illegal cohabitation. When the state prison was built in Draper in the late 1940s, the one in Sugar House was demolished.

EAST SALT LAKE VALLEY
Holladay
Holladay was one of the first settlements outside of Salt Lake City (it was called Spring Creek at the time). John Holladay and a number of other families who had arrived in the Salt Lake Valley the previous autumn moved to this bench in 1848, attracted by the mountain streams. They constructed a number of crude log cabins near Spring Creek and 4800 South (close to Highland Drive). The homes were built of logs, but because rattlesnakes invaded them, adobes became preferable for their tighter walls. Among these adobes was one belonging to John D. Lee, a later settler of Washington County who was executed for his part in the Mountain Meadows Massacre, in which some Mormons assisted some Indians in murdering members of a wagon train. His home was near the southwest corner of the intersection of 4800 South and Highland Drive.

With urban growth, Holladay has become another suburb of Salt Lake City. Many housing developments in the Holladay area were built in the 1950s and 1960s.

Murray
Two smokestacks, relics of the old American Smelter and Refining Company, cast their shadows over Murray. The future of these stacks is uncertain, as most citizens don't want to pay for stabilizing the structures and cleaning up the contaminated soils that surround them. Developers would like them removed so they can utilize the site, which is prime real estate. Historic preservationists, on the other hand, scramble to find some way to hang onto the last reminder of Utah's old mining and refining era.

Midvale, 1949. —UTAH STATE HISTORICAL SOCIETY

Murray was first settled in 1849 as people moved from Salt Lake City out to their own farms. It became an industrial center in 1869, when the smelter was constructed to process the ore from the nearby mines. Murray was incorporated in 1902 and named for former Utah territorial governor Eli H. Murray.

Murray became a popular suburb of Salt Lake in the 1940s and 1950s. It has also become the car dealership capital of the Salt Lake Valley. You can buy just about any make of car on State Street in Murray. The town is also the home of the Salt Lake County Fair, held each August.

Midvale

People were living in Midvale (in the middle of the Salt Lake Valley) long before it was organized as a city. Immigrants first moved to farms in this part of the valley in the 1850s. When miners found silver and lead in the surrounding mountains, smelters were built in Midvale. The town built up around smelting operations in Little Cottonwood and Bingham Canyons. In 1958 the smelter closed, and in 1972 the Sharon Steel Mills closed.

Sandy

Sandy grew up at the base of the Wasatch Mountains as a processing center for the ore mined in the mountains. A number of smelters were built, but only the Mingo lasted. The first trains came into town in 1871–72, and, with ore coming down from the mountains, the small settlement quickly boomed. In its early years, Sandy had only one well, and every train hauled in drinking water. It sold for five cents a bucket. Demand for water was kept down by the town's thriving saloons.

Some say the town was named for the quality of its soil. Others say it was named for Sandy Kinghorn, the engineer of the first locomotive that arrived in town, on September 23, 1871. The station was known as Sandy's Station for some time, and that name even appeared on some early maps.

A number of ore smelters operated in Sandy before 1900, but the town's smelting days are long forgotten. In the past two or three decades, Sandy has become one of Utah's most densely populated suburbs.

Draper

In the early development of the Salt Lake Valley, Draper (or South Cottonwood, as it was called) covered the southern end of the valley between the mountains to the east and the Point of the Mountain, including Riverton and Bluffdale. The first families, who subsequently named their settlement for ecclesiastical leader William Draper, moved to the area in 1849.

Draper is currently going through a change of identity. Even while its neighbor to the north, Sandy, blossomed into a suburb, Draper maintained its image as a farming community for a number of decades. Today, Draper farms are finally succumbing to mighty development dollars. Even the once remote foothills at the extreme south end of the valley, where only sagebrush grew and hang gliders soared, have been scored with new suburban roads.

Just west of I-15 in Draper stands the Utah State Prison. Covering 2,000 acres, the prison houses approximately 2,600 inmates. The complex was built in the 1940s when the Sugar House prison closed.

Brighton

Brighton began its life as a resort and has continued on this course for nearly 150 years. The pioneers considered Brighton a beautiful playground with clear mountain streams and beautiful lakes. Its first name was Silver Lake.

On July 24, 1857, the ten-year Pioneer Day Celebration was held in Silver Lake. Hosea Stout recorded the scene in his diary on Thursday, July 23, 1857:

We started about day light with our breakfast and proceeded on but soon found our way hedged up by the road being full of waggons & teams so proceed in on afoot about a mile I came to the gate at the first mill. Here preparations were making to number the persons teams & animals going up which resulted as follows 2587 persons, 464 carriages & waggons, 1028 horses and mules, 332 oxen & cows We arrived at the Lake about one p.m. A large number had already ariven, and teams continued to come all the evening.

It was here, at one of the new territory's biggest parties, that word reached the pioneers that federal troops were approaching to destroy them.

William Brighton chose to prospect at Silver Lake in 1870. He didn't get rich on his findings, but he did build a store and hotel for prospectors traveling between Alta and Park City. In winter, rugged travelers and miners glided back and forth between the mountain towns on cross-country skis.

In 1936 a tow rope was set up for pleasure skiing, and Brighton's ski resort was born. It has expanded into a major Wasatch Front ski destination.

Alta

Today, Alta is a first-class ski resort, but it started out as one of the wildest mining towns in Utah. Silver was first found in Alta in 1865, but the big discovery in the Emma Mine came in 1868. The town blossomed. By 1872, 3,000 people lived in Alta (some reports say the number was more like 9,500). But the townspeople had never filed for the property, and the Walker brothers of Salt Lake City (of banking fame, and always ones to capitalize on a good business opportunity) filed on the entire town. They offered to sell the land to the residents for $50 to $250 a lot. Some paid up, others left.

Alta was not a quiet town. In its brief boom time, 150 men died violent deaths. One hundred and ten of them were killed in two of the town's twenty-six saloons, the Gold Miner's Daughter and the Bucket of Blood. Entanglements and disputes simmered, easily boiling over.

In the spring of 1873 a stranger came to town and volunteered to resurrect all the bodies in the cemetery. As there had been a great deal of killing recently, a lot of fresh bodies lay in Boot Graveyard. The town held a meeting to discuss the idea. Some citizens were for it, until they began contemplating the consequences of bringing back all the dead. Widows and widowers who had remarried and people who had inherited property felt that bringing their dead back to life would cause a few complications and possibly more killings, so the whole town got up a collection and gave the man $2,500 (another account says $25,000) to leave town. He did so, and was never seen again.

Later in 1873 the value of silver fell. The ore was getting more difficult to bring out of the mountain. In 1874 a disastrous snowslide killed sixty men and started fires that destroyed much of the town. It never recovered completely, though another boom occurred between 1904 and 1920.

In 1937 the Alta United Mines Company gave the U.S. Forest Service surface rights to develop the area for camping and skiing. The new Alta ski resort opened for business in November 1938. During World War II mountain paratroopers trained on the ski slopes of Alta.

In the 1960s and 1970s major development in Alta turned it into one of the best ski resorts in Utah and one of the most popular in America, renowned for its deep powder snow. Some years, total snowfall at Alta exceeds 700 inches.

WEST SALT LAKE VALLEY

Saltair Resort

Not long after homes and farms were established in the Salt Lake Valley, local folks started looking for entertainment. They found recreation on the beaches of the Great Salt Lake. A number of beach resorts existed west of Salt Lake City, and the most famous of these was Saltair.

Though bathing at the beaches had been a popular pastime for decades, the LDS Church felt its members needed their own wholesome place for recreation, so the church sponsors built Saltair in 1893. The

Saltair Resort, undated. —UTAH STATE HISTORICAL SOCIETY

resort included a wide variety of amusement park rides, hot air balloon rides, swimming, vaudeville acts, and dancing on what was claimed to be the world's largest dance floor. In 1906, the owners sold it to a group of Mormon businessmen. The resort remained popular for many years, though it struggled financially during the Great Depression. Saltair finally closed in 1958. The abandoned dance hall burned down in 1970. Another company rebuilt the resort in 1982, but rising lake levels that year put the new dance floor under five feet of water and destroyed their investment. The building is still used occasionally for concerts, though.

The Salt Industry in the Saltair Area

Pioneers began utilizing the salt deposits around the Great Salt Lake almost immediately after their arrival in Utah. While some commodities were difficult for pioneers to obtain, salt was free for the taking on the beaches. In some spots the salt could be taken directly from lakeshore to table, but in most instances processing was necessary. Approximately four barrels of briny sand yielded one barrel of refined salt.

In the mid-nineteenth century, entrepreneurs took advantage of the lake's salt. Perhaps the first to make money from salt was Charley White, who boiled down the brine on the south shore of the lake from 1850 to 1860. Various companies built factories between 1880 and 1900 around the southern part of the lake, near the site of what became Saltair. Among the companies were Inland Salt Company, Royal Crystal, the North American Salt Company, and Morton Salt. A village for the factory workers was built near the lakeshore. About 200 people, mostly European immigrants, lived in humble homes there. When one of the salt companies closed in the 1920s, the workers all moved away.

By 1928 Morton Salt dominated the market, pushing out all the other companies. Morton originally operated a plant near Saltair. However, lake fluctuations of the 1980s caused the company to move its operation to nearby Grantsville, Utah, and in 1991 it tore down the old Saltair plant.

Bingham

Bingham is no longer a town. It has been covered over by the tailings of a huge copper mine.

In 1850 brothers Sanford and Thomas Bingham discovered gold in the canyon that bears their name. When they took the nuggets to Brigham Young, he told them to cover up their find. Young is quoted in *Boomtowns of the Great Basin* as having said, "Instead of hunting gold let every man go to work raising wheat, oats, barley, corn, and vegetables and fruit in abundance that there may be plenty in the land."

Those who rejected Brigham Young's leadership had no hesitation in taking advantage of the earth's riches. In 1863 an apostate Mormon sent a sample of gold from Bingham Canyon to General Connor, the commander of Fort Douglas and an open opponent of Brigham Young. The sample was so rich in gold and silver that Connor published the news of the find in the East, promising military protection to any who would come prospecting; thus, he defeated Young without firing a shot.

Bingham became a wild mining town complete with prostitutes, fights, killings, and thirty saloons. Women were not only employed in the town's brothels, they were among the prospectors, staking out a claim called the Women's Lode. Silver and gold were the primary metals mined at Bingham in its early years. No one considered copper a serious mineral at the site until 1896, when a rich vein was struck. Open-pit copper mining started in 1904.

The Kennecott Corporation took over the operation of the Bingham Copper Mine in 1936. As the mine expanded in area, it took over the town's land, pushing the residents out. The population of Bingham Canyon dwindled from 15,000 in the early years of the boom to 31 in 1970. The last buildings were demolished in 1972, and the expanding pit buried the canyon. Today the copper mine produces 14 percent of the nation's copper supply and is the world's largest open-pit copper mine. It continues to expand as more ore is taken from the mountain. The mine produces 900 tons of ore a day. Gold and silver are by-products of the copper-refining process.

Bingham, Utah, 1926 or 1927. —UTAH STATE HISTORICAL SOCIETY

The ore is crushed and extracted at a site north of the town of Copperton. A museum and viewing area above the enormous pit are open to visitors during the spring, summer, and fall months.

Copperton

Located near the Bingham Copper Mine, Copperton was built by Kennecott's predecessor, the Utah Copper Company, between 1926 and 1941 to house its employees. Salt Lake architectural firm Scott and Welch designed all the bungalows with similar floor plans, but the different exterior treatments make them appear unique. The Utah Copper Company used the homes to feature different uses of copper. They were rented only to more highly paid married employees, in an attempt to make the town stable and peaceful. When Copperton was completed, it had more than 200 houses, a community park, schools, and other facilities. It is the only remaining town of those connected with the Bingham Copper Mine.

I-84
Echo–I-15
38 miles

I-84 splits from I-80 at the mouth of Echo Canyon.

Echo

Echo was named for the echoes that reverberate off the walls of Echo Canyon. As the Mormons traveled down the canyon on their way to the Great Salt Lake Valley, a chorus of echoes rumbling off the steep canyon walls accompanied them.

The first resident of Echo was James Bromely, who came in 1854 to operate a Funk and Walker Stage Station at the mouth of Echo Canyon. The Overland Stage came through here, as did the Pony Express.

Echo boomed while the railroad was under construction. The first locomotive on the newly laid track went through Echo on January 16, 1869. Temporary saloons followed the railroad along its road to completion. At each saloon, the saloon owners dug a big cellar so they could bury their garbage before moving on. When one such cellar was excavated later, seven unidentified skeletons were found among the bottles.

Echo became a busy railroad town in the 1880s, when it served as the hub of the Echo and Park City line. Between Ogden and Evanston, Wyoming, the tracks climbed a steep grade. Trains used up two-thirds of their fuel supply between Ogden and Echo, and had to take on fuel at Echo for the thirty-mile push on to Evanston. The railroad was the town's main employer, but none of its workers were well paid. The saying in the town was, "Uncle Peter [the nickname for Union Pacific] keeps us, but keeps us poor."

With the invention of the diesel engine, the coal and steam engines were gradually phased out and the services at Echo became obsolete. The last coal locomotive was serviced in Echo in 1960, when an era and a lifestyle came to an end.

Echo Canyon is also the site of the Echo Canyon Reservoir. By the late nineteenth century, hundreds of farmers depended on Weber River water for irrigation. With increasing demand, the supply didn't meet all the needs. Soon after the turn of the century serious water disputes arose between those who used the water of the upper Weber River and those who wanted water downstream. The lower-river users wanted the upstream users to shut off their canals so more water would flow downstream. The upper-river water users felt they had first rights to the water. Numerous lawsuits were avoided when LDS Church president Joseph F. Smith called the presidents of the affected stakes together to solve the problem. They decided to build a reservoir to provide plenty of water for all. After years of studying various potential sites, construction was begun on Echo Canyon Reservoir in 1927. The work was completed in 1930.

Morgan

I-84 rounds another bend into a verdant mountain farming valley. In 1852 Thomas J. Thurston of Centerville was logging in the mountains east of Davis County. At the summit of the mountains he was able to look down into the beautiful Morgan Valley. It so reminded him of his native Ohio, he decided to make the valley his home. Thurston's desire remained a dream for the next three years until, in 1855, he convinced some friends to help him break a road through the Weber River Canyon. With picks and shovels they chipped their way through the treacherous gorge and built a rough road into the beautiful mountain valley that would become their home.

Between 1868 and 1869 the Union Pacific Railroad built its tracks along the Weber River in its urgent effort to cover the most land before it met up with the Central Pacific Railroad somewhere in the desert. The influence of the railroad is seen in the layout of many of the towns of Morgan County.

Morgan itself is a railroad town. The businesses on its main street face the railroad. The town was set up by the territorial legislature in 1868, when the Union Pacific Railroad was under construction. People already inhabited North Morgan, or Mount Joy (established in 1861), and South Morgan. Both towns became part of the new city because they were within the boundaries specified by the legislature. While the railroad was being built, Morgan was the only incorporated city on the line between Omaha, Nebraska, and Ogden, Utah. It is still the only incorporated city in Morgan County. The town's original name was Monday Town, but the residents changed it to Morgan in honor of LDS Church leader Jedediah Morgan Grant, father of Heber J. Grant, seventh president of the church.

The Mormon citizenry of Morgan didn't want a wild railroad boomtown, but a quiet pioneer city that benefitted from the commerce the railroad brought. But by Mormon standards alcohol flowed a little too freely among the railroad workers, so one of the first laws passed in the new city was a strict liquor code.

Mountain Green

The last town in Morgan Valley before I-84 enters Weber Canyon is Mountain Green. An incident occurred here that could have sparked a war between Great Britain, Mexico, and the United States, had a report not been filed incorrectly. The Hudson's Bay Company's Peter Skene Ogden and his group of trappers were camped at Mountain Green when a group of American trappers rode into their camp on May 23, 1825. The British-owned Hudson's Bay Company and the Americans competed for trapping grounds. The American leader Johnson Gardner announced that Ogden's group was trespassing on American soil and said they must leave

Peter Skene Ogden.
—UTAH STATE
HISTORICAL SOCIETY

immediately. Gardner was mistaken—the area was legally occupied, jointly, by Mexico and Great Britain—but Ogden believed him and moved back to the Snake River. In addition to Gardner's threats, Ogden was faced with the reality that British trappers received less for their furs than American trappers. Twenty-three of Ogden's men took 700 beaver pelts and defected to the American side.

When Ogden filed his report of the incident several months later, it located the disagreement at the headwaters of the Missouri. His superiors assumed the incident had occurred east of the Continental Divide on U.S. soil, so they let it pass rather than try to collect for damages. Had the Hudson's Bay Company officials known the incident occurred outside of the United States in their own jurisdiction, they probably would have pursued the matter, possibly causing an international dispute.

For the next three decades, the little valley remained peaceful and relatively untouched. In 1859 George Higley moved here, naming it Mountain Green for the beauty of the meadows, valley, and hills. Mountain Green is still a beautiful spot in a high valley of the Wasatch Mountains. City dwellers are beginning to realize what a choice spot it is, and the serene mountain town is rapidly becoming a commuter suburb of Ogden.

North of Mountain Green, the Trappers' Loop Highway commemorates an interesting part of Utah's history. This was the route by which Ogden came into the Weber Valley and left it to head back north. Osborne Russell followed this same route during a hunting trip in January 1841, after his Christmas dinner with the Indians near present-day Ogden.

Weber Canyon

The interstate squeezes through Weber Canyon, crossing the Weber River several times. In pioneer times the canyon was truly treacherous. In 1846 Lansford Hastings convinced three migrating parties to use this route on their journey to California. Their descent into the canyon was disastrous. The rushing torrent of the river occupied the whole rocky chasm in many places, leaving no room for wagons and oxen to pass. The travelers had to tie ropes to their teams and wagons and haul them through the canyon, losing some to the river in the process.

From Weber Canyon, I-84 emerges into the lower valleys of the Great Salt Lake.

Uintah

North of the Weber River, Uintah fits nicely between the railroad tracks. The town enjoyed its brief moment of glory in 1869 during the construction of the Union Pacific Railroad. It was the end of the line until tracks were completed farther west.

Long before the site was a railroad boomtown, a tribe of Shoshone Indians known as the Weber Utes (hence the name Uintah) occupied this site. When Mormon settlers first built their homes and farms across the river in South Weber in the fall of 1851, they were unaccustomed to some of their neighbors' burial practices. The Indian way of honoring the dead was not the white way, and pioneers had to get used to the other culture's traditions. The Daughters of the Utah Pioneers' history of Davis County, *East of Antelope Island*, includes this description:

> Across the river from South Weber on the side of the hill among some trees was an Indian cemetery. When an Indian died they would wrap the body in a blanket and hang it in the top of a tree and tie it there with buckskin strings. . . . The bodies were left there to dry or decay and when they dropped from the trees . . . they were left for nature to take its course.

White men did not leave the Indians alone long in Uintah after South Weber was organized. Soon the settlers were moving across the river, and in 1854 they constructed a fort there.

When the railroad pushed out of Weber Canyon in 1869 Uintah grew to a population of about 5,000, with twenty-five saloons and over seventy-five businesses. Even with the rail lines connected at Corinne, Uintah

The Snowflake Hotel in Uintah, 1869. —UTAH STATE HISTORICAL SOCIETY

remained an important freighting station until 1872, when the Utah Central Railroad opened, taking the lines directly between Ogden and Salt Lake City.

As with many other boomtowns, Uintah relaxed into existence as a farming community with a few agriculturally based businesses. It has remained fairly stable for the past century, though influenced in recent years by the amazing growth experienced all along the Wasatch Front.

South Weber

South Weber was the site of a religious war in 1862. That year Joseph Morris, a pioneer who had lived in various Utah communities, came to South Weber dressed all in white and riding a white horse. Claiming to be a prophet, he said Christ would soon come so the townspeople didn't need to bother planting crops. He was persuasive enough to induce many, including the LDS bishop, to leave the LDS Church and deed all their property over to him. Morris and his followers claimed they were no longer subject to laws or taxes, and, heavily armed, they took over Kingston Fort in the settlement. There they drilled daily to prepare for war.

By the time the Morrisites had been in the fort a year, food supplies were getting low. Dissatisfaction became strong. When some members tried to leave with their possessions, the Morrisites hunted them down and held them hostage. A 500-man posse came from Salt Lake to fight the Morrisites.

The William Kendall family, part of the Morrisite group in South Weber.
—UTAH STATE HISTORICAL SOCIETY

A battle ensued but few people were killed. In the midst of the battle, a cannon was fired. The cannonball killed a woman nursing her daughter and shot off the child's jaw. (The baby later grew to maturity, married, and raised a large family, but she always covered her face when she met a stranger.) The cannonball wounded someone else before it landed in another woman's lap. Several other men were killed. After three days of fighting, Morris surrendered, only to order his men to arms again.

Morris was finally killed, and his followers were taken into custody. Some were tried for murder and convicted, but they were all pardoned and went to live quietly in various locations throughout the West. Some went to work at Fort Douglas when Patrick Connor's anti-Mormon forces came from California, as they were the only population of non-Mormons available to help the soldiers. The cannon used in the battle is now on display in Farmington on the city hall grounds.

I-15
I-84–Salt Lake
27 miles

I-84 joins I-15 in a very populous area of Utah. Numerous pioneer towns, once distinct entities, have grown into each other so they are practically indistinguishable.

DAVIS COUNTY

I-15 enters Davis County just beyond Sunset. Davis County is one of the fastest-growing areas of Utah. Because of the housing shortage in the Salt Lake area, new neighborhoods are quickly climbing the foothills and a large number of expensive new homes occupy the east bench. Davis County has some of the highest household incomes in the state, so this trend is likely to continue.

In 1826 Jedediah S. Smith traveled through the Davis County area with a group of trappers. Captain John C. Frémont also visited the area, and in 1845 he gave Antelope Island its name. The Lienhard party passed through Davis County in 1846 after struggling down Weber Canyon on their way to California. Lienhard was favorably impressed with the area and would have settled there if just one other white family had lived there. Instead, he left it free for the Mormons.

Davis County was a prospect for immediate colonization by the Mormons after they arrived in Utah. Within a short time, they began pasturing livestock, and the first full-time residents moved north from Salt Lake in 1848.

Hill Air Force Base, Clearfield.

The first settlers in the county found a valley filled with a series of long, deep ravines, cut by hundreds of years of heavy spring runoff from the Wasatch Mountains, running down to the Great Salt Lake. Gradually the streams were harnessed and many of the lower ravines filled in.

Daniel Davis, for whom the county was named, was one of its first settlers. He made his farm on Davis Creek, about a half mile south of Farmington, in the fall of 1848.

Clearfield

In 1940, Clearfield changed almost overnight from a farming town to a bustling military community. The U.S. government built Hill Field (originally an army air base but now an air force base) nearby. They also built the U.S. Naval Supply Depot at Clearfield. This depot shipped supplies totalling over $580 million to bases on the West Coast. After World War II, the depot was phased out and resurrected as the Freeport Center, which now contains about seventy-five manufacturing and distribution companies and employs between 5,000 and 6,000 people.

The Clearfield bench was known for many years as Sand Ridge. Only prickly pear and sagebrush grew there, and the hot, dry winds from Weber Canyon offered the only relief from the intense summer heat.

In 1878 Richard and Emily Hamblin, the first to homestead in the area, had to haul all their water in barrels from Layton. For two years Richard Hamblin dug wells up to 100 feet deep without finding water. When he finally struck water, he moved his home to the well site. At night, Hamblin pumped water into a cistern with a wind-driven pump, and by day he watered his crops. He was especially successful at growing strawberries. Later, with the coming of the Davis and Weber Canal, more settlers found the site attractive. There was now ample water to irrigate all the farms on the bench, transforming it into an important agricultural area.

Hill Air Force Base

Hill Field was activated on November 7, 1940, as an arm of the U.S. Army. By 1943 it was Utah's largest employer, with some 15,000 civilians and 6,000 military personnel providing maintenance and other needs for an air force that was expanding into all parts of the world.

The Hill base is still Utah's major employer and one of the most important and largest air force maintenance depots in the world. Aviation fans can look at their favorite aircraft at the Hill Aerospace Museum, located east of I-15.

Antelope Island

Antelope Island is a dominant feature of the Great Salt Lake, easily visible from almost anywhere around the lake. A causeway connects the north end of Antelope Island with the mainland. (Take the I-15 exit for Freeport Center if southbound; northbound, the exit is at Antelope Drive, Layton.) John Frémont found antelope on the island during his early explorations. Pioneers also explored the island soon after they arrived in the valley. Despite its desolate appearance, some natural fresh water flows on Antelope Island, and ranches have existed there since pioneer times. Brigham Young had a ranch there for his sheep and horses; one of his families managed the ranch. The Fielding Garr Ranch House, built for Young, is the longest continually lived-in building in Utah, occupied from its construction in 1848 until the 1960s, when the state took it over.

In 1854 Young launched the Timely Gull, a forty-five-foot boat designed to transport sheep back and forth from the Jordan River in Salt Lake City to Antelope Island. It functioned for four years until it crashed against the south shore of Antelope Island in a terrific windstorm. Its traces could be seen until the early 1950s.

Antelope Island was used as a temporary prison for one of Salt Lake's nineteenth-century criminals. In 1862 authorities arrested a man named John Baptist for robbing over 300 graves in the Salt Lake City Cemetery. He was sentenced to banishment on Antelope Island. "Grave Robber" was branded on his forehead, his ears were cut off, and he was left on the island. But sandbars between Antelope Island and the mainland made escape too likely, and Baptist was soon moved to Fremont Island, farther out in the water. Several months later, when someone visited the island, John Baptist was gone. People thought he had probably made a raft from some planks and floated away. He was never seen nor heard from again.

Antelope Island was the setting for a buffalo-hunt scene in the 1923 silent film *The Covered Wagon.* During filming, one of the cameramen was nearly killed when a buffalo charged him. A quick cowboy shot the animal just before it ran over the terrified man, and the whole crew ate buffalo steaks for dinner.

Layton and Kaysville

Layton and Kaysville grew simultaneously in the area north of Farmington. Kaysville had been used by native tribes for many years before the Mormons came. When settlers arrived in 1849 they found a large amount of evidence of the previous residents: arrowheads, stone cooking implements, toys, and other items. Pioneers also found two dugouts where trappers had probably lived.

Kaysville was named for William Kay, the first Mormon bishop of the new settlement. Gradually the northeastern area became known as Layton and the southern portion retained the name of Kaysville. Christopher Layton was an early bishop and member of the Mormon Battalion. He and his family were influential in the establishment of Layton.

In 1858, upon hearing of the approach of General Johnston's troops, residents of Kaysville and Layton abandoned their towns, as did the rest of northern Utah's population. One little girl drove an entire herd of turkeys all the way from Kaysville to Pleasant Grove and when the danger was past, she herded them back north again.

Layton never really wanted to belong to Kaysville, but it took thirty-four years for the town to obtain its divorce. Kaysville officials claimed Layton as part of Kaysville from 1868 to 1902. They also tried taxing Layton residents, though the people living outside of Kaysville received no services for their money. In 1889 Kaysville leaders announced plans to build a new city hall. This outraged Layton residents, who would have to help pay for the structure. One lawsuit between Kaysville city and a disgruntled Layton tax protestor went all the way to the U.S. Supreme Court. Relations became so bad that in 1899 Mormon apostles Francis M. Lyman, Marriner W. Merrill, and Anthon H. Lund were called on to solve the problems at a meeting in the Kaysville LDS chapel. The church leaders suggested making Kaysville's boundaries smaller. But they had no legal jurisdiction, and they left the matter up to the courts to decide. Finally on March 1, 1902, Layton became an independent municipality.

Many businesses began to grow in Layton, and a lot of houses were constructed. With the coming of many defense-related industries in Weber and Davis Counties at the time of World War II, Layton expanded rapidly. In 1985 Layton succeeded Bountiful as the largest town in Davis County. Many families have recently discovered its beautiful home sites, and the green hills and pastures of Layton are rapidly becoming upscale suburbs.

Farmington

I-15 turns east and joins US 89 at Farmington.

In the fall of 1847 Hector Caleb Haight moved his cattle to this well-watered pasturage for the winter. Farmington grew into a farming town and became the Davis County seat. Rock buildings became a trademark of Farmington, and the most prominent of these were the city hall and an old LDS church. Numerous walls and houses were also constructed of rock. A city ordinance now requires all public buildings to have some stone on the outside.

Because of its position against the dry Wasatch foothills, Farmington gets spring runoff. Heavy winter snows can cause problems. The heavy snows of 1983 lasted well into May. Sudden ninety-degree temperatures during the last two weeks of May pleased the winter-weary citizenry, but brought the runoff rushing down the mountains. Streambeds overflowed, bringing trees, mud, and huge boulders toward the town. All the force met homes built high into the foothills throughout Farmington and all of eastern Davis County. Many homes were evacuated as the raging water and debris tore out windows and filled basements with mud. Some homes were demolished entirely. An amazing effort, mostly on the part of private citizens led by church groups, was launched to help sandbag and clean out mud-and-debris-filled basements. In all of the flooding, only one man (in Bountiful) was seriously injured.

In recent years Farmington has experienced the same growth as the rest of the Wasatch Front. New housing developments surround the old part of the town. But Farmington proper retains its pioneer flavor, and the old, quiet residential community seems to want to remain the peaceful town it was in the beginning.

Lagoon Amusement Park

Lagoon Amusement Park is a prominent landmark just south of the US 89–I-15 junction. In 1886 the Denver & Rio Grande Western Railroad built a resort on the shores of the Great Salt Lake about two and a half miles west of the present lagoon. Due to fluctuating lake levels, the resort closed in 1895. Simon Bamberger, who ran a railroad through the area, later purchased the rights to the park and moved some of the buildings to the present site of the amusement park. He named his property Lagoon for a pond already at the site. He built swimming and dancing facilities and in 1906 added a forty-five-horse carousel that is still in use. The prominent wooden roller-coaster was built in 1921. Many other attractions were added over time, and Lagoon Amusement Park is now a large operation. The only structure remaining from the original 1886 buildings is the cupola of the old dance pavilion.

Centerville

It's hard to tell where Farmington ends and Centerville begins. Though it is becoming a tightly packed suburb, Centerville was once a pioneer town.

Settlers came in 1848 for the rich meadowland, watered by four mountain streams. After several name changes, the town was called Centerville for its position between Farmington and Bountiful.

In the spring of 1849, as the new crops were just beginning to grow strong, thousands of crickets descended on the fields, consuming everything green. The whole town attacked the crickets, trying to burn, drown, and bury them, but they kept coming. In despair, the people prayed for help, and suddenly, flocks of seagulls appeared from the Great Salt Lake. At first the pioneers were afraid the gulls would wreak more destruction, but instead, the birds gobbled up the crickets. Many gulls disgorged crickets into the lake when they got full and went back to eat more. Hundreds of the early pioneers in Davis County witnessed the miraculous event. Because of this incident (and similar, though less dramatic occurrences in Salt Lake and Tooele), the California gull became the state bird. Visitors to Utah can see the event commemorated in various statues and publications.

In the early summer of 1854 winged grasshoppers descended on the pioneers' new crops. The pioneers tried prayer again, as all their other efforts had failed to discourage the insects. The next morning the grasshoppers all rose up in the air at sunrise. At that moment a strong east wind blew down from the mountains and swept them into the lake, drowning the voracious insects. Thousands of dead grasshoppers later washed up on the shores.

The pioneers saw these occurrences as miracles on a par with those experienced by Moses and the Israelites who fled Egypt.

Bountiful

Bountiful was the second city the Mormons established in Utah. Just three days after the Saints' arrival in the Salt Lake Valley, Perregrine

Sessions explored the valley to the north. That fall he and his family herded the church cattle into what is now Davis County, and he built a cabin about where 300 North and 200 West Streets meet in Bountiful. The following year a number of families moved to what was then called Sessions Settlement in order to farm.

When the city was finally laid out in blocks in 1855, the name was changed to Bountiful. The Book of Mormon tells of a city near the sea called Bountiful, where milk and honey and a variety of fruits are plentiful.

When President Buchanan's troops were about to arrive in 1858, the city of Bountiful was abandoned along with other northern settlements, whose residents moved south to Utah County. The people left guards behind to burn the homes and fields if necessary, but the incident was settled peacefully, and the people returned to their homes in the late fall.

The pioneers constructed a tabernacle in Bountiful between 1857 and 1863. Located on Main Street and Center, the impressive building is the oldest church in Utah in continuous use, which it has been since its dedication.

Bountiful has become a suburb of Salt Lake City during the last thirty years. Since 1980, Bountiful has seen an unprecedented boom as new housing developments climb ever higher against the mountains. The new LDS temple (dedicated in January 1995), which glows white against the mountainside, has particularly drawn new, expensive houses, which encircle and reach out from the temple in all directions.

UT 65
Henefer–Mountain Dell/ Emigration Canyon
34 miles

Henefer

Henefer is the only incorporated town built directly on the old Pioneer Trail. Before the Mormons trudged into Utah, several other westward-bound groups blazed the trail down Echo Canyon. Henefer was an important junction for the 1846 companies traveling to California. The first several groups chose to travel north through Weber Canyon; they met with catastrophe as they tried to force their teams and wagons through the narrow rocky passages. At Henefer, Lansford Hastings left a note tacked to some sagebrush warning the Donner party not to attempt Weber Canyon, but to head south to find a better route. The Donner party opened the way, and the Mormons also took the southern route into the lower valleys.

On July 19, 1847, Brigham Young, ill with spotted fever, camped near present-day Henefer on the east bank of the Weber River. In 1859 the brothers James and William Henefer started a blacksmith shop to service not only the pioneers, but the Overland Stage road. After awhile they started farming at Henefer, too. By 1861 other permanent settlers lived nearby.

As in all early pioneer settlements, cooperation was essential for survival in Henefer. Yeast starters for bread and live coals for fires were shared between neighbors. For some time, the community had only one sewing needle, which was carefully guarded and passed from household to household as the need arose.

During the summer of 1868, grasshoppers descended on the growing fields of Henefer, devouring most of the crops. The Union Pacific Railroad, however, in their push toward Promontory and the meeting with the Central Pacific Railroad, saved the residents of Henefer from starvation by providing jobs. It was a year of both catastrophe and blessing for the town.

Today Henefer is a pleasant little town set against the steep rocky buttes that divide it from Morgan County to the north.

PIONEER MEMORIAL HIGHWAY

The road from Henefer is gentle until it rises into the Wasatch Mountains. Here the Donner party blazed new trails, cutting through forest and digging out brush. They spent two and a half valuable weeks forging a new road—lost time that would ultimately cost half of them their lives.

The Donner Party

Though not the only group to cross Utah before the Mormons, nor the first, the Donner party is certainly the most famous. Like many other migrant parties crossing the United States in the 1800s, this group was made up partly of families who were related or acquainted, and partly of others who happened to be traveling at the same time and considered it best to travel in a large group. George Donner, elected head of the party because of his age and wealth, was sixty-two and had left his grown children in Illinois. Tamsen Donner, age forty-five, was his third wife. With them were their three girls, ages six, four, and three, and two children from Mr. Donner's second marriage. The Donners had servants, twelve yokes of oxen, five saddle horses, milk cows, beef cattle, and a dog. The family took three wagons filled with food and supplies.

Equally prosperous was the Reed family. James Reed had acquired the most fantastic rig possible for the comfort of his family in the long pull across the country. Called by some the "Pioneer Palace," this wagon was entered from the side, up steps built for the convenience of elderly and invalid ladies. There was an iron cooking stove with a pipe through the canvas top. Spring seats ensured the travelers ultimate comfort, and a sleeping loft had been laid above the living quarters.

The Reeds were joined by their four small children and Mrs. Reed's ailing mother, who died during the journey. Other well-to-do families accompanied the Donners and Reeds, eager to see what life in California would offer them. In all, eighty-seven people left Fort Bridger in late July 1846, led by famed trail guide Lansford Hastings. Though Donner's wife had some misgivings about taking the experimental, unknown route to the south of the Great Salt Lake rather than the better-traveled Fort Hall road, the rest were anxious to save time this way, as Hastings had assured them they would. So southward they pushed—with Hastings's promise that he would help guide them across. Hastings went ahead, however, and when the Donner party reached the bottom of Echo Canyon they found a note from Hastings telling them not to attempt Weber Canyon. They set up camp and sent James Reed and two other men ahead to intercept Hastings and ask him what to do. The company waited anxiously for five days. Finally Reed returned alone; the other two had decided to stay with Hastings.

The route down the Weber River was too treacherous, Reed explained, and they would have to build a new path through the Wasatch Mountains. Breaking a new trail through steep and heavily wooded terrain was a new type of work for this group of midwestern farmers. It proved strenuous and difficult, and the group, never really a cohesive unit, began bickering.

James Frazier Reed and his wife, Margaret Keyes Reed.
—UTAH STATE HISTORICAL SOCIETY

Some complained the work went too slowly, others refused to do more than they were already doing. After two and a half weeks of hacking their way through the wilderness, they found themselves at the top of a canyon clogged with thick brush and oaks. Sick of chopping through timber, they decided to go over the steep mountain rather than cut any more. The brush they left untouched, less than half a mile in length, was the only new trail the Mormons had to forge on their entire journey to Zion.

The time the Donner party had spent cutting through timber put them behind schedule, and by the time they arrived in the Sierra Nevada, violent winter storms had already set in, trapping them in the mountains. As members of the group began to die of cold and starvation, the survivors resorted to cannibalism. By the time rescue parties reached them in early spring, only half of the original group was still alive.

EMIGRATION CANYON

Eleven months after the Donner party struggled over the rugged Wasatch Mountains, Brigham Young's group chose the same path. The Donner group had by no means built a paved road through the mountains. Pioneer men hacked through brush and trees, smoothing the road and searching for the best stream crossings. They were interested not only in their own passage, but also in the thousands of migrants they knew would follow.

By the time the pioneers reached Henefer, Young had contracted Rocky Mountain spotted fever. The group divided into three separate parties: the advance company, which would scout out the best road; the main body; and the rear guard, a small group that stayed with Young while he was ill. Knowing his people could waste no time before planting if they were to harvest any crops that year, Young sent the advance company ahead under the direction of Orson Pratt and ordered the rest to follow as quickly as possible.

On July 19, 1847, Orson Pratt and John Brown gained their first glimpse of the Salt Lake Valley from the top of Big Mountain. Two days later Pratt, along with Erastus Snow, climbed Donner Hill. Upon reaching the summit they saw the whole valley spread at their feet, as if welcoming them after the tremendous journey. Pratt recorded, "We could not refrain from a shout of joy which almost involuntarily escaped from our lips the moment this grand and lovely scenery was in our view."

Young followed a few days behind. On July 24 the Mormon leader declared from the mouth of Emigration Canyon, "This is the right place, drive on."

Later, in the late 1800s and early 1900s, demand for sandstone, needed for building foundations, was very high. Hauling the heavy stone from

Emigration Canyon was cumbersome, so in 1907 an electric rail line was constructed: the Emigration Canyon Railroad. Its fourteen miles of track crossed and recrossed Emigration Creek many times. After a couple of years of operation, the railroad added open passenger cars for picnickers wishing to escape the city into the canyon. The rail line had a short life. The invention of concrete outmoded the use of stone in building foundations, and passenger use was not heavy enough to support the railroad. The line was dismantled at the beginning of World War I.

This Is the Place State Park

On July 24, 1847, Brigham Young emerged from Emigration Canyon and got his first good view of the valley of the Great Salt Lake. He declared, "This is the right place," and the Mormon capital was unofficially established. In 1937 the state of Utah commissioned Mahonri Young, a grandson of Brigham Young, to create a monument commemorating the event (erected in 1947). The area surrounding the monument eventually became a state park, and between 1994 and 1996 it underwent extensive renovations. The park includes the Old Deseret Village, a living history museum that features original and reconstructed pioneer homes, businesses, and other buildings where people in period costumes reenact pioneer life and answer questions. Refreshments are offered in the stores, as well as other items for sale.

Emigration Canyon railway, July 24, 1909. —UTAH STATE HISTORICAL SOCIETY

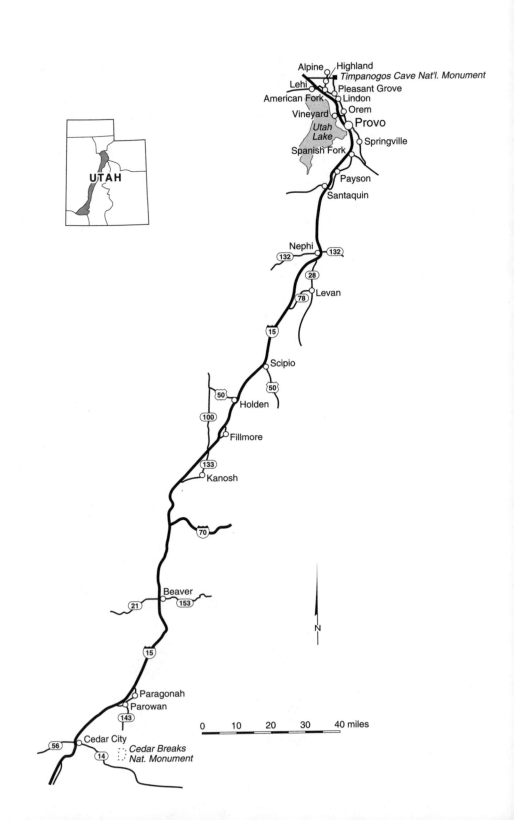

PART III
The Mormon Corridor

Soon after the Mormons' arrival in Utah, Brigham Young announced his intentions to spread his Zion from the Rocky Mountains west to the Sierra Nevada. The northern border of the territory would be Oregon and the southern border Mexico. A small part of California near Los Angeles would be annexed as well, to bring Mormon immigrants by sea rather than over the rough land crossing from the east. Young ordered the establishment of towns and way stations all approximately one day's journey apart, along a "Mormon Corridor" meant to connect Salt Lake City with the Pacific Ocean. Many of the towns along I-15 in Utah are a result of this plan.

UTAH VALLEY

Like the Salt Lake Valley to the north, Utah Valley was once filled with ancient Lake Bonneville. After Lake Bonneville broke through barriers in southern Idaho, its level dropped drastically. Later, weather patterns changed, resulting in the levels of Utah Lake and the Great Salt Lake we see today. Old lake shorelines are visible along the benches to the east and west.

After the lake waters receded, vegetation began sprouting in this broad valley. Grasses and shrubbery grew abundantly. The area became favored hunting grounds for the Desert Culture from 10,000 B.C. to A.D. 300–500, then for the Fremont Indians until about A.D. 1400. Later, the Ute tribes favored the valley for its fine hunting, fishing, grazing, and farming lands.

The Utes

Utah's first native inhabitants had their initial contact with white men in the 1700s, when Spanish monks traveled through the region. The

encounters were generally brief and infrequent and had little effect on the
Utes and Paiutes. However, the era of the fur traders in the 1820s drastically changed the lifestyle of the Indians. The traders took advantage
of the Utes' hunting skills and profited greatly from the furs they obtained
from the natives. The Indians learned to trust the white men and look
on them as a source of food, guns, and other supplies. Jedediah Smith
wrote the following of the Utes:

> I found these Indians more honest than any I had ever been with in
> the country. They appear to have verry little disposition to steal and ask
> for nothing unless it may be a little meat. . . . The Uta's are cleanly quiet
> and active and make a nearer approach to civilized life than any Indians
> I have seen in the Interior.

The Utes were also well-armed and well-supplied with horses.

Father Escalante visited Utah Valley in 1776 and found it to be "the
most pleasant, beautiful, and fertile in all New Spain." The Dominguez-
Escalante party spent three days camped on the shores of the Lake of the
Tympanocuitzis (Utah Lake). They were greatly impressed with the amount
of water for irrigation, the climate, the wildlife, and the good pasture.
They also described the native peoples there as the most peaceful they
had met, and were anxious to convert them to Christianity. Later, when
John C. Frémont and his men visited Utah Valley, they found it a very
favorable spot for settlement. In 1847 Brigham Young considered Utah
Valley for his people, but rejected the area because of the strong Ute
presence, choosing the Salt Lake Valley instead.

The Utes may have looked with wary eyes on the hundreds of
Mormons trekking into the valley to the north of them—and with good
cause. It soon became evident that the Salt Lake Valley could not accommodate the thousands still arriving, and exploration parties were sent to
other valleys to investigate their potential for permanent settlement. In
March 1849 Young sent pioneers to settle Utah Valley. The first fort was
built at Provo.

Young's initial policy toward the Indians, even before the Saints
completed their westward journey, was recorded by one of his clerks in
March 1847:

> If any of the brethren shot an Omaha Indian for stealing, they must
> deliver the murderer to Old Elk to be dealt with, as the Indians shall
> decide, as that was the only way to save the lives of the women and
> children. I felt that it was wrong to indulge in feelings of hostility and
> blood-shed toward the Indians, the descendents of Israel, who might kill
> a cow, an ox or even a horse; to them the deer, the buffalo, the cherry
> and plum tree, or strawberry bed were free. It was their mode of living
> to kill and eat.

After the Mormons arrived in Utah, their attitude toward the Indians changed. They found the native people to be both noble and cruel. They thought the northern Utes' dealings in Paiute child slavery a horrible cruelty. At the same time, they admired the natives' skill at adapting to life in such an unkind climate.

From the Mormons' first incursions into the valley, relations with the Utes were strained at best. Utes were happy to receive gifts of food and clothing from the pioneers, but they resented white society taking over their hunting, gathering, and farmlands. Utes believed they had the right to take the white settlers' cattle and did so, which often resulted in battles and loss of Ute life.

Brigham Young's advice to deal diplomatically with the Indians was sometimes ignored—resulting in drastic consequences. In 1850 three Utah Valley men shot "Old Bishop," a member of a local tribe, when he stole a shirt. To finish the deed, the men cut open the Ute's stomach, filled it with rocks, and deposited the body in the Provo River. Because of this incident and others, the hostility of local tribes increased to the point that Mormon leaders asked Brigham Young for help. He held the whites responsible for killing Indians, but had to finally allow the settlers to either defend themselves or be driven out. Young reluctantly ordered Daniel H. Wells to exterminate the men, allowing women and children to live. Subsequent battles in Utah County saw the deaths of between twenty and thirty warriors.

In December 1850, Young bemoaned the Indians' lack of desire to adopt a more "civilized" lifestyle:

> We have spared no time or expense in endeavoring to conciliate the Indians, and learn them to leave off their habits of pilfering and plundering and work like other people. But habits of civilization seem not to be in accordance with their physical formation; many that have tried it, pine away, and unless returned to their former habits of living, die in a very short time. Could they be induced to live peacefully and keep herds of cattle, then conditions would be very materially ameliorated, and gradually induce a return to the habits of civilization.

The Mormons had wanted to look on the natives as fellow Israelites, but they ended up treating the Indians much as the rest of white America did at the time.

The Walker War

Most of the communities in Utah Valley were established between 1850 and 1851. They were set up around the plentiful mountain streams and structured so the outlying pastures and farmlands touched those of

Chief Wakara.
—UTAH STATE
HISTORICAL SOCIETY

the next community, thus presenting a united front against any Indian attack. These settlements disturbed the hunting, fishing, and farming activities of the natives who already lived in the valley. Hostilities arose, some coming to blows, others just smoldering until a catalyst caused them to erupt.

In 1852 the territorial legislature provided the catalyst, in the form of a law preventing Utah Indian tribes from kidnapping women and children from other tribes and selling them to New Mexico slave traders. The slave trade had been very lucrative for the Utes and the Navajos. Since the Indians in the region were already resentful, the ban on slave trading drove them to arms. Thus began the Walker War in 1853.

The Walker War, which afflicted all the settlements south of Salt Lake City, was precipitated at a homestead about one mile north of Springville in July 1853, when several Ute Indians came to trade some trout for flour. Flour was scarce and a dispute arose over the amount the pioneer was willing to give for the fish. During the altercation that ensued, one of the Indians was injured and later died. Because of this, the Indians declared war. They stole cattle and raided communities in Juab, Utah, Sanpete, Millard, and Iron Counties. Fewer than twenty white casualties but many more Ute deaths occurred before Brigham Young and Chief Walker (or Wakara) signed a peace treaty at Chicken Creek in Juab County in May 1854.

The Walker War was not the first period of conflict for Wakara. In 1840 the chief joined some down-and-out trappers in raiding southern California ranches. They stole hundreds of horses and mules, later trading them with trappers in the Rocky Mountains. The group continued the periodic raids until the United States took control of California. Wakara became adept at trading. For him, stealing and trading became the road to riches and power. Other Utes followed his example, which made them better off as far as worldly goods were concerned, but increased their dependence on the white man. After a number of years of hostilities alternating with uneasy peace with the white settlers, the Utes were banished to reservations in the Uinta Basin, depriving this once-proud tribe of their favorite hunting grounds and leaving the Mormon settlers to prosper.

Modern Utah County

Peace in Utah County facilitated its continued growth. In 1850, 2,026 people lived in the county; by 1900 the population was 32,456, and in 1940 it had risen to 57,382. The 1996 population of Utah County was approximately 310,000, and it remains one of the fastest-growing counties in the state. It has changed from the agricultural area of fifty years ago to a highly specialized, technology-oriented county with a number of computer-software manufacturers in residence. Nearby Brigham Young University provides a well-educated worker pool; that, along with an abundance of available land, has convinced many companies to relocate to Utah County. But with the new business opportunities have come increased housing costs, heavier freeway traffic, and other urban afflictions. Farms have rapidly disappeared, but Utah County officials have been able to encourage new development in the local economy.

I-15
Draper–Cedar City
231 miles

Utah Lake

As you cross the Point of the Mountain between Salt Lake and Utah Counties on I-15 heading south from Draper, Utah Lake comes into view. Covering about 150 square miles, this somewhat murky body of water is the largest freshwater lake in the United States west of the Mississippi. Its average depth is only about eight feet, though, so it does not have the greatest volume of water.

The lake has sustained many people for hundreds of years. It fed native tribes for centuries before providing fishing and hunting opportunities to

Mormon settlers. They survived, in great part, off the fish they caught in the lake. They also dried and sold fish to other communities in exchange for much-needed supplies.

Starting in about 1864, reports that a giant eel-like monster lived in Utah Lake began to circulate. The animal was supposedly twenty-five to thirty feet long and had a head like a greyhound. Every time there was a sighting, someone stepped forward to refute it. Still, intermittent reports of terrifying experiences persisted into the early part of the twentieth century. The monster has been at rest since then.

The lake continues to attract fishermen—though their needs are not as urgent as those of previous generations—and it is a popular recreation spot. Though murky, the water is not polluted, just heavy with silt washed down by mountain streams.

Alpine

Just after rounding the bend of the Point of the Mountain, UT 92 exits I-15 with signs to Alpine, Highland, and Timpanogos Cave. Alpine has one of the most desirable settings of any town in the state. Sheltered in the arms of the Wasatch Mountains, the town faces south over Utah Valley. Because of its beauty and relatively easy access to Salt Lake City and the towns of Utah County, Alpine is losing its farming atmosphere and becoming a thriving suburb. The first settlers to graze their cattle in the place they called Mountainville would be dumbfounded at the mansions being constructed today in their fields. Even then, people were

John Moyle's fort tower, Alpine.

impressed with the mountain scenery, and when Brigham Young suggested they change the name of the place to Alpine for its Swiss atmosphere, they all concurred.

The first families to set up homes in Alpine moved to the area in 1850. As in all new communities, life was hard. Settlers had to pull sagebrush, carry water long distances, and survive the long, cold winters. Repeated grasshopper infestations destroyed most of the crops between 1854 and 1864, but the pioneers stayed on. The warm sun of a southwesterly exposure helped them to overcome the obstacles in their lives.

In 1866 John R. Moyle settled outside of the Mountainville Fort. He built his own fort for protection from the Indians, which included a circular rock tower. He planned to dig a tunnel from his home to the tower. The Indian threat died down, and he never completed the tunnel. The property was donated to the city of Alpine for use as a historic park. The park includes picnic and horseshoe areas, nature trails, an amphitheater, and museums. In Alpine, follow signs to Peppermint Place, then to Moyle Park.

Moyle was a dedicated Mormon who helped construct the Salt Lake City Temple. For many years he walked the twenty-eight miles from Alpine to Salt Lake City, then home again on weekends, to help with the temple construction. One weekend a cow kicked him, badly breaking his leg. The leg didn't heal properly. With nothing for the pain except a thick nail between his teeth, Moyle had his leg cut off with a sharp ax. After his wound had healed, he whittled a wooden leg, padded it, and strapped it onto the stump. When he could walk again, Moyle recommenced his work on the Salt Lake Temple, hobbling back and forth from Alpine each week as he had done before losing his leg.

UT 92 runs through the Wasatch Mountains between I-15 and Provo Canyon. A mile or two of the western portion of this road is open farmland (though development encroaches more and more). UT 92 rises through the towns of Highland and Alpine, then enters the mountains just east of Alpine at American Fork Canyon. At this point UT 92 becomes a spectacular mountain drive, known locally as the "Alpine loop." It is especially beautiful in the fall, though summer is another nice time to take the drive. During winter the highest portions of the road are blocked by snow.

Highland

Highland meets Alpine at UT 92. This pleasant suburban town was homesteaded after its neighbors—American Fork, Lehi, and Pleasant Grove—so there were no water rights left. The Lehi canal ran through Highland, and residents tried taking water from it to save their crops.

One woman went so far as to jump into the ditch; catching water in her skirt, she threw it onto the parched land. A lawsuit between the people of Lehi and John Pool, who had taken water from the canal, ended in Alpine residents obtaining rights to some of the water—enough to scratch out small farms from the parched soil.

Highland remained a small farming community for many years, until the 1960s and 1970s, when it started attracting more suburban dwellers. In recent years it has distinguished itself as one of the fastest-growing communities in Utah. Like Alpine, its neighbor to the north, it was named for a mountainous location in Europe, the Highlands of Scotland.

Timpanogos Cave National Monument

A few miles up American Fork Canyon from Alpine and Highland are the ranger station and trail to Timpanogos Cave National Monument. The first of the series of caves was discovered in 1887. Further exploration revealed other caverns, which were eventually connected by man-made tunnels. The site was declared a national monument in 1922. The first cave discovered, Hansen Cave, was stripped by a Chicago onyx company of most of its ornamentation, but the caves discovered in subsequent years are decked with stalactites and stalagmites. Tours are available from May to October (reaching the caves necessitates a fairly steep one-and-a-quarter-mile hike). Be sure to carry warm clothing to wear in the caves.

Thanksgiving Point

To the west of the Alpine exit a decorative water tower marks Thanksgiving Point, a not-for-profit enterprise. WordPerfect originator Alan Ashton and his wife, Karen, created a 550-acre green space here in 1996 as a token of appreciation of God and the community.

The park complex has restaurants, nurseries, gift shops, and a petting zoo, as well as numerous different gardens. A number of family-oriented activities have been added since the park's opening: a fishing pond, pony and wagon rides, garden tours, and various classes. The complex also operates a professional golf course designed by golfer Johnny Miller. Planned as the crowning jewel of Thanksgiving Point, the sixty-five-acre Thanksgiving Gardens is scheduled to open in 2000.

Lehi

Traveling south on I-15 from the Timpanogos Cave exit, you'll soon see the exit for Lehi. This quiet town was named for a Book of Mormon prophet who moved often with his family. The people who settled the north end of Utah Lake felt a certain kinship with Lehi. After moving many times in the east, coming to Salt Lake, and then to Utah Valley, they had established a city. And, as if that weren't enough, they had to move their new settlement several times before they found the right place. Feeling they had moved as many times as Lehi, they named their town for the prophet.

Lehi, founded in September 1850, was originally called Sulphur Springs because of the taste of the springwater there. As was done in most new communities at the time, the crude cabins were built to form a fort, with the spring in the middle. The settlers survived mostly on fish they caught with nets in Utah Lake, plus some ducks and geese. They traded fish with other communities for provisions.

Though today Lehi is a quiet community, it had its share of excitement in the nineteenth century. A Pony Express station occupied the settlement; later it was an Overland Stage stop. In 1863 soldiers from Fort Douglas who were vacationing at Camp Floyd (deserted in 1861 with the start of the Civil War) caused a number of deaths through their senseless harassing and wounding of several Indians. The Indians swore revenge on the "bluecoats," and, making no distinction between the soldiers and other whites, ambushed a passing stage. They killed and scalped the passengers and, because of the bravery he displayed in the battle, ate the heart of the driver.

Lehi was a boomtown for a year in 1872 when the railroad had its terminus there. Overnight, hotels and saloons went up, and new jobs in freighting and related industries were created. The next year the railroad was extended farther south, and Lehi has been pretty quiet since.

The Utah Sugar Company

The first successful sugar factory in Utah was constructed in Lehi in the years 1890–91. The site was chosen for its easy access to railroads: the Rio Grande Western Railroad passed on one side and the Union Pacific on the other. The plant opened in 1891. On the night of October 15, 1891, a crowd gathered to see if sugar could actually be produced from beets. They watched as the dark molasses boiled, some incredulous that white sugar could emerge from the dark, sticky substance. Quoted in Leonard J. Arrington's *Beet Sugar in the West*, witness James Gardner recalled:

> It was after midnight when the strike was dropped, but they all waited for that important event. Then everyone rushed to the centrifugal and when the first machine had spun off the molasses, Mr. [Ed] Dyer could hardly get room enough to perform the washing. However, he soon passed out the clear white sugar, giving each one of his audience some "right in his hand." Immediately "hurrahs" and "hosannas" filled the air.

By morning 20,000 pounds of sugar had been bagged and sent to Salt Lake City. A yoke of oxen hauled the wagonload of sugar through the town with a sign reading "First Carload of Granulated Sugar Made by the Utah Sugar Company." Within two hours the sugar was sold, and candy companies were displaying signs advertising the "First Candy Made from Utah Sugar."

During the first few years of production, the plant had some success, but had a great deal to learn. Difficulties included poor-quality seed obtained from Europe and a lesson in growing beets in the dry Utah climate. However, within a few years, production increased, and farmers and the sugar plant started showing profits.

Before mechanization increased efficiency, sugar beet production was very labor intensive. Beets were a "stoop crop," requiring many helpers. Fortunately, Utah had a high birthrate and teenage boys were available in abundance. T. F. Kirkham and Al Yates told of their experiences in the beet fields:

> We aimed to be in the fields to begin work at seven in the morning, took an hour out for noon, and quit at six in the evening. For that day of ten hours we received 50 cents—5 cents per hour—and were very glad for the job. The beet gang consisted of men and boys. Older boys with long-handled 4-inch hoes would block the beets, that is, chop the compact row of plants into bunches. The younger boys crawled behind on their hands and knees, with a short-handled hoe, thinning each block to a single good plant. To save wear and tear most of the boys wore knee pads—i.e., sack-like cushions tied with strings above and below the

Utah Sugar Factory and Beet Field, Lehi, circa 1895.
—LDS CHURCH HISTORICAL DEPARTMENT

knee. Every thinner had for his highest ambition the time when he would have a crawler following him on hands and knees. Twenty rows 40 rods long was a good day's work and parents had no trouble getting boys to bed by suppertime. One person could thin from a fourth to a half of an acre per day.

Harvesting the beets was equally work intensive.

Because of Lehi's success, many other plants were built at various locations around the country within ten years. Most notable was the establishment of the Utah-Idaho Sugar Company, with twenty-nine factories throughout the West.

Unfortunately, the plant at Lehi became outdated and nematodes infested the beet fields because of poor crop rotation. By the 1920s more efficient operations took over sugar production, and in 1925 the Lehi plant closed. It was demolished in 1939.

John L. Hutchings Museum

Lehi boasts a natural history museum that is comprised mainly of the collection of one family. The John L. Hutchings Museum, located at 685 N. Center Street, started because Scranton, the small town where John and Eunice Hutchings and their family lived, had no school. They encouraged their children to explore their world and collect items they could look at and discuss. After the family moved to Lehi, they continued to collect objects, and soon their shed overflowed with birds' eggs, minerals, beehives, and other treasures. H. C. Hutchings, one of the children, went on to earn degrees in biology and geology from Brigham Young University. In 1968 the town found a building to house the Hutchings collection. It has recently been moved to the old Carnegie library.

American Fork

A few miles south of the Lehi exit is the one for American Fork. American Fork took its name from the rushing mountain river that shoots out of the canyon at the north base of Mount Timpanogos. The river was named before settlers arrived in 1850, although accounts differ as to what inspired the name. According to one report, the Dominguez-Escalante party entered Utah Valley by way of what they called the El Rio de Santa Ana—later named the Spanish Fork River—and subsequent explorers called the northern river the American Fork River to distinguish it from the Spanish Fork to the south. Others believe it was named by American trappers (great competition existed between the American and Canadian trappers) who inhabited the region as early as 1822.

Mary Ellen Pully was a pioneer wife and mother who lived in American Fork in the 1890s. One day while her husband was away in the

Strawberry River valley herding sheep, her log cabin caught fire and burned. Neighbors wanted to go get her husband to help rebuild their home, but she didn't want him disturbed. She decided she wanted a better home than the one she'd lost in the fire, so she built it herself out of cinder bricks. Her cousin promised to help plaster the walls but he never showed up. That didn't stop her from finishing her new home. She plastered the walls herself. Her father-in-law happened by while she was doing the work and told her she was doing man's work. "Well it's woman's work when you can't get a man to do it," she replied.

In 1866, American Fork opened Utah's first free public school. Not only has the town been a leader in public education, it has been the home of a school for the handicapped for many years. The Utah legislature established the Utah State Training School at American Fork in 1929. The school was built on 400 acres of tillable land. Disabled children and young adults were schooled whenever possible, and some were trained to do agricultural work. Today the institute, now called the Utah State Developmental Center, continues to care for the developmentally disabled. It no longer serves children, but some 325 adults are currently enrolled in the program.

In 1996 the LDS Church dedicated a new temple in American Fork. The white structure dominates the bench, particularly at night, when the brightly lit temple is visible throughout much of Utah Valley. Though the temple itself is not open to the general public, a visitor center offers information and video viewings.

Pleasant Grove

Just south of American Fork, another old pioneer settlement looks down on Utah Valley from its seat in the foothills of the Wasatch Mountains. The most renowned landmark in Pleasant Grove is not Mount Timpanogos, which towers behind the town, but the Purple Turtle, a local fast-food restaurant. If you ask directions from townspeople, they will reference the point of departure from the Purple Turtle.

In February or March 1849, before Pleasant Grove had any white settlers, a skirmish took place between thirty or forty Mormon men and a group of Ute Indians at Battle Creek. Some Indians had stolen cattle belonging to the Mormons camped at the Provo River. Another group of Indians led the Mormon men to the creek where the culprits were camped with the cattle. During the confrontation that ensued, four Indians were killed.

Grove Fort was built on the site in 1850. The name was changed to Battle Creek to commemorate the famous fight. Finally, in 1851, the name

Pleasant Grove was chosen because of a grove of cottonwoods that stood at the original settlement.

Orem

The towns in Utah County are strung tightly together like beads on a necklace. The next bead is Orem. The benchland between Utah Lake and the Provo River was called the Provo Bench for many years. People from Provo farmed there long before any permanent residents moved to the area. Settlers attempted to dig wells for a number of years unsuccessfully; in 1863 a canal was dug to bring water to the farms. Families spent summers on the bench, returning to Provo for the winter, until 1877, when the Thomas and Mary Ann Cordner family moved there permanently.

A name for the community didn't seem very important until 1919, when Oscar Anderson called a group of men to a meeting for the purpose of naming their town. These men were mainly orchardists concerned with getting their fruit to market. They reasoned that if they named the town for Walter Orem, who owned the railroad, he might make a stop so they could load their fruit onto the trains. They called the town Orem—and they got their train stop.

Unlike other Utah Mormon communities, Orem never really had a center. Rather, it grew as scattered homes and businesses along the highway. Lorna Anderson Larsen, who was born in Orem in 1930, recalled wondering as a young girl with her friends where the real town would develop. Orem has grown dramatically since that time. Many businesses, some of them known throughout the world, and massive shopping complexes characterize the city, but it still lacks a real downtown to call the center of the community.

A number of computer software companies have made Orem their home. The first of these to become really successful was WordPerfect, followed by Novell, Caldera, and a number of others.

The Osmond Family

Orem is home to one of America's most famous singing families. George and Olive Osmond reared their eight boys and one girl in Orem. The eldest two sons, Virl and Tom, who are hearing impaired, became the first deaf missionaries to represent the LDS Church, serving in Canada. They were also the inspiration for the Children's Miracle Network, a fundraising program that benefits disabled children.

The next four Osmond boys, Alan, Wayne, Merrill, and Jay, began singing barbershop-quartet-style music when they were very young. While working at Disneyland in the early 1960s, they were spotlighted in a Disney television program. After this exposure the brothers were featured on the *Andy Williams Show* for seven seasons. Donny and Marie Osmond, younger siblings, also made appearances on television as very young children. They both went on to very successful musical careers, including their own television show in the 1970s.

Though the family base is still in Utah, the Osmonds work out of a studio in Branson, Missouri, owned by the youngest brother, Jim. In the 1990s Donny again earned kudos with his portrayal of Joseph in Andrew Lloyd Webber's Broadway musical *Joseph and the Amazing Technicolor Dreamcoat.*

Vineyard

Sugar beets were the first big cash crop in this former agricultural area, but the town was named for the grapes grown there. Dairying was also an important business in Vineyard. Farmers gathered at the old milk house every day to discuss the latest news. Geneva Resort, a bathing resort on Utah Lake, was a popular summer recreation spot. With the coming of World War II, however, Vineyard was destined to change dramatically from a quiet farming town to an industrial center.

In early 1942 the U.S. government announced the projected construction of a steel mill on the shores of Utah Lake west of Orem. The site was chosen because of the ready availability of coal, iron ore, limestone,

The rural and industrial meet in Vineyard: Geneva Steel.

and dolomite in the area; the proximity of the railroad; the quality of the local workforce; the availability of water; and the distance from potential West Coast invasion or bombing sites. Construction of Geneva Steel took place from 1942 to 1944 and displaced thirty-seven families. The government paid pre–World War II prices for the land and condemned the farms of those who refused to sell. However, many more people benefitted from the plant than were hurt by it. The thousands of jobs created at the steel plant brought Utah County out of the Great Depression and into a period of unprecedented prosperity. The plant, the largest fully integrated steel mill in the United States at the time of its construction, built steel plates for ships during World War II. Steel from Geneva went into thousands of merchant and naval ships. In the postwar years Geneva employed more than 7,000 workers and had a payroll of over $30 million annually. Geneva closed for a time in the early 1980s, but a group of private businessmen resurrected it in 1987.

Rulon Gammon, the Vineyard town mayor, calls his city "Utah's best-kept little secret." The town wasn't incorporated until 1989—at Geneva Steel's request. The company had been paying enormous taxes to Utah County and wanted to lower its tax assessment. Now Vineyard has the highest per-capita tax base of any town in the state (in other words, it is the richest!).

Provo

Provo was the first settlement in Utah Valley and one of the first outside of Salt Lake City. In 1825 French-Canadian trapper Etienne Proveau (also known as Provost, Provot, and Provaux) and his men fought an epic battle with the Snake Indians here. Most of the white men were killed, but Provost and three or four of his companions escaped. Both the Provo River and the city of Provo were named for him.

In 1849 Brigham Young called a group of thirty-three families to build a fort in Utah Valley. In March of that year the families traveled south from Salt Lake City. As the group entered Utah Valley, an Indian brave barred their way. After about an hour's delay the pioneers convinced him to let them pass. They built a fort on the south side of the Provo River at approximately 100 North and 1800 West. When President Young visited the settlement a few months later, he advised them to move to higher ground where floods wouldn't be so prevalent. They did so and settled the current site of the city, which was incorporated on February 6, 1851.

Conflicts with area Indians recurred several times, initially because the new settlers killed a local tribesman during the first winter. A group of Utes had made a camp about a mile upstream from the fort on the

Provo River. After the Indians had stolen and killed many cattle and horses and made numerous threats, the army took action. Captain Howard Stansbury, who was in Salt Lake City at the time, approved sending the militia to attack the Ute camp with cannons. One white man and forty Indians were killed. The Indians subsequently abandoned their camp.

In 1872 Thomas L. Kane, an easterner with high government connections, his wife, Elizabeth, and two of their children journeyed to Utah with Brigham Young. Kane never became a Mormon, but he had used his influence to help the Mormons during their trek westward and again during the Utah War. Elizabeth Kane left a fascinating account of her travels and stays with polygamous families in her book *Twelve Mormon Homes*.

In December 1872, Mrs. Kane described Utah towns, and Provo in particular:

> Hardly any "clap-boarded" houses are to be seen in Utah. The Mormons have an ugly, English-looking, burnt brick; but adobe ("dobies") or unburnt brick is most commonly used. I prefer the adobe— its general tint is of a soft dove-color, which looks well under the trees. Sometimes the Mormons coat the adobe walls with plaster of Paris, which, in their dry climate, seems to adhere permanently. Its dazzling whiteness commends it to the housekeeper's, if not to the artist's eye. The walls of the best houses in Provo were white or light-colored, and, with their carved wooden window-dressings and piazzas and corniced roofs, looked trim as if fresh from the builder's hand.

The first fort built by Provo settlers was near the Provo River at approximately 100 North and 1800 West. —UTAH STATE HISTORICAL SOCIETY

Thomas L. Kane.
—UTAH STATE
HISTORICAL SOCIETY

As one of Utah's major cities, Provo qualified for a state institution. In 1880 the territorial legislature set aside $25,000 for building a mental hospital in Provo. The first building was completed in 1885 at the east end of Center Street. The complex today is quite different from what it was a century ago, but it is still the primary mental hospital in the state.

Brigham Young University

Provo is probably best known as the home of Brigham Young University (BYU), which began in 1875 as Brigham Young Academy. The original buildings were in downtown Provo. In the late nineteenth century the academy constructed buildings on Academy (later University) Avenue. Later the campus expanded on the bench to the northeast, where the university is located today. The Church of Jesus Christ of Latter-day Saints has continued to own and operate the school since its inception. In 1903 the school became a university. Since that time, it has become the largest church-sponsored university in the United States, with a student body of about 28,000. The old Brigham Young Academy buildings have stood vacant for a number of years. Though in severely deteriorated condition, some of the old buildings are being rebuilt into a new Provo City Library.

Brigham Young University has a number of excellent museums. The Monte L. Bean Life Science Museum features animal exhibits ranging from elephants to butterflies. The Museum of Art, dedicated in 1993, was built to house BYU's art collection along with traveling displays. Such exhibits as the Ramses Egyptian Exhibition, Etruscan artifacts, the Imperial Tombs of China, and many others have been brought to the public by the museum. Brigham Young University also operates the Peoples and Cultures Museum, as well as the Earth Sciences Museum.

Springville

Springville is a pleasant town a few miles south of Provo. It best known for its art museum and even calls itself the Art City. One reason for its pride in the arts may be that Springville is the birthplace of Utah sculptor Cyrus E. Dallin. Born in 1861, Dallin achieved prominence through his portrayals in bronze of Native Americans and other subjects. Dallin's works include *Massasoit*, *Signal of Peace*, and the Angel Moroni statue located atop the Salt Lake City Temple.

The first settlers who moved to the mouth of Hobble Creek Canyon in 1850 set up a fort named for the canyon. Gradually, because of the abundant mountain springs flowing out of the Wasatch Mountains, the town came to be called Springville.

The Calico Railroad

In 1869 the railroad reached Utah, and spurs were soon built in many directions. The railroad south into Utah County in the 1870s opened up opportunities to develop mining fields in that part of the state. One of

Springville Art Museum. Sculpture is by Dennis Smith.

these was in Scofield, in Carbon County. When Springville merchant Milan Packard built a narrow-gauge railroad from the Union Pacific tracks in Springville to the Scofield coal fields, railroad workers were paid in large part with goods from Packard's store. One of the major items the men received in lieu of cash was calico fabric, hence the line was dubbed the "Calico Railroad."

Springville was a very important, thriving railroad community for many years. However, with the increased use of automobiles, better roads, and the construction of I-15 to the west, it became a quiet, sub-urban Utah community, dependent on the larger towns in the county for employment.

Spanish Fork

In 1776 the Dominguez-Escalante expedition passed through Span-ish Fork Canyon and named the river El Rio de Aguas Calientes for the hot springs that enter the river in the canyon.

The first people to live on the banks of the Spanish Fork River were men who herded cattle. They planted some fields, and by 1852 enough additional settlers had arrived to form a town.

Between 1855 and 1860 fifteen Mormon converts from Iceland made Spanish Fork their home. It is thought to have been the first permanent Icelandic settlement in the United States.

In 1858 about 400 families fleeing General Johnston's invasion of the Salt Lake Valley took refuge in Spanish Fork. Many stayed on after the call came to return to their Salt Lake City homes.

Though this was primarily an agricultural area, such industries as ironworks, milling, and canning have been important sources of revenue. The city currently has a number of different manufacturing concerns as well as a healthy tourist trade promoted by its position at the junction of I-15 and US 6/89.

Payson

The next pioneer town along the old Mormon Corridor is Payson. Payson was first called Peteetneet after the creek that fed the little town. Brigham Young selected this site as a good spot for settlement in 1850. James Pace was an early settler, and the town was called Pacen until 1853, when the spelling was changed to Payson.

With the outbreak of the Walker War in 1853, the Pacen settlers constructed a fort for safety. One guard was shot to death early in the conflict. The Nebo Stake Tabernacle now stands where the center square of the fort was.

Peteetneet School, Payson.

The Peteetneet School, first constructed in 1901, was abandoned by the Nebo School Board in 1988. Spurred on by the threat of its demolition, the citizens of Payson joined together to save the old building and restore it to its original dignity. The building was reopened in 1991 under the name of Peteetneet Academy. It is currently used for public displays and classes.

Santaquin

The last town in Utah County, Santaquin enjoys the views of mountain valleys from the crest of the hills.

Originally named Summit City for its position on the divide between Utah and Juab Valleys, the name was changed to Santaquin in about 1875 to honor a peaceful Indian chief. First settled in 1851, Summit City was abandoned due to Indian troubles in 1853. When the settlers returned to the town three years later, they found it full of Indians, who fired from the houses at the white men as they rode through town.

When the news reached Utah in 1857 that a great army was coming to destroy the Mormons, the northern settlements evacuated south to Summit City the following spring. One refugee, young Josiah Gibbs, had been ill with inflammatory rheumatism all winter. As he grew healthier,

Gibbs's father moved him outside to recuperate. Though young Josiah felt better, his legs were still weak and he had to sit in the sun under a quilt most of the time. In an article published by the Utah State Historical Society, "Boyhood Memories of Josiah F. Gibbs," Josiah recalls "one of the most cherished memories" of his life:

> Presently there came to my super-sensitive ear drums the faint pit-pat of human feet. With easy, swinging strides a slender Indian boy was approaching from the south. He paused at the foot of my cot and keenly looked at the rheumatic invalid.

Using a combination of speech and sign language, the boys communicated that Josiah felt all right, but his legs were not working.

> After setting a target at a distance of about 25 feet, he returned to the side of my cot and gave me my first lesson in . . . bow and arrow shooting. During an hour or two the Indian boy chased arrows for his pupil, manifesting as keen delight when, by accident, I made a close or center shot, as if made by himself.
>
> At about the same hour next morning my Indian friend was at my cot-side. Again he chased arrows for me, and shared my boyish pleasure at evidences of rapid improvement.
>
> A few days of penetrating sun-rays, exercise of my arms and body, and mild perspiration—thanks to the ingenious method of the Indian boy, figuratively, 'put me on my feet.' With his aid I was soon able to walk, and then began our hunting trips for rabbits and other small game. One morning my companion surprised me with a gift of a beautiful bow, made from mountain sheep horn, backed by sinew, and a dozen or so cane arrows, tipped with greasewood spikes. It was a priceless token of friendship that in memory has never dimmed.

Nephi

Nephi, the next stop on I-15, is the major town of Juab County. Nephi sits under the shadow of magnificent Mount Nebo. At 11,877 feet, it is the highest peak in the Wasatch range.

Like many other Mormon places, this town was named for a Book of Mormon prophet. Originally named Salt Creek, the town was first occupied by Mormons called by Brigham Young in 1851 to settle the valley.

Because of danger from the Walker War, the residents of Nephi built a fort in 1853. While the fort was under construction, Chief Walker came and asked them to stop building, saying, "I cannot shake hands over a wall." They finished the fort, however. As it turned out, they were able to live there peacefully and lost no lives during the war.

Residents of Nephi began mining salt at the foot of Mount Nebo. This proved a great boon to the local economy, with people coming from

Joseph L. Heywood.
—LDS CHURCH
HISTORICAL DEPARTMENT

as far as St. George to trade for the precious commodity. In the 1880s a gypsum mine was also started at the base of Mount Nebo. A gypsum plant still operates in the same spot where gypsum was processed a century ago.

Joseph L. Heywood, the LDS Church leader who led the settlement of the town, had a vision during the first night he camped on Salt Creek. He saw a railroad coming from the east to Salt Lake City, extending south to Salt Creek, and branching through Salt Creek Canyon into Sanpete County. This was the exact path the railroad finally took.

The first train arrived in Nephi in May 1879, and the line connecting Nephi with Sanpete County was constructed in 1880. The junction of the railroads brought prosperity to the town.

For many years the main highway ran through the city of Nephi, making it a thriving place. In recent years the freeway has bypassed Nephi, but a number of businesses hug I-15.

Levan

The strip of freeway from Nephi that bypasses Levan and goes on to Mills was not completed until the mid-1980s. Because of the loneliness of the two-lane highway that wound through the foothills and the high volume of traffic in this corridor, accidents were too common, giving this stretch the appellation "Nephi Death Strip." I-15 now bypasses Levan to the west.

Although the origin of the name Levan is not certain, it is doubtful that the original intention was to spell *navel* backwards (Levan is in the center, or "navel," of the state), though folklore gives this as the rationale for the name.

In 1851 Brigham Young and a group of men on their way to find an appropriate place for a territorial capital camped on Chicken Creek, about three miles southwest of present-day Levan. Three years later, on the same spot, Young and Chief Walker signed the treaty ending the Walker War. Afterward, a few Mormon settlers moved to Chicken Creek. Here, they struggled with poor soil for several years, and in 1868 moved to the present site of Levan.

Perjury Farm

In the late 1800s Utah State University experimented with dry farming: planting crops when soil was moist and harvesting them before everything became too dry. Levan was an important dry-farming district early on. Between Nephi and Levan, farmers pioneered the science of raising wheat without the aid of irrigation. In 1887 David Broadhead filed on 160 acres between Nephi and Levan. In his claim he stated that the land would raise crops without irrigation. A U.S. grand jury indicted him for perjury, but he was acquitted after a trial. Thereafter his land was called "Perjury Farm."

Scipio

Scipio is the first gas stop on I-15 after Nephi. It was also an important resting place in pioneer times for travelers on this long road. Scipio was first settled in 1857 by Benjamin Johnson, who set up a mail station. Thirteen families came in 1859 and 1860 and settled near the stream. Scipio A. Kenner was one of the early settlers. The town may have been named for him or for the Roman soldier Scipio, or for a town where George A. Smith (an LDS apostle) once lived.

From its inception, Scipio was an important dairy, grain, and livestock area. As elsewhere, the long drought years of the early 1930s were hard on the farmers of Scipio. In the worst year, 1934, the town recorded less than half the normal snow and rainfall. By May things were desperate. The *Deseret News* for May 11 and 12 said of Scipio, "Most of the grain is burned up and alfalfa is making little growth. The watering place where local cattlemen summer their stock on the forest reserve is dry. This is the fifth year of drought in this place."

Despite the horrendous drought and Depression years, the people of Scipio endured, and continue to farm the area. Today Scipio is a quiet farming community with a couple of gas station/convenience stores located near the I-15 freeway and US 50.

Holden

I-15 climbs through some hills, then travels into the major valley of Millard County. Holden was settled in 1855 by families from Fillmore who were attracted by the mountain springs. They built a fort, completing it in 1856. It was called the "Buttermilk Fort" because travelers who stopped there were given buttermilk to refresh them. Later the people changed the name in memory of Elijah E. Holden, a member of the Mormon Battalion who froze to death in the mountains near the town.

Fillmore

In October 1851 Brigham Young and a group of men set out with the express purpose of finding a spot for the Utah territorial capital city. They chose the site of present-day Fillmore, and Young suggested a name: Millard for the county and Fillmore for the town, in honor of the president who had signed the bill creating the Territory of Utah. They hoped the distinction would help them in their campaign to become a state, but they were to wait more than forty years to realize that dream.

The first group of settlers to head for Fillmore left Salt Lake City in October 1851. After setting up their households, they began work on the territorial capitol building. They quarried red sandstone in the mountains east of Fillmore. The original plan called for a building with four wings and a dome in the middle. However, they had only enough money to build the south wing. Though not entirely complete, the building was dedicated in December 1855.

It turned out that Fillmore, even with its fine new building, was not a convenient place for the legislature to meet. It was too far from most of the settlements, and with its better accommodations, Salt Lake City was just more comfortable. The fifth annual legislative session was the only one held entirely in the statehouse in Fillmore. Other sessions started there, but the legislature passed resolutions to move them to Salt Lake City. The building was turned over to the city of Fillmore, which used it for various purposes until it was finally abandoned. In the late 1920s the building was restored and made into a museum. Now a state park, it features pioneer artifacts and artwork.

Fillmore remained quiet until 1858, when the northern settlements were abandoned at the advance of the army sent by President Buchanan.

Territorial capitol building, Fillmore. —LDS CHURCH HISTORICAL DEPARTMENT

Because of fear that the troops would destroy everything in their path, even the *Deseret News* moved to Fillmore for a few months in 1858. When the danger of destruction was past, the *News* returned to Salt Lake City, along with most of the other settlers who had fled south.

Today Fillmore is the business center for the surrounding communities. It is also a farming town and way station for travelers on I-15, with a number of motels, restaurants, and service stations.

Kanosh Indian Reservation

On the Utah highway map, the Kanosh Indian Reservation is east of I-15 between Meadow and Kanosh. Chief Kanosh was the head of the Pahvant Ute Indians. Kanosh, who had had contact with the Spanish before the Mormons arrived, was a member of the group that Escalante called the "bearded Utes." Kanosh was fluent in Spanish and English. He and his people were growing corn at Corn Creek when the Mormons came. Because of his great respect for Brigham Young and his hopes of avoiding conflict, Kanosh allowed the Mormons to settle in his valley. The Mormons didn't need to protect themselves from the Indians because of the great control Kanosh had over his tribe. Kanosh and many of his people joined

Chief Kanosh.
—UTAH STATE
HISTORICAL SOCIETY

the LDS Church, and Kanosh occasionally preached at church meetings. In 1865, when the Uinta Basin was set up as an Indian reservation, the Corn Creek or Kanosh Reserve was also set aside for the Indians. Kanosh's people moved back and forth between both reservations as drought and grasshoppers destroyed their crops in Millard County. A terrible influenza epidemic in the winter of 1918–19 wiped out more than two-thirds of the 300 Indians living on the Kanosh Reservation at the time.

Elizabeth Kane wrote the following of her impressions of Kanosh:

> There was something prepossessing in the appearance of Kanosh. . . . Kanosh has bright penetrating eyes and a pleasant countenance. He cultivates a white moustache, and carries himself with a soldierly bearing. He wore a dark-blue uniform coat with bright buttons, yellow buckskin leggings, and moccasins, and had a black carriage-blanket thrown over one shoulder.

In conversation with Elizabeth's husband, Thomas, Kanosh mourned the U.S. government's treatment of his people. They had not been provided with promised supplies and were constantly threatened with removal to the Uinta Basin. However, they were eventually allowed to remain in their home at the base of the mountains, and the reservation has endured to the present.

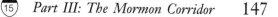

Kanosh

In late 1850, when Brigham Young sent colonizers on the Iron Mission to mine and process iron in southern Utah, the group passed by Corn Creek and saw about two acres where the Indians had farmed. They found corncobs—evidence that the corn had ripened fully, one of the major prerequisites for colonization. In making their report, the group recommended the entire area as suitable for future habitation.

Before Kanosh was settled, nearby Hatton was a changing station for horses on the stage line between Salt Lake City and Pioche, Nevada. A lot of traffic passed there. The original town site was largely deserted in 1867 at the suggestion of Young, who felt farms would have fewer early and late frosts and better water higher on the bench. Most of the people moved up to Kanosh.

Kanosh is a sleepy little town with a small business district and one gas station. Hundreds of deer roam the fields around the town during the winter. The town has some nice old pioneer homes and lots of cattle. Because it is on the bench, it commands beautiful views of the Cricket Mountains and the valley to the west.

Old Cove Fort

From Kanosh I-15 climbs juniper-covered hills and then descends slightly into a small mountain valley. Old Cove Fort is about one mile east of I-15. Old Cove Fort is an impressive structure, with volcanic-rock and limestone walls reaching eighteen feet above the ground. The fort was built as a pioneer rest stop. Travelers on the road from Salt Lake City to the southern settlements needed a safe place to spend the night between Fillmore and Beaver. After the Black Hawk War broke out in 1865, this lonely stretch of road was particularly treacherous. In 1867 Brigham Young called Ira Hinckley to establish a fort on Cove Creek. A small fort had already been built nearby by another man.

Hinckley and his family built the new fort of timber and volcanic rock. They lived there for ten years, aiding travelers with shelter, food, and water. A ranching family bought the land, and eventually the descendants of Ira and his brother Arza purchased the property and donated it to the LDS Church for restoration.

Elizabeth Kane described Cove Fort in her book *Twelve Mormon Homes*:

> The sun was sinking when we reached COVE CREEK FORT, and drove in under its archway. . . . The fort lay in a volcanic basin, geologically esteemed to be the crater of an extinct volcano. All round it were oddly-peaked, ragged-looking mountains glowing in purple and gold, looking no more substantial than the cloud-mountains of sunset

Cove Fort, circa 1900. —LDS CHURCH HISTORICAL DEPARTMENT

with which they mingled. . . . Round the fort were fields with unusually strong and high fences; outside it on the north was a very large barn with a well-filled yard, surrounded by a stockade. . . .

Two wells had been dug, each one hundred feet deep, but without striking water. It seemed to me a foolish thing to build a fort where a besieged garrison would suffer so much from want of water. But I was answered, when I hinted this, that the fort was only meant to defend travelers and the family of the ranch against Indian forays. It was too far from any settlement for a single family to be safe in the open country, and there was too little water for irrigation to warrant the placing of a settlement.

In 1992 the LDS Church opened the newly restored fort to the public. It reflects the period between 1867 and 1877, and is beautifully furnished with quilts, clothing, dishes, and furniture of that time. As well as the original fort, the property includes a rough log bunkhouse where cowboys slept, a blacksmith's cabin, vegetable plots and orchards, and an old cabin that belonged to Ira Hinckley when he lived in Coalville (it was moved to the Cove Fort site in 1994). A beautifully constructed barn has been erected at the approximate location of the original structure. (At the dedication of the fort, LDS president Gordon B. Hinckley is reported to have said he wanted to see the most expensive barn the church ever built.) Public restrooms and picnic grounds are also available. The fort is open daily to visitors year-round.

Beaver

Exploration of the valleys of southern Utah started in 1849. Settlement had already begun in Iron and Washington Counties to the south as well as in Millard County to the north when Mormon leaders decided it was time to settle the area along Beaver Creek. Timber and good grazing land was in demand, and settlers looked to the area around Beaver for expansion. The first group of about twenty men came from Parowan and moved to Beaver in February 1856. They built a twenty-by-twenty-foot cabin in which they all lived for a number of months while they laid out a town and prepared for the arrival of other settlers from the north. The number of settlers in Beaver City was greatly augmented in 1866 when Piute County was abandoned during the Black Hawk War. Robert Leroy Parker, alias Buch Cassidy, was born in Beaver during this period.

In 1870 the Second Judicial District Court of the Territory of Utah was established at Beaver City. After the Mountain Meadows Massacre of 1857, in which a wagon train from Missouri was attacked by a band of Indians and Mormon settlers, concern grew among people outside of Utah over the apparent lawlessness of the territory. One of the major missions of the courts was to prosecute the perpetrators of the massacre.

Cove Fort, 1997.

After years of searching for those responsible for the atrocities at Mountain Meadows, authorities made an arrest. John D. Lee, who participated in the attack, was tried in Beaver between 1875 and 1877 for instigating the horrible episode in one of Utah's most famous trials. Though others were equally or even more responsible for the incident, Lee was the one finally apprehended and he served as the scapegoat for all. Lack of witnesses and disagreements among jurors resulted in numerous delays. Finally, Lee was found guilty in September 1877, and he was executed at Mountain Meadows on January 26, 1878.

In mid-1872 Fort Cameron, a military establishment, was built about two miles east of Beaver to house 250 U.S. troops. A non-Mormon district judge requested the troops to help execute the perpetrators of the Mountain Meadows Massacre. That, as well as the continual Indian raids on the community, necessitated a military presence in southern Utah. Building and supplying the fort provided a great economic boon to the small pioneer community. But with the fort came saloons, prostitutes, and other ignoble diversions for the soldiers.

Elizabeth Kane passed through Beaver in her travels and described it thus:

> We entered the town. Something reminded me of our own villages. Was it the unpainted clap-board shanties?
>
> "No, mamma," cried Will, "they must be going to have a railroad built here. Look at the signs!" They were the signs which the child had noticed at every railroad station from Omaha to Ogden. There were the familiar letters, SALOON; the red curtains behind windows reading without spelling,—Rum-Hole; and round the corner was BILLIARDS. . . .
>
> I asked [our companion] why there was this difference between Beaver and other Mormon settlements, and she replied with her usual gentle brevity, and without the ghost of a smile, "There is an Army-Post here."

It was probably with relief that the people of Beaver witnessed the closing of Fort Cameron in 1883 when all the troops were moved back to Salt Lake City.

A woolen mill, built in Beaver in 1870, gave employment and income to many of the town's citizens. The local sheep ranchers often accepted woolen blankets and clothing as payment for their wool, so the mills operated without large quantities of cash. About 1890, however, ranchers started expecting cash payments. Production soon declined, and around the turn of the century the mill closed. The building was later used to manufacture mattresses, but a fire in the machinery burned the entire structure in 1920.

A great tradition in Beaver was the annual Wood Dance. In the fall, after the harvest, men went out and cut loads of firewood. They received tickets to the dinner and dance in exchange for the firewood they brought. In this way everybody had a wonderful meal and a dance, and the widows and church were supplied with wood for the winter.

Paragonah

Approaching the lonely stretch of road between Beaver and Parowan, then called Red Creek Village, Elizabeth Kane wrote:

> The afternoon was wearing on to the sunset when we came to a blood-red land,—cliffs, soil, and a crumbling old adobe fort, all red. Beside it a rushing stream dashed up wavelets of turbid red. Then came three or four red adobe houses, and some stacks of the brilliant straw-colored hay, with freshly-opened green hearts. The dreary wind howled and whistled among the walls and palings, and shook our carriages when we halted for a few minutes. Thankfulness overpowered me that, wherever else my lot in life might be cast, it was to be neither at Buckhorn Springs, nor Red Creek Village!

Paragoonah, an Indian word for the valley's marshes and springs, was the original spelling of this small Iron County town. It is still pronounced pare-ah-GOO-nah, but the spelling has changed.

Men from Parowan started farms here in 1851, soon after they moved to southern Utah, but they didn't feel it a safe place to move their families until the following year, when there were more settlers. In 1853, however, with the onset of the Walker War, the families in Paragoonah all moved back to Parowan for safety. Those who built cabins hauled them to Parowan, and those who built adobe homes tore them down. In 1856 the settlers built a fort in Paragoonah, and the families all returned.

Paragonah was built on the site of an ancient Indian village, and many skeletons and remains of Indian houses have been unearthed in excavations of the town.

Parowan

A few miles beyond Paragonah, the interstate quietly bypasses southern Utah's first settlement. Parley P. Pratt led an exploration party into southwestern Utah in the years 1849–50. When he discovered iron ore in January 1850 on his return trip, it was seen as a blessing from God that would help the Saints in their quest for independence from the outside world.

In January 1850, Pratt's company camped near the present location of Parowan. They considered it an excellent site for a new colony and christened it the City of Little Salt Lake. When a group came to establish a town a year later, they were equally impressed with the place.

At the October 1850 LDS general conference, apostle and church president George A. Smith announced the opening of the Iron Mission. All who heard the call to mine and process the iron ore of southern Utah waited in trepidation to be summoned during the coming month to move once more, this time 250 miles from Salt Lake City and 200 miles from Provo, the closest settlements, into the unknown wilderness. John D. Lee, who was called to move many times both before and after his call to the Iron Mission, told Brigham Young:

> The whole idea is repugnant to me! If I could pay as much as two thousand dollars in money or goods, if I could furnish and fit out a family to take my place, I would rather do it than go.

President Smith led the first group south, departing in December 1850. The party consisted of 110 men, 31 women, 101 wagons, 2 carriages, 100 horses, and many cattle and other supplies. They arrived in the Little Salt Lake Valley in January 1851. The journey went well and all arrived in good health, with the only illness reported to be homesickness. Generally, the entire company found their new home agreeable. However, one man returned north as "he could not leave off swearing and chose to go where he could exercise his liberty."

Parowan was isolated, far from any other settlement, and those who lived there always practiced extreme caution. In February 1854 when Parowan Stake president John Calvin Lazell Smith heard a call for help in the evening, he ventured forth carefully into the dark, snowy night to investigate. He found a weak, hungry, nearly frozen John C. Frémont, who had been on an expedition to survey the best route to California. Caught in a severe winter storm, he and his men were starving. One had already died. The people of Parowan took the group in and nursed them until they were able to continue on their journey.

During the time that Frémont was on this expedition, his wife, Jessie Benton Frémont, stayed at the home of her father, Senator Thomas Benton, in Washington D.C. When she hadn't heard from her husband for some time, Jessie was sure he was starving. After several days of worry, she heard her husband's voice say "Jessie" and she knew he must be safe at last. Several weeks later she received a letter from her husband, brought east by a Mormon man. Reading the letter, she found that February 7, the day she had heard her husband's reassuring voice calling her name, was the day the Smiths had taken him in (and he had expressed a desire to let his wife know he was safe).

The old rock meetinghouse on Main Street was built between 1862 and 1866 and seats 800 people. It was designed to hold large congregations of people traveling from other cities in Iron County. Although the building is no longer used for religious purposes, it has not been abandoned. The Daughters of the Utah Pioneers now use it as their Iron County headquarters.

When Elizabeth Kane visited Parowan, music greeted her and she recalled how

> the gusts of wind soon brought the sound plainly. It was the brass band from Parowan come out to meet us, escorted by a troop of many youths. The horses danced and plunged as the bandwagon fell into line, and we entered Parowan in great state to the music of "John Brown's Body." ... Next morning, too, the brass band made their appearance as we took our departure; somewhat to the discomposure of the nerves of one of the horses, who broke away from the groom who was harnessing him, and after careening round the yard, leaped the fence, and galloped off to the open country. The time occupied in recapturing him enabled the band to give us a number of airs, and superbly well they played them.

Though Parowan was far from the state capital, its citizens enthusiastically celebrated Utah's becoming the forty-fifth state on January 4, 1896. In an impromptu celebration, a group of young men stood on the main street of the town and grabbed any older settler who happened to pass by. Lifting him up high, they elicited a speech from the pioneer, after which they gave three cheers and let him go. This ceremony was repeated as long as they could find old-timers ready to give their reminiscences on the occasion.

Parowan is no longer the center of activity for Iron County as it was over 100 years ago. It has become a quiet, seemingly unchanging little Utah town. Its old houses and buildings have seen few alterations.

Brian Head

A scenic highway from Parowan switches steeply up the mountainside to Brian Head ski resort. Brian Head (elevation 9,700), the highest town in Utah, was developed as a ski resort in 1964. In pioneer times the high mountains east of Parowan and Cedar City were an important place for pioneers to harvest timber and game. They also provided a popular summer escape from the desert heat.

Cedar Breaks National Monument

A few miles above Brian Head is the colorful Cedar Breaks. At 10,500 feet, it is one of the highest attractions in Utah. Cedar Breaks was dedicated as a national monument on July 4, 1934.

Breaks is a term for an abrupt wall or break in a canyon. Cedar Breaks is a natural amphitheater of brilliant orange, red, and cream-colored limestone cliffs. The area is at its most spectacular with a light dusting of snow, witnessed from the quiet solitude of cross-country skis.

Cedar City

The Mormon pioneers called to the Iron Mission had been assigned to create a community that would mine ore and process iron. The Parowan settlement was not close enough to the source of ore, so in November 1851 a group left Parowan and established a fort in Cedar City.

The first work in a new settlement always centered around shelter, food, and protection, but even with all the necessary tasks of setting up a new community, the men were able to produce their first iron in September 1852. They made enough iron to forge some horseshoe nails and a pair of andirons.

The work of producing iron progressed slowly because of a number of setbacks. The Walker War to the north necessitated building a strong fort. Then a dam broke, taking more time away from the production of iron. Grasshoppers devoured crops, causing efforts to turn to survival rather than iron production.

The Iron Mission also had difficulties associated with the smelting process. The first oven failed and another had to be constructed. One winter the stream used as the power source froze, so roads to a source of coal had to be built. More men were called in to assist the effort. The resources available to build furnaces were limited, and in the summer the makeshift bricks melted and crumbled in the extreme heat. No entirely reliable furnace was ever constructed. Then, in 1857 all work on iron production ceased while the Saints prepared for the invasion of Johnston's army.

In 1858 a few more efforts were made to produce iron, but after repeated difficulties the endeavor was finally abandoned. During World War II, however, iron ore from Iron County was once more in demand and it supplied the Geneva Steel Mill in Utah County.

The LDS Church not only directed the iron production, but most of the other community affairs as well. The bishop's calling was about the most important in the community. A bishop had to be a married man. As bishops were unpaid, they continued their regular vocations concurrently with their service to the church. When a new bishop had to be chosen, a man in authority from the general headquarters of the LDS Church came to make the selection. The following 1888 incident occurred when LDS Church leader J. Golden Kimball came to Cedar City to call a new bishop:

President Kimball looked over the audience seated before him very carefully and long. He was a tall, thin man, and his long Prince Albert coat intensified his height. At last he pointed a long finger toward the men seated on the south side (the men sat together apart from the women). "I mean you with the dark mustache and dark hair. You come up on the stand by me. You will be the new Bishop." "Why in the world did you choose Will Corry?" he was asked later, "He isn't a Church man." His answer has gone down through history. "I wanted a man who could lick hell out of them, and he looked like the one to do it."

Corry was Cedar City's bishop for more than twenty-five years.

In 1897 the Utah state legislature established a school at Cedar City. Sixteen years later the school became a branch of the Utah State Agricultural College and was known as Branch Agricultural College. In 1953 the name changed to the College of Southern Utah, and in 1971 it changed again to Southern Utah State College. With rapid population growth and increased enrollment, the school was elevated to a university in 1992. Approximately 3,500 students are enrolled at Southern Utah University.

The university sponsors its Shakespeare Festival each summer, which has grown into a major event. Thousands of people from all over the United States flock to Cedar City to attend the productions, which include works of Shakespeare and other playwrights. The festival features period dinners and other celebrations. It has grown so large that new theaters and buildings have been constructed to house the performances.

Pioneer cabin at Iron Mission State Park in Cedar City.

Enterprise

Mountain Meadow
Massacre Site

New Harmony

UTAH

NEVADA

Central

Pine Valley

Gunlock (18)

Leeds

Toquerville

(15)

ZION
NAT.
PARK

(9)

Ivins (300)

(15)

(17)

Virgin

Mt.
Carmel
Jct.

Santa Clara

(9) Hurricane

La Verkin

Springdale

(89)

Washington

St. George

(59)

(15)

ARIZONA

0   10   20   30 miles

PART IV
Dixie

The character of southwestern Utah is greatly influenced by its altitude. At 2,880 feet above sea level, St. George, in the Virgin River basin, is more than 2,000 feet lower than cities in most of Utah's other valleys. Many see Utah's southwestern corner as either a wonderful winter oasis, far from the bitter cold and snows of the state's higher elevations, or as a dry, hot oven where summer temperatures of over 110 degrees Fahrenheit are common. However we think of it, Dixie is full of scenic wonders and is rich in a history of sturdy people determined to surmount all obstacles in their paths.

THE SOUTHERN PAIUTES

Ancient Desert Culture Indians roamed the valleys and mountains of this region thousands of years ago. The area was untouched by the Fremont and Anasazi cultures, but later, Southern Paiutes moved into the area and were already living in the southwestern corner of Utah when the first white people arrived. The Dominguez-Escalante party came in 1776 on their search for a route to California. In 1826 Jedediah Smith arrived, and a number of other explorers passed through in the 1830s and 1840s. Finally, in 1844, John Frémont traversed southwestern Utah, heading east from California.

The Southern Paiutes did not follow the Northern Utes in obtaining horses and arming themselves. As a result they fell prey to the Utes' greed. The Utes engaged in an Indian slave trade with Mexicans, and the unarmed Paiutes were vulnerable to Ute raids on their people. The Paiutes had initially been friendly when trappers led by Jedediah Smith first encountered them in 1826. Later they became frightened, suspicious, and finally hostile. Because of their vulnerability, the Southern Paiutes were

Southern Paiute camp. —UTAH STATE HISTORICAL SOCIETY

happy to invite the white men to settle their land, partly as a means of protection against the invading Utes, and partly as a ready source of food.

MORMON SETTLEMENT

The Mormons traversed southwestern Utah for a number of years before they made permanent settlements there. In the fall of 1847 Mormons passed through on their way to obtain seed from California. In 1848 members of the Mormon Battalion brought the first wagons over the Spanish Trail as they headed east to meet their families. In 1849 Brigham Young sent a party out to explore the area south of the inhabited valleys of northern Utah. In December of that year Parley P. Pratt and twenty other men entered the Virgin River basin. They camped at the confluence of the Virgin and Santa Clara Rivers on New Year's Day, 1850. Pratt found the area favorable for farming. Indeed, the Paiutes were farming there already and encouraged the Mormons to come and settle among them.

In the 1850s Mormons established colonies on the Spanish Trail from San Bernardino, California, all the way to Salt Lake City. They had plans to bring newly converted church members by boat from the East Coast to Panama, across the isthmus and up to California, then overland to Utah.

John D. Lee.
—LDS CHURCH
HISTORICAL
DEPARTMENT

This southern route, unlike the trail from Nebraska to Salt Lake City, was generally passable year-round. The Virgin River basin was a logical way station on the road.

A few years later, in the late 1850s, another route presented itself as feasible. Both the Mormons and the U.S. government (which needed to bring military supplies into the area) explored the possibility of bringing supplies and people up the Colorado River from the Pacific Ocean to Black Canyon (southeast of present-day Las Vegas), where the Colorado River became unnavigable. From this point it was only about twenty miles to the already-established Mormon road between Utah and California. This plan was kept alive in St. George well into the 1860s, giving residents hope of the spot becoming a boomtown, even during their struggle through severe shortages of food and supplies from 1863 to 1865. Although some goods were brought up the river, construction of the railroad finally ended hopes of using the Colorado River as a highway to Zion.

Another reason for settling the Virgin River basin was that it was an important place to establish contacts with the Indians, whom the pioneers hoped to convert to Mormonism. Scripture in the Book of Mormon told church members that American Indians, or Lamanites, were descendants of Joseph in the Old Testament, transplanted many centuries before from Jerusalem. The Saints felt it their responsibility to teach the Indians the doctrines of Christianity and Mormonism, and to baptize them.

In February 1852 the John D. Lee party explored the Virgin River. They wrote Brigham Young that the trees were already leafing out, and that any manner of fruit would surely grow there. Once again the resident Indians were friendly and encouraged white settlement. The Lee group built Fort Harmony on Ash Creek. They set to work immediately clearing land and planting crops.

In 1854 Jacob Hamblin started working with the Indians on the Santa Clara River near what is now the town of Santa Clara. The following year they planted cottonseed and grew a successful crop.

The Cotton Mission

Past experiences with other local white inhabitants, whose anti-Mormon attitudes often forced the religious settlers to pick up and move after much hard work, brought Brigham Young to the conclusion that Mormons should be as independent as possible, with little or no contact with the outside world. He was continually experimenting with ways to produce more goods in Utah so they would not have to buy them from the East. Young called a few families to Dixie in 1857 to ascertain whether cotton could be grown in large enough quantities to supply Utah's needs.

Young visited the settlements of southern Utah four years later. Envisioning a great city with many people at the present site of St. George, he returned to Salt Lake with a plan to call many more families to Dixie. Subsequently, at an LDS general conference in October 1861 in Salt Lake City, he called 300 men and their families to the Cotton Mission. The following year more were called.

Those living in northern settlements did not always welcome the news that they'd been called to Dixie. After moving so many times, they were finally building successful homes and farms. Elizah Averett was called with his family to settle Dixie. He records his father's reaction when he came home from working the fields all day to learn they had been called. Averett's father "dropped in his chair and said: 'I'll be dammed if I'll go!' After sitting a few minutes with head in hands, he stood up, stretched, and said, 'Well if we are going to Dixie, we had better start to get ready.'"

Starting a new settlement so far from any other civilization called for people with a wide variety of skills. Juanita Brooks made an inventory of those called to the Cotton Mission in 1861, which included thirty-one farmers, fourteen blacksmiths, ten coopers, and more than seventy others with various skills.

The lifeblood of Washington County was to be the Virgin River, which would provide plenty of water to all the communities. However, this river proved a better fighter than any of the soldiers who had been called to tame it. In the late fall of 1861 a large group of Swiss converts arrived in Washington County. Early in the winter of 1862, just as they were starting to settle into this harsh new environment so different from the lush valleys they had left behind, flash floods decimated all of the communities on the Virgin and its tributaries. Damming the river proved a nearly impossible chore that took years of continual work.

Other troubles were associated with the water of Washington County, including the malaria carried by mosquitoes that bred there. The horrible disease crippled some of the communities for many years. It was also difficult to control the water for irrigation, and as a result, crops were not always plentiful.

Starvation was a real problem in Dixie. Cotton was planted on much of the land, reducing the amount of food crops. Many winters were spent with no wheat or bread, the people scrounging whatever they could find to sustain life until the next harvest. After a few years, less land was planted to cotton and more to food crops.

I-15
New Harmony–Arizona State Line
36 miles

From Utah's high altitudes, I-15 drops rapidly down through dramatic canyons to the lower, warmer valleys of Washington County.

New Harmony

Just before I-15 crosses the Washington County line heading south, there's an exit for New Harmony. Five miles to the west of the exit, the little town is pushed against the Pine Valley Mountains, one of the most spectacular backdrops in Utah. The mountains encircle the town to the north, west, and south. The vermilion Navajo-sandstone fingers of Zion National Park's Kolob Canyon beckon to the east.

Harmony, the original settlement situated on Ash Creek, was established in 1852 by John D. Lee and Elisha H. Groves. It was the first settlement in Washington County and the first county seat. In 1854 missionaries came and started clearing the land. Their objective was to teach the Indians better farming methods in order to improve their standard of living. They also wanted to secure the Indians' friendship so they wouldn't have any problems with them. For the most part, this strategy succeeded. The local Indians were happy to help the Mormon settlers in their work in exchange for food, clothing, and protection from other hostile Indian tribes.

The settlers built an adobe brick fort at Harmony downstream from the current town site. It was considered the finest fort in Utah until the rains started falling in late December 1861. The storm continued into January and the adobe bricks in the fort's houses and walls began to dissolve. After several days the walls merged with the earth again, and water in the underground rooms raised to three feet. The devastated, freezing pioneers tried to save their belongings, and most importantly their food, as they fled the crumbling clay that had been their homes. On January 9 the rain turned to snow. It was soon ten inches deep and still falling fast. In the dead of winter, with snow still falling, they built shacks and tents that would be their homes until spring. The storms continued through February with little respite.

Not willing to give up and move away, the people of Fort Harmony rebuilt New Harmony a few miles away on higher ground—the site of the present town.

Pintura

Continuing south from the New Harmony exit, I-15 winds through a steep canyon lined with ancient black volcanic rock, evidence of lava flows from millennia past. Just to the east, in the shadow of the freeway, lies the dusty town of Pintura, lined with old farming equipment. In the spring of 1863 several families moved to the area, pitching tents and building log cabins as they started tilling the land and planting crops. Because the water in the creek dried up during the summer, the place was abandoned in 1864. In 1867 James Sylvester led another group to a permanent settlement here, which he called Bellevue. A few families were able to coax wheat and fruits to grow, but the water was never plentiful enough to support more than those few, and the land in the narrow valley wasn't broad enough to accommodate large fields.

Leeds

Established in 1867, Leeds struggled to survive along with the rest of Washington County. Then in 1869 silver was discovered at Silver Reef, and during the boom of the 1870s the people of Leeds were able to get a good price for anything they could sell. When the boom ended, the prosperity Leeds had enjoyed declined, but farming continued.

In 1933 the Civilian Conservation Corps (one of President Franklin Roosevelt's programs to create jobs during the Great Depression) built a camp in Leeds to aid southern Utah's public works projects. Utah was one of the hardest-hit states in the union during the Depression, with unemployment reaching 36 percent. A few of the camp's stone structures still stand at 96 West Mulberry Street in Leeds. These served as an infirmary, a dispensary, a blacksmith shop, and the camp commander's headquarters. The site has been placed on the National Register of Historic Places.

Silver Reef

Silver Reef got its name from a silver lode discovered in a sandstone ledge in 1869. John Kemple, who made the discovery, couldn't get any financial backers because everyone said silver couldn't be found in sandstone. The silver went unmined until 1875, when William Barber made another discovery and sent the silver to Salt Lake City for analysis. Within a month, a boomtown was born. The town grew immensely, with hotels, saloons, and even three cemeteries to handle all the men killed during the short period of Silver Reef's boom time.

When the price of silver dropped in the early 1880s, so did miners' wages. The union ordered the miners to strike. With no one working the mine shafts, they flooded and closed for good. Soon the town closed down, too.

The 1870 census showed no one living in Silver Reef. In 1880, the town had 1,040 inhabitants. By 1890 the population had dropped to 177. In 1900, once again, no one was listed in Silver Reef.

The silver boom gave a big boost to the economy of southwestern Utah, where starvation had been the rule since the first people were called to settle Dixie. However, Mormon Church leaders continually urged members to

Mrs. Gramb's Boarding House, Silver Reef, 1880s. Mrs. Gramb is shown standing. —UTAH STATE HISTORICAL SOCIETY

stay with farming. Brigham Young, at the dedication of the St. George Temple, told the members to "let those holes in the ground alone."

Silver Reef has become an exclusive residential district. The Silver Reef Museum and Jerry Anderson Art Gallery are now housed in the old Wells Fargo building in the center of the historic town.

Washington

I-15 continues to drop down to Washington's elevation of 2,600 feet. Today the town resembles many other suburbs that are the product of a recent boom—strip shopping malls, condominiums, and retirement centers have popped up everywhere. Few people whizzing by on the freeway know of Washington's rich history and the arduous trials experienced more than 100 years ago in the new cotton colony.

Washington was the first community established in Utah for the purpose of growing cotton. Several families were called here in the spring of 1857 to plant cotton crops. As in all the settlements, water was Washington's first priority. The people built countless dams in the area, only to have them washed out, sometimes several times a year. They also constructed dams on the Virgin River. Settlers spent so much time rebuilding dams that they could hardly tend to their thirsty crops. In 1890, after a new dam that was thought to be indestructible was flushed down the Virgin River within a few months of its completion, the authorities in

Washington cotton mill, date unknown. —UTAH STATE HISTORICAL SOCIETY

Washington finally decided to build a dam upstream in solid bedrock. After the tens of thousands of dollars spent building other dams, this was the one that held.

Like those in much of Washington County, the residents of this small settlement were plagued with malaria almost from the beginning. The illness drove many people away from the area. It left those who survived weak and barely able to deal with their rigorous pioneer life. The disease was a recurring problem until well after the turn of the century, when most of the mosquitoes' breeding grounds were cleaned out.

When the new members of the Cotton Mission passed through Washington in late fall of 1861, they met many people sick with malaria. Quoted in Andrew Karl Larson's *I Was Called to Dixie*, new settler Robert Gardner wrote in his diary, "This tried me more than anything I had seen in my Mormon experience, thinking that my wives and children . . . would have to look as sickly as those around me."

Because of its central location and ready water power, Washington was the site chosen for a cotton mill. Construction on the new mill began in 1867. Though the factory was never a financial success, it rewarded the community in the accomplishment of self-sufficiency. When the Civil War ended, the southeastern states began to produce cotton again and prices fell dramatically from those of the war years. Growing cotton in a place where irrigation cost so much no longer made economic sense. Still, the mill continued to operate and in 1874 the United Order, the Mormon plan that each participating community would produce everything its members needed, was introduced there. The production of cotton was central to this plan. Even after the order was dissolved, the mill continued to operate. By 1890, though, it was no longer economically feasible to keep the mill running, and the stockholders agreed to lease the factory to Thomas Judd of St. George. He worked it until 1898, when it went idle. The machinery was sold in 1910. The Washington Cotton Factory, located on US 91, is now a retail nursery, with a display of pioneer artifacts on the second floor.

St. George

In 1861, when Brigham Young came to the spot of present-day St. George, he paused for a long time, looking at the river and the red cliffs all around him. His companions paused and waited for him to speak. Finally he said, "There will yet be built, between these volcanic ridges, a city, with spires, towers and steeples, with homes containing many inhabitants." His hearers were incredulous, recalling the struggles of the communities already in the area. Numbers of residents were dwindling rather than increasing.

George A. Smith.
—UTAH STATE
HISTORICAL SOCIETY

While church leaders were calling people to southern Utah, word had spread of the struggles of those already there. Quoted in *I Was Called to Dixie*, Mormon settler Charles L. Walker records the feelings he had when he was called in October 1862:

> Well, here I have worked for the last seven years, through heat and cold hunger and adverse circumstances, and at last have a home and fruit trees just beginning to bear and look pretty. Well, I must leave it and go and do the will of my Father in Heaven . . . and I pray God to give me strength to accomplish that which is required of me.

At a general conference, George A. Smith, an important leader in the movement to settle southern Utah, chastised church members, telling them a call to the Cotton Mission was just as important as a call to proselytize.

The first settlers arrived in St. George on November 25, 1861. They already knew the name of their town; it was to be named for apostle George A. Smith. Erastus Snow headed the mission and oversaw the work there.

The first camp was set up about a half mile east of what are now Temple and Tabernacle Streets. Unfortunately, the settlers chose a wet year to start. While they camped, "forty days and forty nights" of rain fell on them and the rivers flooded. Through the dreary rains of January 1862, the settlers kept their spirits high by dancing to fiddles between storms. After the rains ceased, the earth rewarded the settlers with abundant grasses and plants for livestock and horses to fatten on, so they would be strong enough to labor through the long, hot summer.

St. George suffered the same problems as the rest of the Dixie settlements. As a result of water troubles and the great deal of acreage planted to cotton, crops were not adequate to feed the population. Food shortages, along with cholera, malaria, and other diseases, greatly debilitated and discouraged the pioneers. Alkaline soil was as much a problem as drought. Often the white salts would rise to the surface of the soil so that a field looked like snow had fallen on it. Many crops were lost to the excessive saltiness of the soil.

In September 1862 Brigham Young visited the struggling young city. After witnessing the challenges of obtaining food in the face of extreme heat, lack of water, and alkaline soil, he saw the need for a "public works" project. He instructed that a large meetinghouse be built that would seat at least 2,000 people. In payment he said all of the tithing—which included grain, molasses, and other foodstuffs, as well as some cash—from Cedar City and other settlements would be at their disposal. On Brigham Young's sixty-second birthday, June 1, 1863, the tabernacle was begun.

The suffering was eased somewhat by the building of the tabernacle, and then of the temple. The tabernacle was under construction from 1863 until 1876. The temple took less time to build—from 1871 to 1877. While building was in progress, those in need received work and payment through the church tithes. The projects helped sustain many families until they were able to improve irrigation and farming methods to the point of being self-sustaining.

St. George Temple.

Brigham Young was the first "snowbird" in St. George: during his later years he spent his winters in Dixie. The house that Young had built between 1869 and 1874 is on the corner of Second North and First West. The state of Utah acquired the house in 1959 and in 1975 turned it over to the church. LDS missionary couples serve as guides in the home. Tours are free.

In 1908 the LDS Church encouraged the local church authorities to start a college in St. George. What is now Dixie College opened for instruction in 1911. The first building was completed in 1913. In 1933 the LDS Church deeded the school to the state of Utah. The original building and the gymnasium at 86 South Main still stand. In 1963 a new campus was built for Dixie College on the east side of the city.

Brigham Young's winter residence in St. George. Cotton is growing in foreground.

UT 18 and UT 8
UT 56–St. George
46 miles

An alternate route from Iron County to Dixie winds through the Pine Valley Mountains north of St. George. This picturesque road was once marked by tragedy.

Enterprise

Enterprise was laid out in 1891, but because the neighboring town of Hebron competed with them for water, they were unable to obtain water rights and no one moved to Enterprise until 1895. In 1902 an earthquake in Pine Valley severely damaged Hebron. Many people sold their water rights to Enterprise, abandoned Hebron, and moved to Enterprise. Hebron also experienced water shortages, as well as erosion and a mine shutdown. The 1906 San Francisco earthquake was felt all the way to southern Utah, and it did enough damage to Hebron to finish it off.

With the influx of people from Hebron, Enterprise grew. Still, no reliable, year-round source of water to support a large community existed. In the 1880s, Orson Huntsman envisioned a dam on Shoal Creek twelve miles west of present-day Enterprise. Huntsman found little support for the project, and it wasn't until 1892 that he started constructing the dam himself, convinced that it must be accomplished. He started building with his own money, and the following year he was able to get others to contribute to the project. Money was still scarce, and the work was slow until 1909, when Anthony W. Ivins of the LDS Council of the Twelve visited and donated $7,300 to finish the project. After sixteen years of work, Huntsman finally had the means to complete the dam rapidly. The dam-formed Enterprise Lake guaranteed a supply of water for the town.

In the years 1898–99 an LDS meetinghouse was constructed at 24 South Center Street. By 1912 the congregation had outgrown it and had built another one on the same block. In 1952 still another church was built next to the other two. All three generations of LDS meetinghouses still stand on the same block in Enterprise.

Enterprise is the trade and market center for the thriving potato and alfalfa industries of the surrounding valley.

Mountain Meadows

A few more miles down this mountain road is a favorite resting spot on the Spanish Trail. Its abundance of lush grasses and clear streams made

Mountain Meadows today is a quiet high pasture.

Mountain Meadows a place where southbound travelers could graze their animals before crossing the desert to California. For those coming from the west, it was a place to rest and recover from the ordeal of desert travel.

Unfortunately, Mountain Meadows is remembered not as a pleasant oasis on a long road but as the site of a horrendous episode that has scarred the history of Utah. The tragic event demonstrates how men caught up in anger and hatred can commit heinous crimes.

In order to understand the Mountain Meadows Massacre, we must first understand some early Mormon history. Joseph Smith started his church in New York, but soon moved it to Ohio, then to Missouri. In the 1830s, Missouri was the frontier, and people there were distrustful of large religious groups. Worried about Mormon political strength (Mormons opposed slavery), Missourians began harassing LDS Church members. In many instances, these acts were tolerated and sometimes encouraged by political leaders. The Saints moved to a different county in Missouri, but the persecutions still escalated to the point of violence. After destroying Mormon property and even murdering Mormons, Missourians finally drove the Saints from the territory in the dead of winter, resulting in bankruptcy and in many cases loss of life. Subsequently, hatred and mistrust of Missourians existed among the Mormons.

Years later, when the church members finally found safety in Utah, they discovered it was not to last. As the Mormons celebrated ten years in their mountain home, they received word that President Buchanan had sent an army to take over Utah. In 1857, as Mormons were preparing for the invasion, a wagon train from Missouri—the Fancher party—was traveling through Utah. After stopping in Salt Lake City, the party headed south, passing through Mormon settlements along the way.

In anticipation of the army siege, the Mormons had been given instructions to conserve their foodstuffs, and they refused to sell food to the passing wagon train. Tension grew as the Fancher party progressed southward, receiving no supplies from any Mormon settlers. In retaliation, some members of the party bragged that they had helped torment the Mormons in Missouri and had been part of the Haun's Mill Massacre, in which a mob killed and mutilated a number of Mormons in Missouri in 1838. Others said they had helped kill Joseph Smith. Some in the party called their oxen such names as Brigham Young and Heber C. Kimball (Young's counselor and close friend), whipping and cursing them as they passed through the Mormon towns. They also threatened the settlers with future restitution, calling them traitors.

Meanwhile, the Fancher party had also greatly angered the Paiute Indians. At Corn Creek, in Millard County, the Missourians had poisoned the spring, presumably intentionally. The water killed an ox that the Indians subsequently ate, resulting in the death of several of their tribe. The Paiutes pursued the wagon train, taunting and threatening the travelers. The tribe

John D. Lee, in his coffin at the site of the Mountain Meadows Massacre.
—UTAH STATE
HISTORICAL SOCIETY

Mountain Meadows memorial.

recruited other Indians along the way to help them harass the wagon train. By the time the Fancher party reached Cedar City in September, some locals, including survivors of the Haun's Mill Massacre, were arguing that the scoundrels should be killed.

A messenger was sent from Cedar City to Brigham Young in Salt Lake for advice in dealing with the wagon train. Another messenger was sent to John D. Lee, a local leader in Fort Harmony, asking for help in controlling the angry Indians. Unfortunately, Jacob Hamblin, the great Mormon Indian negotiator, was away in the north getting married at the time; otherwise history might have been quite different.

Some of the Mormons decided to allow the Indians to attack the Missouri emigrants, who were now camped at Mountain Meadows, telling the Paiutes that the Mormons were at war with the non-Mormons. After the initial attack, the Mormon men realized they would be in serious trouble if word reached California that they had instigated the incident. They reached a decision to kill all the emigrants old enough to go to California and tell tales. After the Fancher party surrendered to the Paiutes, the Indians then separated the young children from the rest of the group. Quickly and decisively the Mormons and the Indians shot all the men, while the Indians also shot the women and older children. The younger children were taken into Mormon homes and eventually returned to their relations in the East.

Young's instructions to let the party pass on to California unharmed came too late. Jacob Hamblin and his new wife, along with another couple, came upon the horrible massacre scene on their way back to Santa Clara.

An attempt to blame the entire incident on the Indians failed. Some of the Mormons involved went into hiding. Eventually John D. Lee, a participant in the massacre, was made a scapegoat and executed, but all the others who were equally or more responsible for the episode got off with no penalty.

The entire territory paid a price for this deed for many years, suffering government recriminations of the LDS Church and its members. The church was also hurt by the tales that were told, despite the fact that Brigham Young had not sanctioned the episode. A heavy gloom still hangs over this part of history, along with a sense of group guilt that members of a large religious family could participate in the cold-blooded murder of an innocent group of people.

Pine Valley

Picturesque Pine Valley is just east of the main highway. In 1855 Isaac Riddle of Harmony was searching for a stray cow when he came upon this beautiful, well-timbered valley with its lush, tall grasses. That fall he and several other men purchased machinery for a sawmill and moved to Pine Valley. Because of the great timber and grazing prospects, the valley soon attracted a number of people from the surrounding area. The lumber harvested in Pine Valley was used throughout southwestern Utah and

The Pine Valley Chapel was designed by Ebenezer Bryce, famous for having discovered the canyon of the same name. The chapel is still used for religious services.

southeastern Nevada. The organ pipes in the Salt Lake Tabernacle are made from Pine Valley lumber.

Pine Valley (elevation 6,500 feet), in pioneer times as now, has always been a favorite recreation spot away from the intense summer heat of the lower elevations. People traveled to Pine Valley from the lower Virgin River valley, sometimes taking two days to traverse the rough roads, and stayed two or three days. In 1865 people from the lower settlements of Washington County came to Pine Valley on July 22, 23, and 24 to celebrate Pioneer Day. They camped in the pines, worshipped, and danced.

During the Nevada and Silver Reef mining boom, Pine Valley also boomed, having found a ready market for all its local products. Brigham Young chastised Pine Valley residents for selling to the gentiles for cash, while those in Zion, who had to pay in kind, went hungry. After the turn of the century, little lumber remained, and Pine Valley suffered. The boom was over and many people moved away.

Ebenezer Bryce, famous for the discovery of Bryce Canyon, designed and built the Pine Valley Chapel in 1868. Bryce, a former shipbuilder from Australia, assembled the walls on the ground, then joined them with wooden pegs and rawhide. Like many early Mormon converts, Bryce revered his church leaders; he built the church in the New England style to honor native New Englanders Brigham Young and Erastus Snow. Of his church he said, "If the floods come, it will float, and if the winds blow, it may roll over, but it will never crash." Still used as a church, the chapel is open for tours in the summer. (You'll find bats roosting in the attic there.)

As in pioneer days, Pine Valley is still a popular place to escape summer heat. Many people from lower elevations have summer homes here, causing the population of Pine Valley to swell during the summer months.

Veyo

At Veyo UT 18 and UT 8 divide; UT 8 follows Gunlock Canyon, and UT 18 traverses Snow Canyon and Ivins. The small community of Veyo lies on the other side of a steep rocky gulch. The first families moved here in 1914 after a canal was completed and a flume constructed to span the deep gulch. Veyo was named by a group of local girls. It stands for Virtue, Enterprise, Youth, and Order. Veyo, like other Washington County towns, has had a long struggle to find adequate water. The Baker Dam has helped alleviate that problem.

Gunlock

Continuing south from Veyo, UT 8 crosses hills lined with black rocks of volcanic origin and enters a narrow valley. Gunlock (elevation 3,650 feet) occupies the southern end of this sloping valley. William "Gunlock"

Hamblin, a brother of Jacob Hamblin, was the first resident here, in 1857. He earned his nickname for his skill with guns. In the floods of early 1862, a few homes were washed away, and the town was rebuilt on higher ground. The community limped along for a century, isolated by its position and limited by the narrowness of the valley. While most people eventually left, the few who remained continued to struggle with the age-old problem of water. However, Gunlock is a spot with a desirable climate and could never remain unoccupied. As in all of Washington County, people are moving back to Gunlock, and several hundred people now live in the once-abandoned town.

Ivins

Ivins, another small town along UT 18 at its junction with the Snow Canyon Road, is framed by the mouth of Snow Canyon.

Ivins was another town that wasn't really settled until the residents could obtain a reliable water source. During the winters of 1911 through 1914, a group of local men from Santa Clara worked together to build a canal on the bench. They camped at the canal site all week, returning home on the weekends. In 1918 they built a reservoir on the canal. The first family moved to the site of Ivins in 1922.

The town was named for Anthony Ivins, an important early pioneer, LDS Church official, and Indian missionary. Today, Ivins is a mixture of farms, modest suburban houses, and expensive new homes. Health retreats and housing developments are creeping in, but the town retains its rural feel. About two miles north of town is the Tuacan Heritage Arts Foundation complex, a performing-arts center that hosts year-round theatrical and musical events.

Jacob Hamblin Homestead

A few miles west of Santa Clara on UT 8, an old farmhouse comes into view. For seven years, it was the home of Mormon missionary Jacob Hamblin. Born Jacob Vernon Hamblin in Ohio in 1819, he became a Mormon twenty-two years later. His devotion to his new faith never faltered. His wife, Lucinda Taylor, refused to travel west with Jacob and their four children when the time came to flee oppression and persecution in the East. The two separated, and Jacob later married Rachel Judd, the first of his plural wives.

The Hamblins were sent to settle Tooele, where Jacob first learned about conducting relations with Indians. On an expedition against hostile Indians in the Tooele Valley in 1853, his and his compatriots' guns somehow would not fire against the Indians:

Jacob Hamblin.
—LDS CHURCH
HISTORICAL
DEPARTMENT

The Holy Spirit forcibly impressed me that it was not my calling to shed the blood of the scattered remnant of Israel [the Indians], but to be a messenger of peace to them. It was also made manifest to me that if I would not thirst for their blood, I should never fall by their hands.

Soon Hamblin and his family were sent to colonize southwestern Utah as missionaries to the Native Americans. They helped establish the fort at Santa Clara in the early 1860s. Hamblin continued to work with the Indians. He made missionary visits to the Hopis in northern Arizona nine times.

During the course of his missionary work, Hamblin reopened the ancient Ute crossing of the Colorado River, known as the Crossing of the Fathers (now covered by Lake Powell). Farther downstream on the Colorado River, he pioneered the ferry crossing later known as Lee's Ferry. In the years 1862 and 1863, Hamblin traveled all the way around the Grand Canyon. Major John Wesley Powell, who led several survey expeditions of the Green and Colorado Rivers, hired Hamblin as a guide in 1870. Powell said of Hamblin, "He is a silent, reserved man, and when he speaks it is in a slow, quiet way that inspires great awe."

Throughout his service, Hamblin was continually called on to settle disputes and avert violence between the Mormon settlers and the Native Americans. He tried to maintain a policy of peace and fairness, and he was trusted by all.

Jacob Hamblin's home near Santa Clara.

Because Hamblin was away from home so much, missionaries were called to build him a house and make sure his wives had what they needed. Between 1862 and 1863 stone masons from Cedar City built Jacob Hamblin's home in Santa Clara. The home, which is now run by missionaries and is open to the public, is unique among surviving pioneer dwellings. Designed for a polygamous family, the rooms on the main floor were for Hamblin's wives, Rachel Judd and Priscilla Leavitt. The women seem to have been very close. Hamblin also had three other wives, one of them an Indian. As many as three or four wives may have lived in this home at the same time, along with their children. The front porch is severely sloped because it was used for drying fruit. Hamblin lived at this home until the early 1870s, when he was called to Kanab to oversee the new settlement on the frontier of Navajo country.

Hamblin and his family remained in Kanab until antipolygamy persecution by U.S. government agents became severe. They moved to Arizona and New Mexico, and on to Chihuahua, Mexico. Hamblin spent the last years of his life hiding from the law, traveling between his families, and trying to supply their needs. He died in 1886 in New Mexico and was buried in Alpine, Arizona.

Santa Clara

Clear blue skies explain Santa Clara's name. Travelers on the Spanish Trail named the Santa Clara River for the area's typical clear weather. In 1854

Jacob Hamblin and other Mormon missionaries built a cabin on the river, where they could work with the Paiutes and help maintain peace for the travelers on the road to California. The following spring the Mormons employed the Paiutes to build a dam across the creek. The Indians were happy to help with the tilling, planting, and construction. In 1855 a Mormon convert from the South gave a quart of cottonseed to Augustus Hardy. Hardy took it to Santa Clara and tenderly cultivated it all summer. That fall he harvested the first cotton in Utah and produced thirty yards of cotton fabric.

Brigham Young visited the settlement in 1861 and advised the residents to move to higher ground. The following January they greatly regretted not having followed his advice. Heavy rains caused flash floods on the Tonaquint Creek in the middle of the night. Dugouts washed away and inhabitants barely escaped. A grandfather held his two grandchildren in a tree all night. At dawn they climbed down, just before the rampaging water pulled the tree along with it toward the Colorado River. The entire fort was washed downstream, leaving the struggling community without shelter. The rains continued until February while the pioneers started building new homes.

The climate in Washington County is one of extremes, with no middle ground between severe flash floods and terrible heat and drought. In 1863 many of Santa Clara's families moved to other places because of extreme drought, famine, and sickness. The same things occurred in other Washington County towns. It was difficult to keep people in places so harsh and alien to human existence.

Malaria also plagued the early settlers living along the lower Virgin River. After a number of unhealthy years, residents of Santa Clara decided a swamp near town might be contributing to the recurrences of the disease, though they didn't know the culprits were the mosquitoes breeding in the swamp. The town's men dug a ditch to drain the swamp, then filled the area in to make farmland. This solved the malaria problem.

Santa Clara, though a fairly large community today and rapidly becoming indistinguishable from St. George, has retained a sleepy, small-town feel.

UT 9
I-15–Zion National Park
40 miles

Hurricane

People traversed the present site of Hurricane (pronounced HUR-i-cun) for many years, but no one stayed. Father Escalante passed through on his exploration of 1776. In the 1860s, when Mormon Church leaders explored the area for possible settlements, they described the Virgin River bench as excellent for cultivation because of its climate and soil, but they didn't believe water could be brought there from the river.

Later that decade, when Erastus Snow and David Cannon were on an exploring expedition in the area, they had to lower their buggy down a steep incline. They had almost reached the bottom when a gust of wind tore the top off of the buggy. Snow called it a "hurricane" and named the spot Hurricane Hill. The hill bench, town, and canal all took their names from that gust of wind.

Over the years a number of different parties examined the feasibility of bringing water to the dry Hurricane bench. Finally, after years of hoping to cultivate that tract of fertile land, a group of men joined together in 1893 to build a dam and canal through the Virgin Narrows to the fields. All those who wished to farm in Hurricane cooperated in the effort.

The canal was dug entirely by hand, as no machinery could be carried down the steep slope to where the work took place. The men carried all their tools down on their backs, including heavy anvils used to sharpen other tools. The workers camped in the canyon during the construction, often in rough weather—most of the work was done during the winter. The men had to tend to their farms during the spring, summer, and fall; they only had spare time for digging in the winter.

The dam was constructed within a few years. Though the men had to use dynamite to blast out the enormous boulders they wanted to use as construction material, the Virgin River washed the boulders away as if they were marbles. The workers staked the boulders with huge juniper trees drilled into the bedrock, but still they washed away. Finally, they wrapped the entire mass in iron mesh, and the dam held.

The work on the canal progressed more slowly. The last mile of the seven-and-a-half-mile channel was by far the most difficult. Much of it was built on a sheer cliff, and the canal bed had to be reinforced with rocks. The men had to do a great deal of tunneling on this stretch. One after another, men gave up on the project. Finally, the Hurricane Canal board decided to appeal to the LDS Church for help. James Jepson went to Salt Lake City and spoke with LDS Church president Joseph F. Smith (a nephew of church founder Joseph Smith) and the twelve apostles. After some discussion, the church leaders decided to lend the Hurricane Canal builders $5,000 to help them finish the project. With that help, more men felt completing the canal would be possible, and the work progressed. The canal was finally finished in 1904, after nearly eleven years of work. A historic marker at the east end of 200 North Street indicates where the canal water was finally turned into the fields. From UT 9 between Hurricane and La Verkin, travelers can see the rocks that support the canal as it circles the cliff and enters the narrow Virgin River gorge. The canal is listed on the National Register of Historic Places.

The first family to live in Hurricane came in 1906. Like at all new settlements, life was difficult at first, but after years of struggle, the place flourished. Today Hurricane is an important agricultural area, producing a wide variety of products. Among other agricultural items, sod is grown here and then exported to faraway places; the red earth on its base testifies to its origins.

Virgin

The trip from Toquerville to Virgin seems easy today, but when the original road was built in late 1858, it was a treacherous journey. The road, called Johnson's Twist for the man who spearheaded the building of it, was sufficiently passable by April 1859 for Pocketville, later Virgin City, to be laid out.

The floods of 1862 caused problems in Virgin as they did in the rest of the area, and the town lost its dam and canal. A new canal was soon dug, but the calculations proved wrong and the watercourse, which ran uphill, was entirely useless.

Rockville

As UT 9 approaches Zion National Park, the red rock walls on the left rise to impressive heights. Rockville is, indeed, a very rocky place. Adventure, a name that could have been applied to many early Utah settlements, was the name first given to Rockville by the people who arrived in the fall of 1860. Coping with the Virgin River was an adventure at best. The floods of early 1862 proved that the first settlement was too close to the river. The residents moved uphill about a half mile to Rockville. As the river took more farmland with it, many of the younger generation left Rockville.

Grafton

An interesting side trip from Rockville lies south of the Virgin River across the Rockville Bridge. Once a prosperous little settlement, Grafton is one of Utah's most famous and most visited ghost towns.

The Rockville Bridge itself was constructed in 1924 by the National Park Service to link Zion National Park with the North Rim of the Grand Canyon. The only bridge of its kind remaining in Utah (technically called a rigid-connected Parker through-truss bridge), it has been placed on the National Register of Historic Places.

After crossing the bridge, follow signs that point west on a graded three-mile road to Grafton. You'll find a number of buildings that are evidence of people who intended to live in their little valley long time. Unfortunately, the residents of Grafton fell victim to the Virgin River's ravages. Flash floods and hostile Indians were enough to force the little settlement to break up in search of a safer environment.

An old adobe church/school and a two-story adobe house are the principal structures remaining in Grafton, along with a few log cabins and sheds. Unfortunately, the adobe buildings have deteriorated dramatically over the last few decades. Though completely intact during the filming of *Butch Cassidy and the Sundance Kid* in 1968, the house is now crumbling. Some of the corrals are still in use, so please respect property rights.

Old school/church in Grafton.

Springdale

Springdale, the next town west of Rockville on UT 9, is the gateway to Zion National Park. Little did the sturdy pioneers who came here in 1862 dream that the town they chipped out of the wilderness would one day be a long string of motels, restaurants, and souvenir shops.

The excellent climate allowed early Springdale settlers to plant a wide variety of crops. Unfortunately, a malaria epidemic so weakened the townspeople that they couldn't collect the harvest. The town limped along with a few families until 1866, when it was abandoned because of fear of attack during the Black Hawk War. In 1869 some people came back. Some of the settlers farmed in Zion Canyon, where they were generally safe from Indians because of the Native Americans' belief that evil gods lived there.

Zion National Park

The mountains and canyons of Zion National Park are indescribable. The grandeur of its spectacular stone monoliths and chasms must be experienced firsthand and from a vantage point that does not include the window frame of an automobile or tour bus. Frederick Vining Fisher, in 1916, described one of the canyon's stone faces:

> Never have I seen such a sight before. It is by all odds America's masterpiece. Boys, I have looked for this mountain all my life, but I never expected to find it in this world. This mountain is the Great White Throne.

In November 1858 Nephi Johnson went to Zion Canyon with an Indian guide. The guide refused to go into the canyon with him and stopped at a spot just above present-day Springdale, where he waited while Johnson went ahead. The Indian told him the place was evil because the sun never shone deep in the canyons. Johnson followed the Virgin River all the way to the Zion Narrows. Entranced, he found it difficult to return to the guide by sunset.

A few years later, in 1862, Isaac Behunin built a cabin and farmed near the site where Zion Canyon Lodge now stands. The canyon was so beautiful, its cliffs and buttes resembling spires, that he called it Zion.

In 1874, homesteaders in Zion Canyon, pooling their resources, organized the United Order there. When the order was dissolved in 1875 they all sold out their interests and moved out of the canyon. Though there was no longer anyone living in the canyon, the residents of Springdale and Rockville continued to farm there until it became a national monument in 1909.

Zion was established as a national park in 1919, making it the oldest national park in Utah.

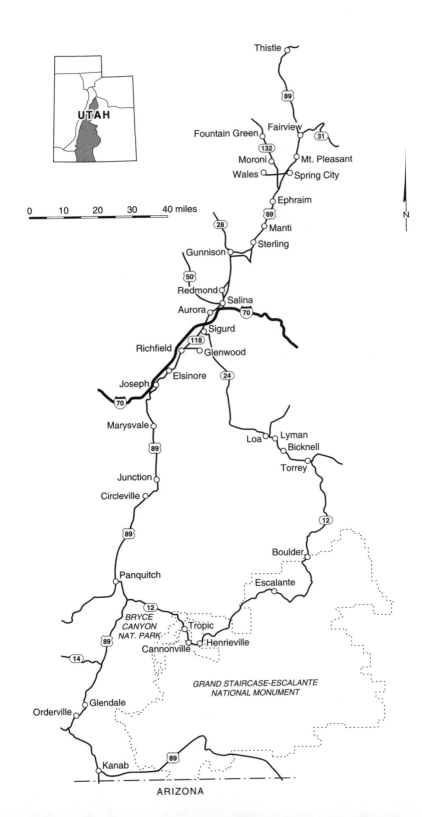

PART V
The Forgotten Corridor

The central portion of the state from Provo Canyon all the way to the Arizona border was initially a source of strength to the territory. Manti was colonized in 1849—just two years after Mormon pioneers entered the Salt Lake Valley. Within twenty years settlements thickly dotted the present-day course of US 89 much of the way to Arizona. These settlements were more numerous than those on similar stretches of I-15 south of Provo. The little towns, well-watered by mountain streams and with favorable soil and climate, prospered into the twentieth century. At first there was great demand for farm products, but the agricultural depression of the 1920s changed that.

AGRICULTURAL DEPRESSION AND RECOVERY

During World War I, nationwide demand for farm products had escalated. Rather than concentrating on local trade, farmers increased their production to meet export demands. Many went into debt to develop new land and purchase machinery. After the war, demand decreased rapidly and prices dropped. Many farmers with large debts were crippled financially, and some local banks closed. Though we think of the national recession as having begun in 1929, in Utah, and particularly in Sanpete County with its agriculture-based economy, the 1920s were very difficult. Prices continued to drop, and in 1932 both farm prices and employment bottomed out.

Some agricultural interests fared better than others. The sheep industry, long important for Sanpete County, kept many families alive. Though wool prices dropped, prize Rambouillets still garnered top dollar on a national market for breeding purposes. Turkey farming was another

185

profitable venture. Many Sanpete County farmers turned to this meat crop when other avenues failed. The area's early cool weather was ideal for firming a turkey's flesh in time for Thanksgiving. Turkeys have proven an important source of revenue in the county for over seventy years. Norbest, a local meat packer, continues to have a major influence on the economy of Sanpete County, both as an employer and as a ready market for farmers' turkeys. As you pass through the valley, notice the long lines of barns and the occasional white feather floating in the air.

In addition to the problems brought on by the agricultural depression, the major transportation routes bypassed the towns of Utah's central valleys. The trains ran across the state north of Salt Lake and through Spanish Fork Canyon. The line to southern California was constructed west of the Wasatch Front. Eventually spur lines were built into the central valleys, but they didn't bring major cross-country traffic.

When Interstate 15 was constructed, it was built along Brigham Young's Mormon Corridor, again to the west of the towns of the Sevier River valleys. The towns there stagnated and lost population. Gradually they stabilized, and in recent years they have experienced some growth. Still, many elements in the towns along this stretch of US 89 and its arteries do not seem to have changed in the last hundred years—it is indeed the "Forgotten Corridor."

US 89
Spanish Fork–Arizona State Line
323 miles

Thistle

From I-15, US 89 follows the steep drop from Billies Mountain to a little deserted valley. Thistle is one of the most unusual ghost towns in Utah. Its residents were forced to leave, and only bits and pieces of buildings remain, some on their original foundations, others broken up and tossed against the hillsides.

The history of Thistle is closely tied with that of the Denver & Rio Grande Railroad. In 1883 the Denver & Rio Grande company constructed their line beside the popular Old Spanish Trail along the Spanish Fork River. Thistle, at the confluence of Thistle and Soldier Creeks, was named for all the thistles growing there. The town grew into an important railroad stop, with 600 residents in 1917. But with the railroad's decline came

Thistle's. The depot was torn down in 1972, and the post office closed two years later. By 1983 only fifty people remained in this once-prosperous railroad town.

The winter of 1982–83 was a particularly long, wet one, and the mountains around Thistle became saturated. In April 1983, the earth in Spanish Fork Canyon began to move. First the road and railroad tracks shifted and buckled at a point just west of Thistle. Road and railroad crews quickly repaired trouble spots. But the movement of the earth quickened, and soon an entire mountain had slipped from its foundation, blocking the Spanish Fork River. The waters rapidly rose, and the natural earthen dam meant certain destruction for Thistle.

Some residents were reluctant to leave their homes, but soon they had no alternative. The water of the new reservoir rose a foot every hour for several weeks, until it reached a spillway. Road crews worked to stabilize the mass of earth, weighing it down with huge trucks. Denver & Rio Grande Railroad officials scrambled to build a new tunnel through Billies Mountain above the anticipated high-water mark of the newly formed lake. The state worked to build an overflow spillway and then a tunnel to drain the lake, while the Utah Department of Transportation (UDOT) hurried to build a new road over Billies Mountain. By the time the lake reached its peak, rooftops were floating in the water. For a time some people wanted to allow the dam to create a new reservoir, but others felt it would be too unstable. The final decision was to drain the water through huge pipes built through the earthen wall.

Flooded Spanish Fork River at Thistle, 1983. Note the floating roof.
—UTAH STATE
HISTORICAL SOCIETY

The Thistle landslide was the first Utah disaster declared as such by a president of the United States. It was also the United States' most expensive landslide. The direct costs of the landslide included $45 million to relocate the railway, $75 million to relocate the highway, and $80 million in lost revenue to the railroad. The indirect costs were incalculable. Because the slide occurred at the junction of two railroads, shipments entirely stopped on the Thistle-Marysvale line and Thistle-Price corridor. This meant layoffs of gypsum workers in Sanpete, Sevier, and Piute Counties. Coal shipments were halted, resulting in layoffs in Carbon and Emery Counties. Coal production in 1983 dropped nearly 30 percent as a result of the slide. Other materials normally shipped by rail sat idle, causing losses in numerous industries. In addition, Utah's tourist industry was affected by worries of inconvenience and actual blockage of a vital transportation route. South-central Utah suffered when the already unprofitable Thistle-Marysvale railroad line shut down forever.

Traces of the temporary lake of 1983 remain. A close look reveals the waterline along with dead trees and other debris, and pieces of buildings are strewn in the small valley at the junction of the highways. A new road has been built through a notch in Billies Mountain high above the Spanish Fork River, and a new railroad tunnel cuts through the base of the mountain.

Birdseye

South of Thistle, US 89 climbs past the dead trees, water-damaged buildings, and high-water mark of the lake that drowned Thistle and into a narrow valley. A few mailboxes and scattered farmhouses indicate that people live here. Birdseye was named for the bird's-eye marble quarries in the mountains east of town. For many years a train stopped in the town to pick up loads of the beautiful pink rock.

Indianola

US 89 next passes through Indianola, once an Indian reservation set up by Brigham Young. Concerned that the Indians would starve because they had no land of their own, Young designated this area as a place where only Indians could own farms. In 1865 the federal government created a reservation in the Uinta Basin, and most of the residents of Indianola were moved to northeastern Utah.

That same year, a white family set up a homestead at Indianola. It was during the Black Hawk War, and the entire family—husband, wife, and four children—were massacred early one morning. The next group of homesteaders moved to Indianola in 1873. Quite a few families lived at Indianola until improved roads and transportation made it possible for them to live in larger towns and drive to their farms, which most do now.

SANPETE VALLEY

US 89 continues through the narrow foothills until it drops down into the Sanpete Valley. This long, narrow valley to the west of the Wasatch Plateau was used for agriculture by the Fremont Indians and later by the San Pitch Indians. The Utes wintered in this mountain valley, and Wakara, a powerful Ute chief, terrorized and enslaved the helpless San Pitch tribe. Wakara invited the Mormons to move into the area in 1849, hoping to profit by trading with them. Because of his invitation, the Sanpete Valley was one of the first areas outside the Salt Lake Valley to be settled by Mormons. Subsequently, in November 1849, fifty pioneer families arrived in Manti to build a new Mormon outpost.

Manti was the first city in Sanpete County, but other towns soon followed. When large groups of Scandinavian Mormon converts began arriving in Utah in 1853, Brigham Young sent many to Sanpete County. By 1870 Sanpete County was 80 percent Scandinavian; the majority of these were Danish. At one time, Sanpete was the county with the most Danes in the United States.

Floods in the Valley

The Wasatch Plateau—in the mountains above the Sanpete Valley—has long been a preferred sheep-grazing range. During the latter part of the nineteenth century, overgrazing became a disastrous problem. People in the valley below could count the sheep herds by the dust clouds that

Floods devastated many Sanpete County towns around the turn of the century. This scene was taken in Manti from about where the Manti garage now stands. The brick building is the old Manti co-op. —UTAH STATE HISTORICAL SOCIETY

A sheep camp in the Skyline Drive area, early twentieth century. Note the tightly packed animals. —UTAH STATE HISTORICAL SOCIETY

followed them. When summer thunderstorms came, huge floods full of mud, trees, and debris—products of erosion caused by the grazing—washed down the mountainsides through towns, farms, and homes.

The worst floods occurred between 1889 and 1910. Before long, the entire town of Milburn had washed away. The center was never rebuilt. In 1903, because of the flooding, President Theodore Roosevelt created the Manti National Forest Reserve to manage the area and correct the erosion problems. Replenishing the mountains with new growth, grading terrain to help it retain water, and limiting sheep herds finally resulted in a more stable environment.

Fairview

Some farmers from Mount Pleasant found the fertile farmland around Fairview very attractive. They obtained Brigham Young's permission to establish a town there in 1859. In 1866, during the Black Hawk War, some of Fairview's residents moved to Mount Pleasant for safety while the men built a ten-foot-high rock wall around the fort in the center of Fairview. This fort gave enough protection so that town residents could return and enjoy relative safety through the remainder of the disturbance.

Fairview grew fairly quickly, surpassing Mount Pleasant in size. At one time the population of the town reached 1,700, but with the emigration from farming communities in the twentieth century, the town census dropped below 1,000.

Fairview was the home of a long-ago social institution, the "poorhouse." Sanpete County residents who did not have the means to take care of themselves were sent to Fairview. There, they lived together and did some farming and other work at a county-run institution for the poor, the Sanpete Infirmary. The infirmary closed years ago, and the building has since been demolished.

Fairview was and still is the center of an important sheep industry area. A. J. Anderson, a longtime Fairview resident, describes some of the more untalked of aspects of sheep ranching in Janet Anderson's book *Bounty:*

> For years and years, for many years, we would dock the lambs. We usually docked them—the operation consisted of putting your ear marks on them and also cutting their tail off. With wethered lambs you'd cut the tail so it was short. Then with the wether lambs, you'd castrate them. And for many, many years, we would use our teeth for pulling the testicles. Of course, that's kind of a bloody operation. I was glad when we didn't have to do that, but I did much of that. Well, my wife says, "That's difficult to have you go out and do that and then you come home and you want to kiss me."

A scenic byway connecting Sanpete and Emery Counties starts in Fairview. East of town, UT 31 ascends a steep canyon. Skyline Drive, running north and south, crosses UT 31 at the summit. High above Sanpete County, Skyline Drive traces the outline of the top of the mountains through sheep country. This sometimes rugged dirt road, over 100 miles long, is one of the most spectacular backcountry roads in the state. At elevations of 9,000 to 11,000 feet, the road seems to sit on top of the world. Only accessible during the summer months, it is well worth a visit.

Mount Pleasant

Continuing south on US 89, you come to the pioneer town of Mount Pleasant. A lumber mill on Pleasant Creek, constructed in 1851, was the first permanent structure in Mount Pleasant. In 1852 several families moved to the site and it became a town. The Walker War broke out in 1853, and Mount Pleasant, too isolated to be safe, was abandoned until 1859.

When Mount Pleasant was resettled, the residents built a fort. All the homes were sixteen feet square, and the fort wall made up the back wall of each house. Pleasant Creek ran through the center of the fort. The one-room schoolhouse was near the stream. When it was time for school to start the teacher would step out and call, "To books, to books, to books."

When peace seemed more certain, people moved out of the fort onto city blocks. As in the rest of Sanpete County, a large portion of the town's population was Scandinavian. Differences between the Danes, Norwegians, and Swedes sometimes erupted into conflict. The Swedes were the minority among the Scandinavians. In 1862 some Swedish LDS Church members apostatized because church leaders refused to hold services in Swedish, even though they conducted them in Danish and Norwegian. The apostate group took on the name "Liberal Party" in 1875. Also that year, a Presbyterian minister arrived to unite them in a new faith. This gave birth to the strong Presbyterian influence in Sanpete County.

Wasatch Academy was founded by the Presbyterians and sponsored by them until 1972, when it became an independent interfaith school. Though it began as an elementary school for the children of apostate Mormons, the academy changed its focus in the early part of the twentieth century, becoming a college preparatory school. It has concentrated on keeping a ratio of one teacher for every eight pupils and has strict entry requirements. Only about 125 students are enrolled each year.

For a time, Mount Pleasant grew faster than all the other towns in Sanpete County and has often been called "The Queen City of Sanpete." Other Sanpete County towns have now surpassed Mount Pleasant in population. In his praises of what he felt was a perfect atmosphere, one historian wrote of Mount Pleasant, "The miasmatic germs of disease cannot exist in the pure ozonified atmosphere."

Spring City

Against the east bench of the mountains just a few miles south and east of Mount Pleasant, Spring City is a time capsule from the early 1900s. In the center of town, a clear, cold mountain stream that never runs dry is caught in a spigot. The spring inspired the name of this unique little town.

Spring City has been preserved almost untouched over the past 100 years because the main highway passes it by. It is a peaceful town with old houses, stores, barns, and other buildings, some crumbling with age. The entire town is now on the National Register of Historic Places.

Spring City was first settled by the James Allred family in 1852. One story about the Allreds illustrates that polygamous families were not always harmonious. When Orson Allred's daughter, Sarah Elizabeth, died in early infancy, he was so heartsick he carved a lavish tombstone for the baby. The child's mother, Sarah, was Allred's second wife, much younger

Old Spring City School, constructed in 1899.

than his first wife. The older sons of the first wife were so insulted at the extravagance lavished on the child of the second wife that they painted the gravestone black. Though the stone was subsequently cleaned, some traces of the black paint still remain.

In 1853, many Danes came to Sanpete County and settled in Spring City. That July, the Walker War broke out and disturbed the peace of the new community. When Mount Pleasant settlers were attacked, they moved to the Allred settlement in Spring City. Here they were held under siege on the meetinghouse block for several days before they were able to evacuate to Manti. That fall, Reuben Allred asked Brigham Young to send more settlers as reinforcements to resettle their town. A large group of Scandinavians had just arrived in Salt Lake City, and the Mormon leader sent half of them (fifty families) to Sanpete County. However, even the larger number was not enough to ensure safety for all, and they moved to Manti and then to the fort at Ephraim. Spring City was finally resettled in 1859, and a large part of the new population was Danish. For many years, "Little Denmark" was a common nickname for Spring City.

In the early days after resettlement, most of the Danish immigrants settled in the north part of the town. Non-Danes often looked down on the Danish residents, even to the point of calling them "north-warders."

Allred child's gravestone from the old Spring City Cemetery.

In 1860, Brigham Young sent apostle elder Orson Hyde to Spring City to serve as the Sanpete Stake president. He had served many missions for the church, among them a trip in 1841 to dedicate Palestine for the return of the Jews. He spent twenty-eight years as president of the Quorum of the Twelve Apostles. He was prominent in the affairs of the town and county until his death in 1878. Orson Hyde's grave can be found in the Spring City Cemetery northwest of town.

Less than a decade after peace came to Spring City, another and more serious conflict arose. When the Black Hawk War began in 1865, Spring City had to fortify against Indian attack. In spite of their precautions, the entire town had to evacuate to Ephraim in the summer of 1866. During the winter they were able to return to their town. The following summer, in August 1867, Black Hawk's warriors attacked several men working in the fields. Two men were killed and another wounded, but the residents refused to abandon the town again.

Spring City boomed for a number of years. At the turn of the twentieth century the population was 1,235, but it started to slip as farm prices went down and families looked to more industrialized areas for employment. In 1920 the population was 1,106; by 1940 it had dropped to 839; in 1950 it was 703; and in 1970 it reached a low of 457. Then the town turned around, and now over 800 people live in Spring City. Many farmers raise turkeys. Some residents are escapees from the cities who find charm

Orson Hyde.
—LDS CHURCH
HISTORICAL
DEPARTMENT

in Spring City's old pioneer homes. However, young residents longing for a more exciting place to start life are not likely to tarry in this quiet county settlement.

Ephraim

The Spring City turnoff returns to US 89 at Pigeon Hollow Junction (no town here), then continues five miles to Ephraim, central Utah's "college town." Ephraim and Manasseh were two of the Twelve Tribes of Israel. When Ephraim was established on the east side of the San Pitch River, it was intended that Manasseh be established on the west side of the river, but Manasseh never materialized.

Although a family farmed in Ephraim from 1852 to 1853, the town really took hold when a group of settlers from Manti and refugees from Spring City fleeing the Walker War established a fort here in 1854. That summer and fall large numbers of Danish immigrants arrived, and the town's primary language was Danish. The fort at Ephraim grew rapidly with new immigrants, and when the danger from the Walker War passed, many stayed in the town. The fort was needed again during the Black Hawk War in the late 1860s.

Indian conflicts occurred throughout southern Utah, and Ephraim was not exempt from these troubles. In 1865 a party of Indians came out of Ephraim Canyon searching for cattle. They stole the entire Ephraim cooperative herd and in the process murdered about seven settlers. One baby was found still alive in his dead mother's arms. These were troubled times for both Utes and Mormon settlers. The Utes, rather than face starvation or expulsion to the Uinta Basin, were determined to drive the white intruders from their lands. White society felt that God had given them the country and that the Indians' depredations only proved their savageness. The whites built stronger forts, kept their rifles loaded, and ultimately won out. The fighting finally ended in 1873.

The Scandinavian population, large throughout Sanpete County, was especially so in Ephraim. By 1860 more Danish-speaking than English-speaking people lived there, and those who didn't understand Danish had to learn the language or not communicate. By 1880, 90 percent of Ephraim's population was Scandinavian and about half the population was surnamed Anderson, Christensen, Hansen, Jensen, Larson, Nielsen, Olsen, or Peterson.

One of the most notable Danes in Ephraim was C. C. A. Christensen, remembered for the huge canvasses he painted depicting the history and life of the pioneers. Born and converted to Mormonism in Copenhagen, he was a handcart pioneer himself, so he could accurately depict life along the trail. He arrived in Sanpete County in 1858, moving from Mount Pleasant to Fairview and finally to Ephraim. He was well known during his lifetime for his writings, lectures, and humorous interpretations of Danish life. He died in 1912.

Artist C. C. A. Christensen painted extensive murals of his pioneer experiences. Shown here is The Handcart Pioneers, 1856–1860, *painted in 1900.* —UTAH STATE HISTORICAL SOCIETY

In 1888 the Sanpete Stake opened an academy in Ephraim with 121 students ranging in age from eleven to thirty. The academy building was constructed between 1899 and 1909. It is now on the National Register of Historic Places. The academy was named in 1902 for Lorenzo and Erastus Snow, early missionaries who served in Scandinavia and showed support for the struggling institution. In 1932 the church deeded the academy to the state of Utah, and it became Snow College. Snow College has struggled for funding through the years, to the point of almost being turned back over to the church. However, after a deciding public vote, the institution remained a part of the Utah state school system.

In 1912, a first-of-its-kind research center was built in Ephraim. The Great Basin Research Center was established to study weather patterns. The center continues to conduct studies in the area, mostly in Ephraim Canyon. You can find the canyon by turning east on 400 South Street from Main Street. As you drive up this well-graded dirt road, watch for the signs along the way indicating the annual precipitation. The amounts climb drastically from the bottom of the canyon to the top, where the road meets Skyline Drive.

Manti

Approaching Manti from any direction, you can see its most visible symbol, the Mormon Temple. It sits on a hill above the town and dominates not only Manti but much of the valley. The temple is a symbol of much of the history of Manti and Sanpete County.

The Mormon Temple continues to dominate Manti.

Manti, looking north. Photo undated. —UTAH STATE HISTORICAL SOCIETY

In November 1849 Isaac Morley led fifty Mormon families and their livestock into Sanpete County. They selected Manti as their town site and built dugouts in Temple Hill (at the base of the hill where the temple now stands) in which to spend the winter. The winter of 1849–50 proved to be the worst in local Indians' memory. The white families living in dugouts and wagon boxes found it especially difficult to endure the hard conditions. The animals fared even worse—127 of the 240 cattle perished in the cold and snow. The spring brought a respite from the weather, but other problems came with it. Thousands of rattlesnakes came out of hibernation. They slithered into the dugouts and hid in beds and cupboards. In one night, the settlers killed 300 rattlesnakes.

It is little wonder that the pioneers complained about the conditions. Seth Taft said of the valley, "This is only a long, narrow canyon, and not even a jackrabbit could exist on its desert soil." Others wanted to find another place to live. Isaac Morley told them, "We behold the stake driven by Parley P. Pratt in his explorations of this valley. This is our God-appointed abiding place, and stay I will, though but ten men remain with me." They all stayed.

Early in the history of Manti, the hill east of town was called Temple Hill. Brigham Young described a vision in which he had seen the Prophet Moroni (who lived in Book of Mormon times) dedicating the spot for the building of a temple. In April 1877 Young dedicated the hillside, and work began on the temple. It was built with volunteer labor from the beautiful buff-colored oolite sandstone quarried on the construction site. Funds were raised by members. All eggs laid on Sunday were set aside and sold as "temple eggs"; the chickens were said to be very busy on Sundays. Men came from every town in the county to work on the temple, walking miles every week. The road between Ephraim and Manti became well-trodden in those days from the Ephraim men's feet going back and forth between home and the temple (some say it was smoother then than it is now). The temple was completed in 1888.

While the temple was under construction, from 1877 to 1888, other building was also taking place in Manti. Some of the stone quarried for the temple was rejected and left for anyone who wanted to use it. Everything from chicken coops, barns, and houses to Manti's Presbyterian church was built from the same stone as the temple. The oolite was later exported to faraway building sites. One of the most notable examples of Sanpete oolite outside of Utah is Hearst Castle in San Simeon, California.

During World War II an unusual industry brought jobs to Manti: a parachute factory. The factory brought many women into the workforce, boosted the local economy, and increased Manti's standard of living. In many homes, indoor plumbing came as a direct benefit of extra money earned in the parachute factory.

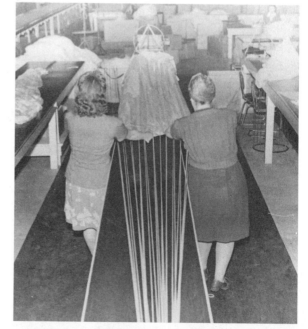

Parachute factory in Manti during World War II.
—UTAH STATE
HISTORICAL SOCIETY

Manti is still a quiet farming community in the shadow of the striking temple on the hill. Two weeks every year the town comes to life with the bustle and activity associated with the Mormon Miracle Pageant, depicting the history of the Mormon Church. It is performed each July on the south slope of the temple grounds. Also within view of the temple, the Sanpete County Fair takes place in late August.

Sterling

Continue south on US 89 to Sterling, through fields overshadowed by the Wasatch Plateau. In 1873 fifteen families from Manti settled Sterling. The town was named for the "sterling" qualities of its citizens. One of the settlers, Gus Clark, received a five-dollar-prize for submitting the best name for the town.

One of the sterling citizens was Daniel Funk, who envisioned a water park in this high mountain desert. In the early 1870s Daniel Funk obtained permission from Brigham Young and Ute Chief Arapien to build a resort lake in Arapien Valley. The Indians were skeptical about the project's feasibility but granted him the land. Funk constructed a canal along the mountainside, and gradually the valley filled with water. The lake was popular with boaters until a tragic storm in June 1878 caused the drowning deaths of eleven young people. From then on the lake enjoyed times of varied prosperity as a recreation, irrigation, and multiuse area. The lake became part of the Utah state park system in 1964, and is now known as Palisade State Park.

A mill on the west side of town produced azomite, used in poultry grit and as a soil conditioner, until it closed in the mid-1980s.

Gunnison

Nighttime travelers know they are approaching Gunnison long before they reach the small central Utah town. The bright lights of the state prison make Gunnison look like a large metropolis.

In 1859 two sites were settled a few miles from present-day Gunnison. When Brigham Young visited in 1862, he suggested both settlements move to higher ground as the lower areas near the river were muddy and prone to flooding. In fact, the original town sites were so swampy that Gunnison was called "Hog Wallow" for a time. When the two sections of the town amalgamated, they decided Hog Wallow and Kearns Camp or Chalk Point (the names of the other town) were not appropriate names for a permanent settlement. They chose Gunnison in memory of Captain John Gunnison, the leader of a United States survey team who had been killed by Indians near Delta in 1853.

The Black Hawk War brought changes to Gunnison. The town was not abandoned during the war like other towns in the area, and it experienced an influx of families from Sevier and Piute Counties in the late 1860s. At the same time, Indians were stealing their cattle and grasshoppers were devouring their crops. With all these conflicting pressures, it was a period of intense struggle for the small town.

SEVIER RIVER VALLEY

US 89 continues south into Sevier County. Sevier's scenery is similar to Sanpete's, but this county was settled after the one to the north and was abandoned during much of the 1860s because of hostilities between settlers and Indians.

Spanish explorers and, later, trappers explored the valley of the Sevier River before the Mormon pioneers arrived in Utah. The Mormons first saw the fertile land along the banks of the Sevier River in December 1849 when Parley P. Pratt led an exploring expedition to the southern part of the territory.

Although the valley was deemed suitable for cultivation, it wasn't pinpointed for permanent settlement until 1863. In January 1864 the first group from Sanpete County started a community at Richfield. Other towns were settled soon after.

Redmond

Redmond is the first town in Sevier County. Named for the red mounds on the west side of the town, Redmond experienced a rough birth. The town, surveyed in 1875, was settled the following spring by families from Salina. When they planted their first crop of grain, rabbits ate the young shoots as soon as they came up. The pioneers watered the grain and it came up again, but once again the rabbits devoured it. Most of the settlers wanted to leave, but John Johnson convinced them to stay. They watered their grain and it came up well again, only to be killed by a heavy frost on the second of June. Johnson had to convince them to try the fourth time, and their persistence paid off; they were finally blessed with a bountiful crop of grain.

For many years salt mining has been an important industry in Redmond. The Redmond Clay and Salt Company specializes in the production of salt blocks for livestock. They also mine clay. In recent years, the American Orsa Company, a division of Redmond Clay and Salt, began producing and packaging table salt at a plant in town.

Salina

Located 145 miles directly south of Salt Lake City, Salina was first explored with a view to a permanent settlement in October 1863. In January 1864 several men arrived and built shanties near the creek. By March of that year twenty families had moved to Salina. One of the first tasks of a new Mormon community was to build a meetinghouse. Salina began constructing its church in 1864, but the building was first used for a different purpose than was originally intended. Ute warriors killed and scalped two men in Salina Canyon in April 1865, and the next year two more settlers were killed. When the conflicts began, the church walls were high enough to offer some protection, and the new settlers used it as a fort. After the troubles ended, the settlers returned to constructing the church. They completed it in 1871 when Sevier County was resettled, and it served the community as both a meetinghouse and a schoolhouse for many years.

Salina was named by the Spanish for the salt deposits east of the town, and salt was produced near the town for a number of years. A Civilian Conservation Corps camp was set up east of Salina during the Depression and corps members worked on roads and dams. In 1944 Italian prisoners of war were sent to the camp, and German prisoners arrived in 1945 and 1946.

On July 8, 1945, a tragedy occurred at the Salina POW camp. Private Clarence V. Bertucci, who was on guard duty, opened fire from the guard tower with a .30-caliber machine gun, spraying several hundred German prisoners with 250 rounds as they slept in their tents. Nine prisoners died and twenty more were wounded. Private Bertucci was declared insane after several weeks of evaluation in Bushnell Army Hospital in Brigham City. The German prisoners were given a Protestant funeral in Salt Lake City and were buried in the Fort Douglas cemetery.

Because of its position at the junction of UT 28, US 50, UT 118, and I-70, Salina has a lot of motels, restaurants, gas stations, and other services. This is the last gas stop for those wishing to travel east on I-70 through the San Rafael Swell to Green River (104 miles).

Aurora

The towns in the Sevier River valley are strung out in a line much like those in the Sanpete Valley. The next town in the string is Aurora. Before Aurora was settled, explorers noted the abundance of water in the area and the tall sagebrush and greasewood that indicated good soil. In 1875 a group of settlers was called by the LDS Church to settle a new town. They immediately started the grueling work of building an irrigation system. It was a difficult task that required cooperation among community members. George Holdaway had to stand shoulder-deep in the river while he worked on the dam, with Jabez Durfee holding onto his hair so he wouldn't go under the water. They survived the wet ordeal and accomplished their goal.

The first crops failed, and travelers passing through the town said the land was no good. One even offered twenty dollars for the first bushel of wheat from Aurora. The settlers persevered, though, and finally prospered.

Aurora was governed by LDS Church officials for many years. The church oversaw the construction of a schoolhouse and an amusement hall, as well as the installation of electricity and a telephone system. In 1914 the townspeople decided to incorporate so they could provide a better water system for the community. The settlement had been called Willow Bend, but the U.S. Postal Service wouldn't accept this name, so the citizens named the town Aurora after the Roman goddess of the dawn. They felt the colors of the surrounding hills looked like the sunrise.

Sigurd

Colorful sandstone cliffs line the valley as you continue south. First called Neversweat for the heat and humidity, the town then took the name Vermillion. When the Vermillion LDS ward was split, the south half became Sigurd and the north half kept the name Vermillion. Sigurd became the official name of the town and the post office, but people living in the northern half still called their area Vermillion.

Before anyone settled this area, two well-known Indian battles took place near the town site. One was the Cedar Ridge battle in 1868. Settlers who had abandoned settlements in Sevier County were returning to Monroe from Sanpete County. They were ambushed by thirty Indians. One white man was killed, another severely wounded, and the rest managed to escape north.

The other incident was an attack on Charles and George Wilson, who were crossing the Sevier River at Rocky Ford. Charles was killed and scalped, but George escaped by burrowing under the riverbank. He dug a hole for his body, flattened out in it, and poked a vent hole through the surface for breathing. He stayed there until the next morning, when he was able to get away.

Sigurd retains the benefits of a rural community, but still has some industry to offer employment to its citizens. Both the Georgia Pacific paper mill and the U.S. Gypsum plant help stimulate the economy of south-central Utah.

Richfield

As the largest city in more than 100 miles, Richfield is the business and shopping center for most of south-central Utah.

The first residents of Richfield lived in cellars topped with willow and mud roofs. Probate Judge William Morrison built the first "aristocratic house" in Richfield in 1865. Its best feature was its shingle roof. The house consisted of a single room that served as kitchen, bedroom, post office, and judge's chambers.

As a polygamist, Judge Morrison left his second wife, Christina, in Richfield when he went to spend the winter with his first wife in Mount Pleasant. When Indians came to Christina's door she gave them beer made from malt and wheat. They liked it so much they returned for more, but she had none to give, so they beat her with rawhide strips. She took the beating so well that they called her a "heap brave squaw." After that she always had beer for the Indians.

Soon after the settlement of Richfield troubles started with Black Hawk and his tribe. The settlers banded together to build a rock fort around the public square. In the spring of 1866 all the settlers from Marysvale, Monroe, and Glenwood moved to Richfield and crowded into homes there. No one was allowed to work alone in the fields. After Indians massacred a family on a supply trip between Richfield and Glenwood, the settlers decided to abandon the entire county. A U.S. Army contingent stationed in Salt Lake City would do nothing to help the hated Mormons. In April 1867, 200 wagons from Sanpete County arrived in Richfield to help evacuate the town and county. They took the families as far as Gunnison, and from there they could go wherever they chose. Many went north to get as far away from the Indians as possible. Others stayed in Sanpete County, returning to reinhabit Sevier County when the years of danger had passed.

Richfield was resettled in the spring of 1871. That year the grasshoppers devoured all the grain that was planted, resulting in more hard times for the already strained group of settlers. They stuck it out, though, and saw their community grow into a flourishing town.

Making Silk

In 1879 a women's association was formed in Richfield for the purpose of making silk. Sericulture (silkworm breeding and silk making) played an important role in Brigham Young's philosophy of self-sufficiency, the United Order. Soon after the pioneers' arrival in Utah they started importing silkworms and mulberry seeds (the worms eat the leaves of the mulberry tree). In Richfield, citizens raised funds and planted twenty dollars' worth of mulberry trees on two town lots purchased specifically for this venture. Thousands of silkworm eggs were placed in the Relief Society Hall.

Young urged women throughout Utah to raise silkworms. He appointed his wife, Zina D. H. Young, who had an abhorrence of worms, to be in charge of the project. She willingly accepted the assignment but suffered from nightmares after working with the wriggly creatures.

Caring for silkworms was a grueling process. One ounce of newly hatched worms required three-fourths of a pound of fresh, chopped, and dried mulberry leaves four times a day. By the time the worms neared their cocoon-making stage six weeks later, they consumed 120 pounds of the chopped leaves eight times a day.

For years Richfield resident Mathilda Westman and her children climbed the mulberry trees and picked the leaves seven or eight times a day to feed the hungry worms. Though they worked ceaselessly, their industry was not a great success. The cocoons were sent to Salt Lake and spun into a few scarves and ribbons. For all her efforts, Mrs. Westman received a silk handkerchief with a picture of the Salt Lake Temple woven into it.

Though the pioneers started in sericulture with enthusiasm, the industry did not endure past the turn of the twentieth century. The work was laborious and failures were common. Producers found no good market for the finished silk, though some was sold in California and the eastern United States. Most of the silk was sold at a loss to the producers.

Women displaying silkworms and cocoons, circa 1895.
—LDS CHURCH HISTORICAL DEPARTMENT

Glenwood

A few miles east of US 89 on UT 119 is Glenwood. This somewhat isolated Sevier County settlement was the site of one of the bloodiest scenes of the Black Hawk War.

The first families in this little town were called there by Brigham Young in 1863 and arrived in January 1864. About twenty-five families spent the winter of 1864–65 living in cellars made of rock walls with a roof about a foot above the ground. During the times of Indian conflict, families huddled together in the dark in these little holes, praying for deliverance.

The entire town lived in continual dread of attack. Men were constantly on watch, and when one of them sounded the warning drumbeat, everyone ran to the bishop's house for shelter. One mother gave birth to her baby in the back of a wagon while she and her family were fleeing an Indian attack. Merrit Stanley, the town blacksmith, was shot several times by Indians when he went outside to fill his coal bucket.

On the morning of March 21, 1867, news came that a fresh shipment of goods had arrived at the Glenwood co-op. Jense Peterson and his wife left their eighteen-month-old daughter with a neighbor in Richfield, and, along with another neighbor, fourteen-year-old Mary Smith, started to Glenwood to purchase supplies. Though they knew travel was dangerous, they couldn't let the opportunity to obtain much-needed supplies slip by.

When the family reached Black Ridge, east of the Sevier River, they saw Indians in the river bottoms stealing cattle. The Indians spotted the Petersons and shot one of their oxen. The Petersons attempted to flee on foot but they were overtaken and killed. The Indians scalped them all and stripped and mutilated the women's bodies. White boys hiding in the river bottoms had witnessed much of the episode and ran for help. Within a month the entire county was evacuated.

In 1874 apostle Erastus Snow traveled to Glenwood to establish the United Order there. All those who wished to participate turned in their property to the bishop and received credit. They received credit only for their labor, so even those who had no property to give received credit. In return, all were given what they needed for their families. During the five-year period the United Order was practiced in Glenwood, production flourished. The community built and operated two grist mills, a saw and shingle mill for producing building supplies, and a cording mill for spinning and weaving wool into cloth. All the town's blankets and wearing apparel were made from this cloth. A tannery produced leather for the townspeople's shoes, and sugarcane was grown and made into molasses. Buildings were built and a telegraph installed, all under the auspices of the United Order. When the order ended, most of these enterprises died out.

An old Zions Cooperative Mercantile Institution with the dates 1878–1930 on it sits at Main and Center Streets. This was the outlet for the United Order in Glenwood. An offspring of the original Glenwood co-op, the store is the only reminder of the fate of the Jense Peterson party on that morning in March 1867.

Central

After passing through Glenwood going southwest toward I-70, you'll hit several small farming communities. One of these is Central. The name Central is indicative of the town's location in the valley. The southwest part of Central was called Little Denmark for many years for the nine Danish families who arrived in 1881. Their lovely gardens and trees distinguished them from the rest of the town. They were especially known for their tidy woodpiles. It was said in town, "You can tell where a Danishman lives by his woodpile."

In the center of town stood a public corral where people brought their cows each morning. The townspeople hired men and boys to herd the cows to pasture every day. In the evening farmers returned to collect their cows. The corral served not only the needs of the cows, but also of the young men and women who conducted courtships on the bars of the corral fence.

Austin

Austin, south of Central, has no businesses—just some houses and farms clustered together. Austin was established when the Elsinore Sugar Factory was built here in 1910–11. However, people lived on their farms in the area from the 1870s until Austin became a town. Originally called Frog Town because of all the frogs in the Sevier River and its ponds, the town changed its name to honor the superintendent of the sugar factory, George Austin. The factory closed in 1928.

Elsinore

Elsinore is a farming town just east of I-70. Joseph A. Young, eldest son of Brigham Young and president of the LDS stake in Sevier County, had a strong controlling influence over all the new settlements under his stewardship. When men from Richfield who were farming in the Elsinore area decided to move their families there in the fall of 1874, they obtained his permission. Then they asked his opinion on a name for the town. He had been to Elsinore in Denmark and thought it would make a good name for the spot. Whether or not he also knew it was the setting of Shakespeare's *Hamlet* is uncertain.

The LDS Church had a profound influence on Elsinore's affairs well into the twentieth century. When the town decided to build a recreation center in the 1940s, the issue was settled with little separation between church and state. The town council decided the hall was needed, and the ward bishopric suggested the church donate money. The citizens voted to bond the town for $6,000. The LDS Church presiding bishopric from Salt Lake City, headed by Bishop LeGrande Richards, visited the site and decided the church would contribute $8,000. A church architect drew up the plans and President Roosevelt's Works Progress Administration (WPA) tore down an old structure and began work on the new building. When more funds were needed to complete the building, they were raised by a cooperation of church and state resources.

Today one of the more prominent landmarks in Elsinore is the Old White Rock School at 200 North and Center Streets, constructed from 1896 to 1898. It operated as a public school until 1958. The school stood empty until 1974, when the citizens decided to use it as a town hall. The school was spotlighted in an episode of the PBS series *Reading Rainbow* that told the story of a young boy in the community who created a public library in the basement of the old building.

Joseph

Little activity is apparent in Joseph, the next town on US 89. Joseph was an on-again, off-again place for a number of years. The first families came in 1864, only to leave again the next year because of Indian problems. More settlers tried again when Sevier County was repopulated in 1871, but it was still not safe and they left in 1872. That fall another group gave the spot a third try and ended up staying for good. The LDS stake president, Joseph A. Young, chose the final town site and named the city in his own honor: Joseph City.

In 1874 John Ross built the finest house in town—a one-room log cabin with a dirt roof. It was used by the whole town for church on Sunday and as a dance hall on other days. The structure later served for many years as a stable.

Dancing was important in all pioneer communities, but especially so in Joseph. Having no fiddlers in their town, they convinced Levi H. Jackman to move from Salem, Utah, to Joseph in 1884. The problem was that he built his home on the east side of the river, and most of the dancing was done on the west side. Jackman played at night for the dances, and when the river ran high he had a hard time returning home. Mrs. Jackman was not pleased with the situation, so the townspeople, unwilling to give up their only recreation, tore down his house and rebuilt it on the west side of the river—all in four days' time.

The early "Josephites" faced another problem: sinkholes. When the people tried to fill a gopher hole with water, the surrounding ground sank two or three feet. Digging canals was difficult—sinkholes continually stopped the progress. The sinking earth even destroyed houses occasionally. As with most troubles they encountered, the settlers learned how to fix, work around, or simply put up with this problem and carried on with their work.

Sickness caused much more serious setbacks than lack of dancing or sinkholes. November and December of 1888 were especially tragic months. A diphtheria epidemic struck the town, killing forty-one children.

Though conflicts with Indians prevented the town from getting an earlier start, the people of Joseph learned to live peacefully with many Native Americans. The Old Spanish Trail went through Joseph, and Indians frequently used it in their migrations. Often as many as 300 to 500 Indians were camped near town. They fascinated the settlers with their packs of dogs and their ponies, each pony dragging long poles that held tents, food, and other supplies. The Indians interacted with the people of the town, trading venison and pine nuts for whatever they needed.

Sevier

The valley narrows at the southern end of Sevier County. Named for the Sevier River, Sevier was not settled by the Mormons. It was founded in 1894 when a railroad station was built at the mouth of Sevier Canyon and called Sevier. A "Y" was built for the trains to turn around, along with a bridge over the Sevier River. In the 1890s gold was discovered in Clear Creek Canyon southwest of Sevier on a spot that became the Kimberly Mine. A boom started in the area and a small town grew up around the Sevier train station. When the gold boom died out in about 1904, the railroad siding was moved. The hotel burned down, the other buildings were removed, and the area reverted to farmland.

Fremont Indian State Park is located about five miles west of Sevier at 11550 West Clear Creek Canyon Road (or take I-70 to the state park exit). Much of the rock art throughout the state was executed by the ancient Fremont culture. The museum helps preserve some of this artwork, and depicts the Fremonts' lifestyle and history. The park has both outdoor and indoor interpretive displays.

PIUTE COUNTY

Prominent along the west side of US 89 as it crosses from Sevier to Piute County is a large multicolored formation called Big Rock Candy Mountain. The mountain, made predominantly of decomposed volcanic rock colored by hydrothermal solutions, has been the subject of stories and the famous song "The Big Rock Candy Mountain."

After passing Big Rock Candy Mountain, the highway squeezes through a narrow gorge into Piute County. Piute County is one of the most sparsely populated areas of the state. Most of the towns' populations are lower than they were at the beginning of the twentieth century. The mountain valleys offer little of what people are looking for these days.

Parley P. Pratt led an exploration party through southern Utah in 1849, starting in Sanpete County. On December 11 the group passed into Piute County near Marysvale.

> We crossed the summit . . . and then had a beautiful descent, still through the forest, the foot of the mountain and entered Mary's Vale, and a beautiful rich valley, densely covered with luxuriant high grass, mixed with fine rushes, and interspersed with willows. There was scarcely a sage brush to be seen. The valley which is from a quarter to one and half miles wide contains perhaps two hundred acres of excellent land, and is connected with more a few miles farther up.

Pratt was impressed with the new surroundings and felt more at home than he had since leaving Juab Valley. But it would be more than a decade before this valley became home to any Mormons.

After the precious-metals boom (mostly gold, with some silver) ended in the 1930s, Piute County went into serious decline. Hope for a strong future glimmered briefly in the 1950s when uranium miners scoured the rocks of southern Utah, but the metal's glory was short-lived and the county sunk even lower into a future of out-migration.

Marysvale

Marysvale sits in the bottom of a narrow ravine. Its houses are built up the steep foothills of the mineral-rich mountains that made this Piute County town an important place 100 years ago. No one knows where the name came from, though general opinion points to the merry times that travelers had sitting around campfires in this little valley. The beautiful mountains, some pioneer homes, and a few businesses remain, but much of the town is boarded up.

Pioneers intent on a permanent settlement first came to Marysvale in 1864. Because of the Black Hawk War, they abandoned the settlement in 1866. In 1868 miners discovered precious metals in the area, and Marysvale was reborn.

A railroad line was built to Marysvale to transport the minerals. It became an important station for most of southern Utah, since it was the farthest point south the railroad reached in the central part of the state.

The town prospered until well into the twentieth century, when the metals boom ended and other forms of transportation were developed, making the railroad less vital in the lives of southern Utahans. Gradually, inhabitants moved out, until the town was left more dead than alive. The railroad line was finally lost in the Thistle mudslide disaster of 1983.

Lizzie and Charlie's Working Loom Museum

A big job in a pioneer woman's life was providing warm coverings for her family in the way of clothing, quilts, and rugs to cover the cold hard floors. Lizzie and Charlie's Working Loom Museum in Marysvale helps us understand the production of pioneer rugs. Charley Christensen came from Denmark to Utah in 1894, bringing with him the skill of weaving old rags into rugs. He continued making rugs and passed the skill to his children, and they passed it to their children, who continue the operation. Visitors are welcome to see free demonstrations of the rag-rug artform at the factory at 210 East Bullion Avenue.

Kimberly

Many rich gold mines have operated in Utah. One of these mines was the Kimberly in the Tushar Mountains west of Marysvale. Gold was discovered here in 1888. In the 1890s Peter Kimberly and a group of ministers from Chicago purchased property and vastly expanded production. The

Kimberly, one of Utah's rich gold towns. —UTAH STATE HISTORICAL SOCIETY

town boomed from 1901 to 1908 with over 500 inhabitants. Nearly $3 million in gold and silver was produced in the fabulous mines of the Tushar Mountains.

Of necessity, Kimberly had the strongest jail in the state to accommodate the rough characters who frequented the saloons and brothels. However, the most famous outlaw in Utah was never jailed in Kimberly. Though Butch Cassidy frequented Kimberly in its heyday, he had friends among the locals and never bothered the company payroll.

Most of the ore was freighted out of Kimberly from 1901 to 1908, but another rich vein was struck in 1932. By 1938 it was played out and the miners abandoned the town, which gradually rotted away.

Recently, Marysvale, Piute County, and the U.S. Forest Service have joined in an effort to bring the history of the Piute County mines to the public's attention. They have identified historical sites in and around Marysvale with markers that explain the history of the area's mines. A new campground, Gold Canyon Campground in Bullion Canyon, was built on the road to Kimberly. It features not only camping, but historical markers that explain the old glory of the riches in the mountains of Piute County.

Junction

Continue through the narrow valley to Junction, Piute's county seat.

Junction has seen a variety of people pass through over the years. The original settlers were farmers, but soon ranchers (and the outlaws who dogged the ranchers) and miners followed.

Junction's outstanding landmark is the Piute County Courthouse. This ornate redbrick building, constructed in 1903, compels travelers to stop and look. Most are amazed that such a tiny place should have such a striking building. The courthouse was gutted by fire in 1944; the county records that were stored there also perished. It was later rebuilt. In the early 1990s it appeared that the building, which was deemed seismically unsound and had other problems, would have to come down. However, funds were procured to stabilize the building.

Circleville

The southernmost town in Piute County is known more for its infamous son, Robert Leroy Parker, alias Butch Cassidy, than for any event in its history. Circleville is situated in a beautiful farming valley surrounded by a circle of high mountains.

Brigham Young called the first settlers from Sanpete County to the Circle Valley in March 1864. Indians killed four of the men in November 1865 at the beginning of the Black Hawk War. The settlers feared the natives were planning an ambush. The men gathered fifteen or sixteen Indians, locked them up, and slit their throats. They felt this would be a warning to other Indians who might want to harm them. The Indians were all buried in a common grave. Young rebuked the Circleville settlers for committing such a horrible crime, and said that the valley would be cursed because of their bloody deed.

Whether or not the valley truly suffered from the curse is a matter of opinion, but it was abandoned in 1866 because of the escalation of the Black Hawk War. Men from Beaver came and harvested the crops, but the valley was not reinhabited until 1873. The first homesteaders to return to Circleville were non-Mormons. The Mormons came back the following year.

Butch Cassidy

Two miles southwest of Circleville, on the west side of US 89, stands an old cabin and several corrals (now deteriorated) where Robert Leroy Parker, alias Butch Cassidy, spent most of his young life.

More fictions than facts are told of this famous outlaw. Western lore is full of exciting and mysterious stories about Butch Cassidy; for all to be true is a logistical impossibility. It is known that Robert LeRoy Parker was born on April 15, 1866, in Beaver, Utah, to Mormon parents. The family moved to Circleville sometime thereafter, and Mike Cassidy, a former horse thief, came to work on the Parker ranch. He taught young Leroy most of his roping, riding, shooting, and branding skills.

Butch Cassidy's abandoned boyhood home south of Circleville.

*Robert Leroy Parker,
alias Butch Cassidy,
on July 15, 1894,
age twenty-eight,
at the Wyoming
State Penitentiary.*
—UTAH STATE
HISTORICAL SOCIETY

Parker ran into his first trouble with the law when he stole some horses, while still living on the Circleville ranch. He fled to Colorado, where he joined Matt Warner in robbing a train at Grand Junction and a bank in Telluride. Parker did do legitimate work as a cowboy and even spent some time in Rock Springs, Wyoming, as a butcher—hence the name Butch.

Cassidy, as he preferred to be known after leaving his religious roots behind, spent two years in a Wyoming jail for cattle rustling. After he was set free he moved on to higher stakes—payroll and train robbing—and formed the "Wild Bunch." The gang specialized in robbing banks and trains; they were very successful at getting away with their deeds.

Though the West was becoming more populated at the time these outlaws were operating, they still found many remote valleys along the Outlaw Trail from Wyoming to south-central Utah where they could hide. One story claims that while Cassidy was living along this trail in the Hanksville area he paid a tithe to the local Mormon bishop.

Cassidy had many famous colleagues, including Harry Longabaugh (the Sundance Kid), Harvey Logan (Kid Curry), Ben Kilpatrick (the Tall Texan), Harry Tracy, and Elzy Lay. Etta Place was a famous lady friend of both Butch Cassidy and Harry Longabaugh. It is possible that Ann Bassett of Brown's Park took the name of Etta Place, though it is also likely that other women also assumed that alias while traveling with these and other outlaws.

Butch Cassidy and Harry Longabaugh traveled to South America in 1902 and ranched for a time in Argentina. They took a trip to Bolivia, where history again becomes murky. Bolivian troops killed two men, but it was never proven that the dead men were Cassidy and Longabaugh. It is very possible (and some say certain) that Cassidy and Longabaugh returned to the United States; people claimed to have seen them in Utah. Stories circulate that Longabaugh served time in the Utah state prison under an alias after his rumored death in South America. Butch Cassidy sightings are also common in early-twentieth-century Utah folklore.

Whatever the truth about these men, the stories are many and fascinating, and abundant publications offer a myriad of different theories as to the outlaws' finish.

Panguitch

US 89 continues into Garfield County, soon climbing to Panguitch (elevation 6,666 feet). In March 1864 pioneers from Parowan and Beaver built a road over the mountains that divided Paragonah from Panguitch. After the road was complete, they built the city of Panguitch. The name, which means both water and fish, was given to the nearby lake by the Paiutes.

The new settlers who moved to Panguitch suffered many hardships because of their isolation. Six months out of the year, the road was impassable because of snow. To get supplies, residents had to travel either 40 miles over the rough mountain road to Parowan or 115 miles north through the Sevier River valley to Gunnison.

Panguitch was a harsh and difficult place to live for early settlers. The settlers made many jokes about the climate. A common one was that Panguitch had "nine months of winter and three months of darn cold weather." The growing season was short. Families went for months without flour the first winter after their crops failed.

Because of the climate and the isolation, commodities were scarce. The residents of Panguitch, like those in many other pioneer settlements, suffered greatly through the lack of the basic necessities of life. They had to be self-sufficient and they wasted nothing. When sheep passed through town from one grazing range to another, women picked off the bits of wool snagged on the rough brush. They then washed, carded, spun, and knit it into children's stockings. They kept their houses spotless using homemade cleaning supplies. They used brick powder and ashes to wash dishes, lime to scrub the hearth, and sand and water to scrub the floors clean. Doubtless women's hands were cracked and terribly sore.

The first dentists in town were two shoemakers who bought pinchers for pulling teeth. Parents took their children to the shoemaker and held them down while their rotten teeth were yanked out.

Relations between Mormon settlers and Indian tribes became increasingly unsettled during the 1860s. In 1866, a battle was fought on Panguitch Creek; one Indian was killed and several white settlers were wounded. The Panguitch residents had built a fort, but it didn't feel safe enough in times of conflict, and they abandoned their new home for the safety of larger communities.

By 1871 white settlers had claimed victory over Black Hawk and his warriors, and Panguitch was resettled. Though few of the original settlers returned, their homes were found undisturbed. Even the crops they had planted were still there.

Food became extremely sparse during the winter of 1877–78. The families lived on gleanings of wild wheat and barley, which they boiled or ground between rocks, along with whatever potatoes, squash, beans, and onions they had grown in their gardens. They made corn into hominy. Milk, sugar, molasses, and any kind of fat for cooking were practically impossible to obtain.

In 1906 the first non-Mormon minister in Garfield County, a Presbyterian, started a mission in Panguitch. Children from an Indian school a few miles outside of town made up most of the congregation. However, the programs of the Presbyterian Church—schools, a mothers' club, service groups—appealed to the Panguitch population. Though only one Mormon family converted to Presbyterianism, the Presbyterian Church made a great contribution to the community until it closed in 1943.

In the early 1900s, Andrew Carnegie donated money to build 1,650 library buildings throughout the United States. Panguitch was one of twenty-three cities in Utah chosen as recipient of a Carnegie Library grant. In 1918 the library, which stands at 75 East Center, was constructed. It has continued to serve as the city library since then and is now on the National Register of Historic Places.

Panguitch today has many old brick homes, untouched by remodeling, that still give it the feel of a pioneer town.

Long Valley

The Long Valley in Kane County is east of Zion National Park and includes Glendale, Orderville, and Mount Carmel. No settlement was ever named Long Valley, but the Long Valley Junction is at the top of the valley.

Long Valley is the dividing line between the Great Basin and the Colorado River drainages. From this point the headwaters of the Sevier River flow north and the headwaters of the Virgin River flow south. Long Valley Junction (elevation 7,513 feet) is the second highest pass in Utah.

US 89 drops from Long Valley Junction into the warmer regions of Long Valley. This part of Utah owes its beginnings to Jacob Hamblin, a Mormon leader whose mission in life was making peace with the Indians. The settlement of Kane County was especially dangerous because the Navajos, many recently released from confinement in New Mexico, were very hostile to the white settlers. Hamblin was able to negotiate with them. He acted as interpreter and peacemaker, helping resolve many disputes and saving hundreds of white and Indian lives.

Cattlemen started coming into the area in the late 1850s and early 1860s. In 1864, tentative settlements were made at Kanab and Mount Carmel, but because of conflicts with the Navajos they were abandoned for several years.

Glendale

In 1862 men from Kanarraville explored the Long Valley and found it ideal for cattle grazing. Robert and Isabella Berry settled here and named their new home Berryville. In 1866 they were killed by Indians, and the town was abandoned. In 1871 settlers moved back to the area. Many were Mormons from the Muddy River Mission in Nevada who had been forced to leave because of tax problems. Because it was such a beautiful spot, and because their bishop was from Glendale, Scotland, they named their new town Glendale.

Orderville

The next town on the road reminds us of religious customs long past. Orderville is one of the best-known remnants of the United Order in Utah. In the years 1870–71, settlers from the failed Muddy River Mission of Nevada moved to Mount Carmel in Long Valley. Brigham Young visited the people in 1874 and invited them to join the United Order. He succeeded in enrolling 190 people, who agreed to combine their worldly goods and share all things in common. Because of land disputes in Mount Carmel, they moved a few miles north and formed the community of Orderville.

Those entering the order turned over all their property and money. Workers were given credit for their labor, and all were reimbursed equally no matter what type of labor they performed. If members were unhappy they could withdraw from the order and receive back what they had put in.

In *Twelve Mormon Homes*, Elizabeth Kane describes the Mormon cooperative practice:

> In Utah they have carried the principle of co-operation very far, and finding how well it pays are pushing it in every direction. Each

settlement has its herd, its dairy, its stores, its irrigating channels, and its fields managed on this basis; and the effort so far to restore the primitive Christian communism is entirely successful in settlements where the brethren live alone, without Gentiles to come in on them. One fence will enclose the harvest-fields or cotton-grounds of a whole settlement, each brother doing his share of the labor and being credited with his portion of the produce.

Soon after its inception in Orderville, the United Order had to purchase more property as additional families joined. Within two years the town's population reached nearly 800. The town was set up somewhat like a fort, with houses in blocks of eight and a central dining hall where the community cooked and ate. The men in the order ate first, followed by the women, and then the children. The surrounding farmland was worked communally. Men in the order received $1.50 a day credit. Boys under eighteen received seventy-five cents a day, as did women. Girls from ten to thirteen years old got twenty-five cents a day, and younger ones were credited twelve and a half cents. From the credit received for work, members of the order were required to pay $50 for board and room, $17.50 for men's clothing, and $16.50 for women's clothing.

The people of Orderville wore clothing made from the same fabric and pattern. One boy wanted a pair of pants like those of the boys in other

UNITED ORDER, ORDERVILLE,,UTAH. ESTABLISHED 1875 UNDER THE ORDER OF BRIGHAM YOUNG. NO. 1-RELIEF SOCIETY 2-DINING HALL 3-BIG HOUSE 4-BLACKSMITH SHOP 5-CARPENTER SHOP 6-COMMISSARY 7-ORDER OFFICE AND SHOE SHOP 8-DWELLINGS 9-STABLES 10-FIELDS.

United Order building, Orderville. —UTAH STATE HISTORICAL SOCIETY

towns where free enterprise reigned. In the spring when the lambs' tails were docked, he gathered them up, saved the wool, and traded it in Nephi for a pair of "store-bought" pants. When he returned home, he wore the pants to a dance, greatly impressing all the young people. He was severely reprimanded for using that which belonged to the order for his own purposes, but the pants were taken apart and used to make a pattern for the town. This caused additional problems. It was soon discovered that all the boys were wearing their old pants out on the grindstone so they could have the new style.

For a number of years the order prospered, producing everything necessary to sustain life in the town. The people did so well they were able to purchase a thirty-acre cotton farm in Washington County. However, after the death of Brigham Young in 1877 new difficulties arose in maintaining the United Order. The leaders didn't feel the same support from the Salt Lake authorities as they had from President Young. The order pay system was changed to give more credit to skilled laborers, which caused new problems. In the 1880s, increasing government tensions over polygamy forced the end of the United Order. In 1884 Orderville was surveyed and individual lots were parcelled out. In 1889 the livestock and ranches were sold to individual stockholders. The woolen factory was held jointly by stockholders until 1900, when the charter expired.

Mount Carmel and Mount Carmel Junction

Just a few miles down US 89 from Orderville, Mount Carmel spreads out on both sides of the road in this narrow valley. First settled in 1864, the area was abandoned in 1866 because of Indian conflicts. It was re-settled in 1871 by original settlers and those from the abandoned Muddy River Mission of Nevada. Originally called Windsor, the town was re-named Mount Carmel after an area in Palestine. The name means "a park or garden land."

In 1890 the territorial legislature mandated free public schools, and many were built at that time. Off US 89 is the combination school and LDS church that was built in 1890 in Mount Carmel. Combining a church with a government-run public school may seem strange today, but it was a common practice in the 1800s, when economic concerns were more important than the separation of church and state. The building burned in 1919 and was rebuilt in 1924. Later, the students were bussed to Orderville, but the building continued to serve as a church until 1961, when the Mount Carmel Ward was incorporated with the one in Orderville. The building served ecclesiastical purposes until 1983, when it was abandoned.

Kanab

US 89 continues to Mount Carmel Junction, where, at a group of motels and gas stations, it is joined by UT 9 coming out of Zion National Park. It then climbs the hills and descends to Kanab.

The hidden canyons surrounding Kanab are replete with ancient ruins from the Anasazi and Desert Cultures that roamed southern Utah. The Southern Paiutes also inhabited these valleys; the word *kanab* is derived from the Paiute word for a willow basket used to carry a baby on its mother's back.

The first non–Native Americans to try to settle the area were cattlemen who lived in dugouts along the creek in the late 1850s and early 1860s. After recurring Indian hostilities, they abandoned the area. In 1864 Mormon pioneers built a fort at Kanab under Jacob Hamblin's supervision. The settlement was deserted in 1866 because of conflicts with the Indians.

In 1870 Brigham Young and several church officials declared the site a fine place for a new town. In fact, Young considered Kanab so suitable he claimed one of the city blocks for himself. The president called several families from the Big Cottonwood area of Salt Lake to Kanab.

Kanab was very isolated, bordered as it was by mountains to the north, the Kaibab Plateau and the Grand Canyon to the south, and the Colorado River to the east. One man called it the most inaccessible place in the United States.

One family's experience in Kanab illustrates life in a polygamous home. Artemesia Snow, daughter of LDS apostle and Cotton Mission leader Erastus Snow, wished to marry her childhood sweetheart. However, because of her father's wish that she become a plural wife, she married Franklin Woolley. He was killed by Indians, and in 1873 she became the second wife of Daniel Seegmiller. The Seegmillers were so poor they could hardly afford food. They lived in a rented two-room adobe with a lean-to kitchen on the back and an attic where the children slept. At first the new wife was a burden on the family because of their extreme poverty, but Artemesia soon proved to be a great help and the women learned to love each other. A daughter, Annie Frost, told of the jokes the wives played on her father, "such as not telling him which room he was to sleep in after returning from some business trip. I remember one night they had him trotting back and forth from one room to the other, each saying: 'No, it's not your turn in here.'"

In 1911 some politically prominent men in Kanab thought it would be funny to ask the townspeople to vote for an all-female town council. The joke was on the men, though, when no one would run against the women. The first all-female town council in the United States—a woman mayor and four councilwomen—was elected. Mary Woolley Chamberlain, a polygamous wife (her husband's fifth), lived in hiding for six years during the 1880s so her husband would not be arrested for bigamy. She didn't take her new position as mayor seriously until her father, president of the Kanab Stake, told her it was important. The local newspaper editor also thought the women had great abilities and encouraged them through his newspaper. The outgoing town council gave the women their support. Because the new councilwomen were mothers with young children, they had to meet in their homes. The women had between two and seven children each, and three of the five gave birth during their tenure. They also took care of their homes and families, doing all the typical women's chores. Being Mormon, they also maintained their busy church schedules.

The council's main efforts in civic office involved cleaning up the town. They rid the town of pigsties, liquor, gambling, stray dogs, and Sabbath breaking. They gave prizes for clean streets and sidewalks and fined those who let their wastewater run down the street. Many said these five women accomplished more than any other Kanab City Council had done before them.

Four of the women declined to run for a second term in office, saying they wanted to give someone else a chance to serve. The fifth ran for a second term, but resigned immediately after the election.

The Kanab area is known for the numerous films, television shows, and commercials filmed here. In 1927 *Deadwood Coach* was filmed in southern Utah. The Parry brothers of Kanab were so enthusiastic about the

All-female town council in Kanab. Left to right: Luella Atkin McAllister, Blanche Robinson Hamblin, Mary Woolley Chamberlain (mayor), Tamara Stewart Hamblin, Ada Pratt Seegmiller. —ROGER HOLLAND

Grand Staircase of the Grand Staircase–Escalante National Monument.

potential of their town as a film location that they brought pictures of the region to Hollywood to promote Kanab as a moviemaking center. They were successful. With the cooperation of the whole town, many movies and television shows were filmed in the area; the entire citizenry served as extras when necessary. The television western series *Gunsmoke* was shot in Johnson Canyon near Kanab, and altogether over 300 movies and commercials have been made in the area.

Kane County's proximity to Glen Canyon National Recreation Area, Grand Canyon National Park, Zion National Park, Bryce Canyon National Park, Coral Pink Sand Dunes State Park, Kodachrome Basin State Park, and other recreation locations make the Kanab area attractive for tourists.

Glen Canyon Dam

In 1956 President Dwight D. Eisenhower signed legislation funding Glen Canyon Dam, which would be built just a few miles south of the Utah-Arizona border. The dam was completed in the mid-1960s, and the resulting lake extended 186 miles north up the Colorado River and 71 miles up the San Juan River. The dam had an enormous impact on the economy of the area, both during its construction and later. After roads were built to connect Kanab with Lake Powell, tourists passed through Kanab on their way to the reservoir.

Grand Staircase–Escalante National Monument

On September 18, 1996, flags in Kanab flew at half mast and businesses closed. President Bill Clinton had just designated 1.7 million acres in the Kanab region as a national monument. This coal- and petroleum-rich area had been the last hope for high-paying jobs in a region where environmental laws had reduced lumber and milling work.

Environmentalists and naturalists applauded the creation of the Grand Staircase–Escalante National Monument. Vermillion sandstone mountains, wide-open sagebrush plains, ancient Anasazi rock art and cliff dwellings, deep gorges cut by the Escalante River, and historic pioneer trails are all part of the national monument, the largest in Utah. The Grand Staircase, named for a series of cliffs that rise from the Arizona border to the Aquarius Plateau, is undeveloped by the federal government. The monument encompasses several Utah towns, including Kanab, Tropic, Henrieville, Escalante, and Boulder. It is administered by the Bureau of Land Management.

Paria

At Kanab, US 89A splits off from US 89 and heads south into Arizona toward the North Rim of the Grand Canyon. US 89 leads west to Lake Powell.

On the way to Lake Powell, a dirt road marked "Paria" leads into the washes of the White Cliffs. A few miles up the road is a western town. If you look closely you'll see that the town is crumbling. It is not as old as it seems. This is the Paria movie set, a western town built for the filming of movies and never occupied. The films shot here include *Sergeants Three, Duel of Diablo, Ride in the Whirlwind, MacKenna's Gold,* and *The Outlaw Josie Wales.*

A few miles past the movie set are traces of the real town. Paria, a Paiute name for muddy water, was named for the Paria River. Located on the banks of Paria and Cottonwood Creeks, Paria was first settled in the 1860s, was abandoned because of Indian conflict, and was resettled in 1870. The town served as a polygamist wives' hideout for a number of years because of its isolation. For a time, settlers prospered in Paria with their orchards, gardens, and livestock, but they were plagued by floods and washouts and had to move their homes several times. After years of struggling with the fluctuating streams, the settlers started leaving one by one until 1930, when the town was empty.

Today a few fragments of homes remain along the creek banks where the town once stood. Behind them are the picturesque sandstone cliffs that once sheltered the small community.

Big Water

Farther to the west US 89 arrives at the last town in Utah. Big Water, a fairly recent addition to the Utah landscape, doesn't look like a Utah town. When President Dwight D. Eisenhower signed legislation to fund the Glen Canyon Dam, a town sprang up north of the dam site: Glen Canyon City. After the dam was built, most of the city's residents moved away. However, the town was not destined to stay vacant. Because of the site's remoteness, a group of Mormon fundamentalists headed by Alex Joseph and his nine wives moved there in the 1970s. In 1983 the town was incorporated and Joseph was elected its mayor. He changed the name to Big Water.

Joseph and his many relatives held all the key positions in Big Water until 1994, when Joseph decided not to run for mayor again. His tenure had been a controversial one, plagued by allegations of favoritism and abuse of power. A 1990 vote to disincorporate Big Water failed amidst accusations of election fraud.

UT 132
Nephi–Pigeon Hollow Junction
40 miles

UT 132 squeezes between Mount Nebo to the north and Salt Creek Peak to the south. This was the route the first Sanpete County settlers took in 1849. Many who came later to establish their families, farms, and towns in the valley of the San Pitch River also followed this route.

Fountain Green

Take UT 132 from Nephi; Fountain Green is the first town in Sanpete County. For many years before it was settled, the area was a favorite camping spot for travelers between Sanpete County and Salt Lake City because of its springs and lush meadows. Fountain Green was named for the fountain of fresh mountain water that created the green meadows at the site of the town.

Because of the mountains on either side, the spot was not only a favorite for camping, it was also dangerous—vulnerable to Indian attack. In 1853 an Indian ambush killed the drivers of four wagons enroute from Manti to Salt Lake City.

In 1859 a few men came to survey a new town site at Fountain Green. While they were running lines for the town site, Utes came and stole their horses. The men walked the thirty-two miles back to Santaquin and prepared to return and settle Fountain Green.

Freedom and Wales

From Fountain Green you can either stay on UT 132 to Moroni or head south through more Mormon settlements that hug the foothills.

Freedom was established in 1870. The site proved to be excellent for fruit trees. Dairy cows were also numerous in Freedom. For a time Freedom had an LDS ward, but it was eventually combined with the one at Moroni.

Wales was the site of the first coal mine in Utah. In the 1850s Chief Tabiona showed some Mormon leaders the vein of coal. A few years later, when new Welsh converts arrived in Utah, they were sent to Sanpete County to start extracting the coal from the ground. Settled in 1859, the town was originally called Coal Bed. The mines operated for a number of years, and when the railroad came to central Utah, a special branch line was built to carry the coal from Wales. Better veins were discovered elsewhere, however, and eventually the mines closed and the railroad tracks were torn up.

Settlers remained after the mines closed, adopting the agrarian and ranching life so common in rural Utah. Cowboying paid off during Prohibition for a bootlegger in Wales. He periodically traveled to the spot where he made whiskey. When he was ready to go, the man filled his horse's packsaddle with whiskey, then turned the animal loose to make the twenty-mile trip back home. He drove home in his car, and when authorities who suspected he was bootlegging stopped him and searched his car, they never found the whiskey.

Moroni

The next town south of Fountain Green on UT 132 is Moroni. In 1859 families moved to Moroni and made their homes in dugouts along the banks of the San Pitch River during the fall and winter. The high spring runoff washed away the temporary dwellings. The settlers moved back from the river and established homes, gardens, and canals. In the spring of 1862 the river flooded, filling canals, swamping fields, crumbling adobes, and collapsing buildings. Brigham Young suggested they move the town north into the hills, which they did—they moved about two miles to Moroni's present site. The town was named for the last prophet in the Book of Mormon. He was the same Moroni who returned as an angel to present the Golden Plates to Joseph Smith, from which the young man translated the Book of Mormon.

The white feathers fluttering in the air, settling on tables in the town park, and collecting along the roadsides give a clue to the economic base of this little town. The economy of Moroni and the entire area has been strengthened by the Moroni Feed Company and the Norbest Turkey Plant, which provide employment for much of Sanpete County. The plant provides not only jobs but also a market for farmers' turkeys. Turkeys became an important farm product in the 1920s when other farm crops were in low demand and the economy was severely depressed.

Chester

A few more miles to the southeast, UT 132 brings you to Chester. Chester is at almost the geographical center of Utah, but it is not central in most people's memory. A small farming village in the middle of the Sanpete Valley's river bottoms, Chester was called The Bottoms when the first settlers started farming here in 1870. In 1875 the families moved permanently to their farms, and they soon wanted a post office. They changed the name to Chester, the town in England that had been the home of founder David Candland.

UT 132 joins US 89 at Pigeon Hollow Junction, five miles north of Ephraim.

Sanpete County turkeys.

UT 24
Sigurd–Torrey
66 miles

UT 24 climbs from the agricultural valley of the Sevier River to an 8,406-foot pass on the Paiute–Wayne County line. It then descends into the ranching land of Rabbit Valley, watered by the Fremont River.

RABBIT VALLEY

After the Fish Lake turnoff, UT 24 climbs a bit higher to the pass and drops into a sagebrush-covered valley known to the pioneers as Rabbit Valley. In 1875 the Richfield Cooperative Livestock Company sent their cattle herd to graze in Rabbit Valley. Soon families came to homestead the new territory.

An early inhabitant of Rabbit Valley, William C. Jenson, related the story of how his mother coped with the need to be flexible and innovative in the face of any crisis. A sow with a litter of young pigs decided to scratch her itchy belly on the sharp blade of an ax left in the farmyard, accidentally cutting herself open. The sow's entrails hung out of the gash. William ran and told his mother, who was a skilled cobbler. Some of the children held the pig down while the others helped their mother clean the dragging intestines in a basin of water. Mrs. Jenson pushed the vital

Rabbit Valley was a lonely place in the nineteenth century.
—UTAH STATE HISTORICAL SOCIETY

organs back into the sow. She tried to sew the skin together but it was too tough, so she sent the children for an awl. With the aid of the awl, the mother managed to sew up the poor struggling pig. When the operation was over, the sow was released and she settled down carefully to nurse her litter. She carried the scar, but survived the ordeal.

Loa

The first town in Rabbit Valley is the Wayne County seat, Loa. Early in the history of the LDS Church, missionaries proselytized in Hawaii. Franklin Young, one of the missionaries, suggested naming the new town for Mauna Loa, the highest peak in Hawaii. He believed a nearby mountain resembled the Hawaiian volcano.

Families started moving to Loa in 1876, but it wasn't until 1880 that the town was surveyed into the typical Mormon plan of blocks and straight grid streets.

Lyman

West of Loa, Lyman is a smaller version of its neighbor. In 1876 families settled the other side of the river from Loa. When LDS apostle Francis M. Lyman visited the town in 1893, he helped them select a better town site on higher ground. The people moved to the site he had chosen,

The old gristmill between Bicknell and Torrey.

dragging their homes with them. They named the new town after the apostle who had guided their decision.

Lyman remains a small farming community and also supports sheep ranching. A mill there manufactures log homes.

Fremont

Looking north from Loa, you can seen the town of Fremont sheltered against the Thousand Lake and Fish Lake Mountains. Named for the Fremont River, Fremont was the first settlement in Wayne County. Utahans have long been known for their large families. This was especially true in the days of polygamy. Though land seemed endless, good farm and grazing ground filled up quickly, and pioneers were always ready to move into new territory. Soon after Sevier County farmers started moving their cattle into Rabbit Valley, homesteaders followed. For a short time people moved into the Fremont area in large numbers. In the 1890s the town had enough children to support five schoolteachers. However, for various reasons, many families moved away, and by 1895 the town needed only two schoolteachers.

Bicknell

In 1875 cattle ranchers Albert Thurber and Beason Lewis built the first houses in Thurber, which would later become Bicknell. In 1895 apostles Francis M. Lyman and J. Golden Kimball suggested that the residents of Thurber move north to where a better water supply was available. The settlers obediently built new homes and abandoned the schoolhouse they had constructed in 1890.

The town was called Thurber until 1914, when Thomas W. Bicknell from Providence, Rhode Island, offered his 1,000-volume library to any town in Utah that would change its name to his. Thurber in Wayne County and Grayson (now Blanding) in San Juan County competed for the library. They each ended up with half the library; Thurber changed its name to Bicknell and Grayson became Blanding—Bicknell's wife's maiden name.

The Old Gristmill

Continuing on UT 24 east from Bicknell, you will pass a weathered two-story structure—the old Nielson gristmill, constructed in 1890. The mill served the grinding needs of Wayne County residents for more than forty years. Not just a place to grind wheat for flour and animal feeds, it also had an old fireplace adjacent to it that was an ideal spot for socializing, roasting hot dogs, and occasional romancing. The mill is not open to the public.

Old log meetinghouse in Torrey.

Torrey

Torrey is the last town on UT 24 before it enters Capitol Reef National Park. From the Teasdale turnoff, UT 24 follows a line of red cliffs, crumbling farms, and grazing cattle. At the western edge of Capitol Reef National Park, against the backdrop of spectacular crimson cliffs, sits the high desert town of Torrey.

Attracted to the waters of Sand Creek, Peter Brown was the first to farm along its banks in the early 1880s. Others followed, but water was never plentiful enough to sustain a large population and many moved away. In 1894 some people from Thurber (later Bicknell) purchased water rights to Sand Creek so that more settlers could farm. To supplement the water supply, they dug a canal from the Fremont River, enabling farmers to the west of Torrey to have water. Later, after many struggles and failures, a pipe was installed across the river that sent water to Torrey.

The town went through many incarnations as Youngstown, Central, Popular, Poverty Flat, and Bonita, until it finally became Torrey in honor of a Spanish-American War hero from Wyoming.

An old log meetinghouse on Main Street was completed in 1898 and served as both church and school. Made of sawed logs that dovetail at the corners, the structure is the only known log meetinghouse still standing in the state. In 1917 the town built a new school and in 1928 a new church, but the old log building continued as a meeting place until the 1970s. In 1991 the structure was moved 100 yards to the west by the Daughters of the Utah Pioneers so the LDS Church could expand its local building.

UT 24
Torrey–Hanksville
51 miles

Capitol Reef National Park

The area that now encompasses Capitol Reef National Park was first inhabited by Fremont Indians. Many traces of this nomadic group have been found in the park. Later the Paiute Indians hunted and gathered in the region. When early white pioneers arrived, they saw this fantastic wonderland as an inconvenience. They had to figure out a way to get through the narrow washes without being washed away by flash floods. On the other hand, the area was perfect for outlaws, who could hide in these same washes, ravines, and rock formations with any horses or cattle they may have recently rustled.

The region first became an important tourist mecca in the early 1900s when "Wayne Wonderland" (it was in Wayne County) was made a state park. In 1937 Wayne Wonderland became Capitol Reef National Monument. The name came from the rock formations in the middle section of the park, where the huge wall of stone (or reef) seems to be carved with domes that resemble the U.S. Capitol building. With the creation of Lake Powell in the 1960s, Capitol Reef received more attention. Its area was expanded, and it became a national park in 1971.

UT 24 travels through the central section of the park, where the dome-shaped Navajo sandstone walls are easily identifiable. The north section of the park is Cathedral Valley, a spectacular and sometimes bizarre no-man's-land accessible only by dirt roads. The southern part of the park is dominated by the Waterpocket Fold, a large bend in the reef. Dirt roads lead to washes bearing old pioneer signatures and other interesting markings. Farther south, the Burr Trail crosses the Waterpocket Fold.

Fruita

Within the boundaries of Capitol Reef are traces of a small town established in 1878 called Junction. The climate here was ideal for growing all sorts of fruits and vegetables. Because of this, and because of the abundance of Utah towns already called Junction, when the town got its post office between 1900 and 1903, it changed its name to Fruita. Built up

Old Fruita one-room schoolhouse.

around its orchards, the town peaked in the 1920s and 1930s. After Fruita became part of the national monument in 1937, the population dwindled.

Today the only permanent residents of Fruita are park rangers. The old one-room schoolhouse, built between 1892 and 1894, still stands, and visitors can push a button to hear of the experiences of one of the teachers who lived in Fruita and taught at the school. The old orchards remain an integral part of the park. Visitors lucky enough to pass through at the right season can pick the fruits and enjoy the sweetness of the harvest.

Caineville

From Capitol Reef, UT 24 winds through odd greenish-tinged hills of ancient volcanic ash to Caineville. The settlers who first came to Caineville in 1882 and 1883 were called there by their church leader, President A. K. Thurber. They traveled through Capitol Wash (now Capitol Reef Gorge) and Grand Wash. Both animals and people found the trip very trying, especially when flash floods came through. Later flash floods destroyed cars and those who drove them through the wash. The Capitol Reef visitor center has pictures documenting the road used by the first settlers.

Though getting to Caineville was tough, the conditions there were excellent for farming. Farmers grew a wide variety of crops.

The Mormons do not pay their clergy. They "call" people to positions, and those who serve do so without pay. Sometimes the calls are not greeted with enthusiasm. When Walter Hanks was called as the bishop of the Caineville Ward he said he would rather go on a mission for fifteen years than be bishop. The stake president told him he could be bishop for longer than that if he behaved himself. He served eighteen years as bishop of the Caineville Ward.

The little community flourished until a series of flash floods washed it away. The first was in 1896, and they continued coming every few years, until the worst one took out the town in 1909. Most of the people sold or abandoned their property and moved away.

Today, much of the area around Caineville is cultivated. You'll see no sign of a town, but scattered dwellings are visible on the farms. The people of Caineville only recently got their first telephones. In order to reach someone in Hanksville, the nearest town, a call has to be routed through Moab, Price, and back down to Hanksville, making it a long-distance call.

Dirt roads between mileposts 98 and 99 from Caineville head north into the Cathedral Valley section of Capitol Reef National Park and into the San Rafael Swell. Both of these areas, so isolated from habitation, are spectacularly beautiful with a romantic feeling of the wonders of nature.

Hanksville

Hanksville was settled by Ebeneazer Hanks, his family, and a group of people from Iron County attracted by the lush grasses along the Fremont River. In 1892 gold was discovered in the Henry Mountains, giving temporary hope of great wealth to local residents. But an outside company came in and mined it, shipping out all that was there via Green River within three years.

Pioneers who came to Hanksville in 1881 said the area had previously been inhabited by a man named John Graves. Graves had been on one of John Wesley Powell's expeditions and had lived here alone, prospecting in the Henry Mountains with Cass Hite. When Hite took a trip down to the crossing on the Colorado River, Graves disappeared, and locals said he became the ghost of Mount Pennel in the Henry Mountains.

At one time Hanksville was a trading spot for Butch Cassidy and other outlaws. "Robbers' Roost," the most southerly of the outlaw stations, was at the extreme east end of Wayne County, about forty miles east of Hanksville. No road leads from Hanksville into Robbers' Roost Country, but primitive roads lead to the Roost from the north and the south.

During the uranium boom of the 1950s, activity in the San Rafael Swell gave a push to the economy of Hanksville. However, the mining activity was not long-lived and the sleepy town returned to business as usual.

Though the 1914 LDS meetinghouse is the only original historic public building remaining in the town, a mill that was relocated to Hanksville from the Henry Mountains is also interesting. The Wolverton Mill was constructed in 1921 by Edwin Thatcher Wolverton, a would-be miner from Maine. He heard stories of lost Spanish gold in the mountains and came west to find out for himself. The mill is unique both in its construction and in its function. Rather than building it by notching and overlapping timbers, Wolverton stacked the logs and braced them with other heavy posts. The mill was used both for crushing ore and for cutting wood. The Bureau of Land Management moved the mill to its present location in 1974 and finished restoring it in 1988. The public is welcome at the mill, and short tours, restrooms, and picnic facilities are available.

Because of its proximity to Lake Powell and Capitol Reef National Park, Hanksville has several gas stations, restaurants, and motels.

UT 12
Torrey–Panguitch
128 miles

From the scarlet pinnacles of Bryce Canyon National Park to the verdant forests of Boulder Mountain, US 12 winds through some of the most magnificent terrain in the United States. Many consider this particular section of the highway to be the most scenic. It climbs to mountain meadows with rugged vistas, traverses chasms, and plunges into red rock country. The road has only been completely paved since the mid-1980s; before that, this was one of the nation's most remote areas.

Today, UT 12 is still isolated. The ranchers like it that way; it keeps their ranges wide open. They don't, however, want their isolation enforced by the federal government and are in a constant battle with groups like the Sierra Club and the Southern Utah Wilderness Alliance over wilderness issues. Many ranchers are angry about the new Grand Staircase–Escalante National Monument, which will control so much of their rangeland.

Grover

Grover is a very sparsely populated area in the low pines and junipers at the base of Boulder Mountain.

In 1880 two men, Alex Keele and Will Bullard, brought their cattle here and planted grain. They settled on Carcass Creek, so named because its steep banks prevented animals from getting out once they had slipped in. In 1884 they sold out for $500, paid in mules and horses, to some men from Escalante. By 1889 five families and three bachelors lived in Carcass. At the turn of the century the settlement had 115 inhabitants, but by 1952 only four families remained.

The people apparently didn't like having their town named for the animal remains they found floating in the creek; when they got a post office they changed the name to Grover for Grover Cleveland, the U.S. president at the time.

In 1935 the Works Progress Administration built a school at Grover. It didn't see much use because of the small population. Students were soon being bussed to Bicknell, fifteen miles away. In 1941 the school was closed down permanently. It is now on the National Register of Historic Places.

Boulder

Boulder sits at the base of Boulder Mountain. Also known as the Aquarius Plateau, the mountain was once a great obstacle between Garfield County and the northern settlements. Now it is viewed as a recreational asset. The fine streams and lakes of Boulder Mountain offer some of the state's best fishing as well as trails for dirt bikers and snowmobilers.

Boulder is perhaps most famous for being the last town in the continental United States to receive its mail by mule. It was called the "last frontier" until 1942, when the first vehicular mail delivery arrived in this isolated Utah town.

As was the case with many other outlying Utah communities settled late in the nineteenth century, Boulder was established by ranchers attracted by the lush grasses. They brought their herds here in about 1879, and made a more permanent settlement in 1889.

For many years Boulder remained unsurveyed, so technically the residents didn't own property and didn't have to pay taxes. In 1933, twenty-one of the town's thirty-one families decided they wanted the privilege of ownership, so they petitioned the Department of the Interior to stake out their town and make them official.

During the Great Depression of the 1930s, unemployment in Utah reached 36 percent, the fourth highest in the nation. As a result, federal spending on public works projects was high in Utah—the ninth highest in the nation. There were 233 Works Progress Administration buildings constructed in the state during the decade. One of these was the Boulder Elementary School, built in 1936. Because only 130 WPA buildings remain in Utah, this school has been placed on the National Register of Historic Places.

Boulder remained completely isolated until 1935, when the Civilian Conservation Corps built a road over Hell's Backbone, a spectacular narrow ridge between Boulder and Escalante. This is now a graded dirt road. The paved highway between Escalante and Boulder was built later. The town received electricity in 1948.

Anasazi Indian Village State Park

Anasazi State Park is at the north end of Boulder. During the construction of the Glen Canyon Dam, the University of Utah's anthropology department was commissioned to document any archaeologically significant sites in south-central and southeastern Utah. As a part of this study, they excavated the site of an ancient Anasazi village at Boulder dating from about A.D. 1050–1150. They discovered eighty-seven structures and large numbers of artifacts in the process. In 1968 the site was designated a state park. The park includes a museum containing artifacts, a re-creation of an Anasazi dwelling, and the actual site of the village.

BURR TRAIL

In a countryside where fabulous scenery is commonplace, the Burr Trail is beyond description. It also epitomizes the struggle in southern Utah between environmental groups and local government authorities. Few roads run east and west across the sandstone and shale reefs and canyons of southern Utah. The Burr Trail, which does so, was developed as a livestock path by John Atlantic (born while his parents were immigrating to Utah across the Atlantic Ocean) Burr.

Recently the trail has been a source of serious controversy between Garfield County officials and environmental groups. Residents of Garfield County had long felt their economy would be improved by a paved road connecting Boulder with Bullfrog Basin at Lake Powell. Government officials wanted to pave the trail, while environmentalists felt the fabulous country crossed by the trail should be preserved in as untouched a condition as possible. Garfield County would start grading the road, and environmental groups would obtain court orders halting the work. The process went back and forth for years, until finally in the 1990s Garfield County won and paved the Burr Trail all the way from Boulder to Lake Powell, except the section that crosses Waterpocket Fold in Capitol Reef National Park. This section, though unpaved, is well graded and easily passable.

Calf Creek Recreation Area

Once you leave Boulder and begin climbing the narrow stone bridge that supports the road over the deep gorges, the reason it took so long for roads to reach this remote ranching settlement becomes clear. The highway plunges from the high rock ledges down to the river bottoms of Calf Creek. Ancient petroglyphs decorate some of the narrow canyon walls here. Take the Lower Calf Creek Falls hike and experience the beauty and ancient wonders of the canyon.

Escalante

The highway ascends to the Escalante Rim, at an elevation of 7,149 feet, then descends to the basin occupied by Escalante. Just before reaching the town you'll see a sign for the Hole-in-the-Rock Trail. This is the point where members of the San Juan Mission departed on their treacherous journey to claim and settle the San Juan Valley in 1879. Adventurous types with a four-wheel-drive vehicle can take this trail (part graded road, part rough terrain) all the way to the Hole-in-the-Rock historic site. Those willing to brave the 100-odd-mile journey will be rewarded with some amazing scenery.

The Potato Valley, so called because of the wild potatoes growing here, was first discovered in 1866 by Mormons in pursuit of Indians during the Black Hawk War. In 1875 a group from Panguitch decided to come and make a community in this rugged section of Utah. They worked for months to build a road through the treacherous country, and the first families moved here in 1876. The name Escalante was suggested by some members of the Powell Colorado River expedition. Father Escalante never actually passed through here, though he did explore much of southern Utah.

Within a few years of Escalante's settlement, ranchers learned of the excellent rangeland in the area and brought large herds to graze. At one point early in the twentieth century, 20,000 head of cattle and 60,000 sheep grazed on the range. Within a short time they had depleted the range, and by the 1930s it was completely devastated. Passed in 1934, the Taylor Act greatly limited grazing on open range, and the restoration of the grasslands was begun.

Escalante still has many old pioneer homes and barns. The Mormon Tithing Office at 40 South Center Street was built in 1884. The law of tithing, in which one-tenth of a member's gain is donated to the church, has been important since the church first organized in 1830. During Utah's pioneer times, cash was scarce, so members donated one-tenth of whatever they grew or produced. Hence, the tithing office and its yard and barns were a vital part of the community. Not only did members bring their produce, milk, eggs, livestock, etc., here to donate, but those in need came to receive help. The tithes were distributed to the poor and used to pay laborers working on church-sponsored projects. Starving members in communities like St. George greatly benefitted from tithes paid in other locations.

Escalante Petrified Forest State Park

The petrified forest is on UT 12 about one mile west of town. The ancient tree trunks may have been preserved by massive volcanic activity then turned to stone by silica carried in the groundwater. Wide Hollow Reservoir, a part of the park, is open to water recreationists. The park also has campgrounds.

Henrieville

After another thirty miles through magnificent country, UT 12 descends to Henrieville. Like so much of Garfield County, Henrieville is in a spectacular setting, surrounded by buff-colored bluffs, with views of the red cliffs of Bryce Canyon to the west. James Henrie was the first president of the Panguitch Stake, and when the first people came here from Cannonville in 1878 they gave the new town his name. Like many communities in southern Utah, where rainfall is sporadic and heavy when it comes, Henrieville has lost valuable farmlands in flash floods.

The towns of Cannonville, Henrieville, and Escalante suffered heavily in the 1930s when years of overgrazing had finally ravaged their land. Completely reliant on the livestock industry, families were left desolate. In 1935, 70 percent of the 1,000 residents of Escalante received government relief. The ranchers slowly dug out of their troubles, but life will never be easy for those who struggle to make a living in this harsh land.

The schoolhouse, built in 1881, remains and now serves as city hall.

Cannonville

Just a short distance from Henrieville, UT 12 rounds a bend at Cannonville. Cannonville occupies a sheltered valley surrounded by red and varicolored sandstone cliffs. It was settled in the 1870s by ranchers who sought the grasses to feed their livestock. The first residents of the town called it Clifton because of the beautifully colored cliffs nearby. They built their cabins a mile and a quarter south of the present location. When they decided to move, they carried their houses with them. They changed the name to Cannonville for apostle George Q. Cannon, but some of the residents thought the town was too small to have the name of such a large weapon, so they nicknamed it "Gun Shot."

The land around Cannonville was good and the Paria River irrigated the fields, but then it started carrying the soil away with it. Up to one-third of the farmland that existed in 1880 was subsequently eroded and carried away by flash floods. Evidence of the floods is visible today in the eroded riverbanks. Irrigation was relatively easy in Cannonville, but the upper part of the valley couldn't be watered by the Paria, so a nine-and-three-quarter-mile canal was built to the Sevier River, which flows north of Bryce Canyon.

In 1949 Cannonville residents dreamed of their town becoming an important tourist spot because of their proximity to Grosvenor Arch, the Paria River Canyon, and the Crossing of the Fathers on the Colorado River (the spot where Spanish monks chipped out steps in the rock bank of the Colorado River). If good roads were built to those areas, tourist dollars would come to town. However, Glen Canyon Dam was built a few years later, flooding forever the historic spot where the Spanish fathers had crossed the Colorado River. The road to Grosvenor Arch is now part of Grand Staircase–Escalante National Monument, so perhaps Cannonville's dreams may finally come true.

Cannonville is the best point from which to access Kodachrome Basin State Park, another display of the geological wonders of southern Utah. A well-graded dirt-and-gravel road heads a few miles southeast to the park. For the more adventurous, this same road continues southeast past Grosvenor Arch, through Cottonwood Canyon, along the Paria River, and all the way to US 89 west of Big Water. In good weather the road is passable by two-wheel-drive vehicles, and well worth the detour.

Tropic

From Cannonville UT 12 heads north to the village of Tropic. It would be hard to order a better backdrop than Tropic's. Immediately to the west are the vermillion cliffs of Bryce Canyon. Surrounding the little town are other brightly colored buttes and mountains, topped with deep green conifer forests.

Though relatively high in altitude, Tropic is slightly lower than Panguitch. The people from Panguitch who settled here felt the climate was downright tropical compared to their own.

In 1890 the people of Cannonville finished building a canal from the Sevier River. It was in a good position to irrigate the fields of what is now Tropic. A town was formed in 1892, and soon after a Mormon ward was organized. The citizens built several sawmills and shipped lumber all over southern Utah.

Today Tropic is in an ideal location to profit from the resorts and national parks of southern Utah. The crude little cabin that once belonged to Ebenezer Bryce, who discovered the canyon of the same name, is now a museum on UT 12 in Tropic.

Bryce Canyon National Park

UT 12 enters a conifer forest as it rises in altitude toward the national park. The pink cliffs and sandstone formations, the most distinctive feature of Bryce Canyon, are especially beautiful viewed from the canyon bottom at sunrise or sunset. The high plateau offers year-round recreational opportunities. Some areas in the park reach an elevation of nearly 10,000 feet.

Ebenezer Bryce built a cabin near the mouth of the canyon (below the park, in Tropic) in about 1875 and raised his cattle there. Utah folklore tells the story of Bryce herding his cows near the canyon when he lost one. He looked down into the richly colored maze of rock and is supposed to have called it a "hell of a place to lose a cow."

In 1916 homesteader Reuben (Ruby) Syrett and his family became early promoters of the canyon's wonders, taking friends out to see it from their ranch a few miles away. Word spread, and soon the Syretts were putting up tents to house visitors. Later the family built Ruby's Inn, now a prominent local landmark.

After the public began to discover the canyon, the Union Pacific Railroad jumped in. The Union Pacific was largely responsible for the development of the park. Hoping to encourage use of its rail lines and other transportation, the company built the Bryce Canyon Lodge and its cabins. The central part of the lodge was built in 1924, the wings in 1926, and the cabins in 1929. All are listed on the National Register of Historic Places. Bryce Canyon became a national monument in 1923 and a national park in 1928.

Bryce Canyon Lodge.

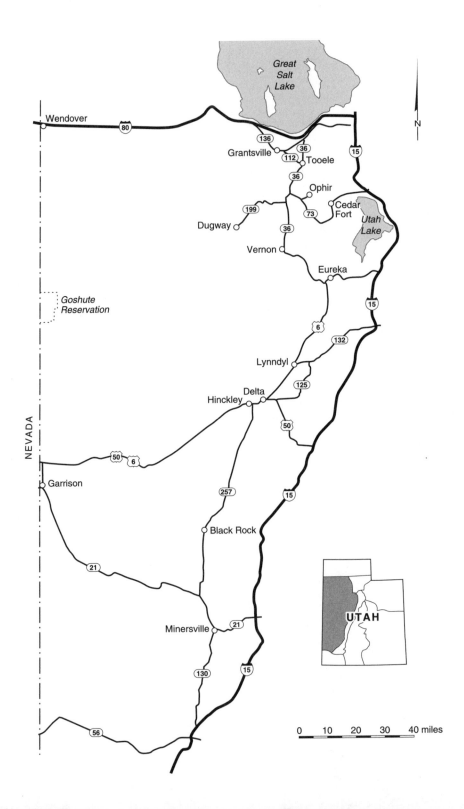

Great
Salt
Lake

Wendover

80

136

Grantsville
36
112
Tooele

15

36

Ophir

199
73

Cedar
Fort
Utah
Lake

Dugway
36

Vernon

Eureka

15

Goshute
Reservation

6

132

Lynndyl

125

Delta
Hinckley

50

NEVADA

50 6

Garrison

257

15

Black Rock

21

Minersville
21

130
15

UTAH

56

0   10   20   30   40 miles

PART VI

The West Desert

The western basins and ranges of Utah include the state's least populated areas. Few paved roads penetrate the flat wastelands and rugged mountains in the region. Mormon pioneers quickly scouted out the few valleys suitable for an agrarian society. Pony Express and Overland Stage riders galloped through the valleys along the Tooele-Juab County line for a relatively short period of time. Later, miners built boomtowns in a few mineral-rich locations. The rest has been left mostly untouched and free from any traces of society.

The section designated as the West Desert is intersected by only one interstate highway: I-80 crosses the desert from Salt Lake City to Wendover. UT 36 connects the Tintic Mining District and the Tooele Valley with I-80. US 6 is the only major road crossing the southern desert; it goes from I-15 through Delta to Nevada.

I-80
Salt Lake City–Wendover
120 miles

From Salt Lake City I-80 quickly rounds the Oquirrh Mountains, passes the populated areas of Tooele County, and travels on to the salt flats.

THE SALT FLATS

The trip across I-80 from the southern tip of the Great Salt Lake to Wendover is an easy hour and a half drive through low mountain ranges and barren, white, salty plains. From a speeding car these plains look like they'd be easy to cross even without a road. Indeed, parts of the salt flats

243

Lansford Hastings.
—UTAH STATE
HISTORICAL SOCIETY

are excellent speedways, and many world records have been set on this seemingly endless expanse.

However, the salt flats can be deceptive. In many places a layer of muddy slush underlies the hard crust of salt. For heavy vehicles, particularly those with narrow tires, sinking into this substance can mean never moving again.

The men and women who attempted to cross this plain in the 1840s discovered the cruel realities of the Great Salt Desert. Trapper Jedediah Smith, along with two companions, crossed the desert in 1827 returning to Utah from California. The men nearly died in the crossing and had to eat their horses along the way.

John C. Frémont was the next to cross the great field of salt in October 1845 after he and his group had explored the region around the Great Salt Lake. Having stopped at the springs near Grantsville to prepare for their journey, they rounded the mountain into Skull Valley and headed straight across the desert toward Pilot Peak, their next source of water. With Frémont were Kit Carson, Auguste Archambeau, and a number of other men. They set out toward evening and traveled through the night in order to avoid the heat of the day. The reflection of the moon on the salt made it easy to see their way. They traveled all the following day, too, to reach the springs at Pilot Peak. Because they had healthy mules and no heavy wagons, the seasoned explorers made excellent time across the desert without any loss of life or property. Others who came later were not so lucky.

Lansford W. Hastings

As a self-proclaimed expert in traveling the West, Lansford Hastings can be held responsible for the difficulties so many pioneers suffered on the salt flats, and ultimately, for the tragedy of the Donner party.

Born about 1818 in Ohio, Hastings made his way west in 1842, first to Oregon, then on to California. In California, with high hopes of a political future, he wrote *The Emigrants' Guide to Oregon and California* in 1845. In a time when few people besides mountain men had ever traveled west, this was one of the first guidebooks for pioneers, and it was used extensively by those who packed their belongings and headed to the promised land of eternal summer. The main problem with the book was that at the time he wrote it, Hastings had never traveled the route he suggested: over the Great Salt Desert south and west of the Great Salt Lake.

Hastings made his first journey over the salt flats in the spring of 1846. He was headed east from California to recruit immigrants, whom he hoped would install him as president of California (which was not yet part of the United States). He and a small group of men traveled by horseback across the desert, unaware of the perils that awaited heavier wagons, which would sink into the mud hidden under the hard crust of surface salt.

James Clyman, who was with Hastings on this trip, wrote in his journal on May 28, 1846, while camped in the middle of the great desert, that

> this is the most desolate country perhaps on the whole globe, there being not one spear of vegetation, and of course no kind of animal can subsist; and it is not yet ascertained to what extent this immense salt and sand plain can be south of where we are now.

Anxious to steer prospective immigrants over this new route, Hastings made light of the difficulties when he encountered pioneers in Wyoming. He managed to divert a number of groups from the Fort Hall (Idaho) road, telling them they could shave 300 or 400 miles off their journey by taking the route south of the Great Salt Lake. Hastings led the first migrant party with wagons into the desert in August 1846. The crossing proved much more difficult than it had been with only horses. The oxen pulling the heavily loaded wagons could not travel as quickly as horses, and the wheels of the wagons stuck in the salt-encrusted mud. In *Salt Desert Trails*, Samuel C. Young, an observer on this trip, gives the following description of what occurred in the white desert:

Hastings had made them believe that the desert was but forty miles across. When they arrived there they . . . filled all their vessels full of water, procured all the grass they could take with them, to feed and sustain their stock. . . . It was a blessing that they were ignorant of what was before them. They were led to believe that they would reach water and grass by noon; full of hope they again started their jaded and trusty teams. They traveled until noon, the stock showing great distress; they stopped to feed them some grass and give them a little water, which comprised nearly all they had laid in.

The emigrants by this time had become very much discouraged. The eye could not detect the end of the plain. But no time was to be lost, so they started again, in the midst of the glare of the sun at noon-day, upon this still, vast, white salt plain. . . . From the middle of the evening one disaster after another happened nearly every step of the way. Wagons were abandoned; such of the oxen as could travel were taken out and driven along; others would give up and lie down, even after the yoke was taken off, and neither persuasion nor the whip could make them budge. These misfortunes continued and increased during that evening, until it seemed as if all were lost. . . .

They struggled on through that long, dark and lonely night, still praying for water and grass; but the morning was again ushered in with the sun's reflection upon the white salt plains, with no signs of the end.

Hastings stayed with his group through the ordeal of crossing the Great Salt Desert, then through the desolate valleys and mountains of Nevada, and over the Sierra Nevada into California. In California he managed to secure a position in John C. Frémont's battalion, and later practiced law during the wild gold rush years.

Though he was born in the free state of Ohio, Hastings joined the Confederacy at the outbreak of the Civil War, during which he proposed an unfeasible plan for capturing California, Arizona, and New Mexico for the South. When the war ended he devised another scheme. He led a group of southerners who didn't wish to pledge their allegiance to the United States to establish a Confederate colony on the Amazon River in Brazil. He published a guidebook to the Amazon, *Emigrant's Guide to Brazil*, in Alabama, and led a group to a place near present-day Santarem, Brazil. On his return voyage to pick up more recruits for his colony, Lansford Hastings died on board the ship.

Some three weeks after Hastings led the first group over the Great Salt Desert, the Donner party made the crossing with equal difficulty. Added to the delays they'd experienced cutting through the Wasatch Mountains, the time spent trudging across the desert was time they could not afford. Thus their tragic fate was sealed.

The Donner party was the last group to cross the salt flats in 1846. The infamy of the Donner party discouraged migrating groups from

Most traces of emigrant parties that crossed the salt flats in the 1840s are gone now, but for many years bones (such as those of this abandoned horse), wagon pieces, and other discarded items could be found encrusted in the salt. —UTAH STATE HISTORICAL SOCIETY

attempting the route for awhile. The year 1849, however, brought new incentives for a quicker route to California. The scent of gold reached all the way to the East Coast. By late summer travelers were flooding into Salt Lake City, where they enjoyed the first fresh vegetables and home-cooked meals they had tasted in many months. Some of them headed north for a safer route to California, but many were afraid all the gold would be gone if they didn't arrive in California quickly. They braved the more direct route across the Great Salt Desert and suffered like those who had attempted it previously. The dangerous and costly route was finally abandoned, and after 1850 those immigrating to California took the southerly road through Los Angeles. In 1854 a new route was surveyed that located water farther south, and in 1859 General Johnston's soldiers, invading Utah, outlined an even better course south of Tooele that was eventually used by the Pony Express and the Overland Stage Company.

In 1907 the Western Pacific Railroad laid its tracks across the salt flats near where the migrant parties had crossed. In 1916 a dirt road for automobiles was laid near the railroad, but most of it washed away in the winter and the underground mud was still a problem. Finally a better road was built in 1924, making it possible to travel straight west from Salt Lake City to Nevada over a safe route.

William Rishel found out that crossing the salt flats on a bicycle can be as grueling as crossing them on horseback. —LDS CHURCH HISTORICAL DEPARTMENT

The Great Bicycle Race

Over time, the trials of the Donner party and others who had crossed the Great Salt Desert in the mid-1840s dimmed for some. One young man who thought he could defeat the desert was William D. Rishel. Rishel, recently moved from Wyoming to Salt Lake City in 1896, was asked by William Randolph Hearst to map the western section of a transcontinental bicycle race. Rishel planned the route across the desert south of the Great Salt Lake. Though warned by many people that it was too dangerous, Rishel and his friend Charlie Emise took their bikes to Terrace, twenty-eight miles southwest of Park Valley, to test the crossing in preparation for the race. With some sandwiches, canteens, and a trail map, they set off at 2:00 A.M. At first they rode quickly, but soon they hit the mud and their tires sunk into the briny goo. They could barely carry their bikes through the sticky mess. The heat of day sapped their strength and they ran short of water. They made it to a drip of water in the Lakeside Mountains that revived them a bit, but it took hours to fill their canteens. They slogged on through the mud and heat. Finally, twenty hours after they began, the bikers dragged into Grantsville. They still suggested the race take that route, but it detoured north of the lake because of a bad storm.

Bonneville Speedway

The Bonneville Salt Flats International Race Track lies a few miles north of the first Wendover exit off I-80. The world-famous racetrack has been the site of numerous speed and endurance records.

The first migrants to cross the Bonneville Salt Flats were out to set their own speed record: they hoped to reach California faster than they would have by traveling the longer road through Idaho. Years later, automobiles set speed records on these white expanses. Ferg Johnson was one of the first to test the speed of his car on the salt flats. He drove his Packard over the vast flatland in 1911.

The first high-speed racing event here took place in 1914, followed by years of eventful records and races on the eighty-feet-wide, ten-mile-long course. The site was developed for better racing in the 1930s. Until 1947, when the record of 400 miles per hour was set, a new speed record was broken every year. Since then, records have been more difficult to break, but the salt flats still see amazing speeds every year when cars come to race on the glaring white stretches of salt. If you choose to drive onto the salt, use caution in venturing too far north, where pioneers of the 1840s became mired in the salty muck.

Wendover

The great expanses of salt stretch all the way to the Silver Island Mountains, where Utah meets Nevada. Straddling this border is Wendover, a town distinctly divided in appearance as well as by the state line. On

Ab Jenkins in his "Mormon Meteor," Bonneville Speedway.
—UTAH STATE HISTORICAL SOCIETY

the Utah side of the line, modest motels, convenience stores, and gas stations offer every amenity to interstate travelers. At Wendover, Nevada, glaring neon signs and casinos announce the border without having to say "Nevada" at all. In recent years Wendover, Utah, has tried unsuccessfully to convince the Utah legislature to legalize gambling so it can compete with Wendover, Nevada.

The town's name is derived from "wending over" the desert. Wendover is the only city in Utah that sets its clocks in the Pacific time zone.

Nothing existed at Wendover until 1907, when the Western Pacific Railroad blazed an iron route across the barren salt flats. The closest available water to the site was in the mountains twenty-five miles to the north. With water so difficult to obtain and the number of people crossing the salt flats restricted mainly to those on trains, Wendover saw little growth until events on the other side of the world made a lasting change in this desert oasis.

In 1940, as worldwide conflict escalated, the United States government started looking for suitable training locations for its air force. Wendover, because of its isolation, good rail access, and year-round flying weather, proved an excellent spot. At first the site was intended to be fairly limited, but after December 7, 1941, the base escalated to a huge 3.5 million acres, the nation's largest military reserve. The 509th Composite, which dropped the atomic bombs on Hiroshima and Nagasaki, Japan, trained at Wendover from October 1944 to June 1945. The air force base, though still intact, closed in 1963, but the training grounds where fighter jets soar over the wastelands west of the Great Salt Lake remain in continual use.

Danger Cave

Northeast of Wendover, against the Silver Island Mountains, is Danger Cave, inhabited many thousands of years ago by desert Indians. This site is one of the oldest known habitations in the United States, occupied long before Mesa Verde in Colorado or Hovenweep in Utah. Evidence collected in Danger Cave and other caves in the area suggests that Desert Culture natives existed in Utah more than 10,000 years ago. These people lived in groups of twenty-five to thirty extended family members. They spent most of their time gathering food for survival—pine nuts and seeds, plants, and meat. Unfortunately, the cave was long ago emptied of any archaeologically significant items, and the state of Utah, which owns it, is considering closing it due to lack of funding.

UT 138
Lake Point–Rowley Junction
23 miles

Lake Point and Mills Junction

The UT 138 exit from I-80 leads into a brief corridor of gas stations and convenience stores and continues through present-day Lake Point and Mills Junction, two adjacent communities whose borders essentially overlap. This corridor was an important meeting place in pioneer times.

Near here, Adobe Rock, a large outcrop at the northwest point of the Oquirrh Mountains, was a favorite pioneer rendezvous spot. Its name came from a small adobe house Captain Howard Stansbury (a U.S. surveyor of the area) had built nearby to house his herders. It was the site of many travelers' camps and a familiar point of reference. The Donner party camped near Adobe Rock in 1846. On July 27, 1847, apostle Orson Pratt and two other men climbed to the top of the rock to get a view of the Tooele Valley. Later, when Brigham Young came to visit the settlements, this was where he was greeted.

Mormon pioneers quickly took advantage of mountain streams in the area to power their gristmills. The mills were eventually closed, and by 1889 the town of Mills Junction was abandoned. The Benson mill, constructed in 1854 by the grandfather of Ezra Taft Benson, an LDS apostle

Adobe Rock, an important pioneer landmark.

Old Ezra Taft Benson mill.

and two-term secretary of agriculture under President Eisenhower who later became LDS Church president, has been restored and operates as a museum. The mill is open from April through October.

Stansbury Park

Though geographically close, Stansbury Park has a very different history from that of Lake Point and Mills Junction. Stansbury Park is unique in its inception as a totally planned community. Named for Captain Howard Stansbury, head of the U.S. Geological Survey team when the area was explored in 1850, the town was built in 1969 by Terracor, a Salt Lake firm that specialized in community building. Everything a community needed was designed into the master plan: roads, houses, a golf course, parks, shops, schools, etc. The market for the homes was mainly people who worked in Tooele County but lived in Salt Lake County. The development was also advertised as a bedroom community for Salt Lake City. Stansbury Park was projected to be Utah's fourth largest community by 1985 with a population of 40,000. Terracor, however, went bankrupt and the original plans were not entirely fulfilled. Now, as real estate prices in Salt Lake County soar, Stansbury Park is once again growing. With rapid overcrowding in the Salt Lake Valley, the community is finally achieving the status envisioned by its planners.

Grantsville

Productive farms line the highway to Grantsville, once an important watering spot for westward travelers. The cemetery in Grantsville pre-dates the Mormon pioneers. Two migrant parties that crossed the Great Salt Desert buried men here in 1846. The Hastings company buried John Hargrave, who died of pneumonia, and soon after the Donner party buried Luke Halloran, who died of tuberculosis, in the same spot.

The Donner party stopped here for water in 1846 before crossing the Great Salt Desert. They called the place Twenty Wells. In 1850 two families moved to Grantsville, attracted by the streams and lush growth of willows. They named their new home Willow Creek, but when Col. George D. Grant came from Salt Lake City to help them deal with hostile Indians in 1851, they changed the name to honor him.

Like many other settlements, Grantsville suffered near-starvation because of the terrible grasshopper infestation of 1855–56. The insects came over the lake in waves and devoured everything that grew. The farmers tried grinding them to death with a huge roller, and burning them, and drowning them, but they kept coming. The creatures left little for the people to eat that winter. Even wild game was hard to find because the grasshoppers had eaten everything the animals used for forage. No government programs existed to give grants to disaster-struck farmers or food to starving people, so the Grantsville residents had to eat whatever they could find, and many people suffered terribly.

At a Grantsville LDS Church conference in 1867, Brigham Young advised the people to build a woolen mill so they could be self-sustaining. Subsequently, the town built a one-and-a-half-story limestone building east of Grantsville, close to an area known as E. T. City (E. T. stands for Ezra Taft, an early church leader). They purchased equipment and expended much time and money. When the factory was completed in 1870, a number of apostles came from Salt Lake to dedicate it at a great festival. In spite of all the money spent and the high hopes of the people, the mill only operated for a few months. The dam holding the stream that powered the equipment gave way and was never rebuilt. The building was subse-quently used as a fishery, a dairy, a sewing factory, and even apartments. The shell of the old woolen mill is still standing near UT 138 at E. T. City.

UT 36
Erda–US 6
60 miles

From its junction with UT 138, UT 36 follows the Tooele Valley south along the west side of the Oquirrh Mountains to the Tintic Mining District. This once rural route is becoming increasingly congested; suburbs are spreading around the mountain from Salt Lake County. Where once only farms and a few scattered villages adorned the landscape, numerous convenience stores, gas stations, housing developments, and other signs of civilization have been built.

TOOELE COUNTY

The Tooele Valley was one of the first areas outside the Salt Lake Valley that Brigham Young explored after the pioneers' arrival in Utah in July 1847. The first permanent settlers in the county were sent in September 1849. They tried the area at the mouth of Settlement Creek Canyon, but soon moved north a mile or two, building a fort in 1854. A nine-foot-high mud-and-straw wall was constructed around two-thirds of the town. The wall was built by soaking dirt and mixing straw and grass into the mud. The mixture was packed into wooden forms by boys who stamped on it with their feet. The forms were removed when the mud was dry. The wall was never completed since the Indians never attacked the town. The only use the settlers made of the wall was as a trap for wolves and coyotes. The men placed animal carcasses outside the wall and waited on the corner bastions, shooting the wild animals when they came to eat. The practice seems inhumane today, but in pioneer times it was part of the fight for survival—when wildlife ate the livestock, the people starved.

Early Tooele Valley residents considered their climate the best in the state, tempered by the Great Salt Lake to avoid the extreme summer highs and winter lows felt in other areas. Early settlers were plagued by cricket infestations, though. They fought them, burned them, beat them—then held prayer meetings before returning to do battle again. Sometimes the crickets miraculously turned back; at other times seagulls devoured them. Often, though, the crickets won, devouring the crops, and the people had to survive on native plants gleaned in the mountains and fields.

Most early pioneers in Tooele County subsisted by farming; some tried other trades. A number of families boiled and refined salt near the Great Salt Lake. After the joining of the transcontinental railroad, others harvested timber in the canyons and sold it in Salt Lake or floated it across the lake to Farmington to be used as railroad ties in the construction of the line between Ogden and Salt Lake.

In the early days of the community only one man owned a clock. He also happened to have a bugle. Thirty minutes before church started he blasted on his bugle so everyone could meet at the same time.

The pioneers who settled Tooele County were all Mormons. In 1858, with the arrival of federal soldiers in the vicinity during the Utah War, gentiles became more common. Brigham Young discouraged his followers from engaging in mining activity, but the new non-Mormon population took advantage of the rich deposits of ore in Utah and Tooele Counties.

Early Politics in Tooele County

The major political party of the early pioneers was the conservative People's Party. As the population of Tooele County grew to include many miners, the Liberal Party began to make itself felt. By 1874 about as many miners as pioneers lived in the county, and Liberal Party members convinced the People's Party to run a Liberal Party county sheriff candidate on the general ticket. When the state leaders of the People's Party heard of the Tooele compromise, they pressured Tooele's leaders to remove the Liberal Party candidate from the general ticket. The name was removed, and from then on it was open war between the two parties.

Because the voting act written by the territorial legislature only specified that a person had to be a resident of Utah Territory for six months before voting, the Liberals decided anyone in Utah could help them vote their candidates into office. They made arrangements with local stage lines to bring people into the county, offering free drinks along the way for anyone willing to vote for the Liberal Party candidates. As a result, Lawrence Brown of the Liberal Party was elected Tooele County probate judge. He had the full support of anti-Mormon Territorial Governor George Woods despite the fact that 980 illegal votes had been cast in the election.

When the county selectmen refused to accept Brown as judge, he went to Salt Lake for support. A delegation of the People's Party also went to Salt Lake to consult with their party leaders. While they were gone the Liberals took over the county recorder's office. When the People's Party officers returned, they discovered they had been replaced, so they offered to take the new Liberal officials on a tour of the county. During the tour, the People's Party recaptured the office. With the aid of the U.S. marshall, the Liberals were able to retake the office, but they soon discovered that all the county records had been hidden. At this point county residents were arming themselves and preparing for battle, but a messenger came from Brigham Young instructing the People's Party leaders to give up.

The Liberals managed to keep control in Tooele County from 1874 through 1878, when the territorial legislature passed a law requiring that voters be registered. This didn't stop the Liberals, however. An election was held in August 1878, and the county clerk refused to count the ballots. Finally, in March 1879, under court order, the ballots were counted, but the clerk declared all precincts except Ophir and Lakeview invalid, giving the victory to the Liberals. The People's Party protested, and finally, three weeks later, all the ballots were counted and the People's Party came back into power. They found county affairs in not quite as good a condition as they had left them. A Tooele County historian sums up the effects of the Liberals' term in Tooele County:

> During the four years that the Liberal Party was in control of Tooele County, from 1874 to 1878, script of the county fell from par to 10% of par, a loss of 90% value. The $2,000 surplus of the county was replaced with a $14,000 indebtedness, and of $51,000 spent during the Liberal incumbency, the only benefit left was in repairs to the court house in the amount of $2,500.

Since the early political fighting, Tooele County has remained conservative. There's been no recurrence of election shenanigans.

Tooele

In the late 1800s and early 1900s, the mountains around Tooele produced huge amounts of ore. The town became a center for smelting, employing hundreds of men in the industry. There is no smelter open in Tooele today.

The U.S. Army base south of town has had a significant impact on the community. For more than forty years, the army base was a major

Abandoned army barracks, Tooele Army Depot.

employer in Tooele. With the 1995 announcement of the base's closure, the future of some of Tooele's industry is in question.

On the courthouse grounds in Tooele sits an old cabin that was moved there in 1933 and surrounded by a protective structure in 1956. Thirty-one different couples lived in the cabin between 1856 and 1917. Sixteen children were born there, including one set of twins, and five people died in the cabin. A number of different businesses were also operated within its walls.

Tooele County Museum

The early pioneers of Tooele County made a living farming and ranching. However, those who came later were more often interested in the glittering riches buried in the earth. The Tooele County Museum displays a re-created mining shaft and old mining tools. The miners had to transport their ores, so railroads were integral to the mining operations. The Tooele Valley Railway ran until 1982, when it donated the old station and a number of old engines, cars, and cabooses to the museum. Visitors can see the original old steam locomotives and ride in a miniature train on a miniature track. The museum is at the junction of Broadway and Vine Streets in Tooele.

Bauer

After UT 36 leaves Tooele, it travels through a sparsely populated area. Bauer, just west of the highway, is the site of a garbage-sorting plant. All the refuse collected in the county is brought here for sorting. Workers separate out recyclables and send the rest to a landfill in another part of the state. Named for local mine operator B. F. Bauer, the town was settled in 1855. It was never a very large place, and no one lives in Bauer today.

Stockton

Stockton was first a military post in 1854 for soldiers sent to investigate the Gunnison Massacre, in which some Indians murdered members of an Army Corps of Engineers survey team. The soldiers named the place after their California home. The men were inclined to chase women, get drunk, cause fights, and create havoc in the normally quiet Mormon settlement. When Brigham Young threatened to bring out the Nauvoo Legion, the whole company retreated to California.

After the soldiers left, several local families occupied the military barracks for some time. In 1862 Colonel Patrick Connor's troops arrived and reoccupied the site, building more barracks for the large army. The soldiers decided to exploit the rich deposits of lead, silver, and gold ore in the nearby mountains. The first non-Mormon community in the state, Stockton was also the first mining town in Utah.

As well as mining, some ore processing was done at Stockton. Evidence of this activity still exists in the form of several charcoal kilns. A lime kiln from the 1870s can be found at Soldier Creek.

Deseret Chemical Depot

Proceeding south from Stockton, UT 36 passes another large military facility, the Deseret Chemical Corps Depot. At night the buildings are lit up like an airport. Built as a storage and shipment site for top-secret chemical warfare material, the depot was converted in 1996 to a chemical weapons destruction post.

Vernon

Vernon is a small town in wide-open ranching country. Named for Joseph Vernon, who was killed by Indians in 1858, Vernon was settled in 1862. Originally settlers living in Faust, four miles to the north, came just to farm, maintaining their homes in Faust. The first house at Vernon was built in the fall of 1863. Farming was difficult in the early years as late and early frosts and grasshoppers destroyed many of the crops. Farmers later learned methods of adapting and improving their crops. Raising livestock became a big business, as horses were in demand and rangeland in the area was good. Cattle and sheep ranches have also succeeded in Vernon.

Deseret Chemical Depot.

UT 196
Rowley Junction–Dugway
40 miles

Exit I-80 at Rowley Junction to see the valley west of Tooele, a lonely place that deserves its name: Skull Valley. Early pioneers named it for the ancient buffalo skulls they found here. The valley's history is interesting and varied.

Iosepa

UT 196 travels south through Skull Valley. The few scattered ranches and clustered houses are the remnants of an old town. Long before the town grew up here, the spot was known as the last watering hole for California-bound travelers before the Great Salt Desert. The members of the ill-fated Donner party were among those who drank their last fresh water near Iosepa.

Iosepa was founded in 1889 by a group of Mormon converts from Hawaii who came to Utah to be close to the soon-to-be-completed Salt Lake Temple. They were given land near a small stream in Skull Valley. The Hawaiians called their new town Iosepa, Hawaiian for "Joseph." Joseph F. Smith, who would become sixth president of the LDS Church, had been a missionary in Hawaii as a young man.

In the 1870s Hawaiian converts to the Mormon Church started immigrating to Utah. By 1889 about seventy-five Polynesians, mostly

A group of Hawaiians in Iosepa on Pioneer Day, July 24, circa 1914.
—UTAH STATE HISTORICAL SOCIETY

Iosepa cemetery.

Hawaiians, had settled by Warm Springs (near Beck Street) in the northern part of Salt Lake City. Because of racial differences and an outbreak of leprosy, the Polynesians didn't integrate well with the predominantly Caucasian population. In 1889 the church established a gathering place in Skull Valley for groups from the Pacific Islands where they could be self-sufficient and preserve their unique heritage. The church bought them a large farm that included 1,920 acres, irrigation rights to five streams, a number of large buildings, and adequate wood, as well as 129 horses and 335 head of cattle.

For a number of years, the Hawaiians struggled to survive in the harsh new climate. They learned to cope with the extreme conditions and began to prosper. They made their small city in the desert beautiful, planting flowers and lawns. One year they received an award for their town's beauty. At one time 225 people lived in Iosepa. During the last few years of the city's life the residents installed a new water system, complete with fire hydrants. A number of factors contributed to Iosepa's gradual decline. The cold winters and scorching summers had always been hard for the Polynesians. In 1896 three members of the community contracted leprosy, causing a general panic. The afflicted citizens were quarantined and the disease did not spread any farther, but the discouragement remained.

In 1916 the church announced that it would build a temple in Hawaii, and the Polynesians returned to their island home. Today all that remains to show a small city once stood here are a cemetery with Hawaiian headstones and a few old homes, reminders of an industrious people who tried to improve their desert oasis.

In 1989, 100 years after its beginning, a monument to the pioneers was erected on the site of Iosepa.

Skull Valley Indian Reservation

Continue south on this long, straight desert road and you pass through the Skull Valley Indian Reservation, home to a small band of Goshute Indians. A few houses against the eastern mountains and a few more to the west are all that is visible of settlement here.

Survival and prosperity for the Goshutes have been tough to come by in a white man's world. With wide-open spaces and few resources, they constantly search for ways to enrich their people. Tribal leaders have seen moneymaking opportunities in the national demand for nuclear-waste storage facilities. However, many of the lawmakers in Utah oppose any more hazardous waste in their state. The issue remains unresolved.

Dugway

Parts of Utah are truly desolate. A European visitor might marvel at the vast stretches without a building or even a tree. About twenty miles south of Iosepa is one such area. The emptiness of this region is largely intentional. Since the 1950s, the United States Army has controlled much

Dugway Proving Grounds. —UTAH STATE HISTORICAL SOCIETY

of this desert land for testing chemical and other weapons. The lead-in of a May 8, 1960, *Salt Lake Tribune* article by Jerry Voros about Dugway read, "Death is the business, silence a trademark and isolation an accepted way of life for the residents of this, Utah's 14th largest community."

The U.S. military began using the West Desert in 1942 for training exercises for the war effort. The Dugway Proving Grounds officially opened on July 1, 1950, under the auspices of the Chemical Corps of the United States Army. The facilities were used extensively in the 1950s and later for testing chemical weapons. The town of Dugway housed the families of military personnel.

During the early years of military occupation, few people raised concerns that chemical testing might endanger animals and humans. But thousands of sheep died in the surrounding rangelands as a result of the tests. By the 1970s, people were asking questions. Today, the military still uses the area for testing, but takes more precautions than were exercised in the 1950s and 1960s. With military cutbacks, the town of Dugway is under constant threat of disappearing.

UT 73
Lehi–UT 36
39 miles

Cedar Fort

When UT 73 leaves the Wasatch Front it enters its own little valley. The first settlers in this remote area of western Utah County arrived in 1852 and built houses around some springs. The next year they built a fort made of cedar posts, hence the town's name. Enough people lived in the valley in 1856 to merit establishing a county, with Cedar Fort as its seat. However, the county didn't last long, and soon the area became a western extension of Utah County.

With the arrival of General Johnston's troops at Camp Floyd in 1858, a period of not entirely welcome prosperity came to Cedar Fort. Though the community needed cash to pay for farm products, they disapproved of the military camp's lifestyle. The locals were relieved in 1861 when the soldiers sold their goods at cheap prices and abandoned Camp Floyd.

As doctors were a rarity in pioneer settlements, midwives delivered all the babies and served many other medical needs as well. Anna Christina Peterson was one of these midwives. Anna was only eighteen months old when her family emigrated from Denmark and crossed the plains to Utah. On the way she contracted cholera and was believed dead. Because Indians were in the area, the party didn't take time to dig a grave for her.

They wrapped the baby in a blanket and placed her under a bush. The next night her grieving mother, not wanting to leave her baby on the prairie, slipped out of camp and, ignoring both the Indians and the wolves, went back for her daughter. She found her baby alive. Anna grew up, married, had nine children, and became the midwife of Cedar Fort. She delivered about 200 babies.

An annual water fight, a tradition since the mid-1900s, is a "cooling" event in Cedar Fort. Every July 23 the citizens gather in the streets to cool down in a townwide, all-ages group water fight. Unsuspecting motorists are likely to get thoroughly soaked if they happen through Cedar Fort on this day. Sometimes the activities get a bit rambunctious, but no one seems to mind.

Fairfield

Fairfield is five miles south of Cedar Fort. Amos Fielding discovered a spring at the site while on a scouting expedition in the 1850s. His group decided it was a good place for a town and named it Fair for its beauty and Field for the man who discovered the spring.

The first families moved to Fairfield in 1855, intending to create a quiet farming community. In 1858, though, General Johnston's troops arrived and changed Fairfield overnight. More than 4,000 soldiers—the largest contingent of U.S. troops in the nation—marched into the small town, bringing 3,500 wagons and teams, more than 40,000 oxen, and 1,000 mules. They built Camp Floyd (named for President Buchanan's secretary of state) on the south side of the spring that fed the little town. Fairfield boomed with every sort of business that could serve an army base. For a time, Camp Floyd's 7,000 inhabitants made it the second largest city in Utah. Some called it "The Hell Hole of the West" because of the multitude of social ills it engendered in its midst.

In 1861, after the outbreak of the Civil War, the camp was abandoned, and $4 million worth of equipment and supplies were sold for only $100,000. Local people with the cash and smarts to take advantage of the situation made fortunes by purchasing cheap merchandise from the military and selling it at a higher price. The Walker brothers were among those who profited from the liquidation of Camp Floyd.

In 1860 and 1861, Fairfield was a Pony Express stop for eighteen months; later it was an Overland Stage stop. The old Stagecoach Inn at Fairfield, built in 1855, was expanded to a hotel and inn in the late 1850s. It later became a stop on the line for both the Pony Express and the Overland Stage. John Carson, the owner, unwilling to follow the wild leanings of the other establishments that catered to the army, refused to

Camp Floyd Stagecoach Inn.

serve alcohol at his inn. The hotel was a respected place and became the favored hotel for important guests. The inn remained in the Carson family until 1959, when they donated it to the state of Utah. The state restored it and in 1964 made it Stagecoach Inn State Park. The original furnished building is open to visitors for a nominal fee. A small museum in the old army commissary building, the only surviving structure from Camp Floyd, features displays about the camp. Camp Floyd's cemetery is nearby.

Mercur

UT 73 turns west from Fairfield and crosses a low divide into Tooele County. Seven miles after the Tooele County line a road to the northwest leads to an old mining town. Gold was discovered in a creek near Mercur in 1869. Findings there were sparse, but prospectors came in search of silver because they knew of other rich silver finds in neighboring mines. Prospecting began and a town called Lewiston sprang up. Both gold and silver were shipped from Lewiston for a number of years, but by 1880 the boom was over. The town was vacated and never rebuilt.

In 1882 a German immigrant discovered cinnabar (mercuric sulfide) near the town and renamed the place Mercur. He was unable to extract the metal, though, and eventually left. The new name, Mercur, stuck. In 1883 more gold was discovered and a new boom occurred.

Until 1895 Mercur had only one small spring, owned by a man who sold water by the cupful. Peddlers went door-to-door selling water. Whiskey was cheaper than water until a spring was discovered at Ophir and water was piped to Mercur.

Mercur was a thriving community until it was devastated by a fire in 1906. Here it is before the inferno. —UTAH STATE HISTORICAL SOCIETY

Mercur after the 1906 fire. —UTAH STATE HISTORICAL SOCIETY

By 1896, 6,000 people lived in Mercur. In June 1906 a grease fire destroyed the town's entire business district. This was the second time the town had burned, and once again it was rebuilt. By 1910 Mercur had between 8,000 and 12,000 inhabitants. Mercur was a boomtown, though, and since its economy depended on mining, when the gold played out, nothing was left. In 1913 the quality of the gold fell, and by 1917 everyone had left. They even disassembled their homes and recycled the bricks. Another brief resurgence of mining occurred in the 1930s, but a permanent town was never again established.

Today few traces remain of the once-thriving city, for a time the largest in Tooele County. A good imagination is required to picture the numerous houses and businesses that lined the streets of Mercur. Gold was still mined at Mercur until 1997, when the supply finally ran out and operations ceased.

Ophir

A few miles up UT 73 after the Mercur turnoff, another mining road heads into the Oquirrh Mountains. When the soldiers who came to Utah in the 1860s with Patrick Connor heard that local Indians had ornaments made of silver, they started exploring. After several years, their search led to rich deposits around Ophir. In 1870 the town of Ophir was built. One of the miners named it for the biblical town where King Solomon's mines were located. The town was replete with saloons, hotels, and brothels. Because the ore was so rich (mostly silver with some lead, copper, and gold content), smelters were built and permanent business

Ophir Town Hall.

structures went up. Organized city government even came into being, which required a town hall. The town's prosperity peaked between 1871 and 1874. People made large fortunes in Ophir, and some already-rich men who invested in the mines and smelters became even richer. Then, as in many other mining towns, the big boom ended and Ophir began to decline. By 1880 only a few people were left in Ophir. Mining activity persisted, but the mines were harder to work and required more specialized equipment and technology.

In 1940 new ore was discovered, but in 1950 Ophir was once again a ghost town. In 1970 Ophir had over seventy residents; in 1976 fourteen families made up the town. These residents installed their own water system. Ophir's population has remained pretty steady since then.

An excellent example of mining-camp architecture, the town hall, built in the 1870s, is still standing and has been placed on the National Register of Historic Places.

Pony Express and Overland Stagecoach Trail
Fairfield–Nevada State Line
145 miles

The Pony Express and Overland Stagecoach Trail tells an important part of Utah's story. Though Pony Express riders carried mail on the trail for only eighteen months—from April 1860 through October 1861—their

The Pony Express was a great service until the Transcontinental Telegraph made the swift riders obsolete after just eighteen months. —UTAH STATE HISTORICAL SOCIETY

fame has lasted for more than 100 years. The old unpaved trail from Fairfield into Nevada is easily traveled in a two-wheel-drive vehicle. The unpaved portion begins at the Tooele County line on UT 73, then follows a southwesterly route through Simpson Springs, Fish Springs, and Callao, through the Deep Creek Mountains, down through Ibapah, then into Nevada. It is a very lonely but beautiful section of Utah, largely untouched and unchanged from the way it was at the time of the Pony Express.

Every year the Pony Express Association reenacts a ride across the Pony Express Trail. The riders are greeted by the Tooele County representatives at Simpson Springs, a stop on the route where several old buildings have been preserved.

Faust

About twelve miles down the trail from the county line is Faust. Dr. Henry J. Faust started out as a Pony Express rider and later settled at the site of one of the stations. Faust is one of the few stops on the trail today that is actually on the map as a town. After Faust the trail crosses UT 36 and climbs to Lookout Pass, between Rush Valley and Skull Valley. The pass was so named because of the frequent warnings to stage passengers of potential Indian attacks.

Point Lookout Station

Just down the hill from Lookout Pass, Uncle Horace and Aunt Libby Rockwell ran a station for the line. Aunty Libby was very fond of her dogs,

Aunt Libby's Dog Cemetery, Lookout Pass.

Reconstructed Pony Express stop, Simpson Springs.

and anyone who happened to die in the vicinity was buried in the dog cemetery. It seems the only true objects of mourning were the dogs: they were the only ones to receive headstones. The cemetery is encircled by a stone wall, just south of the trail.

Simpson Springs Station

Among the benefits of the Union army's presence in Utah were its contributions to the search for a new route to California. Captain J. H. Simpson was the chief explorer who scouted out a route through the desert that included water holes and grazing for livestock. The site named for him—Simpson Springs—was the most dependable spring along the route. Soon after Simpson discovered the spring in 1858, George Chorpenning established a mail station here that became a stop for the Pony Express the next year, and later served the Overland Stage.

Because of the availability of water here, a number of people built structures in the vicinity, most of which have since fallen apart. Today it is hard to tell which one was the Pony Express station. However, a replica has been constructed on the site of one of the ruins. Simpson Springs is the best-preserved and documented of all the stops on the trail. Between Simpson Springs and Fish Springs were a number of crude stations, but all traces of them are long gone.

Fish Springs

With its scenic mountains and wide-open vistas, Fish Springs is a beautiful spot on the Pony Express Trail. Hot springs bubble up here as well as cold springs filled with fish.

Fish Springs has never been an active community, but has been inhabited periodically for the past 135 years. It was an important stop on the trail, but the riders complained about the condition of the road here. One called it "the muddiest, slickest, dirtiest place man was ever in."

After the Pony Express period, Fish Springs saw some mining and ranching activity. In 1947 people raised muskrats in the swamps around the hot springs.

Today the road is much better than it was at the time of the Pony Express. Though still unpaved, it is raised and graveled where it crosses slick mud.

There is now a national wildlife refuge at Fish Springs. A few houses that serve as park-service housing nestle against the east slope of the Fish Springs Mountains.

Callao

Approach Callao from the east across the Pony Express Trail and you will be amazed at the grandeur of the 12,000-foot mountain backdrop behind the small frontier town. Isolated even from paved roads, Callao still has the look of a pioneer town, with many homes made of logs. Residents have to travel to Wendover and Salt Lake City for supplies.

Log structures, Callao.

When it was a Pony Express and Overland Stage station, Callao was called Willow Springs. Permanent settlers had arrived in 1870. They kept the name of Willow Springs until around 1895, when a post office was established. The postal service said too many towns had the name Willow Springs already. A prospector who had been to South America proposed Callao because the town reminded him of a place in Peru.

Callao has the last operating one-room school in Utah. Classes were held in the highway department building until recently, when the school district acquired the old LDS Church house. Now, Callao's kindergarten through eighth-grade students attend school there.

Gold Hill

From Callao, the dirt road turns north to round the Deep Creek Mountains (southbound, the road leads to Trout Creek). You can either bypass Gold Hill as the old trail did, or drive the few extra miles to see this interesting, semi-inhabited town. In 1858 prospectors bound for California discovered gold in the mountains near the Nevada border. However, real mining didn't begin until 1869. The town alternately boomed and busted through the 1930s as people discovered more gold, silver, lead, copper, and finally arsenic. The Deep Creek Railroad from Wendover arrived in Gold Hill in 1917. The railroad brought the town a period of prosperity. Gold Hill was laid out in blocks. Businesses, hotels, saloons, and a daily newspaper, the *Gold Hill News*, flourished. Copper was a hot item during World War I, as was cotton, and when the boll weevil started devouring all the cotton in the South, arsenic was needed to fight it. These minerals were readily available in Gold Hill.

Old store converted to residence, Gold Hill.

After the war arsenic from abroad became cheaper, and the Gold Hill boom died. In 1938, the trains stopped running to Gold Hill, and the tracks were taken up in 1940. World War II created another boom from 1944 to 1945, but it was short-lived and the last one the town would experience.

Gold Hill was never the garden spot of Utah. It was a boomtown, and residents knew they would soon be moving on to better finds, so they didn't try to improve their surroundings or keep up their yards. They also built their privies over any old mine shaft that was available. Mine shafts were everywhere, even in the middle of the street. As Stephen L. Carr describes the situation in *The Historical Guide to Utah Ghost Towns*, "At least the [outhouses] kept automobiles from falling into the mine shafts."

Though some consider it a ghost town, a few people and even more horses and chickens still live in Gold Hill. Residents of Gold Hill are friendly and like to tell you about the history of the town. Ernie Cadler says the two-lane bowling alley and the movie theatre were the first ones in Utah outside of Salt Lake City. Both are closed today. The bowling alley is used to store mining samples. Alongside the crumbling old buildings, several dozen rusting automobiles with sagebrush growing in and around them attest to the mostly abandoned state of Gold Hill.

Ibapah

The Pony Express Trail meets pavement just above Ibapah. Ibapah was once a rip-roaring frontier town that catered to the Overland Stage passengers and miners. The town was originally called Deep Creek, but the name was changed to Ibapah, a derivative of a Goshute word for white clay water (referring to the creek). The first white settlers in Ibapah were Mormon missionaries who came in 1859 to teach the Indians farming methods. Soon thereafter the town became a Pony Express station and later a stop for the Overland Stagecoach. A number of families connected with stage-related businesses lived in town, and several sheep and cattle ranchers settled here. Ibapah had stores that traded with the Indians, and it was a business center for miners and prospectors in the surrounding mountains, so several saloons did thriving business.

Then known as Deep Creek, Ibapah experienced some growth in the late 1870s because of troubles in Nevada. In September 1875 a dispute erupted between two white men and a Goshute Indian near Mount Moriah, just west of the Utah-Nevada border. One of the white men was killed, and the other reported that the whole Goshute nation was on the warpath against the whites. Rumors also circulated that white Mormons were inciting Indians to kill non-Mormons. Neither assertion was true, but in the hysteria white men killed a number of Goshutes. The Nevada governor called for the army to come and fight the Indians. However, before military leaders would wage war, they conferred with the two sides to learn if there really was a conflict. They found no cause for war, and after the Indian who had shot the white man was hanged, peace returned. The whites who had killed the Goshutes were never punished.

White settlers in Nevada were nervous about Indian uprisings, and they urged their leaders to send the Indians away. Most of the Goshutes were sent to the Deep Creek area of Utah.

After the Goshutes left, Nevadans felt their loss. On January 8, 1876, the editor of the *White Pine News* lamented:

> What has become of all the Shoshone [Goshute] Indians? We have not seen one since the first storms commenced this winter. Who is to saw our wood? Who is to shovel paths in the snow? Who is to do the drudgery work for our wives? When they are around we think them a great nuisance, and do not appreciate their services until they are badly needed. They will probably return from the valleys when the snow is gone.

But they did not. Most remained in Utah, as do many of their descendants today. The present Goshute Indian Reservation straddles the Utah-Nevada border.

Goshute girl,
Goshute Reservation.

Ibapah is no longer the bustling town it was in the days of the Overland Stage. The town had no telephones until 1968. Some ranchers remain, many descended from the original ranch owners. One resident calls it "kind of lonely and desolate," but a wonderful place to live. It still has a trading post and a few scattered houses. Some of the old buildings are boarded up. The Goshute Indians own most of the land in the area.

Tom Irvin and Henry Goldsmith can no longer be found sitting on the front porch as they did here in 1915, but little more than the faces in Ibapah have changed with the passing of time. —UTAH STATE HISTORICAL SOCIETY

US 6
Santaquin–Nevada State Line
158 miles

This stretch of road begins in the farmlands of central Utah, climbs through the historic Tintic Mining District to the farmlands around Delta, traverses vast unpopulated ranges and valleys, and reaches the Utah-Nevada border near Great Basin National Park.

TINTIC MINING DISTRICT

After skirting the south end of Utah Lake and passing through several small towns, US 6 climbs into the historic Tintic Mining District. Soon after Mormons started digging in the virgin soil of their new home, it became evident that this was a rich spot, not only in agricultural potential but in mineral wealth. However, church members were encouraged not to spend their valuable time and resources in the pursuit of wealth. To those who asked what they should do with the riches of the earth, Brigham Young replied:

> There is no happiness in gold. . . . Not the least. . . . We have the real wealth here. . . . We have the good, fine flour, good wheat, horses, cattle, beef, vegetables, fruit, sheep, and wool. . . . This is real wealth. This people is a rich people.

Young felt that basic, life-sustaining needs must be met first. The people must have food, clothes, and shelter. After these requirements were met, they could go in search of gold. Church leaders also feared that wealth from the mining of precious metals would lead to materialism and bring in undesirable populations, so they discouraged members from mining the rich ores that abounded in the area. When soldiers moved into Utah in the 1860s, they were the ones to start mining, and Utah did indeed change dramatically.

US 6 climbs from Utah Valley through juniper-covered hills. Five towns are shown close together on the Utah highway map. The only one with much visible habitation today is Eureka. In 1869 ore was discovered in the Tintic Mining District, which straddles Juab, Tooele, and Utah Counties. The Tintic turned out to be one of the richest districts in Utah, and many fabulous fortunes were made from its gold, silver, and lead. The district produced nearly $600 million worth of precious metals during its history.

Dividend

Dividend is the first of the Tintic mining towns listed on the map, but there is no evidence today of its fabled past. The town name was chosen because of the high dividends the Tintic Standard Mining Company paid its stockholders. Though it is hard to imagine a town here, stores, saloons, a pool hall, and a schoolhouse once thrived on the spot. A huge smelter stood guard on the hill above the town well into the 1970s, when it was torn down by the owners to avoid the taxes on the structure.

Dividend was in its heyday from about 1916 through the mid-1920s. In 1921 four masked men held up the Dividend store. They didn't manage to get any money, but they killed two men and wounded two others. The villains escaped and were never apprehended, nor were their identities ever discovered.

Eureka

Up and over the hill, Eureka is the largest and most famous of the old Tintic towns. Eureka was known as one of the quietest boomtowns in the West. The wealth of its numerous mines meant that Eureka was not just a passing fancy; its residents felt it was there to stay, and they wanted to maintain a sense of the future.

In times when Brigham Young made the decisions, a man named Shadrack Lunt discovered silver near Eureka. He asked his bishop what he should do, and the bishop went to Young. The church president followed his usual course and advised against mining. Lunt obediently went on with his farming activities and never realized the riches that others who didn't follow the prophet's counsel would gain.

In 1869 a cowboy and some local farmers searching for firewood independently discovered silver at the surface of the hills around Eureka. The Eureka Hill Mine ("Eureka, we have found it!") opened in 1870, and soon numerous fabulously rich mines were operating in the district, named the Tintic after an Indian chief who had lived in the area.

Eureka grew quickly, and soon its population was over 3,000. Buildings sprang up all over the hills of the little valley and canyons, practically overnight. They weren't all saloons, either. There were hotels, theaters, a Carnegie library, department stores, and schools. Religion was important to the miners as well as the Mormons. The Catholic priest, the Reverend Lawrence Scanlon, who rode circuit between the Tintic District, Deep Creek on the Utah-Nevada border, and Silver Reef near St. George, was in charge of 2,000 square miles, the largest parish in the nation.

The mines near Eureka paid well for many years. Not until 1930 did the high costs of mining and the low returns on the mostly silver ores make it necessary to start shutting down operations, leaving huge mine shafts tunnelling everywhere under the ground. One plunges 3,300 feet into the depths of the earth. By 1940 most of the major mines had closed.

Some mining activity persisted through the 1950s, though, and even today there is talk of reopening some of the mines around Eureka.

Eureka is an interesting kind of ghost town—one that still has many inhabitants. Old headframes—used by the mines to haul ore, men, and mules in and out of the mines—still dot the landscape, seemingly ready for use. If you drive through the town just before twilight it will be hard to tell which buildings are inhabited and which are just full of the spirits of miners long gone.

Knightsville

Knightsville no longer exists and it isn't on any maps, but the town was too important in the history of Utah not to receive a mention.

Two miles east of Eureka, Knightsville was unique among mining camps. A "dry" camp, it was the only mining town in the West with no saloon. It also had no prostitutes, and the mines were closed on Sundays. Everything was respectable.

During the 1880s, after years of legal trouble and government confiscation of property over the polygamy issue, the LDS Church was deep in debt. Jesse Knight felt it was his mission to get the Mormon Church out of debt. He had had a vision of obtaining the wealth out of the

Miners in a Knightsville mine. —UTAH STATE HISTORICAL SOCIETY

mountains, and vowed he would use it for the good of the church, not for his own enrichment. He started digging when he heard a voice telling him to, even though he saw no sign of ore. He hit silver 150 feet down. The same phenomenon was repeated in many spots, and Knight became a multimillionaire. His mines paid off fabulously, as did other mine-related industries he owned. Knight was generous with his employees and still had money to donate to Brigham Young Academy (later Brigham Young University) and the LDS Church. He made the statement, "The earth is the Lord's bank, and no man has the right to take money out of that bank and use it extravagantly upon himself." His employees called him "Uncle Jesse."

By about 1915 Knight's mines were played out. He was a rich man and had helped many people along the way. Knightsville soon disappeared, but Jesse Knight's home (now a mortuary) still stands on East Center Street in Provo.

Mammoth

Around a bend from Eureka and up a short road is a west-facing valley where a few scattered homes climb the surrounding hills. This is Mammoth. In 1870, the shout at the discovery of a mine of the same name was "Boys, she's a mammoth strike! We've got ourselves a mammoth mine!" The town exploded, and within a few months the population had reached 2,500. Soon a mining engineer named Robinson moved downhill from Mammoth and started a new town, Robinson. Both towns grew until they turned into one huge town with two post offices. The confusion was great until one post office was formed on the towns' borders called Middletown. The name didn't last, and finally the whole "metropolis" was called Mammoth.

Mammoth had its share of wild times, just like other mining towns. One of the wildest resulted not from liquor or fighting, but from boredom. Some teenagers looking for fun soaped the railroad tracks just before a heavy locomotive headed down the town's steep hill. When the train started sliding, everyone bailed out, but the engineer survived the curving hill and returned and pick up his passengers.

The mines were gradually played out, costs rose, and other troubles came. By 1930 the town was dying. Most residents left and Mammoth became a ghost town.

Mammoth still has a few residents, but it is difficult to imagine it as a boomtown with thousands of people. The few families that call Mammoth home are rewarded with wonderful views of the valley and mountains to the west.

Tintic

Across the valley to the west you can see mostly junipers. When this valley was first discovered, it was a beautiful place full of lush grasses. Because of overgrazing by sheep, sagebrush and Utah juniper encroached, covering over much of the original beauty. Hundreds of junipers now cover the foundations of the old mining town.

Unaware of the riches that lay under their feet, Mormons grazed their cattle here until 1869, when they discovered silver and gold deposits. In less than a year, they sold out at a very cheap price to an English syndicate.

Silver City

The last of the Tintic mining towns was also one of the smallest. Over the mountain south of Mammoth more silver was discovered in 1869, and the town of Silver City sprang up. Though Silver City boomed, it was never as big as Eureka or Mammoth. Water flooded the mines, causing big problems, and by 1900 people began to leave. However, Jesse Knight, one of the few active Mormon mine leaders, took an interest in the area and resurrected it for a time. He built a smelter and over 100 homes for the miners. In 1908 more than 1,500 people lived in Silver City.

The operations became unprofitable, and Knight moved his smelter to Murray in the Salt Lake Valley. The town was finally abandoned in the early 1930s.

Little Sahara Recreation Area

US 6 leads from the Tintic Mining District into a sagebrush valley. After about fifteen miles it enters a land of sand dunes. Hundreds of years ago the Sevier River crossed this valley on its way to the Great Salt Lake. Over the years sand and silt deposits changed the course of the river, turning it into the desert southwest of Delta. Where the river once flowed, 60,000 acres of white sand dunes now offer recreational opportunities. The dunes are administered by the Bureau of Land Management and include campground facilities.

Lynndyl

Seventeen miles past the Little Sahara turnoff, US 6 passes Lynndyl, a town named for a badly fitted shoe. One day in 1904, soon after the station was installed, a woman tried to send a telegraph. Her shoe was bothering her while she waited in line, so she took it off and held it in her hand. When asked where she was calling from, she glanced in her shoe, saw the words Lynn, Massachusetts, where the shoe was made, and said "Lynn." The town was named Lynndyl because there was already a Lynn in Utah.

In 1904 Lynndyl was the main junction of the Union Pacific Railroad between Salt Lake City and Los Angeles. The town grew up when railroad workers brought their families here in about 1907. The train was only supposed to stop at Lynndyl if it was flagged. Someone flagged it by mistake, and after that it stopped every day.

Lynndyl is now a quiet farming community with a gas station and a convenience store.

Delta

In 1906 residents of Millard County decided to construct a canal through this area and establish a town. They named the new town site Melville in honor of one of the canal organizers. The first house was built in 1907, and the town was officially established in 1908. The Melville area was heavily promoted by developers, and the resulting development pushed area farms farther out of town. At the insistence of the U.S. Postal Service, the new area was quickly given the name of Delta (for the old river delta). A large number of families moved to Delta to farm in the first few years after the canal was built.

Delta became an important region in the growing of sugar beets and alfalfa seeds. For a time a sugar factory operated in Delta, but the production of alfalfa seeds proved more profitable, so farmers eventually quit growing sugar beets.

Delta profitted in 1942 when the U.S. government built Topaz, a Japanese relocation camp northwest of town. During this time, Delta was flooded with construction workers and other people connected with building and operating the camp.

Today Delta is the largest town in the region. People from surrounding communities travel many miles to conduct business here.

Gunnison Massacre Site

Millard County has been the scene of some of the tragic events in Utah's history. In 1853 seven members of an Army Corps of Engineers survey team were massacred by Indians about five miles west of Delta. The leader of the team, Captain John W. Gunnison, was among those killed.

A few days before the survey team camped here, a group of pioneers traveling to California had killed some Indians. In revenge, their tribesmen massacred the unsuspecting survey party. A Mormon guide who was killed was taken to Manti, where he was buried. Captain Gunnison and his men are buried at the site of the massacre, which is marked by a monument.

For years controversy surrounded the incident. Members of the eastern press alleged that the Mormons were responsible for the deaths of the survey party. Extensive investigation, however, proved that Mormon settlers had no hand in the tragedy.

Topaz

Topaz, a World War II Japanese internment camp, is located about seven miles northwest of Delta on a well-graded dirt and gravel road.

Topaz is listed as marshland on the Utah map, but it should be remembered as the site of a Japanese relocation camp. In 1942 more than 8,000 Japanese Americans were moved to this spot in the desert. The total number of prisoners reached 8,255, making the camp the fifth largest city in Utah at the time. Sixty-five percent of the people interned in Topaz were U.S. citizens; most of these were from the San Francisco Bay area. They were held in this camp until October 3, 1945.

People of Japanese heritage were allowed to work only on farms or in other jobs not connected with the war. Their children were not accepted into either the University of Utah or Utah State Agricultural College in Logan while they were in the camp.

Topaz residents near barracks. —UTAH STATE HISTORICAL SOCIETY

High school graduation exercises at Topaz in 1945.
—UTAH STATE HISTORICAL SOCIETY

Conditions in the camp were not terrible, but neither were they pleasant. Winters were cold and bitter. Summers were equally uncomfortable—the hot desert wind blew dust everywhere and through everything. The prisoners were unable to keep their quarters clean. To make things more difficult, the restroom facilities were separate from the living quarters. The government provided adequate food and some opportunities for learning.

A monument and some concrete foundations partly overgrown with sagebrush and tumbleweeds are silent reminders of the people who were imprisoned in this lonely Utah desert.

Hinckley

Southwest of Delta, Hinckley is the last sign of civilization on US 6 before the highway crosses the desert to Nevada. The area was first visited by Father Escalante in 1776, then by the Gunnison survey expedition in 1853. First called Deseret Number Three, Hinckley was renamed for Ira N. Hinckley, the president of the Millard Stake. The town was established in about 1876. Early settlers had to fight grasshoppers, scorpions, coyotes, and rattlesnakes. They hauled the lumber to build their homes from Oak Creek Canyon, thirty miles away.

After Hinckley, US 6 traverses some lonely country for sixty-odd miles before reaching the ranching valleys on the other side of the state. Here, roads are unpaved and people notice every car that goes by. Life is different out on the ranches than in the cities of Utah's more populous regions. These areas started out isolated and have remained so despite the march of time.

UT 257
Delta–Milford
78 miles

This stretch of road seems to run in a straight line forever. There are a few communities near Delta, but south of there UT 257 becomes completely uninhabited.

Deseret

After Delta, Deseret is the last town on UT 257 for many miles, but it was the first settlement in this section of Utah. Names from the Book of Mormon are prevalent throughout Utah, and Deseret is one of the most common.

In 1859 settlers from Fillmore came to establish farms, and in 1865 the people built a fort to keep their cattle safe from the Indians. It took

Old Fort Deseret. Made of mud and grass, the fort probably would not have stood for more than 130 years in a wetter climate.

ninety-eight men eighteen days to construct it out of mud and straw trodden by oxen. It protected the residents as well as their cattle during the Black Hawk War of 1865–67.

When food was scarce the early residents of Deseret subsisted mostly on fish from the Sevier River. The water was full of suckers, and men waded into the river, picked the fish up, and tossed them on the banks. Barrels full of the suckers were salted for use all winter. Deseret settlers traded fish for supplies in the other settlements.

Today Deseret is a peaceful farming community. The remains of the old 1865 fort still stand south of town. About one-third of the fort is intact, an amazing thing considering the fragility of the mud and straw walls.

Clear Lake

On the road between Milford and Delta, Clear Lake may disappoint travelers looking for signs of human life. You may wonder why a town with no residents is listed on the map.

In 1897 a New York City developer established a town on the railroad line. He had a canal built, and the little town thrived for a time with ten families, a hotel, and other buildings. However, the soil was poor, and the settlers had other problems. The people soon left, and some of them moved their houses with them. The Utah Division of Wildlife Resources now operates the Clear Lake Waterfowl Management area.

Black Rock

In the 1770s, the Dominguez-Escalante party stopped at Black Rock while scouting an easier route to California. A century later the area became popular winter grazing land. Some people established ranches at Black Rock, and for awhile the settlement had a store and a school. But the school and store closed during the first year of World War II, and gradually everyone moved away. Now there's nothing at Black Rock but a railroad siding.

Milford

Unlike other Utah pioneer towns, Milford is not laid out on a uniform east-west, north-south grid. It is a railroad town, and the streets correspond with the most important feature of the town—its rails.

During the mining booms of the 1870s and 1880s mines lined both sides of the Beaver River. People on the east side had to ford the river to reach the ore-processing mills. They called the crossing point the "Mill Ford," and the settlement eventually took the name Milford.

In the 1870s, before Milford became a town, a few cattlemen and miners lived in the area. Arvin Stoddard started Milford in 1880 with a 160-acre homestead. He built his own home, then sold lots to other settlers.

The Utah Central Railway reached Milford the same year on its way to the silver and lead mines of Frisco. Because of the numerous mining camps in southwestern Utah and eastern Nevada, Milford became the terminus through which all freight passed.

The surrounding territory was not just mining country. A large number of ranchers raised animals in the valleys of southwestern Utah. Milford served as the shipping point, not only for precious metals, but for thousands of head of livestock—sheep and cattle—from the surrounding territory.

Milford is in the middle of the desert, and its residents have always fought dirt. In the summer dust filtered everywhere. In the winter when it rained, mud filled the streets of the mining/railroad town. Pedestrians sank to their knees in mud and had to hang onto fences and hitching posts to keep from becoming hopelessly mired.

Milford reached its peak in 1950 with a population of 1,673. The town continues to rely on the railroad, but other activities, including hog-feeding operations, have more recently boosted its economy.

The old Hotel Milford, though still a prominent landmark, is no longer open.

UT 21
Beaver–Garrison
107 miles

This solitary highway crosses a land filled with mining legends and interesting stories from Utah's past. One of them is about the Bradshaw (or Cave) Mine, and gold discovered as the result of a dream. John Bradshaw dreamed one night that he went hiking in the mountains and found a cave. In the cave was a pack-rat's nest filled with golden nuggets. The dream was so real that he searched the mountains north of Minersville for the cave. He found it and the nest, and the cave was lined with gold and silver. Within a few years the cave was stripped of its wealth and was once more deserted. John Bradshaw, who knew nothing of the business aspects of mining, never got rich from his "dream" mine.

Beaver County has a very colorful mining history. In the second half of the nineteenth century, more than a dozen mining towns sprang up in the desert. Most have been forgotten, but a few live on in legend. Two or three are still viable communities.

Minersville

Minersville is a small town at the edge of the desert. If you can imagine a town in the Old West with blowing dust and rolling tumbleweeds, you'll have a pretty clear picture of Minersville.

Years before the Mormon pioneers entered the valleys of Utah, the Spanish worked mines in its mountains. About five miles northwest of present-day Minersville, the Spanish had chiseled a lead and silver mine out of the rock. This mine was abandoned long before the Saints came, but it was still in good condition.

In 1858 Bishop James Rollins rediscovered the mine, with a very good grade of lead ore still inside it. It became Utah's first lead mine; many believe it was the first American mine of any kind in Utah. The lead was mostly used to make bullets. The silver content in the ore was so high, reports spread throughout the east that Mormons used silver bullets. The spring after the mine opened, Mormons sought a suitable town site near the mine and founded Minersville.

The mine was named for Bishop Rollins, but when non-Mormons came to work the mine a few years later, they changed the name to honor President Abraham Lincoln. The town that grew up around the mine prospered, and nearly 500 people lived there at one time. The mine was productive until depressed silver prices, water in the mine shafts, and smelting problems slowed it down. Then in 1900 a British syndicate purchased the property. They mismanaged the mine, and soon everything closed up.

This rusting truck in Minersville is great for target practice, but probably would not carry passengers very far.

Water was always a problem in this part of Beaver County. A farming town grew up on the present site of Minersville soon after the Lincoln Mine became productive. Because of water shortages, the settlement never grew very large. The population, mostly farmers, could raise only a small amount of hay because of the lack of irrigation water. After the town built a canal, and later a reservoir, irrigation improved and more farms prospered.

Farming is still important around Minersville, and alfalfa is the most important crop.

Frisco

Frisco, west of Milford, is the most famous of the Beaver County mining towns. Silver and lead ore were struck here in 1875, and the town boomed. It grew to include 6,000 people, twenty-three saloons, and a wide variety of mining-town-type vices. When the railroad arrived, the town grew even more disreputable. A large number of scoundrels traveled on the rails, looking to find pleasure or profit by any means, regardless of law. A number of mines were built at Frisco; the biggest was the Horn Silver. It produced fabulously until a fateful morning in 1885. The night shift had just come to the surface and the day shift was waiting to go down when the foreman felt the ground shake. He stopped the men from going into the mine for a minute, and the entire shaft caved in. The majority of the town's men worked in the Horn Silver Mine, and most of them left. Some mines still operated, unearthing much

A child's grave in Frisco. This little boy died December 27, 1887. He was one year, four months, and twenty-seven days old. The inscription reads, "Tis a little grave, but Oh have care; For world wide hopes are buried here. How much of light, how much of joy; Is buried with my darling boy."

As with many ghost towns, the most visible remains of Frisco's inhabitants are in the cemetery. Many of the graves here belong to children. This little plot is occupied by four children of the same family.

valuable ore between 1885 and 1913, but the life of the town was gone. By 1920, it was abandoned.

Newhouse

Newhouse, northwest of Milford, was a model mining town started by Samuel Newhouse and finished by his brother Matt. The miners lived in nice homes. The town awarded fifty dollars for the first child born each year and at Christmas gave gifts to all the children. The only saloon was a mile outside of Newhouse. The town thrived quietly until 1910, when the ore was exhausted. Gradually the buildings were moved or burned. In 1922 *The Covered Wagon*, a famous silent movie, was filmed at Newhouse, and the place has been silent since.

Garrison

UT 21 travels west through Utah's legendary mining country to the Nevada border. The last town on this stretch is Garrison. In the 1850s, the area was ruled by cattle rustlers and outlaws, who chose the location for its remoteness from lawmen. They could fatten stolen cattle and sell them to Nevada miners without being asked any questions. In the 1870s ranchers came to this lonely western Utah valley and built a town. When they got a post office they named the town for Emma Garrison, the schoolteacher who also handled the mail. The town is now the center of an important winter grazing area. Garrison is also the Utah settlement closest to Great Basin National Park in Nevada. A small LDS church, a post office, a gas station and grocery store, and a Utah Highway Patrol building make up Garrison.

UT 56
Cedar City–Nevada State Line
63 miles

UT 56 is another lonesome West Desert highway, passing through a handful of dusty towns before wandering into even lonesomer Nevada.

Iron Springs and Irontown

The first settlements in the area were built by pioneers trying to follow their prophet's counsel to be self-sufficient. All are now located off the highway. Parley P. Pratt discovered iron ore in this part of Utah in 1850 while exploring the territory. He gave the name to the springs that flowed near the ore source. When he reported back to Brigham Young that there was iron in southern Utah, Young put together a mission based on the dream of manufacturing every tool possible from the Utah iron.

The initial settlement, however, was not close to the source of iron. The settlers needed to set themselves up with food and shelter before they could try to produce iron. So they made their home in Parowan, about twenty miles northeast of Cedar City. As soon as the men had plowed and planted the land and built some cabins in the mother settlement, they turned their efforts to the original mission. In November 1851, some of the Parowan settlers moved to Cedar City. Though they did produce iron, floods and other problems made them abandon the Iron Mission in 1858. A decade later, in 1868, interest in producing iron revived and production began in the 1870s, this time at Irontown, a site twenty-two miles west of Cedar City. Again, problems plagued the operation, and it lasted only a few years. Much later, during World War II, iron ore was mined here for production at U.S. Steel in Orem. The remains of the old ovens and furnaces are preserved at Old Irontown, telling a silent story of the pioneers' hopes for independence from the outside world.

A different product that came out of the area was more successful than the Iron Mission. Southern Utah has been popular with filmmakers for many years, and parts of the motion picture *Union Pacific* were shot at Iron Springs in 1938.

Oven at Old Irontown.

Newcastle

One of only two viable towns on this route, Newcastle is the first town after Cedar City. A group of people from Pinto, in the Pine Valley Mountains south of Newcastle, bought land out in the desert and moved onto their ranches early in the twentieth century. Two mountain peaks called the Castle Peaks overlooked the town. The name Newcastle comes from these mountains.

Modena

The last town in Utah on UT 56 is just south of the highway. Modena (pronounced mo-DEE-nah) sits dusty and practically abandoned, begging the question: Is Modena dead or alive? Modena was once an important railroad town. In the latter part of the nineteenth century, the Utah Southern Railroad built its line through the southwestern part of the state, connecting many mining towns by rail. Anyone traveling to southern Utah (including St. George) got off the train at Modena and took overland transportation to their destination. Today the town is almost a ghost—boarded-up buildings and houses dot the streets. A few houses remain occupied, and a general store services the few inhabitants.

Modena was probably named by one of the Italian railroad workers for a town west of Bologna in the Emilia-Romagna region of northern Italy.

Modena still has a handful of residents, but most of the buildings are occupied only by memories.

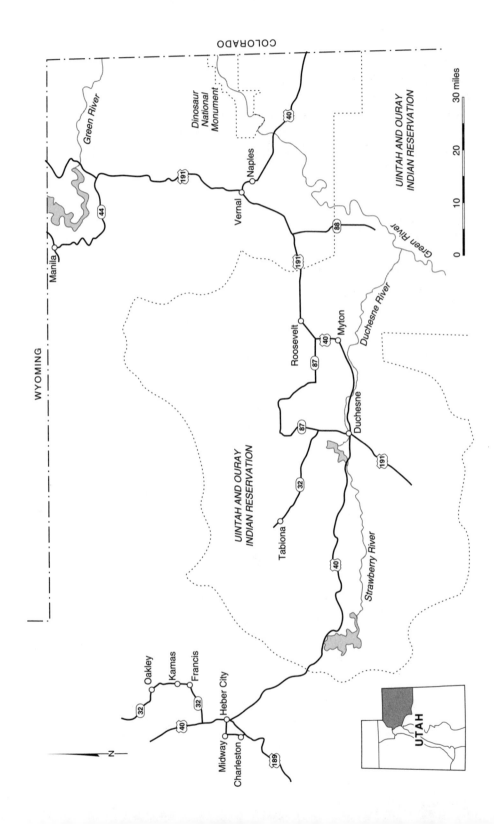

PART VII

The Uinta Basin

The Uinta Basin is a huge bowl 300 miles long and 127 miles across that extends into three states—Utah, Colorado, and Wyoming. The basin is bordered to the north by the Uinta Mountains (Uintah was the original spelling; when the *h* was later dropped, Uintah County had already been named and it retained the original spelling). The Wasatch Mountains lie to the west, and the vast Tavaputs Plateau to the south. The Colorado Rocky Mountains form the basin's eastern border. Ancient Lake Uinta filled the basin many thousands of years ago, and in its wake left a rugged sagebrush-lined bowl dotted with limestone buttes and mesas, intersected by life-giving mountain streams. Deep below the surface of this broad land lie rich oil deposits, while dinosaur fossils hide under sometimes only a few inches of stone against the flanks of the mountains.

The Uinta Basin has long been separated from the rest of Utah by mountain ranges and distance. For many years roads into this corner of the state were poor, and the closest railroad was in Price, accessible only over a long, rough dirt road.

EARLY EXPLORATION OF THE BASIN

The Dominguez-Escalante party passed through Uintah County in the summer of 1776 on their westbound expedition to California. A number of other explorers followed. General William N. Ashley's exploration party visited the Ashley Valley (where Vernal is now) in 1825 and named it after their leader. A man named Green in that party gave his name to the Green River. Jim Bridger, who became famous as an explorer and trapper, was also a part of the group, which subsequently formed the Rocky Mountain Fur Company.

After their arrival in Utah, the Mormons sent out exploration parties in all directions from Salt Lake City. One group went to the Uinta Basin, but returned without hope of creating permanent settlements there. They reported in the *Deseret News* that the area was "one vast contiguity of waste, and measurably valueless excepting for nomadic purposes, hunting grounds for Indians, and to hold the world together." Since the Mormons didn't want the land, Brigham Young, acting as the Indian agent for the Utah Territory in 1861, convinced the Ute Indians living near Spanish Fork to move there. President Abraham Lincoln made the Indian reservation official, signing it into law in 1864. He created the Uintah Indian Agency, and the first agent arrived in the Uinta Basin in 1868.

The basin was meant to be the Utes' home. Young had promised them safety and freedom in the great stretches of the basin, and they had a document signed by President Lincoln giving them full rights to the lands in eastern Utah. However, as more people moved west and rangelands in other states became increasingly crowded, ranchers discovered that the wide-open, well-watered fields south of the Uinta Mountains were perfect for ranging cattle. After Young and Lincoln died, others involved in the promise to the Utes either had no power or didn't care. In the 1870s cattlemen started moving into the northeast corner of the state, leasing rangelands from the Indians. Later that decade Mormons settled around Vernal, and in the 1880s a small section of the Uintah and Ouray Indian Reservation known as the Deep Creek area was opened to homesteaders.

NATURAL RESOURCES IN THE BASIN

Mormons began leasing reservation land from the Indians in 1876. More homesteaders came in 1877, settling the area around Vernal. Before the turn of the century, Gilsonite had been discovered on the reservation, and pressure mounted to open the Indian lands to mining and homesteading. In 1905 the federal government allotted each married male Indian 160 acres of land, with lesser amounts going to unmarried men, women, and orphaned children. After the Indians received their allotments, homesteads were opened to the rest of the population.

Small towns sprang up quickly from Duchesne to the Colorado border. The greatest challenge to early residents was bringing water to the land. Settlers had to dig canals, often at a great cost of time, money, endurance, and, sometimes, lives. The canals of the Uinta Basin are now considered so significant that many of them are on the National Register of Historic Places.

Late in the nineteenth century, farmers in the area began digging up huge bones in their fields. Paleontologists explored the area and discovered enormous deposits of dinosaur bones. Though desolate and worthless on the surface, the area had been blessed with ancient underground wealth.

In the late 1940s and early 1950s the U.S. Bureau of Reclamation proposed building two dams in Dinosaur National Monument on the Green River. A group of conservationists, led by columnist Bernard DeVoto, sparked a national controversy that eventually quashed the dam proposals.

During World War I oil companies explored for oil shale in the area. They conducted tests and were satisfied that there was oil in the region, but no one did any serious drilling until the end of World War II. Major oil fields were tapped around Altamont and Roosevelt, bringing a new source of revenue to previously poor ranchers of the Uinta Basin. The Uinta Basin benefitted from a brief uranium boom in the 1950s, and another oil boom in the 1970s. The oil industry has been a major employer in the basin for many years. Like many other industries, this one has had its ups and downs, and in recent years the Uinta Basin has known more lean times.

Oil pump near Tabiona.

US 40
I-80–Colorado State Line
179 miles

US 40 exits I-80 a few miles past the Park City turnoff. This is still open country, though the buildup along the Wasatch Front is creeping even this far into areas previously isolated from Salt Lake City. This stretch of road is fairly new, since the construction of the Jordanelle Dam required US 40 to be moved in 1990.

Keetley, Hailstone, and the Jordanelle Reservoir

The remains of two small towns have disappeared under the waters of the new reservoir. Keetley and Hailstone were little more than a few pastures and farmhouses when the dam was built, but they did have a history.

Keetley started as a Pony Express station and a mining camp. It was named for one of the Pony Express riders, John B. Keetley, who later returned to the place as a mining supervisor. Keetley was known for several decades only as a mining shaft. The town was surveyed in 1887, making it the last community settled in Wasatch County.

During World War II many Japanese Americans living in Pacific Coast states were ordered to leave out of fear they would assist Japan in the war effort. Some leased land and farmed in Keetley. Nearby Heber City

Jordanelle Dam.

residents, angry at having the Japanese Americans so close, soon learned that they were good, peaceful neighbors. The school board hesitated to accept Japanese American students, but when the U.S. government refused to fund a separate teacher, the staff of the Heber schools were told to treat the outcast children with tolerance. When the war ended, the Japanese Americans all left Keetley.

In the 1950s and 1960s the town was in serious decline, and by the time the Jordanelle Dam was built, little was left for the water to cover.

Hailstone, now deep under the waters of the Jordanelle Reservoir north of Heber City, will appear only on maps that are a few years old or older. Hailstone was homesteaded in 1865 by the Hailstone family. A few other families built homes and farms there, but as more highways were constructed, the roads pushed out the little farms, and Hailstone decreased in size until it was just a junction in the roads. In memory of the small settlement, the state park on the west side of the new reservoir has been named Hailstone.

Preparations for the Jordanelle Dam began in 1956. The plan was to build the reservoir on land belonging to the Jordan family. As with many government projects, this one did not progress quickly. In 1978 research into the impact and benefits of the dam was still being conducted. Many looked forward to the irrigation and recreational opportunities the dam would make available. Others (particularly the residents of Keetley) were concerned about losing farmland and businesses. Heber and Midway residents worried that the dam would not be stable and might flood their towns. A rumor spread that the dam would be built on a fault line, and that an earthquake could destroy the Heber Valley. Despite complaints and concerns, however, studies progressed, and construction began on the project in 1990. By 1995 the state park at Hailstone was open to the public and had already become one of Utah's most popular boat launch sites.

HEBER VALLEY

The new section of US 40 descends into the valley and meets the old section a short distance south of the new dam. Mount Timpanogos dominates the west side of Heber Valley, and the reflection of its white peaks glistens in the waters of Deer Creek Reservoir. Until recent times, the towns in the valley have been small farming communities separated by beautiful green meadows where black-and-white magpies are more plentiful than people. Now, suburbs and summer homes encroach more and more as the rest of the Wasatch Front becomes more crowded.

In 1857 men from the Provo area hiked to a point where they could view the "Provo" (Heber) Valley. The following spring, cattlemen drove herds into the south end of the valley, establishing the first cattle ranches there. That year a bridge over the Provo River and a road into Provo Canyon were built, making the Provo Valley more accessible to settlement.

Though cattle grazed successfully in the valley, settlers feared that crops wouldn't ripen there. Most believed that the area had frost twelve months of the year and winters so harsh no one could endure them. Nevertheless, a group of families willing to try it set out from Provo on the last day of April 1859 to start farms for their families in the upper Provo River valley.

Despite the frosts and long winters, Wasatch County proved an attractive place to settle, and by the summer of 1860 more than 200 people lived in the valley. By 1862 enough people had settled there to form a county. The original county borders reached all the way to the Colorado state line.

Heber Valley is becoming increasingly popular as a suburb for commuters who work in Utah, Summit, and Salt Lake Counties. Where once farms spread among meadows, many new houses crowd together in this beautiful mountain valley.

Heber City

Heber City, named for Brigham Young associate Heber C. Kimball, who garnered many conversions to the Mormon Church in England, was the first settlement in the valley. As soon as they had cleared the fields of sagebrush, planted crops, and built log homes to make a fort, the men

Chief Tabby was instrumental in keeping peace with the whites.
—UTAH STATE
HISTORICAL SOCIETY

returned for their families. Most spent the winter of 1859 in the lower towns, and year-round habitation did not start until 1860.

The construction of a fort at the location now bounded by 100 and 400 West and 200 and 500 North Streets was of the first importance for the vulnerable families living in this remote country. Worship and recreation needs had to be met next, so in 1860 the town built a combination church/community building/dance hall/theatre on the corner of what is now 300 North and 200 West Streets.

Along with the rest of Utah, Heber City experienced the terrors of the Black Hawk War in the 1860s. However, residents had a friend in Chief Tabby, who preferred negotiations to fighting. In 1867, at the height of the conflict, Chief Tabby's son, Tom Tabby, died in a hunting accident. The great man carried him to Heber City for a Christian burial. Joseph Stacy Murdock conducted the services, which were followed by a traditional Indian ceremony. Today a piece of sandstone with T. T. carved into it marks the grave.

Theatrical productions were an important part of Heber City from the very first. On days when a play was scheduled the men in the play would dress up—some as gentlemen wearing stovepipe hats and cutaway coats, others as Indians—and chase each other through the streets of the town in their sleighs and wagons, firing guns and waving a banner that read "Theatre Tonight."

As the town and county grew, so did the need for a more permanent place to hold church services. The Wasatch Stake Tabernacle was built from 1887 to 1889. The red sandstone for the building was hand quarried in Lake Creek, east of Heber City. Originally the building was set up much like the Salt Lake Assembly Hall, with a balcony wrapping around three-quarters of the upper hall. In the 1930s it was remodeled and the side galleries were removed. The seating for the tabernacle was arranged with ladies on the north side, men on the south, mixed couples in the middle, and women with babies around the corner stoves. The building was later remodeled into an office building.

The railroad connecting Heber City with Utah Valley was completed in 1899. This enabled Heber City to increase its economic base as a shipping center for local products. A few mines operated in the county, which enriched Heber as the county seat and the shipping point for the ore.

Midway

A few miles west of Heber City, Midway is one of the most picturesque old pioneer towns in the state. Its charming homes are sheltered by the Wasatch Mountains on the west side of Heber Valley. Though it is currently known to most Utahans as the location of Wasatch State Park and the Homestead Resort, where hot springs have become secondary to a wide variety of other recreational opportunities, Midway was a pioneer and farming town for many years.

The town began as an effort at cooperation. The first settlers in the area chose a site at Snake Creek (southwest of the subsequent town site) for its warm springs, fertile soils, and beautiful views of the mountains. In the summer of 1859 they harvested their first crops of grain. Four families wintered along Snake Creek in 1859. The following summer more families arrived, most of them settling about two miles north of present-day Midway. They named their settlement Mound City for the area's geological formations.

By the spring of 1862 more than fifty families had wintered in the two settlements. They stayed separate until 1866, when the Black Hawk War threatened the peace of most of Utah. The two groups decided to strengthen their position by moving together to a point "midway" between the two settlements.

The original fort housed seventy-five families living in log cabins built to form the walls of the fort. This fort was constructed where the town's main square is today. It was never attacked by Indians. By 1868 the threat was over, but the families had become very close and didn't want to go back to their individual settlements. Instead, they stayed in the vicinity and eventually built their homes around the fort square. The square became a community area with schools, churches, and stores.

Many Swiss settlers came to Midway soon after its establishment. Soon the Swiss could attend church meetings held in German. Official announcements were often read in both German and English. Swiss Days is now an annual event in Midway during the first weekend in September.

Midway was primarily a farming community, but it was close enough to the mines of Park City and American Fork Canyon to be influenced by the ready income. Work in the mines wasn't the only benefit to Midway residents; the mine workers provided a ready market for the eggs, milk, and produce the farmers had to sell. This meant steady cash and a relatively good living.

From the beginning, Midway was a peaceful settlement. In February 1867 David Van Wagonen reported that residents had passed a comparatively mild winter and that not a single person had gotten drunk (there were no liquor stores in the entire valley).

The Watkins-Coleman House

A number of impressive homes were built in Midway during the nineteenth century. The most notable of these is the Watkins-Coleman

House at 5 East Main Street. John Watkins, a noted Utah architect, designed and built the home in 1869 for his polygamous family. His grandson, Arthur V. Watkins, became a U.S. senator from Utah. One of Midway's most famous daughters, Lethe Coleman, lived in the house until her death in the 1980s. Lethe became interested in the stage as a young girl, when the Chautauqua movement for traveling performing artists was popular. She wrote speeches and traveled a Chautauqua circuit. With another local performer, Maud May Babcock, she went on a world tour and presented such topics as the home as the foundation of the nation; one of her talks was entitled "A Young Woman Looks at Her World." Mrs. Coleman later performed in many LDS Church movies, including *Windows of Heaven*, and *The Mailbox*. The home she lived in, still in excellent condition, is privately owned.

The Homestead Resort

The area known as the Hot Pots was first homesteaded in 1875. For a time it was called Schneitter's Hot Pots. In 1886 the Schneitters built the two-story Virginia House, with twelve rooms for guests and a dining room where fried chicken was a popular specialty. They also dug two swimming pools: a small hot pool and a larger, cooler pool. The place changed hands several times, and in 1952 the name was changed to the Homestead.

Virginia House (the Homestead) in Midway.

Wasatch Mountain State Park

To the west of Midway lies Wasatch Mountain State Park. By the late 1950s Utah residents had realized they needed to set aside some of their beautiful mountain retreats as public-use areas. The state, appreciating the incomparable beauty of the east side of the Wasatch Mountains, started acquiring land there to develop recreational facilities. By 1962 the state owned over 22,000 acres. An eighteen-hole golf course opened in 1967, and nine additional holes were added in 1972. A section of the park is being developed with cross-country ski trails in anticipation of the 2002 Winter Olympics.

Strawberry Reservoir

US 40 exits Heber Valley going southeast through Daniels Canyon. At the summit of the tree-lined canyon, the horizon opens onto a sage-brush basin through which the Strawberry River once flowed. The basin now holds a large lake, one of the most popular fishing spots in the state. The Strawberry Valley reservoir was the first irrigation project in Utah to receive federal funding. Strawberry Valley was part of the Uintah Ute reservation. The Utes experienced continual problems with white settlers from Heber Valley, who grazed their cattle in Strawberry Valley without the Indians' permission. Disputes also erupted over illegally diverted irrigation water. When a massive water-storage project was proposed for the Strawberry Valley, the rights of the Utes were ignored. The project was approved in 1905, and construction began on the dam in 1911. The project engineers' biggest challenge was figuring out how to get the water from Strawberry Valley to southern Utah County. They managed to construct a 20,000-foot-long concrete tunnel from the reservoir to the Diamond Fork of the Spanish Fork River between 1906 and 1915. The irrigation water greatly enhanced the agricultural capacity of farms in southern Utah County.

Fruitland

The country between Heber Valley and Duchesne is pretty much devoid of settlement. Fruitland is the only site that might qualify as a town along the entire stretch. Rabbit Gulch, the name the original set-tlers here chose, was probably a more appropriate name for this outpost on US 40 near Wasatch County. In 1907, a group of lawyers and doctors from Nebraska decided to develop the town, and they needed a better name to lure investors. The climate wasn't suitable for growing fruit, but "Fruitland" was a more inviting name than Rabbit Gulch. Over the years a number of colorful characters have lived in Fruitland, including some of the original mountain men. It is primarily a ranching community with one general store and a small LDS church.

Duchesne

US 40 comes out of the hills and crosses the sagebrush flats, and the waters of Starvation Reservoir glisten in the sunlight. A few miles farther, US 40 meets US 191 at the first Uinta Basin town, Duchesne. In 1776 the Dominguez-Escalante party camped at the confluence of the Duchesne and Strawberry Rivers (the Strawberry was named not for any abundance of fruit, but for the color of the valley through which the river flows). They were on an exploratory expedition to find a better route from New Mexico to the Spanish missions in California. Later, trappers traversed the region and named the Duchesne River, possibly for Sister Rose Duchesne, who had started schools in Missouri that a number of the early explorers' and trappers' daughters had attended.

In 1905, when settlers were filing for homesteads, A. M. Murdock received permission to start a trading post at the confluence of the two rivers. He started his business in a large circus tent and sold food, hay, and grain. According to the Duchesne County historian's records,

> Murdock's store served as a social center the winter of 1905. It was built in the late fall of that year, and was the first business house. They danced between the counters to the tune of Bud Winslow's guitar, and it was after the Christmas Eve dance that Bill Pickering froze to death. He had left the store for some reason, and when he returned, the store was locked, so he started home without his overshoes and coat. He was living four miles east of town in a cabin with Reuben Whitehead, which they had built in August of that year. He was found dead by Charlie Pitt, the mail carrier, about 9 o'clock Christmas morning.

Murdock's daughter, Dora, was the only woman in a place with fifty-two men, and the town was named for her. Later the name was changed to Theodore, for Theodore Roosevelt. When the government surveyed the site, they renamed it Duchesne, but people continued to call it Theodore for many years.

Many of Utah's first towns were nearly 100 percent Mormon, but Duchesne was not one of these. People of a number of different faiths worshipped here. The town also had quite a few saloons. The first barber worked in a saloon, making it a convenient place to get refreshment, a shave, and a haircut all at the same time.

The first steel bridge in town was completed in 1911. On the day the bridge was finished, two men were waiting, one on either bank, both impatient to be the first to drive his team across the new bridge. Both were so determined that when they leaped forward and met, their buggy wheels locked, and one buggy dragged the other back over the bridge.

Duchesne is now an important business center for the western part of the Uinta Basin. Though not large, it has all the services the surrounding farms and passing travelers require. A few miles northwest of town, Starvation Reservoir offers picnicking, boating, and camping facilities.

Myton

Myton, an ordinary jumble of farmhouses today, once had more importance. For many years, all traffic between the Uinta Basin and the nearest railroad station in Price had to pass through Myton, which had the only bridge over the Duchesne River. After crossing the river, the old dirt road went southwest through Nine-Mile Canyon and on to Price. Supplies and passengers traveled this road for many years until paved highways and motorized transportation became common.

Myton was one of three original town sites designated by the government when Indian lands were opened up for homesteading. Named for Major H. P. Myton, who served at Fort Duchesne, the town quickly flourished, with many businesses springing up to serve the needs of the Uinta Basin.

After severe flooding in the spring of 1909, the course of the Duchesne River changed, leaving the bridge at Myton high and dry. By then the entire Uinta Basin's mail and supplies came through Myton from both

The Wells stage changing station, Nine-Mile Canyon Road, about 1905. One of the few watering places along this long stretch between Myton and Price. —UTAH STATE HISTORICAL SOCIETY

Petroglyphs and pictographs left by ancient Fremont Indians abound in Nine-Mile Canyon.

Fort Duchesne and Price, so a new bridge was essential. When the new bridge was completed on September 10, 1910, the town held a celebration and proclaimed the day Bridge Day, with the slogan, "All roads lead to Myton."

Myton residents were used to seeing people hurry by in various forms of transportation, but an airplane was a different thing altogether. The first airplane ever seen in the basin, an army bomber, arrived in Myton on August 21, 1919. The town had expected the plane several days earlier; a landing strip was ready and waiting on the bench. To entertain the large crowd that gathered to see the plane, rodeos, horse races, and ball games were held until it finally arrived, to the joy of the cheering people.

During the 1920s, traffic switched to Indian Canyon Road (US 191) and a better road that had been built from Heber (US 40), so use of the Nine-Mile Canyon Road declined sharply. By the time the Great Depression hit in 1929, Myton was already in decline. A number of devastating fires had destroyed parts of town, both banks had already failed, and many people were leaving the area. After the Depression, better irrigation systems were built, water became more available to farmers, and life improved all around. However, the town never regained the glory of the old days.

Roosevelt

A string of gas stations and agriculture-related businesses along US 40 announces another town. Roosevelt is in the geographic center of the Uinta Basin, and also serves as the center for a number of businesses conducted in the basin, though it shares that role with Vernal.

Before Indian land was opened to homesteading in 1905, a number of sawmills operated around Roosevelt, some run by the government for the building of Fort Duchesne (about seven miles to the east). A. C. Harmston and his wife pitched their tent at the site that became Roosevelt on January 1, 1906. This was their homestead, and they decided to turn it into a city. Mrs. Harmston chose to name the town for President Theodore Roosevelt.

The winter of 1905–6 was the worst the Uintah and Ouray Reservation had seen in many years. It was hard on the new homesteaders, who were mostly living in tents. They spread cedar shavings on the ground under their beds to try to keep the cold from creeping through, but it was a long, anxious wait for spring to come and alleviate the cold.

The town enjoyed its first big celebration on July 4, 1906. The pink lemonade was an especially big hit until someone discovered a dead cow in the stream just above the spot where the water was taken for the lemonade.

Lemonade was not the only popular beverage in the Uinta Basin. Saloons were big in many towns. When Woody Alexander built the first log cabin in Roosevelt, the local Indians thought it would be a saloon. They called it "Whoopee Kahn." However, they were disappointed. The saloons came later.

Fires were common catastrophes in Utah's early towns. In 1915 a fire burned the Roosevelt Drug Store and all of its stock, valued at $88,000. It was insured for $3,000. The same fire burned the Commercial Club. In 1917 the amusement hall/church house caught fire. It was saved by three young men in the rafters and a group of people outside who flung snowballs into the burning building. The save was a temporary one, however. The structure succumbed to fire in 1930.

Farming was the major occupation of the Roosevelt settlers, and the men were always looking for new inventions to make their work easier. The first tractor in the Roosevelt area was a large steam contraption. It was so heavy it broke most of the bridges and got stuck in the muddy roads. Most farmers decided to rely on their horses and plows until a better invention came along.

In recent times Roosevelt has enjoyed sporadic prosperity. The oil boom of the 1970s seemed to promise eternal jobs and ever-rising property values, but a depression hit the industry in the 1980s and slowed growth in the Uinta Basin. Lately, the town has been a busy commercial center. Its Pennzoil oil refinery is a major employer for much of the basin.

One of Roosevelt's notable daughters was Lorraine Johnson, a popular movie star in the 1930s and 1940s. Known as Lorraine Day, she starred with John Wayne in a number of pictures. Among her most famous movies were *Foreign Correspondent, The Trial of Mary Dugan, Journey for Margaret, The High and the Mighty, Wassail, Tycoon,* and the *Doctor Killdaire* series of the 1930s.

Whiterocks

A few miles north of Roosevelt on the bench close to the Uinta Mountains, you'll get a view of high mountains and beautiful canyons that beg to be explored.

Whiterocks has been inhabited sporadically for more than 1,000 years. Long ago, a Fremont Indian village was located near Whiterocks. Evidence suggests it was the largest Fremont village in the Uinta Basin.

Whiterocks was probably the site of the first white settlement in Utah; it was certainly the first in eastern Utah. Between 1826 and 1830 the Reed family established a trading post near the confluence of the Whiterocks and Uinta Rivers about a mile south of the present town. This post did not last many years, but in about 1832 Antoine Robidoux came to the area and built a trading post called Fort Robidoux. Robidoux and his family had previously established a fur trade in Colorado with both white men and Indians. Kit Carson spent the winter of 1833–34 in Whiterocks, Marcus Whitman came by in 1842, and John Charles Frémont stopped in 1844.

The fort saw a lot of trading activity. One Indian remembered seeing hundreds of buffalo hides drying in the sun in the meadow near the fort. Furs were not the only commodity traded at the fort; Robidoux also traded in slaves. For many years the Spanish and various Indian tribes made fortunes selling captive Indian women and children to other tribes. Robidoux is reputed to have been an unsavory character who only valued human life for what he could gain from it. He traded Indian women and children with other Indians and white men. Some reports say he used Indian children for target practice. It's no surprise that the Indians hated Robidoux and finally became so angry that they attacked his fort, killed the men there, took the women captive, and burned the buildings. Robidoux was away from the fort at the time, so he escaped unharmed. Some reports indicate that he was warned ahead of time of the impending attack.

Utah State Agricultural College home economists with Ute women, 1927. —UTAH STATE UNIVERSITY

Whiterocks became the first permanent white settlement in the Uinta Basin in 1868, when an Indian agent was stationed there. Since that time the residents of the area have been primarily Ute Indians.

Uintah and Ouray Indian Reservation

After the 1879 Meeker Massacre, in which reservation Utes murdered Indian agent Nathan Cook Meeker and the entire agency staff, the White River Utes were moved to the Uinta Basin reservation in 1882. Their leader, Chief Ouray, was born in 1833 in New Mexico. Fluent in English, Spanish, and a number of different native languages, he became a great negotiator. He was conciliatory to the whites, though, and often angered his own people. In 1868 he traveled to Washington D.C. to help with the peace process. However, peace came at a great cost to Ouray's people. Finally in 1880, following the Colorado Indian uprising of 1878, Ouray again traveled to Washington to sign a peace treaty that banished the White River Utes and Uncompahgre Indians from Colorado to Utah. Ouray died soon after he returned home and was buried in southern Colorado, leaving his beloved wife, Chipeta, to move to the Utah reservation with her people.

For a number of decades, whites and natives lived peacefully together. Until 1934 white settlers used some of the reservation's irrigation water.

During a severe drought in the 1930s, however, the Indians protested, and settlers received no more Indian water. Their canals ran dry and many families left the area.

The Uintah and Ouray Indian Reservation is currently home to nearly 3,000 members of the northern Ute tribe and is the largest reservation in Utah. Its border runs along the foothills of the Uinta Mountains north of US 40 and includes scattered areas south of US 40, extending on the east side of the Green River into Grand County.

Fort Duchesne

About a mile south of the highway, Fort Duchesne is both a reminder of the basin's former reservation days and a tribal government center for the Utes. Fur-trading posts were fairly abundant in the Uinta Basin in the first half of the nineteenth century. Besides the ones at Whiterocks and Ouray, Fort Duchesne had a trading post prior to 1841. In August 1861 the Lincoln presidency established Fort Duchesne as the headquarters to oversee the Indian reservation. It was probably one of the most expensive forts the government ever built and maintained; the freighting costs for materials and supplies were tremendous. Along with everything else transported into Duchesne and Uintah Counties, the goods had to be sent by train to Price (after the railroad reached that city), hauled by wagon and team to Wellington (in Carbon County), carried over the rough

Fort Duchesne.

road through Nine-Mile Canyon to Myton, then transported to their final destination.

In 1912 the U.S. Army abandoned the fort and it was reestablished as the headquarters for the Uintah and Ouray Indian Reservation. A few of the old fort buildings remain in use. The old military hospital is now the Ute tribal courthouse. Other buildings serve as a juvenile courthouse and a police station.

Vernal

US 40 climbs through some foothills before it descends into another farming valley. Vernal was named for its green, springlike setting. To easterners, this dry land would hardly have seemed lush, but for pioneers used to sagebrush and dry sand, any moisture and greenery made a spot a paradise.

The first rough cabin was built here in 1873, and the settlement that grew around it was named Ashley. Four years later Thomas Bingham received permission from LDS Church president John Taylor to lead a party from Huntsville to the Ashley Valley. The party consisted of approximately a dozen families, and others joined them in Evanston. When Bingham reported back to President Taylor in 1878, he said about 100 families were living in the area.

After the Meeker Massacre, the residents of Vernal banded together to build a fort. However, the local Indians posed no threat. They told the settlers that if there was ever any trouble, they should raise a white flag, and they would not be harmed.

The winter of 1879–80 brought disaster. The previous summer grasshoppers had decimated the crops, so the pioneers had managed to store little food for themselves or their livestock. The snow was deeper than usual and the temperatures were colder. The settlement was so new that it had no barns to shelter the animals. Cattle died by the hundreds.

By spring the people of Vernal were starving. Early settler Archie Hadlock's son had been killed in the Civil War, and the U.S. government sent Hadlock $400. The settlers borrowed the money from him to buy supplies at Green River, Wyoming. In *Builders of Uintah*, A. Reed Morrill describes how his contract was agreed for the loan:

> My share was $100 and for security I mortgaged my new Peter Schuler wagon. It was a very odd contract. Archie picked up the tongue of the wagon and raising it to the sky said: "Know all things by these presents, this wagon is mine if this debt is not paid." Lowering the tongue to the ground our bargain was made and sealed.

When the group returned from Green River with the much-needed supplies, two of their daughters ran out to meet them. The first thing the men asked was who had died while they were gone. When the girls answered that no one had died, the men burst into tears. Morrill was able to repay his loan plus interest, so he did not lose his new wagon.

In 1905, when the U.S. government opened the Uinta Basin to homesteading, Vernal became a boomtown. The land office was located in the county courthouse in Vernal, and everyone had to go there to file for their land and buy supplies.

In spite of the boom, Vernal was isolated for many years. In a time when all vital supplies were carried by train, Vernal was more than 100 miles from the nearest railway station. Any product not grown or manufactured in the basin had to be freighted in. The roads between Vernal and Myton (southeast of Roosevelt), and between Myton and Price (where the station was), were well-traveled.

Freighting was so expensive that people began sending supplies via the U.S. mail. In 1916 a bank building in Vernal was built of brick. The builders discovered that sending the bricks by freight from Salt Lake City would cost four times their worth, so they wrapped the bricks in fifty-pound packages and sent them by mail. The limit was 200 pounds a day, so every day packages were mailed to different people in Vernal, who

Woolly mammoth, Utah Field House of Natural History State Park.

voluntarily carried their contents to the building site. By the time they were all delivered, there were 5,000 parcels containing all the bricks for the building. Zion's Bank, at 3 West Main Street, is a reminder of an isolated but innovative people.

With the construction of better highways, trucks, and cars, access to goods and services in Vernal improved greatly.

Utah Field House of Natural History Park

Vernal's most prominent landmark is the group of dinosaurs in front of the Utah Field House on Main Street. Inside the museum, visitors can travel through the various prehistoric periods and learn about the creatures that inhabited the earth long ago. An outdoor dinosaur garden gives children an idea of what dinosaurs may have looked like. The museum also has a gift shop, a tourist information bureau, and a large sandbox where youngsters can dig for dinosaur bones.

Vernal Utah Temple (Uintah Stake Tabernacle)

A major landmark in the Uinta Basin has come full circle from a prominent church building to a derelict structure and back to the most important religious building in the area. The impressive craftsmanship of the Uintah Stake Tabernacle, built by members of the LDS Church between 1899 and 1907, represented the dedication of church members to their religion. The edifice served as a regular meeting place until 1948, when a more modern structure was built next to it. The tabernacle continued as both a church and a community meetinghouse on an irregular basis until 1984, when it was closed completely. Local citizens feared that their beloved tabernacle would be demolished, so they were thrilled when the church announced in 1994 that it would convert the historic structure into a temple. It was the first such project undertaken anywhere by the church. The exterior of the building was preserved intact and the interior was completely gutted. With the November 1997 dedication of the newly refurbished building, the people of eastern Utah not only had a temple, but a proud monument to the efforts of their pioneer forebears. The temple is open only to members of the LDS Church.

Naples

A few miles south of Vernal, US 40 passes through Naples. People started coming to Naples in 1879, about the same time Vernal was settled. They planted fruit trees, lilacs, and rosebushes and raised sheep, spun wool, and knitted. One woman knitted over 100 pair of socks for soldiers during the First World War. The settlers tried to make a happy home with some beauty to relieve the hard work and difficulties of life.

Jensen

The name Jensen is not well known outside the Uinta Basin, but is nevertheless a destination for many tourists headed to Dinosaur National Monument.

The first white settlers came to Jensen in about 1877. The town grew up around a ferry operated by Lars Jensen on the Green River. The ferry provided a vital transportation link until 1911, when a bridge was built. The bridge cost $25,000 and took six months to complete. When it was finished the town's residents celebrated for three days.

Jensen people didn't need a bridge to have a party. They loved to celebrate for any reason, and often danced until dawn. It is difficult to understand how people with so much work to do could stay up all night, until you realize that they had to keep dancing until daylight came so they could find their way home on the rocky, potholed roads.

Jensen didn't get modern conveniences until well into the twentieth century. Electricity was installed in 1941. Aside from the traffic connected with the national monument, Jensen remains a primarily agricultural area in a lush setting.

Dinosaur National Monument

In 1893 Jensen farmers discovered the first dinosaur fossils a few miles north and east of town in what would become Dinosaur National Monument. The men were too busy making a living to spend time digging for ancient history, so the first real excavations started much later, in 1909. Woodrow Wilson declared the dinosaur quarry a national monument

The author's daughter with dinosaur bone in quarry wall at Dinosaur National Monument.

in 1915. Though over 350 tons of fossils were shipped to the Carnegie Museum in Pittsburgh, Pennsylvania, thousands of dinosaur bones remain on display. The public can also watch paleontologists at work at the dinosaur quarry. Connected with the monument, a series of trails lead to petroglyphs and other historic sites near the Green River.

UT 32 and UT 35
Rockport–Duchesne
84 miles

Rockport

This little town used to sit along Three Mile Creek where boaters now zoom over the waters of a reservoir. Rockport was named for a rock fort built in 1867 for protection from the Indians. The U.S. government relocated the residents of Rockport when they built the reservoir in 1950.

Peoa

Peoa is a farming town in a bend of the Weber River. Early pioneers found a log near the site with the Indian word *peoa* (pronounced pe-OH-a), meaning "to marry," carved into it. No one knew who carved the word, but it inspired W. W. Phelps to chose the name Peoa for the settlement in 1857.

The first permanent settlers were not sent to Peoa until 1860, when Brigham Young called a group of people from Salt Lake City to establish a town in the well-watered valley. In 1866, during the Black Hawk War, settlers from Peoa and Kamas joined together at Sage Bottom, about a mile south of Peoa, and built a fort, arranging the log houses around a central church. One side of the fort was for the Peoa people and the other side was for the group from Kamas.

Oakley

Turn another corner on this winding highway and you arrive at Oakley. Oakley is a familiar name to many Utahans, mostly because of its rodeo, held annually on the Fourth of July. It's a big event that always sells out, so if you plan to go, order your tickets in advance.

This pretty farming community was known as Oak Creek for a number of years until its name was shortened to Oakley. The first rancher here, Thomas Rhodes, came in 1853. He found the abundant grass and water perfect for his cattle herd. Others came in 1864 and 1865 and lived in dugouts on the banks of the Weber River.

By 1893 summer homes in the Oakley area were already popular with Salt Lake City residents. This part of Utah continues to grow as a recreation refuge from the cities.

Marion

The Kamas Valley opens into wide fields at the feet of rugged mountains to reveal Marion. Marion received notoriety in the early 1980s when the Singers and the Swapps, polygamous families living in the town, bombed a Mormon church. Law enforcement officers tried unsuccessfully to arrest the offending family members. The standoff ended in the death of a police officer and the arrests of several members of the families.

Thomas Rhoads, a trapper, came to Marion with his family in 1856. The Blythe family also settled nearby for trapping. When the number of furbearing animals dwindled, the trappers left the valley. In 1861 Samuel P. Hoyt, a well-to-do cattle rancher, moved to Marion. He provided work for many men, and he paid them in meat: a hog's head for a day's work. A beef head with the tongue in it was worth $1.50, while the head without the tongue was worth seventy-five cents.

Once called Denmark because of all the Scandinavians who lived there, Marion took its current name in honor of two people: LDS Church bishop Francis Marion Lyman and Mrs. Marion Sorenson, a leading woman in the community.

A future rodeo contestant at the Oakley arena.

Kamas

Ranches line both sides of the road as it leads into Kamas. The name Kamas is derived from an Indian word for edible bulbs. Trappers used the area in the 1850s, hunting the beaver in the mountain streams. Soon families came searching for good farmland. Though the area was too high for most farm crops, hay did well, and pastures were good for cattle and horses.

Kamas residents were delighted when Utah finally became a state on January 4, 1896. A sleigh parade with nearly 400 participants jingled merrily down the main street to the city park, where the men of the town celebrated statehood day with a game of ball. The single men defeated the married men as spectators watched the game from the sleighs.

Kamas remains a peaceful ranching community. The *SS* on the mountainside stands for South Summit High School.

Francis

Francis is a ranching community of about 450 people south of Kamas on the Summit-Wasatch County line. Homesteaders first came to Francis from Peoa and Kamas in the mid-1860s to farm. The land was quite dry and the springs were small, so most culinary water had to be carried from the Provo River. A canal constructed in 1873 alleviated most of the water problems, and the town grew from the 1880s through about 1905.

Cowboys repair a livestock truck in Francis.

Woodland

Woodland is the last town before the beginning of a lovely stretch of road that crosses Wolf Creek Pass into Duchesne County. The Wolf Creek Road was unpaved and fairly rough in spots, but recent improvements have made it passable for passenger cars.

In 1867 settlers from Salt Lake came to make their homes in the "Woodland Alley," this narrow, wooded, well-watered valley. The Provo River provided plenty of water and the area had abundant timber. The winters were severe, though, with two feet of snow on the ground most of the time.

Because of the heavy timber, a number of sawmills were built. Lumber was floated down the Provo River for use in mines and as railroad ties. Logging provided a good source of income until most of the trees were cleared out of the valley. Then farming and ranching took its place as the prevalent occupation of this small mountain town. By the late 1940s, many summer homes had been built in the mountains around Woodland.

Stockmore

UT 35 climbs through pristine pine meadows and mountains over Wolf Creek Pass into Duchesne County. Stockmore, the first settlement in the Uinta Basin, is not much more than a dot on the map just northeast of Hanna. Its name is a reminder of two swindlers named Stockman and Moore who tried to sell lots in the town by showing gold nuggets that

Sheep on Wolf Creek Pass.

Hanna's tiny post office.

purportedly came from the area. They were discovered to be crooks, but they managed to escape the federal marshals who came after them in 1905.

Hanna

Hanna, named for its first postmaster, is another farming settlement. In Hanna's early days, goods had to be hauled in over Wolf Creek Pass. Doctors had to be brought over the rough road from Summit County.

In 1902, before the Uinta Basin was opened to white settlement, local rancher Chancey Lee captured wild horses in the area and sold them in Heber, Park City, and Salt Lake City for five to fifteen dollars a head. Horses were both profitable and dangerous for early Hanna residents. When Thomas Roades was struck in the leg by a horse's flailing hooves in 1909, no medical help was available. With the help of a neighbor, he set his own leg, which was broken in two places.

Tabiona

A few miles down the road lies Tabiona, a larger settlement. In 1867 the U.S. government built a military fort here and called it Tabiona. In the fall of 1905 the first homesteaders came and built cabins. They were humble dwellings, but the men who built them had dreams of bringing their families to Tabiona and prospering. Before one settler left to spend the winter with his family, he wrote "God Bless Our Home" on the outside of his door. When he returned in the spring, someone had changed it to "God What a Home."

Despite the difficult circumstances, the families moved to Tabiona in August 1906. It was a lonely place, far from any towns. The nearby mountains offered striking scenery, but not a lot of comfort for a family in the winter. Indians lived in the area, and the settlers' relations with them were generally peaceful.

Early dwellings were crude at best. One family decided they needed more space, so in February they built a room onto their cabin out of green cottonwood. The room felt awfully damp, and the family realized why when, in the spring, their home started leafing out.

UT 35 continues through farmland along the foothills of the Uinta Mountains until it joins UT 87 six miles north of Duchesne.

US 189
Heber City–Provo
25 miles

US 189 leads from Heber through Provo Canyon into Utah Valley. Provo Canyon is an important link not only between Utah Valley and Heber Valley but between Utah Valley and I-80. The opening of the canyon in 1859 made it possible for Utah Valley residents to bypass the Salt Lake Valley when traveling between eastern locations.

Charleston

The first settlers came to Charleston in 1859 and planted a crop of grain. They lost it all to frost but stuck with their plan to settle in the valley, building the first log house that fall. The next spring several families started homesteads. Charleston was blessed with lush pastures—good grazing land for the award-winning Hereford cattle the settlers raised here.

The town grew well until the Deer Creek Reservoir project began in 1938. Within three years the dam was completed, flooding over most of Charleston's farmlands. A number of families had to move, businesses and the post office closed, and the town went into a general decline.

Charleston is now a tiny farming community in a picturesque setting. The fields stretch right up to the reservoir waters, which reflect the image of Mount Timpanogos.

Charleston was named either for Charles Shelton, who surveyed the town, or because a local sheepherder had heard of Charleston, South Carolina, and put up a sign with that name on a tree.

Deer Creek Reservoir

This large reservoir is located just west of Charleston. Severe water shortages along the Wasatch Front during the early 1930s resulted in an increasing demand for additional water-storage facilities. Studies were submitted to the Federal Emergency Administration of Public Works, and the state received $2.7 million to dam the Provo River in Wasatch County. It took several years to negotiate water districts and property purchases from those farmers and homeowners affected by the reservoir. Construction began in 1938. The dam was built by 1941, but the onset of World War II caused delays. The state couldn't obtain the pipes and build the canals to carry the water to the Utah and Salt Lake Valleys until after the war was over.

Sundance Ski Resort

The verdant eastern slopes of Mount Timpanogos are home to one of America's favorite actors, Robert Redford. Born August 18, 1937, in Santa Monica, California, Redford married Utah native Lola Van Wagenen. After success in such films as *Barefoot in the Park* and *Butch Cassidy and the Sundance Kid*, Redford purchased Timp Haven ski resort north of Provo and changed its name to Sundance.

Redford has remained in Utah, expanding his ski resort and participating in local environmental causes. One of Redford's greatest contributions to the community has been the founding of the Sundance Film Institute.

Sundance Film Festival

Robert Redford established the Sundance Institute in 1981 to support emerging independent screenwriters and directors. The festival spotlights independent documentary, short, and feature films from all over the world.

Some films premiered at the festival since its inception have been *The Spitfire Grill*, *Hoop Dreams*, *Like Water for Chocolate*, *Paris Is Burning*, and *sex, lies, and videotape*. The Sundance Institute is also involved in producing films. Some of its more notable projects have been *Trip to Bountiful*, *El Norte*, *Yosemite: The Fate of Heaven*, and *Impromptu*.

The Sundance Film Festival begins the third Thursday of January and runs for ten days. Theaters in Park City, Salt Lake City, and the Sundance Resort screen the various films. The festival is open to the public.

US 191
Wyoming State Line–Vernal
54 miles

US 191 skirts the Uinta Mountains to the east, crossing the Green River at Flaming Gorge Dam and dropping into the Uinta Basin. The Green River, one of Utah's major rivers, enters the state west of US 191, wanders out of the state into Colorado, then comes back into Utah about twenty miles north. The thirty-six-mile stretch of road between the Flaming Gorge Dam and Vernal is noteworthy, even in a state where the spectacular is commonplace. Cut through slickrock and sandstone, US 191 traverses rock rich in geological history. Markers along the way indicate the rocks' origins and age and prehistoric artifacts found in the various layers.

FLAMING GORGE NATIONAL RECREATION AREA

In 1868 and again in 1871, Major John Wesley Powell explored the Green River from Green River, Wyoming, down through the Colorado River. The Green River was known before Powell's time by the Indians and by the trappers who explored the area. Powell named Flaming Gorge Canyon, where the river cuts through the mountains, after the spectacular red cliffs that rise hundreds of feet above the river. He returned in 1874 and 1875 to explore both the north and south slopes of the Uintas with a pack train.

Major John Wesley Powell, the great river explorer, about 1872.
—UTAH STATE HISTORICAL SOCIETY

Today the northernmost part of the Green River forms the backbone of the Flaming Gorge National Recreation Area, which extends from southwestern Wyoming into northeastern Utah. In 1956 work began on the almost-600-foot-high Flaming Gorge Dam. It was completed in 1963.

Dutch John

The next town around the bend, a few miles from the Wyoming border on US 191, is Dutch John. "Dutch" John Honselena was a prospector and cattle rancher in the Browns Park area in the early 1860s. Though he was Prussian, people called him Dutch because of his strong accent. He left his name on several landmarks in the area.

The U.S. government built Dutch John in 1957 during the construction of the Flaming Gorge Dam. It is now home to employees of the Flaming Gorge National Recreation Area and others who provide services for recreationists who come to fish and boat on the reservoir. The town has two lodges, along with other tourist facilities.

In 1991 the U.S. Forest Service began a study pursuant to the sale of Dutch John. The town, wholly owned by the Forest Service since its construction, has become too expensive for its owners to maintain. Daggett County wants the sale to take place, since government-owned property is not taxed. Manila is the only other town in Daggett County, so the county's tax base is extremely small.

Browns Park

About one mile past the Wyoming border on US 191, a road heads east into a sparkling valley; it will take you back to an era talked of only in legends. The Browns Park (also called Browns Hole) area, east of Flaming Gorge Canyon, encompasses parts of Wyoming, Utah, and Colorado. A significant stop on the outlaw trail, this long, narrow ranching valley is still secluded from the rest of the bustling world.

Unlike other sections of Utah, where the LDS Church oversaw colonizing efforts, early settlers in Browns Park were non-Mormons who came for the excellent rangeland for their cattle. By 1872, well-established cattle outfits thrived within the county. Rustling was also a booming business, and the valley offered ample places to hide stolen cattle. Butch Cassidy, the famous outlaw who seems to have been everywhere in the state at one time or another, was living in Browns Park when he formed the Wild Bunch. They had their headquarters in the area from 1896 to 1900. Browns Park was a favored hideout for cattle thieves and outlaws because of its inaccessibility and its year-round grazing.

This photograph of Harry Longabaugh (the Sundance Kid) and Etta Place was taken in New York City in 1902, before the couple went to South America with Butch Cassidy. Etta Place was the alias of Ann Bassett of Browns Park.
—UTAH STATE HISTORICAL SOCIETY

Another sometime cattle rustler, Ann Bassett, was born in Browns Park. She later used the alias Etta Place when she rendezvoused with the Sundance Kid and Butch Cassidy in such diverse locations as Texas, Emery County, and South America.

Bassett was born in 1878. Her mother died in 1892, and her father tried sending her to Catholic school in Salt Lake City to settle her down. It didn't work, and the nuns sent her home a year later. During the winter of 1896–97 she met Butch Cassidy in Browns Park. For the next twenty or so years she periodically left home to rendezvous with the famous outlaw. She always called herself Etta Place when she was with the outlaws and Ann Bassett when in Browns Park, so some mystery surrounded Place's true identity until recently, when a definite identification was made. In 1923 Bassett married Frank Willis and moved to Leeds (in southwestern Utah). She died in 1956.

Ann's sister Josie had as wild and interesting a life as her younger sister. She married several times and was suspected of killing at least one of her husbands. She ended up building a cabin near the Green River inside the present-day Dinosaur National Monument.

Jarvie Ranch

The Jarvie Ranch is a collection of historic and reconstructed buildings in Browns Park that belonged to Scottish immigrant John Jarvie

A number of buildings at the Jarvie Ranch have been restored or rebuilt. The stone house is from Jarvie's time.

The dugout is also original.

around the turn of the twentieth century. Jarvie set up a trading post/post office and ran a ferry on this beautiful site on a bend of the Green River. His place was frequented by the famous outlaws of the day as well as many other interesting characters and explorers.

John Jarvie was born in Scotland in 1844. Arriving in America in 1870, he moved west to Wyoming and married Nellie Barr in 1880. The same year, they moved to Browns Park and opened their trading post. After Nel died of tuberculosis in 1895, Jarvie ran the place by himself until he was shot and killed in a holdup in 1909.

The ranch has been restored by the Bureau of Land Management and is open to the public from May to October. The site has a number of buildings, some of them furnished, and offers guided tours.

UT 43 and UT 44
Manila–US 191
36 miles

UT 43 and 44 pass through the heart of Daggett County. Most of the early settlers in the area were ranchers. They moved their cattle where the good feed grew, tilling very little soil themselves. After the hard winter of 1887–88, they realized they needed to store feed for their stock in case of hard times. In the 1890s homesteaders came to the area and started farming. Though they were not always successful, the homesteaders brought a different lifestyle and a tendency to prefer law and order over the lawlessness that had prevailed in the past.

Manila

Manila, next to the Utah-Wyoming border, is the smallest county seat in Utah. The town is now closely tied with Flaming Gorge Reservoir, but it actually predates the reservoir by forty-four years. In 1893 Adolph Jessen surveyed the area. He felt it would be an ideal agricultural area if he could bring water to it, so he found backers to help form a company to build a canal. By 1896 the canal company had distributed brochures expounding on the bounties of the newly developed area, and families started arriving. Most of the families came from Beaver, lured by the brochure's pictures of thick, lush grasses. Despite the pictures, the canal didn't go far enough to water most of the new settlers' crops, and the first few years proved difficult until they built their own canal.

After several years the people in the valley decided to form a town. Just as the town was being laid out they heard of the U.S. victory at

Manila Bay in the Spanish-American War, so they named their town Manila. Most of the settlers built log cabins in town so the children could attend school, while the men lived on the ranches all winter tending their livestock. Women and children went for months without seeing their husbands and fathers.

The wind blew incessantly in Manila, whipping up the sands of the freshly plowed fields. It filtered into every home, making its way through cupboards, into food, onto clothing, everywhere. Many early settlers referred to Manila as Sandtown.

The construction of the Flaming Gorge Dam changed the face of Manila considerably. While ranching retained its importance, residents also reaped the benefits of tourist dollars spent by the many people who came to the new reservoir for fishing, boating, and other activities.

OLD CARTER TRAIL

Though in this part of Utah natural boundaries played a much larger role in day-to-day life than political boundaries, government obligations had to be met; to meet them residents had to travel over the Uinta Mountains to Vernal, their county seat, any time they wanted to get married, purchase property, obtain a building permit, or perform any official business. Because they were so isolated from the government to which they paid taxes, the settlers didn't receive any services in return.

In 1881 Judge William Carter, a longtime resident of Fort Bridger, Wyoming, contracted the construction of a rough road over the Uinta Mountains. He felt that, if speculation at the time was correct and some of the Uinta Basin Indians were to be transferred to Fort Bridger, a road would facilitate the move. While helping with the construction of the road, the judge became chilled, contracted pleurisy, and died on November 7, 1881. On detailed maps the road is still called the Old Carter Trail.

The road, icy in winter and a muddy mire in summer, did link those living north of the mountains with Vernal on the south side—but traveling it was often impossible. Finally in 1918 the northern residents formed their own county, Daggett County (named for Ellsworth C. Daggett of the company that originally surveyed and developed the Lucerne Valley), and the road fell into disuse. Today the road is just a foot trail in the Ashley National Forest.

Greendale

The community of Greendale, now part of the Flaming Gorge National Recreation Area, has left some evidence of what life was like for early homesteaders in the wilderness. At the Swett Ranch, visitors can see the progression of one family's success: from a one-room log cabin, where the entire family first lived and shared a bed, to a two-room log cabin to a five-room home, where the family grew and prospered with the times. The outbuildings where the work on the farm was conducted still stand, along with traces of the schoolhouse where the children came to learn the three R's. The Swetts reared nine children in this isolated place. The ranch gives visitors a clearer picture of homesteading life.

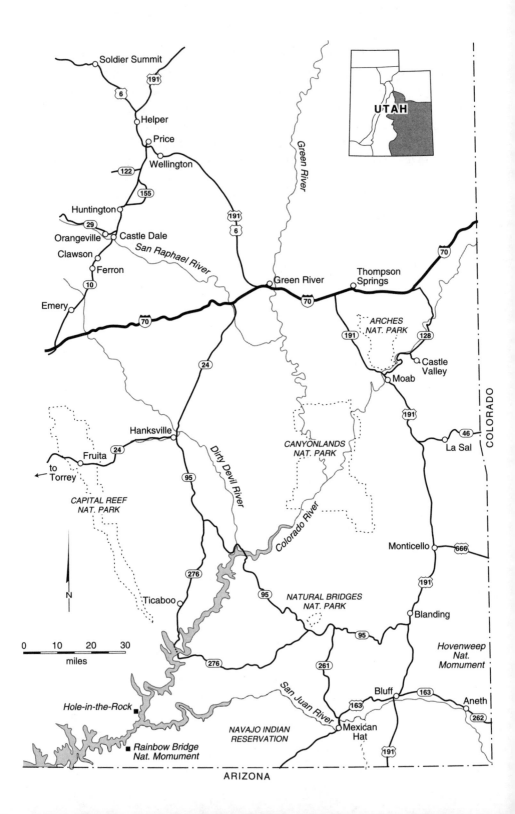

PART VIII
Canyon Country

Southeastern Utah's geographical features cut it off from the rest of the state until the last two decades of the nineteenth century. The rugged cliffs and gulches of the Green and Colorado Rivers were practically insurmountable obstacles. Also, the Four Corners region was Navajo territory. Settlers were wary of traveling through hostile lands in order to claim new ranges. As cattlemen from Colorado began moving their

A family traveling through a narrow wash in the Canyon Country.
—UTAH STATE HISTORICAL SOCIETY

329

herds into the land north of the San Juan River, Mormon colonizers realized they must either claim this corner of Utah or lose it.

Because of their remoteness and wild landscape, the canyons of southeastern Utah were a favorite hideout for outlaws. The large cattle herds attracted them. Many of the cowboys employed by the bigger cattle outfits were on the shady side of the law.

As the territory became more settled, people discovered valuable mineral deposits in the land. Booms were born and died—but the ranchers endured steadily through every economic swing.

PREHISTORIC HABITATION IN SOUTHEASTERN UTAH

Prehistoric tribes hunted in southeastern Utah as early as 10,000 B.C. Different groups came and went, as evidenced by ancient tools and hunting points that have been found. Between 7800 and 6000 B.C., the Archaic people started inhabiting the Colorado River plateau, leaving behind many traces of their civilization. Between 2000 B.C. and A.D. 500 the Archaic people turned from a primarily hunter-gatherer lifestyle to a more agrarian society that depended on crops—mainly corn, squash, and beans—for survival.

The Anasazi or Ancient Ones were in the region from about 600 B.C. to approximately A.D. 1200 and left the most visible marks on the area in the form of cliff dwellings, villages, and rock art. The Anasazi are thought

Anasazi ruins abound in southeastern Utah. This one is at Hovenweep National Monument.

to have been descendants of the Archaic culture. They farmed the mesas and built a dam in the Glen Canyon area that trapped water to irrigate their crops. After centuries it filled with silt. The Anasazi left numerous ruins that still remain in the washes throughout the country. About A.D. 1300 the Anasazi disappeared from the region and Numic-speaking tribes (ancestors of today's Utes and Paiutes) appeared.

CATTLEMEN AND DESPERADOES

Because of its desolation and rugged geological features, the canyon area of the Colorado River was a favorite hiding ground for desperadoes in the second half of the nineteenth century and into the early twentieth. The southeastern corner of Utah was the last section settled, and men ran wild in it for many years. When cattlemen came in, they frequently hired disreputable characters to work for them—outlaws hiding from eastern lawmen. These men became criminals in Utah as well. Poorly paid county sheriffs rode long and hard to catch some of these criminals, and many on each side of the law lost their lives in the process. Such outlaws as Butch Cassidy, Matt Warner, Mont Butler, "Kid" Jackson, Al Akers, and "Kid" Parker were among the more famous ones. These men were difficult to catch. They rarely killed anyone and were often on friendly terms with the locals. They specialized, for the most part, in robbing the big outfits, thus keeping peace with the common folk who befriended them. Countless books have been written and movies made about the wild life in southeastern Utah around the turn of the twentieth century. Many are fictional, but a lot of truth can be found in the rugged legends of this part of the Wild West.

US 6
Spanish Fork–Green River
125 miles

US 6 and US 89 exit I-15 together at Spanish Fork. The highway soon enters the Spanish Fork Canyon and travels along the riverbed for about ten miles. The hillside and cut of the roadbed are evidence of a newer stretch of road between Billies Mountain and the split of US 6 and US 89. The old road follows the Spanish Fork River, while the newer one climbs. Across the canyon to the south, part of the mountain slid across the riverbed a number of years ago. This was the site of the great Thistle landslide of 1983.

Tucker, when there was a town. —UTAH STATE HISTORICAL SOCIETY

Tucker

After US 89 turns south, US 6 winds along the riverbed until it reaches a rest stop. The land occupied by the stop was once Tucker, a Denver & Rio Grande Railroad town. Though a dot on the map marks the place, no road sign indicates that a town once thrived where now there are only a rest stop and a few dirt roads leading into the mountains.

Tucker grew up as an important railroad junction. Carbon County coal was loaded onto the Salt Lake trains in this prosperous town built around a small stream. Tucker had as many as 500 residents for a brief time. However, the railroad changed its course, and the town was abandoned.

Soldier Summit

After Tucker, US 6 climbs quickly to Soldier Summit, another forgotten railroad town. In 1861 General Johnston's invading army was returning east at the beginning of the Civil War. At the top of Spanish Fork Canyon, they were caught in a storm. Some of the men died and were buried here, and the site was named Soldier Summit.

When the Denver & Rio Grande Railroad was built through Spanish Fork Canyon, the company used Soldier Summit as a turnaround and storage stop for engines. In 1919 the railroad built a freight station and yards at Soldier Summit and moved a lot of its employees in from Helper.

A real estate developer started selling property at Soldier Summit. The town grew and several businesses started. Ozokerite, a type of paraffin wax, was mined nearby. From 1925 to 1930, 2,500 people lived in the town. Houses crowded along the highway and pushed up the hillsides.

Severe winters made life at the summit difficult, and finally the railroad stopped using its Soldier Summit stations, moving most of the services and houses back to Helper in 1930. The town gradually died.

When county lines were drawn, Soldier Summit fell within Wasatch County. However, no roads led directly from Soldier Summit to Heber City, the Wasatch County seat. To conduct official business, residents had to travel down Spanish Fork Canyon, all the way through Utah County, and up Provo Canyon, a distance of more than seventy miles that traversed two mountain passes. In 1923 a countywide vote was held to determine if Soldier Summit should remain in Wasatch County. Despite the inconvenience to the townspeople, county residents voted to retain the isolated hamlet as part of Wasatch County because the railroad paid so much in taxes to the county.

By the 1970s, little of Soldier Summit remained. Four part-time police officers still lived in the town: one for every seven residents. Their duties mostly consisted of issuing speeding tickets on the highway. A slower speed limit was posted through Soldier Summit, and officers collected an av-

Soldier Summit, undated. Pictured is the Denver & Rio Grande Western Railroad depot. —UTAH STATE HISTORICAL SOCIETY

erage of $4,500 a month in revenues. In a statewide scandal, a Utah Police Association investigation of the Soldier Summit police department ended in the resignation of the town's police chief and the final disbanding of the department. The town itself was disincorporated in the early 1980s, and today only a gas station and a convenience store exist at Soldier Summit.

CARBON COUNTY

US 6 drops quickly from Soldier Summit into coal country—Carbon County. The name evokes images of coal mines belching black smoke, but the true picture is different. From the peaks of the mountains on its northwestern border to the Green River's Desolation Canyon on Carbon County's eastern edge, this part of the state showcases nature's geological wonders. Because Utah contains so much of the spectacular, Carbon County has no national parks, but its stark cliffs are awe-inspiring to those who will pause to contemplate them.

By the 1870s the western valleys of Utah were filling up. A few Mormon pioneers moved into the more arid lands of eastern Utah, but no one rushed to inhabit this unappealing desert until the Denver & Rio Grande Railroad came through in 1883. Railroad employees discovered rich veins of coal in the mountains, guaranteeing the wealth of the future county. The railroad opened up the coal mines and controlled most of them for many years. Emery County had been pioneered the decade before when land in Sanpete County became overcrowded. Before that time, the eastern part of the territory was considered uninhabitable.

Coal mining is still a vital part of the county's economy. Because of the mines, Carbon County's demography is different from the rest of the state's. Most of the population of the mining towns has been made up of ethnically diverse people who came for work rather than for religious freedom. While most of the Mormon pioneers were English or Scandinavian, the majority of the coal miners were Greek, Polish, Italian, or Irish. The area has traditionally had fewer Mormons, and the Democratic Party in Carbon County has been the strongest in a predominantly Republican state since the 1930s. In 1911, when most of Utah adopted prohibition, Carbon was the only county that voted to stay wet.

The coal camps of Carbon County were unique establishments. The coal company built towns, schools, stores, and even saloons for its workers. The company saw to its employees' every need. But it also held the monopoly in these isolated towns, controlling the prices in the stores and saloons, so miners had no choice but to patronize company businesses. Few people owned automobiles, so if miners wished to shop elsewhere they had to carry their purchases home on the train, where company bosses might see them. Anyone disloyal to the company could lose his job. The monopolies and the fixed wages led to strikes and labor disputes in the 1920s and 1930s. Some areas of Carbon County became hotbeds of worker unrest.

Castle Gate

Castle Gate is just north of the junction of US 191 and US 6. Formerly a striking rock formation, the gate resembled closed castle doors from a distance that appeared to open up as the traveler drew closer. Half of the gate was destroyed when blasting was done for the highway.

In 1883 construction on the Denver & Rio Grande Railroad came through Castle Gate, and in 1888 a coal-mining town sprang up.

In the most famous incident in the town's history, Butch Cassidy and his gang held up the coal company's paymaster, taking $7,000 in gold. Plenty of men in the vicinity could have stopped the robbery, but no one did. The newspaper account says the holdup was carried off with so much "bravado and daring" that everyone was taken by surprise. A shoot-out took place in which two of the outlaws were killed. The lawmen reported to the public that one of the dead men was Butch Cassidy. However, at

Castle Gate before blasting for the highway removed part of the gate.
—UTAH STATE HISTORICAL SOCIETY

the inquest, when the bodies were displayed to the public, Butch Cassidy showed up to see them. The authorities realized they had made a mistake, much to the famous outlaw's amusement. Cassidy escaped to rob other payrolls in other towns.

Mining was dangerous work, and women had to face the fact every morning that they might never see their husbands again. Fears were justified in Castle Gate in 1924 when a mine explosion killed 172 men.

Castle Gate ceased to exist as a town in 1974. The Pleasant Valley Coal Company expanded its mines and had to remove the town's houses. Mines still operate at Castle Gate, but the workers live elsewhere.

Helper

From Castle Gate, US 6 descends into a valley. Helper is the first town after the canyon opens up. The spirit of Helper is symbolized by "Big John," a large black statue of a coal miner in front of the city auditorium.

In the early 1880s Teancum Pratt and his two wives, Annie and Sarah, homesteaded at Helper. Soon the railroad came through, and a town formed. The town's name came from the helper engines stored there that helped the trains climb the steep mountain grades to Soldier Summit.

United Mine Workers in Helper, June 8, 1919. —UTAH STATE HISTORICAL SOCIETY

Helper became a railroad and mining center. Many different European immigrants moved into the area to take advantage of the mining and railroad jobs, bringing ethnically diverse businesses with them. Helper's ethnic groups included English, Scandinavian, Italian, Greek, Japanese, and Chinese.

Helper was known as the "Hub of Carbon County." Price was the major commercial city, but Helper was the center of all the mining activity, with a number of mining towns in the surrounding area forming the spokes on the wheel. It was also the heart of Carbon County's labor movements, where most of the major organizing took place. Other towns had their biggest celebrations on July 4 and 24. The most important day of the year in Helper was Labor Day, when parades and speeches honored the laborers. Leona Turner, a young girl in Helper in the 1930s, remembers the city park as the center for the area's labor activities. Her mother wouldn't allow the children to go to the park for a time because of the danger posed by angry, rock-throwing miners.

The Helper Post Office on 45 South Main is adorned with a mural painted in 1941 under the Public Works of Art Administration. Entitled *A Typical Western Town*, the mural won a prize in a national contest for post-office wall designs in each of the forty-eight states. One of only three public buildings in Utah containing a mural, it is the only post office in Utah graced with one of the prizewinning paintings.

Helper has become a quiet town in recent years. Many of the mines and towns that formed the spokes around the hub have closed. A few businesses remain, but most people go to Price to shop and work.

Kenilworth

A few miles away east of US 6, Kenilworth once thrived as a mining town. A hunter discovered coal veins at Kenilworth in 1904. The mines that opened in 1905 were named either for Kenilworth, England, or for an old English word for coal. Kenilworth was the first mine in the area that was not owned by a large corporation.

Though racial diversity was an accepted fact of life in Carbon County, integration was not. When boardinghouses were built in Kenilworth for the mine workers, one housed the black workers, one the workers of Japanese descent, and yet another housed the rest, who were predominantly white. Despite the racial differences, the residents of Kenilworth felt their coal-mining camp was the most attractive in Carbon County.

The mine at Kenilworth is no longer in operation, and the town is in serious decline.

Spring Glen

Another spoke radiating from the Helper hub, Spring Glen is between Helper and Price. The first homesteaders were Mormons who arrived in 1879. They settled on a beautiful spring that inspired the name of their town.

By 1886 enough people lived in Spring Glen to merit building a school and church. In 1889 charcoal kilns were built here and were used for about fifteen years.

In the 1890s eastern European Slavs migrated to the coal fields of Carbon County. They were single men, free to travel to wherever the pay was best. In 1906 one of these men, Martin Millarich, settled in Spring Glen and built a home and tavern near the railroad tracks. Millarich's Hall became a gathering spot for Slavic miners. The building burned in 1919, and in 1922 the spot became a gathering place for striking miners. These men helped rebuild the tavern, even though Prohibition precluded the selling of alcohol (they bottled soda pop at the tavern for a time). After Prohibition ended, the tavern again sold alcohol and served as a gathering place for Slavs and disgruntled miners. Communist party organizers met in Millarich's Hall during the most heated periods of dispute. Gradually, political activities became less leftist-oriented, and eventually some LDS Church meetings were held in the hall. However, it continued to serve as a Slavic gathering place for many years and is now the Slovenian Hall.

Price

In 1869 Bishop William Price of Goshen (in southern Utah County) explored the eastern side of the mountains. He found a barren land that was white with alkali in spots. However, a fairly good river and agricultural possibilities gave the place promise. The river was named for him, and the town later took its name from the Price River. Late in the 1870s men from Salem (also in Utah County) tried trapping along the Price River. They built a cabin in Price and later decided to make a permanent move with their families to the east side of the Wasatch Mountains.

Like in all pioneer settlements, the people of Price struggled to farm in a dry and isolated location. The new community was many miles from any other town, and trips for supplies were long and hard. Medical services were also difficult to obtain. Anyone with dental problems went to John Pace, a dentist who had the hazardous job of extracting teeth. He gave his patients a club to grip when he pulled their teeth. One young boy let go of the club as the tooth came out, hitting the dentist full-force in the face.

A lot of the town's problems were solved in 1883 when the Denver & Rio Grande came through eastern Utah and built a station at Price.

It became an essential freighting and passenger station for the eastern side of the state from Vernal to Bluff (in San Juan County). Along with the business came some prosperity, and soon new mines brought a wide range of people to settle in Price.

The mines attracted hungry workers from various parts of the world. Most of these were men, but some brought their families; eventually women followed to marry the single men. Price's mining history has rendered it more diverse than the rest of Utah—more religions and political persuasions are represented here than in Utah's other small towns.

The Hellenic Orthodox Church of the Assumption at 61 South Second East Street is a dominant structure in Price. The church represents a group of people who immigrated to the United States in the twentieth century. In 1900 only three Greeks lived in Utah; by 1916 there were over 3,000. The church, built in 1916, gave its congregation a feeling of permanency in the community. Single men who had come to mine began sending for Greek women to marry. In 1940 and 1941 some exterior remodeling was done on the church, and in 1945 a fire necessitated further reconstruction. In 1961 the church was enlarged, but the building kept its stylistic integrity.

A Greek family portrait.
—UTAH STATE
HISTORICAL SOCIETY

College of Eastern Utah

Carbon College, the first two-year college supported by the state, was established in 1937. Its name changed to the College of Eastern Utah in 1959, but it has taken many years for the school to grow from a few hundred students to an enrollment of 2,000.

In connection with the college, a fine museum exhibits displays relating to ancient inhabitants of the region, as well as some dinosaur casts from the area. Displays are user-friendly. The museum is a must for anyone interested in dinosaurs and Utah's ancient inhabitants.

Wellington

Continuing southeast from Price, US 6, now concurrent with US 191, passes through Wellington. Wellington is a somewhat depressed farming and mining community. The first settlers were men who arrived about 1878 and lived in dugouts on both sides of the Price River. They tried growing grain, but their irrigation efforts failed and the site was abandoned until 1882.

Food was scarce in Wellington, so the men hunted. They drove their wagons into Whitemore Canyon and returned when their wagons were loaded with game. One trip brought back 120 deer, which were hung in a granary. Anyone who needed meat could help himself. Wellington was named for Judge Justus Wellington Seeley Jr. of Emery County.

The Nine-Mile Canyon Road to Myton joins US 6 in Wellington. This route was used to transport goods and passengers from the railroad in Price to the Uinta Basin until the 1920s.

Green River

US 6 from Wellington to Green River is a long, lonesome stretch. This interesting, desolate country is full of ghosts from the old outlaw days. The land is devoid of water, and in the West, where water isn't, neither is population.

Green River is an oasis in the eastern Utah desert. It has served travelers since early in the nineteenth century. One of the few breaks in the steep-walled canyons of the Green River, the spot has been an important fording point for a number of centuries. The Old Spanish Trail crossed the river here and was used by numerous explorers, Indians, and trappers. The overland mail used the crossing in the 1870s, and Green River became a station for the mail between Salina, Utah, and Ouray, Colorado.

The first Mormon settlers at Green River came in 1879, when the rest of Emery County was being settled. When the Denver & Rio Grande Railroad connected with the Western Railroad in Green River, the town

Pioneer family homestead in Green River.
—UTAH STATE HISTORICAL SOCIETY

boomed, but the railroad later transferred most of its big engines and workers to Helper, reducing Green River to just another stop along the way.

Green River was destined to know a number of boom-and-bust cycles through the years. Shortly after the turn of the century an oil boom hit southeastern Utah, but it didn't last long enough sustain a large population in Green River. It was followed by an ill-fated attempt at orchard development, the discovery of uranium, and a surge in military missile production that lasted from 1964 to the mid-1970s.

Through all the ups and downs, agriculture has remained constant in Green River. The proximity of the river makes irrigation water readily available, and Green River is blessed with a long, hot growing season, excellent for ripening melons and other heat-loving crops.

Green River is strategically located for the tourist trade. It is a jumping-off point for I-70 west to Salina, a 105-mile stretch of road that—though one of the most spectacular—is the longest in the entire interstate system without any services. This fact assures Green River a constant supply of dollars at its gas pumps and other tourist-related businesses. Green River has benefited from the popularity of river rafting and is an excellent spot for starting a wild, wet adventure.

Appropriately, Green River is home to a museum celebrating river transportation. The John Wesley Powell Museum at 885 East Main Street, explores the history of John Wesley Powell and Utah's river exploration.

The Western Meets the Denver & Rio Grande

In the fall of 1881, railroad contractors of the Denver & Rio Grande Railroad, under the leadership of powerful William Jackson Palmer, hacked away at the wilderness west of Gunnison, Colorado, bound for the Utah line. In the face of mounting obstacles, Palmer was determined to reach Salt Lake City to complete a 600-mile link between Pueblo, Colorado, and Salt Lake. He wanted to service mining districts and capitalize on general traffic between Colorado and Utah. In the final lunge toward Utah, General Palmer had more than 1,000 men and 175 teams at work grading and laying track. At the same time, his officials were busy in Utah making plans to begin construction eastward from Salt Lake. Western workers began grading and laying track through the mountains and deserts of southeastern Utah. On March 30, 1883, construction crews of the Western met those of the D&RG a few miles west of Green River, where the traditional last spike was driven and the two rails were formally joined. Commercial men of Utah and Colorado rated the merger as next in importance to the completion of the transcontinental railroad in 1869.

UT 96
US 6–Clear Creek
17 miles

Scofield

Scofield is known today for its popular trout-filled mountain reservoir rather than as the large town that once rivaled Price as the county seat.

Settlers first came to Pleasant Valley in the 1870s, attracted by its lush grasses and fine timber. Trees grew tall in this well-watered mountain valley, and lumber was in demand in the bare lower valleys. The town that was later established here was named for Charles Scofield, a timber and mining contractor. Lumber and shingle mills prospered in the early days of Scofield until importation of cheaper Oregon lumber drove them out of business.

Winter Quarters Mine

In 1877 men who lived in Sanpete County opened Scofield's first coal mine. They worked the mine and carried the coal back down to the Sanpete Valley. The winter of 1877 came early, stranding the men on the mountain. They named their mining camp Winter Quarters, a reminder of the cold, hard winters many had passed in the Mormon camp in Iowa before

This group of men from Provo volunteered to help dig graves after the Winter Quarters Mine disaster in 1900. They brought their own shovels. —UTAH STATE HISTORICAL SOCIETY

traveling on to Utah. The name attached itself to the mine, which grew to be large and productive. As the Winter Quarters Mine grew and others started, Scofield grew up nearby.

In 1900 people considered the Winter Quarters Mine the safest in the territory because it was free from gases. A spark lit the coal dust, however, and caused a terrible explosion, killing 199 men, either by fire or suffocation. The bodies filled all the town's public buildings. Salt Lake City couldn't provide enough coffins to hold all the dead, so a carload was sent from Denver. The men left 107 widows and 268 fatherless children. In spite of the disaster, the mine continued operating until 1928.

Clear Creek

A few miles past the junction of UT 96 and UT 264, the small settlement of Clear Creek hides in the forest. In the 1870s loggers were sent into the mountains to harvest logs for mine props. This place was called Mud Creek (the streams of Mud Creek and Clear Creek ran quite close together). After a few years of logging, workers discovered they were actually standing on a coal mine. The rich coal right at the surface was easily extracted from the ground. For a time, this was the cheapest coal

Clear Creek. —UTAH STATE HISTORICAL SOCIETY

in Utah because of its accessibility. About thirty years later, the coal was deep enough to make mining it unprofitable. Mining operations stopped in about 1950. The town that had grown up around the mine died, but in recent times has been partly revived to serve nearby summer homes.

UT 10
Price–I-70
106 miles

UT 10 leaves the mining areas of Carbon County behind and enters Emery County, a more traditional, agrarian-based region. Emery County is one of the most geologically interesting and least-known parts of the state. Emery encompasses Goblin Valley State Park, with its unearthly rose- and orange-colored Entrada sandstone cliffs, as well as the San Rafael Swell. A rugged and remote land of deep crevices and dramatically colored buttes, the county stretches for 100 miles from Castle Dale to Capitol Reef National Park. No wonder outlaws found this an incomparable land for escaping justice.

The outlaws were not the only people who appreciated the hideouts of this rugged country. During the Black Hawk War of 1865–71, Sanpete and Sevier County settlers became familiar with the area east of the mountains that they called Castle Valley for its fabulous rock formations. A common trick of the Indians was to steal the settlers' cattle and horses and drive them over the mountains into the no-man's-land of the San Rafael Swell. The pioneers recovered very few of these animals, though they gave the Indians some good chases.

After peace came, A. D. Ferron surveyed several town sites for the federal government. Settlers were hesitant to relocate, however; they were convinced the water was insufficient, and the soil looked strange.

Because of its inaccessibility, many outlaws hid in the San Rafael Swell and neighboring mountains. "Robbers' Roost" was in the rugged country toward the Colorado River, and the county had a reputation as the safe harbor of the rough characters who concealed themselves there.

CASTLE VALLEY

By the 1870s large Mormon families had taken over most of the available farmland in Sanpete County, and they needed new territory for their children to farm. Though earlier Mormons had found the area east of the mountains uninhabitable, by 1877 it was starting to look pretty good. At the fall 1877 LDS conference of the Sanpete Stake, people were called to settle Castle Valley. Brigham Young had issued the call on August 22, 1877, just a week prior to his death on August 29. It was his last directive for the settlement of new territory.

The pioneers set out the next year for Castle Valley, some reluctant, others happy to be pioneering new land. The first towns settled were Huntington, Castle Dale, and Ferron. By 1880, 556 people lived in Emery County.

The region remained sparsely settled in spite of the Mormons' need for new land. On May 20, 1905, with an obvious desire to recruit more settlers to the area, H. T. Haines wrote in *The Emery County Progress:*

> To the many thousands of our subscribers in Oklahoma and Kansas (that we would like to have), let us advise you to come away from the blizzards, tornadoes, floods, droughts, sunstroke, etc. Come out to the God-blessed valley of Eastern Utah, where the land is rich and fertile, where there is just enough and never too much water, where the sunshine is tempered just right almost every day in the year, where blizzards, tornadoes, sunstrokes and earthquakes are impossible. What is the use of living in states where it is necessary to spend nine months in the year in chasing your hat, and the other three months in a cellar while good old Emery County has a home and a warm welcome for you?

Perhaps Haines's advice had some effect on the area's settlement, because the valley's population grew steadily until the 1930s. From 1940 to 1970, poor economic conditions caused a rapid population decrease; the county lost a third of its inhabitants. Then, Utah Power and Light built an electric power plant in Huntington, and the 1974 Arab oil embargo helped raise the price of local energy sources, bringing Emery County another growth spurt.

Wilberg Mine

The mountains west of Castle Valley are rich in minerals. Coal is plentiful, but mining it always involves risks. On December 19, 1984, many families learned about the risks firsthand. Twenty-seven men and one woman were trying to set a twenty-four-hour production record in the Wilberg Mine when a parts runner discovered heavy smoke in the Fifth Right section. The call went out to evacuate the tunnel, but fire cut the telephone line. The miners were trapped inside. Some, not aware of the danger, failed to use their oxygen masks. Of the twenty-eight people trapped in the mine, one managed to get out by a route he later could not clearly describe. The rest died in various tunnels, trying to escape.

Huntington

Present-day Huntington is in a favored position at the junction of UT 10, which leads to Price, and UT 31, which climbs over the Wasatch Plateau to Fairview in Sanpete County. Named for William Huntington, an early explorer, Huntington was one of the first towns in Emery County. Stockmen first settled here in 1875. In 1877 Mormons from Sanpete County joined them.

Huntington's early population was predominately male—ranchers setting up homesteads for their families. A story is told of the first dance held in the town, which took place in a Mr. Avery's log cabin, the only building with a wooden floor. Forty-two men and seven women came to dance; the men divided into six groups, and took turns dancing with the women.

As happened in other settlements in the area, Huntington residents soon discovered the rich coal deposits in the mountains west of Castle Valley. Coal-mine operations in lower Huntington Canyon brought some prosperity to the area; it also brought the influence of the outside world in the form of saloons. The women of Huntington decided to act on their hatred of the local saloon. Using bricks and stones, they assailed the offending establishment with such fury that the customers thought an earthquake had struck. Some of the men were so frightened they tried to climb the walls and hide in the attic. No one knows if the women were prosecuted, or if the saloon closed down.

Castle Valley has always been primarily farming and ranching country, and a mill was a necessity for the people who lived here. The Huntington Flour Mill's long service to the community is unusual: it has operated since 1896. People from all over Emery and Carbon Counties used the mill for many years to grind their wheat into flour. Located at 400 North, the mill continues to produce a variety of flour products.

Castle Dale and Orangeville

UT 10 continues south through Castle Valley, with the Wasatch Plateau on the west and the San Rafael Swell on the east, to Castle Dale. Mormon bishop Orange Seely was called to oversee the settlement of eastern Utah. Stories say he rode around visiting his flock on a mule, pulling another behind him laden with food to give to needy families.

In 1878 Sanpete County residents were called to settle the Castle Valley. They named their new home Castle Vale. Later, the settlement split into two towns: Orangeville, named for Orange Seely, and Castle Vale. United States postal officials made an error, changing Castle Vale to Castle Dale, and no one ever changed it back.

Naturally, some rivalry existed between Orangeville and Castle Dale. Most of the people in Orangeville came from Manti, where it was important to dress stylishly. The Castle Dale community, mainly from

Castle Dale City Hall.

Ephraim and Spring City, said the people from Orangeville "put everything they had on their backs." The Orangeville residents said the Castle Dale people put everything they had into their bellies. Castle Dale was made the Emery County seat.

This section of Utah was settled after 1869, which is the year some historians consider the end of the pioneer period because of the coming of the railroad. But the people who settled this new territory were very much pioneers; they faced trials comparable to those faced by the migrants crossing the plains. The trek from Sanpete County wasn't easy. When they arrived in the barren Castle Valley, the settlers didn't find enough trees for building, so they built their cabins of mud and straw adobe bricks. Some early brick structures remain today, with numerous additions tacked on.

Castle Dale grew for a number of years, but declined between 1940 and 1970. In recent years, energy-related industry has improved the economy of Castle Dale, and its population has topped 2,000.

Castle Dale is one of the gateway towns to the San Rafael Swell. A dirt road just north of town (near some large old corrals) leads into some of the most spectacular country in Utah.

Clawson

Seven miles south of Castle Dale, UT 10 passes through the hamlet of Clawson. Settled in 1897 between Ferron and Castle Dale, the town was named for Mormon apostle Rudger Clawson, who organized the town's first ward.

The original town was about two miles east of present-day Clawson. The settlers irrigated their farmland, but the water increased the soil's alkalinity and made it useless for agricultural purposes. In 1902 the residents wanted to move the town site to the west. They requested ecclesiastical advice, as was usual at the time. The Mormon bishop from Ferron, Bishop Nelson, came in his new buggy to help them decide. He drove west a couple of miles searching for the proper town site, climbing to the top of a hill to look around, but the clip on his singletree broke. He wired it together and started his horses off again, but the other clip broke. Deciding it was a sign, he appointed that very spot as the new town site.

Ferron

Continuing southward along the Wasatch Plateau, UT 10 arrives at a small town set against the backdrop of beautiful Ferron Canyon. The town and canyon were named for the man who surveyed the county before settlers arrived in the late 1870s.

Like all of southeastern Utah, Ferron was isolated from the more civilized areas where pioneer settlements abounded. Establishing a new community in the middle of the desert was no easy task. The first settlers arrived in Ferron in the late fall of 1877 and immediately set to work making dugouts and preparing an irrigation canal.

Early Ferron residents tried to enjoy themselves, even in the early, difficult days. The first Christmas was a time of merriment. The women did the best they could to make a feast with their limited provisions. To add some fun to the day, the men and women switched clothes, the wives dressing in their husbands' trousers and the men in their wives' dresses.

Life was still more work than play in Ferron, though. Men went away for weeks on end, herding cattle on the range. These cattlemen lost some of the more refined ways of their neighbors west of the mountains. They let their hair grow long and became rough in speech and manner like the rest of the cowboys. However, these men didn't stray from their belief in the Mormon Church. When their leaders called, they obeyed.

Emery

Muddy Creek, the town's first name, was settled by Spring City pioneers in 1879. Some didn't stay long because of the scarcity of water. Those who stayed tunnelled 1,200 feet through the mountain until they struck the Muddy River, which supplied them with ample irrigation water.

Emery residents discovered coal soon after they settled the town. A number of years passed, though, before coal mining became an important

The old clapboard church in Emery.

industry here. When the coal was determined to be of a high quality, mining operations began, providing much-needed cash to the town's agrarian economy.

Emery's LDS chapel, constructed in 1898, is the oldest church building in Emery County and the best example of the New England clapboard style in Utah. The building was used until 1956, when the church dedicated a new chapel in town. The city bought the original chapel for use as a town meeting and recreation hall.

I-70
UT 10–Colorado State Line
160 miles

In the 1970s and early 1980s, I-70 was built through the San Rafael Swell. This stretch of interstate is one of the most spectacular in Utah, if not in the United States. With its rock cliffs, gulches, ravines, and canyons, the swell has defied humans for centuries. Two terms are used in reference to this area. The San Rafael Swell is the entire area where a huge rocky uplift has eroded into cliffs, towers, buttes, and chasms. San Rafael Reef is the backbone of the swell, a long cliff that runs along the swell's eastern edge. Like a reef in the ocean, the cliff hindered those who tried to cross it.

Men who didn't want company have spent years in this landscape, and outlaws have found temporary refuge here. Numerous interesting but mostly forgotten characters have inhabited the area. The names they left on the swell's geographical features tickle the imagination: Secret Mesa, Oil Well Flat, Drowned Hole Draw, Jackass Benches, Cactus Flats, Eagle Canyon, Big Wild Horse Mesa, Old Woman Wash, Rattlesnake Bench, Blue Castle Canyon, Humbug Wash, and many more. In order to really experience the San Rafael Swell, take one of the numerous unpaved but graded roads that wander through the washes and canyons of this fascinating country.

URANIUM DAYS

Throughout the San Rafael Swell appear traces of old mines. These are not from a century past when the world was gold hungry, but from the 1950s when the nation wanted uranium. The region is rich in uranium. Old shacks, outhouses, and abandoned vehicles on dirt roads in the secluded canyons are reminders of a time when the southern part of Utah was thick with Geiger-counter-toting uranium miners searching for the ore that would make them rich. A few got wealthy, some later developed cancer, and all were out of a job before 1960.

BLACK BOX

One especially interesting feature of the swell is the Black Box, a dark canyon on the San Rafael River where a deep gorge has developed. A man named Sid Swazy inhabited these wild lands in the late 1800s. A bit of a daredevil, he leaped the chasm of the river on his horse at a point about three miles north of I-70's current path. The drop to the river was said to be about 100 feet at the time. Both man and horse survived to ride on to other amazing adventures. The spot is listed on some maps as Swazys Leap.

Crescent Junction

I-70 bypasses Green River, Utah, then crosses the river of the same name. Twenty miles after Green River, an exit affords an opportunity to visit Crescent Junction. In the 1920s entrepreneurs drilled for oil in the vicinity of Crescent Junction. Though they found some traces of oil and gas, they installed no permanent wells.

Crescent Junction was just a railroad stop until after World War II, when improved highways brought more cars, tourists, and freighting dollars to southeastern Utah. In 1947 Charles and Erma Wimmer built a service station at the junction of the two main highways. The station and subsequent cafe have expanded over the years to employ a staff of between nine and thirteen people.

Crescent Junction is now a service stop at the junction of I-70 and US 191 to Moab and southeastern Utah. The area has some service stations and a few residences near the businesses. The name comes from the crescent-shaped curve of the Book Cliffs to the north.

Thompson Springs

E. W. Thompson moved to the springs here sometime in the early 1880s. About the same time that Thompson set up housekeeping, the railroad came through and established an important stop about a mile from Thompson's home. This stop was the closest the railroad came to Moab, so Thompson Springs was a crucial stop for Moab and all points south and became a major loading site for cattle and sheep riding the trains. Numerous corrals were built, and soon hotels and saloons flourished as well. For a time anyone traveling to Moab had to get off in Thompson Springs.

With the coming and going of trains, Thompson was the site of excitement and activity—especially with a war on. During World War I, towns throughout Utah had to fill quotas for the armed forces. Many men were drafted; some volunteered for duty. After a farewell dance in Blanding for some boys bound for war, others felt the patriotic call and set off for Thompson Springs to catch a train to enlist. Some of the boys' girlfriends intercepted them before they got to the train and married them on the way home.

When the highway came through, filling stations sprang up at Thompson. Then, when I-70 was built in the 1970s, it bypassed Thompson, causing businesses to close. The one-room school in Thompson closed in 1962. Some gas stations and a few residents still inhabit Thompson, but the children are bussed to Moab to attend school.

US 191
Crescent Junction–Arizona State Line
179 miles

Twenty-five miles from Crescent Junction, US 191 leaves I-70 and travels through scenery too spectacular to ignore. The red rock cliffs and formations of Arches National Park are legendary. Visitors marvel at Dead Horse Point's fabulous plunge to the Colorado River. The chasms and rock walls of Canyonlands continue to defy four-wheel-drive enthusiasts, and the buttes of Monument Valley in the Four Corners have been the backdrop for more automobile commercials than anyone can count.

The history of this corner of the state is equally impressive. Centuries before anyone kept written records, Native Americans roamed the canyons and mountains of this area. The famous Mesa Verde National Park cliff houses are echoed in the lesser-known Anasazi dwellings at Hovenweep National Monument. Recorded history has passed down the journals of Spanish monks, who ventured through the canyons of the Colorado River in their quest for a better route to California. Mormon pioneers attempted to colonize this region—first in the failed Elk Mountain Mission to Moab, and later in the legendary Hole-in-the-Rock Mission to the valleys of the San Juan River. The struggles between white society and Indian cultures have been the overriding story of this land for the last 100 years. From its red cliffs to its rich history, this region is indeed rewarding to visit.

Dead Horse Point State Park

Twenty-one miles south of the junction of I-70 and US 191, UT 313 turns west toward Dead Horse Point. Millions of years of erosion have created some amazing geographical features in this region, and Dead

Horse Point is one of the most spectacular. A roughly football-shaped mesa, Dead Horse Point is connected with the rest of the upper plateau by a thirty-yard-wide neck of land. Around the perimeter of the point, vertical drops of up to 2,000 feet connect the top with the canyons of the Colorado River below. For many years bands of horses roamed the mesas around the Colorado River. The mesa made a convenient corral; cowboys had to fence only a thirty-yard section to keep the horses from running away. They selected the best horses, broke them, and sold them in eastern markets. One story tells of a group of culled mustangs left on the point with the fence open to find their way back to the open range. They never found the opening and died of thirst 2,000 feet above the Colorado River.

In more recent years this towering peninsula has become a recreation spot. Dead Horse Point State Park, established in 1959, affords one of the best views of the Colorado River available from a paved road. High above a gooseneck of the river, the park offers not only wonderful vistas of the river, but also of the surrounding countryside. A road on the high butte of Canyonlands National Park is accessible from Dead Horse Point, as are some unpaved roads into the depths of the river canyons. Dead Horse Point has an excellent campground and picnic areas.

Arches National Park

A dusty old log cabin and a root cellar hug the ground next to Salt Creek at the Delicate Arch trailhead in Arches National Park. John Wesley Wolfe and his family homesteaded this barren patch of earth in 1898. Wolfe, a Civil War veteran, was already getting on in years when he built the place on Salt Creek, and in 1910 he sold it to J. Marvin Turnbow. Turnbow later became custodian of Arches National Monument.

It was neither Wolfe nor Turnbow who first brought the grandeur of Arches to the public eye. A Hungarian immigrant and local prospector, Alexander Ringhoffer, stumbled on the place in 1922. So struck was he by the towering sandstone cliffs and over 500 arches, that he talked the Denver & Rio Grande Railroad into promoting the area as a tourist attraction.

Railroad officials subsequently pushed for national recognition, and in 1929 Herbert Hoover designated 4,500 acres as Arches National Monument. In 1938 President Franklin D. Roosevelt increased the acreage to 34,000. When President Richard Nixon made the monument a national park in 1971, it covered 73,233 acres.

Arches remains one of the least developed of the national parks. It has no lodges or restaurants within its boundaries. A paved road accesses the visitor center, campgrounds, and trailheads.

Moab

Spanish explorers first entered southeastern Utah in the eighteenth century, crossing the Colorado River near present-day Moab. This route became known as the Spanish Trail, and later other explorers and trappers used it. The valley where Moab was settled was known for many years as the Spanish Valley.

The Mormons were not immediately interested in the country around Moab, but in 1855 a group of forty-one men were sent on a mission to teach the Indians farming methods. The group, led by Alfred W. Billings, was commonly called the Elk Mountain Mission. They built a rock fort and planted crops. The soil was very fertile and farming was successful, but relations with the Indians were not always good. Though the Mormons baptized many Indians, most Utes resented the intrusion into their territory, where they had already been farming. When the Indians killed three of the Saints, the rest of the group decided that continuing the mission was too dangerous. The men only stayed a few months, then returned to Sanpete County.

Though the fort was abandoned, it remained intact, and various groups used it as they passed through the Spanish Valley. In 1877 William Granstaff and a man known only as "Frenchie" came into the area prospecting. (The locals called Granstaff, who was a black man, "Nigger Bill," and Negro Bill Canyon is named after him.) Bill had some cattle, and he and Frenchie

Ferry crossing the flooded Colorado River at Moab.
—UTAH STATE HISTORICAL SOCIETY

took over the fort, each living in half of it. Later that year the Rays came from Sanpete County, with their eight children and their cattle, looking for a place to make their home. They set up housekeeping at the fort until the following spring, when they headed for the south side of the La Sal Mountains and formed a permanent settlement.

In the spring of 1878 the LDS Church sent another family, the Wilsons, to begin the permanent settlement of Spanish Valley. A few other families joined them, and by the end of 1879, they had dug a ditch and begun a new life.

In 1880, when the new community petitioned for a post office, they chose the name Moab for their town. In the Old Testament, Moab is a remote place in the desert. Moses spent many years exiled from Egypt at Moab, working as a sheepherder. Another possible source for the name is the Paiute word *moapa*, meaning "mosquito." Millions of mosquitoes breed in the swamps near the Colorado River.

Life in Moab was not all hard times. In *Bounty*, Janet Alm Anderson quotes Lydia Taylor Skewes on the old-time dances held in Moab:

> They had dances down there, and everybody would bring their babies. And of course, everybody had a great big wool shawl they'd wrap them up in. They had one little room in the back where they always put their babies on a bed in there. One night Tom Trout got in there and changed all the babies around in different shawls, and of course when the women went in to get their babies, they'd picked up their shawl, but they had somebody else's baby. When my mother got home, she had Arthur Loveridge. My brother Peck . . . had big black eyes and was real dark, and Arthur Loveridge was redheaded and freckle-faced. . . . It took the women nearly all next day to go around and find their own babies.

Moab is one of only three places in Utah where a bridge crosses the Colorado River (the others are just south of Cisco and at Hite). Crossing the river was difficult and dangerous for early settlers. A ferry was built in Moab in the early 1880s, and the bridge was constructed in 1911.

Moab was struck hard by the terrible influenza epidemic that swept the world at the end of World War I. Though city officials imposed a strict quarantine of four days in a hotel room before anyone visiting town could mingle in public, the disease still came to Moab. By January an estimated 500 people—two-thirds of the population—had been infected with the virus. However, dedicated midwives, nurses, and doctors aided in most patients' recovery; less than a dozen people died in Moab during the epidemic.

Moab was a boomtown from the beginning. In the 1890s, gold discovered in the La Sal Mountains brought many people to the town. Though not many found gold, a lot of them stayed in the warm southern Utah town. In the 1910s a fruit boom hit Moab. Peaches measured twelve inches in circumference, and many prospective growers wanted to get in on the business. Grape production also exploded in the early part of the century. Unfortunately, circumstances were against the fruit grower in Moab: unpredictable frosts, flash floods, and expensive irrigation systems all worked against agricultural success. In the 1920s oil was discovered, bringing more residents to Moab.

The Uranium Boom

The biggest boom in Moab came in the 1950s with the discovery of uranium. The town became the headquarters of the southeastern Utah mining region. Prospectors searched everywhere for the mineral, some flying planes equipped with special Geiger counters. During the boom, Howard Balsley, one of the major proponents of uranium, kept one and a half tons of the yellow mineral in a shed in his backyard, just because he felt it was pretty.

The school population in Moab exploded from just 300 students to 2,000, bursting the budget. School was held in double sessions, two students sat at each desk, and all students shared books. The schools didn't have enough restrooms for all the students. Many families had come to the area after hearing a fortune could be made, only to lose what little they had when they couldn't find work. As a result, many children lived in horrible conditions, some without shelter or food.

In 1951, the U.S. government raised the price it would pay for 0.2 percent ore to $3.50 a pound to encourage uranium prospecting and mining. Government officials promised to buy all the uranium produced for at least eight years. Unfortunately, a lot of strings were attached to the promise, and many miners went hungry. By 1956 the government had quit encouraging uranium production, and in 1959 it announced it would only purchase reserves. The boom was over.

Uranium mining continued at a much slower pace through the 1960s. Another problem arose when the government failed to warn people of the dangers of the radioactive ore. By 1954 knowledge of uranium-associated health hazards spread, and the government began examining uranium mines. In the 1970s increased health problems among uranium miners finally brought an official acknowledgment of the danger.

The uranium boom lasted only five years and many of the prospectors left, but Moab was never the same little town again. Increased oil drilling helped maintain the economy, and potash was developed around Moab. Many evaporation ponds (some visible from Dead Horse Point) continue to operate around the town.

Sagebrush Rebellion

For a number of years southern Utah ranchers, developers, and other citizens have been wary of the federal government. They felt the U.S. government was butting in: taking over land and regulating affairs in southern Utah. Starting in 1934 with the Taylor Grazing Act (legislation intended to curb the severe overgrazing of the rangelands), individuals became increasingly resentful of government interference in their land decisions. National parks and monuments took substantially more area from the public domain. Then the Federal Land Policy and Management Act (FLPMA), passed in 1976, greatly restricted the uses of federal land and mandated that wilderness areas be reserved. This was too much for some people to endure passively.

In August 1979 the Bureau of Land Management set aside Negro Bill Canyon for wilderness consideration. The Grand County commissioners publicly proclaimed their opposition by tearing down the barricades at the entrance to the canyon. However, the area remained in the wilderness study. On July 4, 1980, all three county commissioners and 300 other concerned citizens met at the mouth of Negro Bill Canyon, and, with a bulldozer flying the U.S. flag, scraped a rough road (on an already existing older dirt road) 200 yards long. The Sagebrush Rebellion was born.

The government didn't do much more than bluster in response to the rebellion's outbreak. Angry words and accusations flew back and forth for years. The wilderness issue remains unresolved, though Negro Bill Canyon is still a likely candidate for wilderness designation.

Moab Today

Since the 1960s, when Canyonlands National Park was established, Moab has been at the center of the southern Utah tourist industry. With 325 sunny days a year, southern Utah is hard to beat for recreation. Motels, restaurants, gas stations, and other tourist-related businesses line Moab's streets. River rafting has become a major business; a flotilla of rafting companies offers everything from one-day outings to week-long excursions on the Colorado River.

Southeastern Utah contains some of the best and most famous slickrock country in the world. Thousands of people travel to Moab each year with their mountain bikes, dirt bikes, and all-terrain vehicles to defy the orange solid-sandstone hills in the surrounding countryside. Moab hosts the Jeep Safari, the Fat Tire Festival (for mountain bikers), and a number of other events that celebrate southern Utah's special attractions. In 1986 the Moab tourism industry promoted Moab's landfill as the "World's Most Scenic Dump," reasoning that if the world could only see the spectacular surroundings of Moab's dump, they would certainly come to see what other wonders the area held.

Hole-in-the-Rock

In the second half of the nineteenth century, southeastern Utah experienced an influx of non-Mormon cattlemen and miners. The arrivals alarmed LDS Church leaders, who wanted to keep outside influence and control to a minimum. In 1878, church leaders called a group of people to settle San Juan County, both to claim the land for Mormons and to act as a buffer between warring Utes and Navajos. The families that were called felt they were on a mission, and for many years they referred to themselves as the San Juan Mission. For this reason, they felt they needed extra spiritual force to accomplish their work—and they did encounter some of the most difficult obstacles faced by any pioneers before or since.

A scouting party left Parowan in the summer of 1878 to explore southeastern Utah for suitable locations for permanent settlement. They traveled by way of Lee's Ferry on the Colorado River, then continued up through northern Arizona to the San Juan River near present-day Aneth (following the approximate routes of US 89A and US 160). This route exposed them to heat, lack of water, and, especially, dangerous encounters with Navajos. Two families remained at Fort Montezuma on the San Juan River to prepare a colony. The rest of the expedition returned to Iron County to lead the larger group to the site. The two pioneer families spent a terrifying year of near-starvation, life-threatening dealings with the Navajos, and constant anxiety over why the main body of the party didn't arrive. Finally the colony disbanded.

The rest of the exploring party traveled home in a northerly direction, hoping to avoid the hostile Navajos they had encountered coming into the area. They passed the site of present-day Monticello then crossed the Colorado River near Moab.

When they arrived home, they advised the rest of the settlers to take a more direct route to southeastern Utah and to avoid Navajo country. Several expeditions went out looking for a different way across the Colorado River. Charles Hall, Andrew P. Schow, and Reuben Collett reported back on what they thought would be the most feasible crossing place. The spot they had found was a 100-foot-deep cleft in a rocky cliff through which the travelers would pass. However, the canyon rose 2,000 feet above the Colorado River, and the drop down to the water would entail clearing two sheer sixty-foot cliffs and rocky inclines of greater than forty-five degrees.

In the late fall of 1879, the company finally left Escalante with 70 families, 83 wagons, and 1,800 head of cattle and horses. Most of the families were young with small children. A few unmarried men and a very few older people joined them. The group faced terrible roads and the prospect of a river crossing that everyone said was impossible. The party camped at Forty-Mile Creek (forty miles from Escalante) and sent scouts ahead to explore.

When the scouts returned, they reported finding the cleft in the canyon wall, but said no one could build a road through it. Only one man said it might be done. By the time the reports came back, it was already December and winter had set in. Camped in the snowy wilderness, the travelers felt it was impossible to go either back or forward. But the company sincerely believed they were on a mission from God, and they voted to press forward, and raised their voices in the hymn "The Spirit of God like a Fire Is Burning." The wagons streamed out of Forty-Mile Creek toward the Colorado River, seventeen miles away.

When they reached the river, the majority of the group camped in front of the crevice in the great cliff, dubbed the Hole. Meanwhile, members of the party traveled back to Escalante for gunpowder and other supplies to widen the crevice and blast a rough track down the face of the cliff.

Hole-in-the-Rock.

Conditions were severe for those who stayed at the Hole. There were no grazing areas, water, or firewood for miles around, and the families and their livestock quickly exhausted the limited resources. The men tried lowering the horses down to the river where grazing was better, but after losing nine of their animals, they gave up. Nevertheless, they managed to survive on whatever food and water they could scrape out of the barren rocks and desert, and in moments of leisure they played their fiddles and danced on the slickrocks. The campers rejoiced when snowstorms came because the "tanks"—indentations in the rocks—caught water for them and their livestock. Families slept in (or even under) their wagons, some draping rag rugs over the top for extra warmth.

When the supply party returned, they set to work right away. Once they'd widened the Hole, they found a forty-five-foot sheer drop. The men working on that section had to be lowered down the drop on a rope to blast out a graded road. They cut dugways, or tracks, in the steepest spots to prevent the wagons from slipping down the cliffs.

On January 26, 1880, wagons started through the gap in the cliff. Ten men lowered each wagon through the Hole with ropes. The women and children slid down the upper portion of the drop because it was too steep to walk. By January 28, most of the wagons were through. Miraculously, no loss of animal or human life occurred in the descent.

Crossing the Colorado River itself was another treacherous experience. The wagons were ferried over, but some of the livestock had to swim across. Once across the river, they had to blast a new dugway out of the 250-foot rock wall on the other side. (That cliff, on which some of the San Juan Mission pioneers carved their names in the rock, along with parts of the road they built are now covered by the waters of Lake Powell.) As the party pushed on, sometimes in battering snowstorms, there was often little feed for the livestock. A number of large livestock companies had joined the group, and disputes erupted over grazing rights along the way.

After struggling for weeks through the slickrock country of the Colorado River, the weary settlers faced San Juan Hill, another sheer rock wall. Charles Redd, quoted in David E. Miller's *Hole in the Rock: An Epic in the Colonization of the Great American West*, told of his father's experience on the hill:

> Seven span of horses were used, so that when some of the horses were on their knees, fighting to get up to find a foothold, the still-erect horses could plunge upward against the sharp grade. On the worst slopes the men were forced to beat their jaded animals into giving all they had. After several pulls, rests and pulls, many of the horses took to spasms and near-convulsions so exhausted were they. By the time most of the

outfits were across, the worst stretches could easily be identified by the dried blood and matted hair from the forelegs of the struggling teams. My father was a strong man, and reluctant to display emotion; but, whenever in later years the full pathos of San Juan Hill was recalled either by himself or by someone else . . . he wept.

By the time the haggard group staggered into the little valley at Bluff, neither the people nor their animals could go any farther. Their food supplies were gone and their livestock were emaciated. Rather than push onward to Montezuma Creek, they decided to make their permanent home at Bluff. It had taken the party from February 1 until April 6, 1880, to travel from the Colorado River to Bluff.

The pioneers abandoned the Hole-in-the-Rock road in 1881, less than a year after its first use. At that time, Charles Hall moved his ferry up the Colorado River to approximately the point where the Hall's Crossing Marina is today. Miners used the Hole-in-the-Rock road in the 1880s and 1890s, however. Because they traveled on horseback instead of in wagons, the miners cut steps in the rock for their animals. In the late 1890s the Hole was widened by crews working for a gold-mining group. Today at the Hole-in-the-Rock historic site the drop to the Colorado River is not as far because of the elevated waters of Lake Powell. Still, those who cross the trail from Escalante and sit and reflect a few moments in the cool, still depths of the crevice are rewarded by the echoes of the creaking wagons, rattling hooves, and hopeful cries of the pioneers of over 100 years ago.

La Sal

South of Moab US 191 passes through some irrigated farmland and then enters red rock country. The La Sal Mountains straddle the Grand–San Juan County border near Colorado. They reach over 12,000 feet in altitude and are green and cool all summer long. A beautiful alpine drive winds from Moab around the west face of the La Sal Mountains, drops down into Castle Valley, then follows the Colorado River back to Moab. After the heat of the dry red desert, this drive feels like a drink of cool mountain water.

Farther down the road, UT 46 leads to La Sal. Founded after Aneth, La Sal was probably the second settlement in San Juan County. La Sal, which means "the salt," was the name given to the nearby mountains by early Spanish explorers. The first permanent settlers here were the Ray family and their eight children. Originally from Tennessee, they moved to California, then to Mount Pleasant, Utah, and finally herded their sixty milk cows to Moab, where they stopped for several months at the abandoned mission. Early in 1878 they headed out, seeking good pasture for their livestock, and ended up at La Sal. Soon other families moved there from Sanpete and Sevier Counties.

Because of the isolation and the hard life, pioneers had to be tough and self-reliant. Early settlers had to travel to Salina, 200 miles away, or to Durango, Colorado, 135 miles away, to get supplies. They made the trip once or twice a year, and everything had to last until they were able to go again. In 1883, when the San Juan County assessor traveled from Bluff to La Sal to collect property taxes, the independent frontiersmen met him with guns. After some negotiations, however, the people paid their taxes and the assessor departed.

In 1885 a group of investors seeking to make their fortunes in the cattle industry formed the Pittsburgh Cattle Company and bought out the largest ranches in La Sal. The original owners moved away. The company changed hands several times, and eventually the cattle were replaced with sheep.

A number of families came to the area between 1909 and 1916 to take up dry farming. Water was scarce, however, and only a few of the families remained permanently. In 1930 the town moved thirteen miles west to its present site because of the flash flooding that occurred during heavy rains. The uranium boom of the 1950s especially affected La Sal—major strikes were made near the town. However, like most booms, this one was followed by a bust and the town returned to its ranching emphasis.

Charles Redd was one of the dominant ranchers in La Sal, and the Redd family still has large holdings of cattle and sheep in the area, plus a large feedlot operation in Kansas.

Canyonlands National Park

Canyonlands National Park contains more inaccessible regions than any other Utah park. Two roads lead into the park from US 191, as well as one from Dead Horse Point and another from UT 24 west of the Colorado River. Roads in the park have for the most part remained unpaved. The first superintendent of Canyonlands, Bates Wilson, said "Come to our wilderness, but be ready to rough it." He didn't mention that if you intend to drive you ought to bring a few extra tires.

The majority of local residents did not welcome the creation of Canyonlands National Park. Opponents were too few in number to have any political clout, however, and the park was approved by Congress in 1964. Local opinions brightened when Moab residents learned they would benefit financially from park offices.

Monticello

US 191 quickly climbs from the valleys of the Colorado River to the higher mesas of southeastern Utah. The atmosphere is less touristy and more ranch-oriented. Like Thomas Jefferson's home in Monticello, Virginia, Monticello, Utah, is set in lush farming country in the foothills of the mountains. Utah's Monticello (pronounced Montisello) sits at the base of the Abajo Mountains, which were called the Blue Mountains in pioneer times. In 1878 the San Juan Mission's exploring party stopped near here on their way home to Parowan. One man caught seventy-five fish in Montezuma Creek and everyone feasted.

Patrick O'Donnell, the first white settler here, came in 1879. In 1887–88, the LDS Church called five families and twenty men from Bluff and the surrounding areas to settle the Blue Mountain Mission. The families farmed all summer and in the fall stored the grain they had harvested in a cabin. They hired a cowboy to guard it for the winter, which they spent in Bluff. However, both the grain and the cowboy disappeared before Christmas.

Cattlemen had used the region for several years before Mormon settlement. They resented the intrusion of the homesteaders and threatened to "annihilate" them. One of the Saints rode to Fort Lewis, Colorado, for help. He returned with fifty soldiers, who stayed until the next year, ensuring the peace of the new community.

The settlers of Monticello continued to have problems with cattle ranchers after the army left. A man named Carlisle who ranched upstream from the Mormons cut off their water supply. When the Monticello people tried to restore the water flow, Carlisle sent gunmen to make sure they did not. The new settlers refused to be intimidated, so Carlisle got a court order giving him rights to all the water in the North Fork of Montezuma Creek. Through eight years of court battles the settlers hauled water one and a half miles during the summer months, when the South Fork went dry, until the court gave them rights to half the water in the North Fork.

By 1889 only about fifteen families lived in Monticello. People were reluctant to settle here because of rumors that the entire county was going to be made an Indian reservation; even more daunting were the continual water problems and the constant harassment of the renegade cowboys. The cowhands on the surrounding ranches far outnumbered the townspeople. These cowboys delighted in frightening and intimidating the Mormons in any way possible. They rebranded their cattle and even killed hundreds of head of livestock. They rode drunk through town and shot out windows.

By the turn of the century the pioneers had worked out their water problems, and fears were allayed that all of San Juan County would become an Indian reservation. Gradually order was imposed on the lawless cowboys, and when the town was incorporated in 1910 it had a population of 365 people.

Hispanic people have a long tradition of sheepherding. As herds in southeastern Utah grew, local ranchers asked Spanish-speaking sheepherders from New Mexico to help them. At first the men came alone and returned south periodically to visit their families. Eventually, though, New Mexican families began moving into southeastern Utah, particularly Monticello. Many kept their own culture and language, and though their numbers have dwindled, some have remained.

Blanding

After Monticello, US 191 descends to Blanding, the last town of any size in Utah before the highway heads south into Arizona. Originally called Grayson, the maiden name of the wife of one of its founders, Walter Lyman, the town changed its name when in 1914 Thomas Bicknell promised his 1,000-volume library to any Utah town that would change its name to his. Thurber, Grayson's competitor, became Bicknell and split the library with Grayson, which became Blanding, the maiden name of Bicknell's wife.

In the 1880s several men traveling through decided the site was a perfect place for a town. Francis A. Hammond, San Juan Stake president, thought it the most beautiful place he had ever seen. Others were concerned that water would be too scarce, so Monticello was developed instead. When Walter Lyman saw the spot, he envisioned a lovely town, complete with a temple on the hill. When a friend asked him later how big the town was, Lyman wouldn't specify lest the friend think him crazy. He and his brothers built an irrigation canal to feed water to farms, marking the unofficial birth of the town in about 1902.

Between 1905 and 1910, Mormons fleeing the revolution in Mexico augmented Blanding's population greatly. These same families had gone to Mexico to escape antipolygamy persecution occurring in the United States.

Blanding has a history of cooperation among its residents. During the influenza epidemic of 1918–19, Blanding had its share of illness. When the owner of the Grayson Co-op caught the flu, customers stopped at his home to retrieve the key, got what they needed at his store, and paid him later. Though medical help was hard to come by, many willing neighbors and friends, and some trained midwives, nursed the sick. There are no records of how many contracted the disease or died in the epidemic.

Edge of the Cedars Park, Blanding.

In the mid-1950s, when the uranium boom hit southern Utah, the population of Blanding swelled again. The boom was brief, though, ending for the moment Blanding's dreams of a rich economy.

Today Blanding is a bustling community with many farms spreading out to the east. It offers travelers ample accommodations.

Edge of the Cedars Park

Edge of the Cedars park in blanding commemorates a site where early settlers found ancient ruins. Here, the Anasazi left traces of their lives—remains of homes, pottery, and other items—before they moved on. The park's museum houses a fine collection of Anasazi artifacts.

The Chief Posey Battle Site

On a small Indian reservation a few miles south of Blanding, a historical monument commemorates the last Indian-white battle in Utah. After a long series of conflicts, the Posey Battle broke out in 1923 when two Ute boys who had robbed a sheep camp escaped from the sheriff. A battle erupted in which Chief Posey, the leader of the tribe, was wounded. He eventually died of his wounds. Other members of the band were

The Posey Battle is considered the last Indian battle in this country. This photograph of Chief Posey's men was taken in 1915. —UTAH STATE HISTORICAL SOCIETY

captured and detained in Blanding. They were later disbanded and given land allotments in local canyons.

Bluff

On April 6, 1880, the first members of the Hole-in-the-Rock party arrived at Bluff. The narrow valley allowed little space for farming. Rather than split up the party, the members decided to have small farms and stay together. The settlers lived in a fort for protection until about 1884, when they moved out on their own lots.

The colony was beset with problems—Indians stealing horses, drought, harassment by renegade cowboys, and recurring irrigation failures. Because of the irrigation problems and the lack of land, many men were forced to seek employment in western Colorado. They found work in sawmills and on roads, railroads, and ranches and brought back much-needed cash and supplies. Many of the original settlers left Bluff, but others stayed after LDS Church leaders promised they would be blessed for sticking with their mission. However, after a few more years of struggle, the leaders released the people of Bluff from their mission and said they were free to move if they chose.

Bluff, looking southwest, November 5, 1895. —UTAH STATE HISTORICAL SOCIETY

In 1885 the Bluff residents organized the "Bluff Pool," in which they formed cooperative cattle herds that challenged the non-Mormons' dominance of rangelands. As a result, a period of relative prosperity came to Bluff. A number of large homes built between 1890 and 1910 offer enduring evidence of this prosperity. Construction on the San Juan County courthouse began in Bluff in 1893, but the building was never completed; the county seat was moved to Monticello in 1895. Out-migration depleted Bluff's population until only a few families remained.

From the time the Mormons colonized Utah, and even before, when Catholic monks traveled north through Utah, many religious faiths saw the territory as a place that desperately needed missionaries. This attitude continued well into the twentieth century, but the emphasis switched to missionary work among native populations. In 1943 the Episcopal Church built St. Christopher's Episcopal Indian Mission in Bluff. The mission, now run mostly by Navajos, continues to serve the people.

Though isolated, Bluff has enjoyed some of the benefits of the booming tourist industry. The town is an excellent jumping-off place for rafting on the San Juan River.

Navajo Reservation

The San Juan River, the northern boundary of traditional Navajo territory, is one of four rivers sacred to this southeastern Utah tribe. For many years the members of the Navajo nation were afraid to cross this river. Some tribal members still sprinkle corn pollen in the river for protection when they have to cross it.

In 1863 the U.S. government declared war on the Navajos. Kit Carson led 1,000 troops on an offensive through southeastern Utah that took thousands of Navajo prisoners. The Indians were held at Fort Sumner, New Mexico. Many of the them got sick and died before they were allowed to return to their native lands south of the San Juan River in 1868.

When the Navajos returned to their lands, their crops were shriveled and their livestock had died or wandered off. The only way they could survive was by raiding the scattered white settlements. The conflicts between the two ethnic groups increased in frequency, with both Indians and whites claiming the land north of the San Juan River. The only people with traditional rights to the area were the Utes, who had been pushed farther north.

In the 1880s proposals were discussed for making parts of San Juan County into reservations for the Paiute, Navajo, and Ute tribes. The area south of the San Juan River was given to the Navajos in 1884, but the rest of the reservation was still tentative. The U.S. Senate passed a bill giving most of the rest of San Juan County to the Ute and Paiute tribes. Before the bill could pass the House, though, various non-Indian groups successfully blocked it, and the reservations were put on hold, leaving the natives in a state of poverty. The white residents of the area, who had been in danger of losing their homes and farms, were relieved.

At one time during the San Juan County reservation debate, the Indian agent in Colorado gave the tribes permission to move onto lands throughout the county. The Indians came with their families and their herds of sheep, believing they were entitled to settle anywhere they wanted regardless of white settlements. They moved sheep onto land already being grazed, cutting fences and destroying property in the process, which infuriated white settlers. After several months of trouble on both sides, the Indians were called back to Colorado. Once again, promises had been made and broken. Finally, with the encouragement of Howard Antes, a Methodist minister in Aneth, the government deeded additional lands north of the San Juan River to the Navajo Reservation in 1905. Conflicts would continue, however, for several decades until final boundaries were established.

A Navajo round house at Oljato.

In the midst of the conflict over reservation location and size, the terrible influenza epidemic of 1918–19 struck the Navajos. The illness took a great toll among the white population, but it devastated the Indians. The Navajos customarily gathered in groups during times of crisis, often congregating in sweats, where they believed they could purge the disease from their bodies. Instead, they passed it on. In addition, the Navajo custom of burning the dwelling of the dead left whole families, many of them also sick, without adequate shelter. Approximately 2,000 Navajos in Utah and northern Arizona died in the epidemic.

In the 1950s new prosperity came to the Navajos in the form of mineral riches. Uranium was the first source of wealth mined from Navajo ground. Soon oil was discovered in the Aneth-Montezuma Creek area. For two decades oil companies controlled the oil and distributed royalties to the tribe. The Navajos felt the small cut they received from the oil companies cheated them of their rightful inheritance. In 1978 tribal members staged a takeover of the main Texaco pump station in Aneth. For three weeks production stopped, until oil companies agreed to increase benefits to tribal members. Despite the concession, tensions continue between the Navajos and the oil companies.

UT 163
Bluff–Arizona State Line
42 miles

Mexican Hat

In a country replete with colorful cliffs and peculiar geological features, it is not unusual to find a town named for a rock formation. Two and a half miles northeast of Mexican Hat is the hatlike rock that gave the town its name.

During an early oil boom 1,000 people lived in Mexican Hat; then the bust came and the population plummeted to one. During the uranium boom the town once again blossomed, then withered. In 1969 some mobile homes bolted together served as a motel. Currently Mexican Hat boasts several motels, two gas stations, and several restaurants and trading posts.

Mexican Hat is a popular jumping-off point for rafting through the Goosenecks of the San Juan River.

Monument Valley

Nearing the Arizona border, the huge stone monoliths of Monument Valley dwarf the reservation town of the same name. In 1923 Harry and "Mike" (his wife) Goulding founded a trading post here. They operated it for forty years, then deeded it to Knox College in Galesburg, Illinois,

Monument Valley.

Gouldings' Trading Post, Monument Valley, about 1945.
—UTAH STATE HISTORICAL SOCIETY

for a perpetual Navajo scholarship fund. They deeded more land to the Seventh-Day Adventists for a hospital that was built in 1958.

The Gouldings brought pictures of Monument Valley to Hollywood in 1938 to encourage filmmaking in the area. The results were John Ford's *Stagecoach*, *My Darling Clementine*, and *War Party*.

The Gouldings devoted much of their lives to helping the Navajos. Unfortunately the hospital facilities, much needed by the Navajos, had financial problems, and had to be closed.

UT 163 and UT 262
Bluff–Colorado State Line
34 miles

Prospectors searched for silver, gold, and copper in the San Juan region from the time it was settled, about 1880, until after the turn of the century. Some were successful, but most went away poorer than they had come. In the 1890s, prospectors discovered deposits of uranium, vanadium, and carnotite in the Four Corners area. Mining of these elements was fairly strong through the early 1920s, when a lull in demand occurred.

With the coming of World War II demand for the metals revived. The boom was short-lived, though, and the miners knew only a brief period of limited prosperity.

With the escalation of the cold war in the early 1950s, demand for uranium again increased. Hundreds of mines opened or reopened, uranium stock soared, and some miners finally made their fortunes. By 1956, however, the boom ended and stock prices fell drastically. Some uranium mining continued through the 1960s with the hope that nuclear power plants would require the mineral. That demand never developed, and uranium is no longer a desired element.

Montezuma Creek

UT 163 hugs the base of the bluffs along the San Juan River as it approaches this reservation town. Peter Shirts, an excommunicated Mormon, was the first white settler in the Montezuma Creek area. He arrived in 1877, along with his brother Carl and Carl's family. Carl and his family left because of tension with the Utes, but Peter returned after a brief retreat. Shirts left shortly after the Mormons came, and died in Mexico three years later.

Two families spent the winter here in 1879–80 while the rest of their party went back to Parowan to lead more settlers to the spot. The larger company, though, ended up at Bluff in April 1880, and it wasn't until September that several families joined the two already at Montezuma. William Hyde came with his family and opened a store. After several years of coping with isolation, river and crop problems, and the Indians, the settlers at Montezuma abandoned ship.

The Navajo Reservation annexed this area in 1933, and in 1953 Humble and Shell Oil Companies signed an agreement with Navajo tribes to pump oil from their lands. Today Montezuma Creek has an elementary school, a high school, a public swimming pool, a cafe, and several other businesses.

Aneth

Though not continuously occupied, Aneth was the first white settlement in San Juan County. For a number of centuries, the Aneth floodplain was an important area to the Navajos because of its agricultural usefulness. It was flat, accessible, and easy to water in times of drought. The Navajos transplanted prairie dogs into the area as an extra source of meat.

The Mitchells, a non-Mormon family, came from Colorado to farm here in 1877. They homesteaded some land just below where McElmo's Wash empties into the San Juan River (near present-day Aneth). They had difficulties getting water to their crops. In 1878 a group of young men sent from Parowan to investigate settlement locations in southeastern Utah stopped at the Mitchell farm. The Mitchells asked the scouts to help them build a dam, promising to share farmland with all those who did. The party did help the Mitchells, but soon moved downstream to Fort Montezuma. In 1884 the San Juan River washed away the Mitchells's home. After years of crop failure and difficulties with the Indians, they abandoned the site. Aneth was named by a Methodist missionary, Howard Antes, in 1895. In Hebrew, Aneth means "the answer." Antes and his family became great friends of the Navajos and were instrumental in the expansion of the reservation lands.

Hovenweep National Monument

Hovenweep, which means "deserted valley" in Ute, straddles the Utah-Colorado border. The fascinating ruins of ancient towers and granaries built around a ravine were occupied by the Anasazi Indians between A.D. 1200 and 1300.

Hovenweep National Monument.

UT 95
UT 24–US 191
80 miles

Goblin Valley

Cowboys ranged through this relatively unknown part of Utah for about forty years before some men from Green River trying to find a faster way to Cainesville officially discovered a strange valley. They told everybody about the unusual little "goblins" in the rocks. One of the men returned to the spot in the 1940s and took pictures, which he published in order to let people know about the rock formations. In 1965 Utah designated Goblin Valley, with its Entrada sandstone formations, a state reserve. The sandstone figures in the valley really do resemble playful goblins. Visit at a time when the sun is not too hot and clamor over the interesting little (and big) creatures.

Robbers' Roost Canyon

Toward the end of the nineteenth century cattle thieves came to work in Wayne County. They established a hideout between Hanksville and the Green River called Robbers' Roost. They stole cattle, changed the brands on them, then sold the animals to eastern cattle brokers. By about 1900 most of the rustlers had been caught, and the country was rid of them.

The rugged cliffs, swells, and mazes of southeastern Utah made a good hideout for the cattle thieves and outlaws of the nineteenth century. It would still be very difficult to locate a person who wanted to stay hidden here, even with four-wheel-drive vehicles and helicopters to help in the search. Entire cattle herds could easily be concealed in this stony wilderness.

Hite

Cass Hite, a former Civil War guerilla, outlaw, and prospector, came to this isolated locale in the 1870s. The spot was considered the best crossing on the Colorado River and was popularly called the "Dandy Crossing." Hite came here to prospect, and though he found an abundance of gold dust along the river, he never garnered enough ore to make him rich. When a ferry was established and a town built here between 1881 and 1883, the community took Hite's name. By 1889 Hite had a post office that served approximately 1,000 miners.

In the 1930s A. L. Chaffin ran a ferry here, powered by a Ford car that pulled cables attached to cliffs on either side of the river. In 1946 a road from Hanksville to Hite was completed.

The Hite ferry. —UTAH STATE HISTORICAL SOCIETY

The warm climate made the location ideal for farming, but because of the valley's extreme isolation and small area, Hite never drew many settlers. In 1949 nine families lived in what was considered a desolate place on the Colorado River. The uranium boom of the 1950s was not enough to make Hite into a town. The proposal to build a dam at Glen Canyon meant the end of the little outpost on the Colorado River that had been far from civilization and the law.

Today the waters at the north end of Lake Powell cover the original site of Hite. A full-service marina, an airport, and a campground, all part of the Glen Canyon National Recreation Area, occupy the northern lakeshore. A bridge on US 95 offers spectacular views of the Dirty Devil and Colorado River Canyons.

Fry Canyon

This is spectacular country, and every canyon and wash probably has a story to tell. Charlie Fry was an early prospector who lived in this canyon. He was more famous, though, as a horse thief. He had a herd of horses, and most of them were generally thought to be stolen. Because it is such an isolated spot, nobody knew Fry had died until some time later when they found his bones. Though the canyon was named for Fry, some people think the searing heat provides a more fitting reason for the name.

During the uranium boom of the 1950s, a lot of people came prospecting in Fry Canyon. Currently the canyon has a service station and grocery store.

Natural Bridges National Monument

From Fry Canyon, continue southeast on UT 95 and take UT 275 to Natural Bridges National Monument. Cass Hite, who was prospecting along the Colorado River in 1883, went on a hike up White Canyon and discovered three natural stone bridges. *National Geographic* magazine highlighted the wonders in 1904, and President Theodore Roosevelt designated the area a national monument in 1908. Today paved roads allow easy viewing of the bridges, though a hike down into the canyons yields even better vistas.

UT 276
UT 95–Natural Bridges National Monument
86 miles

An alternate route over the Colorado River crosses Lake Powell at Bullfrog Basin.

Ticaboo

Ticaboo is a Paiute word for "friendly." Ticaboo started as a uranium-mining town during the short boom of the 1950s. It was deserted for many years, but recently a lodge was built here that serves people going to Lake Powell. Ticaboo now has a number of full-time residents.

Bullfrog Basin

The name Bullfrog has become associated with Bullfrog Marina at Lake Powell, but it was a local moniker long before the Glen Canyon Dam was built. Bullfrog Creek (named, of course, for all the frogs in the creek) originates in the Henry Mountains and winds around until it drops down into the Colorado River—now Bullfrog Basin in Lake Powell. The marina was constructed in conjunction with the dam in the 1960s.

Hall's Crossing Marina

Charles Hall was a member of the famed Mormon Hole-in-the-Rock expedition to San Juan County in 1879–80. One of the party that explored plausible crossings of the Colorado River, he approved the hole high above the river where the party eventually dropped down the cliff. The Hole-in-the-Rock road was abandoned by the pioneers in 1881, less than a year after its first use. In its place, Hall established a ferry crossing at approximately the point where the Hall's Crossing Marina is today. He became the first permanent resident of Glen Canyon since the Anasazi lived here about 700 years before.

Selected References

Books and Articles

Alexander, Lana. "The History of Farr West." Manuscript, 1968. Daughters of the Utah Pioneers Library, Salt Lake City.

Alexander, Thomas G. *Utah, the Right Place: The Official Centennial History.* Salt Lake City: Gibbs Smith Publisher, 1995.

Allen, M. D. "History of Kingston." Manuscript, 1969. Utah State Historical Society Library, Salt Lake City.

Anderson, Mable. "History of Bothwell, Utah (Six Miles West of Tremonton, Utah)." Manuscript, 1975. Daughters of the Utah Pioneers Library, Salt Lake City.

Andrew, Lydia L. "History of Tremonton, Cache County, Utah." Manuscript, ca. 1970. Daughters of the Utah Pioneers Library, Salt Lake City.

Antrei, Albert C. T., and Ruth D. Scrow, eds. *The Other 49ers: A Topical History of Sanpete County, Utah, 1849–1983.* Salt Lake City: Western Epics, 1982.

Arrington, Leonard J. *Beet Sugar in the West: A History of the Utah-Idaho Sugar Company, 1891–1966.* Seattle: University of Washington Press, 1966.

———. *Brigham Young: American Moses.* New York: Alfred A. Knopf, 1985.

———. *Great Basin Kingdom: Economic History of the Latter-day Saints, 1830–1900.* Lincoln: University of Nebraska Press, 1958.

———. "Utah's Pioneer Beet Sugar Plant: The Lehi Factory of the Utah Sugar Company." *Utah Historical Quarterly* 60, no. 4 (spring 1966).

Athearn, Robert G. *The Denver and Rio Grande Western Railroad.* Lincoln: University of Nebraska Press, 1977.

———. *Union Pacific Country.* Lincoln: University of Nebraska Press, 1971.

Bachman, J. R. *Story of the Amalgamated Sugar Company, 1897–1961.* Caldwell, Idaho: Caxton Printers, 1962.

Barney, Lewis. "Personal History." Manuscript, n.d. Utah State Historical Society Library, Salt Lake City.

Brian, Donald Faust. "Notes on the Early History of Fremont Valley, Wayne County, State of Utah." Manuscript, 1917. Daughters of the Utah Pioneers Library, Salt Lake City.

Brown, Dee. *Hear the Lonesome Whistle Blow: Railroads in the West.* New York: Holt, Rinehart & Winston, 1977.

Buhler, Ruby Lee. "Localities History of Highland." Manuscript, 1991. Daughters of the Utah Pioneers Library, Salt Lake City.

Cache Valley Centennial Commission. *The History of a Valley: Cache Valley, Utah-Idaho.* Ed. Joel E. Ricks. Salt Lake City: Deseret News Publishing, 1956.

Carr, Stephen L. *The Historical Guide to Utah Ghost Towns.* Salt Lake City: Western Epics, 1972.

Carroll, Elsie Chamberlain. *History of Kane County*. Salt Lake City: Utah Printing, in association with the Kane County Daughters of the Utah Pioneers, 1960.

Carter, Harvey A., Rex R. Pugsley, and Norine K. Carter. "Park Valley, Utah." Manuscript, n.d. Daughters of the Utah Pioneers Library, Salt Lake City.

Casper, Warren O., and Jesse A. West. "Town of Bluffdale." Manuscript, 1963. Daughters of the Utah Pioneers Library, Salt Lake City.

Child, Blanche Mayberry. "Kanesville Wards Celebrate 100th Birthday." Manuscript, 1987. Daughters of the Utah Pioneers Library, Salt Lake City.

Chittenden, Hiram M. *The American Fur Trade of the Far West*. Vols. 1 and 2. 1902. Reprint, Lincoln: University of Nebraska Press, 1986.

Christensen, Beulah Nielsen. "Axtell, Sanpete County, Utah." Manuscript, 1979. Daughters of the Utah Pioneers Library, Salt Lake City.

Christensen, James P., Elias Anderson, and J. Walter Green. "History of Elwood, Utah." Manuscript, 1927. Daughters of the Utah Pioneers Library, Salt Lake City.

Cistercians of the Strict Observance, Order of. "Abbey of Our Lady of the Holy Trinity." Pamphlet. Trappist monastery, Huntsville, Utah.

Cline, Gloria Griffen. *Peter Skene Ogden and the Hudson's Bay Company*. Norman, Okla: University of Oklahoma Press, 1974.

Cook, Betty R. *Here Are the Counties of Utah*. N.p.: privately printed, 1983.

Crane, C. B. "Memories of Circleville, Utah." Manuscript, n.d. Utah State Historical Society Library, Salt Lake City.

Dalton, Luella Adams. *History of Iron County Mission, Parowan, Utah*. Salt Lake City: Daughters of the Utah Pioneers. 1962.

Daughters of the Utah Pioneers. *Daughters of the Utah Pioneers Marker Directory*. Salt Lake City: Daughters of the Utah Pioneers, 1990.

Daughters of the Utah Pioneers, Beaver County. *Monuments to Courage: A History of Beaver County*. Ed. Aird G. Merkley. Beaver: Milford News, 1948.

Daughters of the Utah Pioneers, Box Elder County. *History of Box Elder County 1851–1937*. Brigham City: privately printed, ca. 1938.

Daughters of the Utah Pioneers, Davis County. *East of Antelope Island: History of the First Fifty Years of Davis County*. 4th ed. Salt Lake City: Publishers Press, 1971.

Daughters of the Utah Pioneers, East and West. *Milestones of Millard: One Hundred Years of History of Millard County*. Ed. Stella H. Day and Sebrina C. Ekins. Springville: Art City Publishing, 1951.

Daughters of the Utah Pioneers, Emery County. *Castle Valley: A History of Emery County*. Ed. Stella McElprang. N.p.: privately printed, 1949.

Daughters of the Utah Pioneers, Garfield County. *Golden Nuggets of Pioneer Days: A History of Garfield County*. Panguitch, Utah: Garfield County News, 1949.

Daughters of the Utah Pioneers, Grand County. *Grand Memories*. Ed. Phyllis Cortes. Salt Lake City: Utah Printing, 1972.

Daughters of the Utah Pioneers, Salt Lake County. *Tales of a Triumphant People: A History of Salt Lake County, Utah, 1847–1900*. Salt Lake City: Stevens and Wallis Press, 1947.

Daughters of the Utah Pioneers, Summit County. *Echoes of Yesterday: Summit County Centennial History*. Comp. Marie Ross Peterson. Salt Lake City: privately printed, 1947.

Daughters of the Utah Pioneers, Tooele County. *History of Tooele County*. Salt Lake City: Publishers Press, 1961.

Daughters of the Utah Pioneers, Uintah County. *Builders of Uintah: A Centennial History of Uintah County 1872 to 1947*. Springville, Utah: Art City Publishing, 1947.

Daughters of the Utah Pioneers, Utah County. *Memories that Live. Utah County Centennial History*. Ed. Emma N. Huff. Springville, Utah: Art City Publishing, 1947.

Daughters of the Utah Pioneers, Wasatch County. *How Beautiful Upon the Mountains: A Centennial History of Wasatch County*. Ed. William James Mortimer. N.p.: privately printed, 1963.

Daughters of the Utah Pioneers, Washington County. *Under Dixie Sun: A History of Washington County by Those Who Loved Their Forebearers*. N.p.: privately printed, 1950.

Daughters of the Utah Pioneers, Wayne County. *Rainbow Views: A History of Wayne County*. 3d ed. Comp. Anne Snow. Springville, Utah: Art City Publishing, 1977.

De LaFosse, Peter H., ed. *Trailing the Pioneers: A Guide to Utah's Emigrant Trails, 1829–1869*. Logan, Utah: Utah State University Press, 1994.

DeVoto, Bernard. *Across the Wide Missouri*. New York: Bonanza Books, 1957.

Dietz, Sadie Morgan. "Locality History of Gosher, Utah." Manuscript, 1967. Daughters of the Utah Pioneers Library, Salt Lake City.

Dillman, Mildred Miles, ed. *Early History of Duchesne County*. Springville, Utah: Art City Publishing, n.d.

Dunham, Dick and Vivian. *Our Strip of Land: A History of Daggett County*. Manila, Utah: Daggett County Lions Club, 1947.

Ephraim Centennial Book Committee. *Ephraim's First One Hundred Years: 1854–1954*. Ephraim, Utah: Ephraim Centennial Book Committee, n.d.

Firmage, Richard A. *A History of Grand County*. Salt Lake City: Utah State Historical Society, 1996.

Gambles, Ruby B. Hansen Pratt. "Condensed History of Bear River City and Added Comments of Hans Hansen." Manuscript, n.d. Daughters of the Utah Pioneers Library, Salt Lake City.

Geary, Edward A. *A History of Emery County*. Utah Centennial County History Series. Salt Lake City: Utah State Historical Society, 1996.

Gowans, Fred R., and Eugene E. Campbell. *Fort Bridger: Island in the Wilderness*. Provo, Utah: Brigham Young University Press, 1975.

Hafen, LeRoy R. *Mountain Men and Fur Traders of the Far West*. Lincoln: University of Nebraska Press, 1965.

Harris, Mable. "History of the Town of Lindon, North Utah County." Manuscript, 1961. Daughters of the Utah Pioneers Library, Salt Lake City.

Hays, Ruth R. "The History of Portage, Utah, Box Elder County, Utah." Manuscript, 1977. Daughters of the Utah Pioneers Library, Salt Lake City.

Hedrick, U. P. *A History of Horticulture in America to 1860*. New York: Oxford University Press, 1950.

History of Sanpete and Emery Counties, Utah, with Sketches of Cities, Towns and Villages, Chronology of Important Events, Records of Indian Wars, Portraits of Prominent Persons, and Biographies of Representative Citizens. Ogden, Utah: W. H. Lever, 1898.

Horan, James D. *Desperate Men.* New York: Bonanza Books, 1959.

Hovey, M. R. "Millville, Cache County, Utah." Manuscript, n.d. Daughters of the Utah Pioneers Library, Salt Lake City.

Hunter, Milton R. *Brigham Young the Colonizer.* Independence, Mo.: Zion's Printing & Publishing, 1945.

Hunter, Milton R., ed. *Beneath Ben Lomond's Peak.* Salt Lake City: Publishers Press, 1966.

Irving, Washington. *Adventures of Captain Bonneville.* Portland, Ore.: Binfords and Mort, 1837.

"Join the UHF in Celebrating Historic Copperton." *Heritage: The Utah Heritage Foundation Newsletter* 30, no. 3 (May/June 1996).

Judd, Mary Grant. "Susa Young Gates." *The Relief Society Magazine* 20, no. 7. (July 1933).

Judkins, Lucille Child. "Riverdale, Weber County, Utah." Manuscript, 1972. Daughters of the Utah Pioneers Library, Salt Lake City.

Kane, Elizabeth Wood. *Twelve Mormon Homes, Visited in Succession on a Journey through Utah to Arizona.* Salt Lake City: Signature Books, 1974.

Kennecott Utah Copper. "Kennecott's Bingham Canyon Mine: The World's First Open-Pit Copper Mine." Pamphlet. Kennecott Utah Copper, Bingham, Utah.

King, V. "The Daily Journal of Kingston United Order." Manuscript, n.d. Utah State Historical Society Library, Salt Lake City.

Korns, J. Roderic, and Dale L. Morgan, eds. *West from Fort Bridger: The Pioneering of Immigrant Trails across Utah, 1846–1850.* Rev. Will Bagley and Harold Schindler. Logan, Utah: Utah State University Press, 1994.

Larson, Andrew Karl. *I Was Called to Dixie, the Virgin River Basin: Unique Experiences in Mormon Pioneering.* Salt Lake City: Deseret News Press, 1961.

Madsen, Carol Cornwall. "At Their Peril: Utah Law and the Case of Plural Wives, 1850–1900." *Western Historical Quarterly* 21 (November 1990).

Madsen, David B. and Brigham D. "One Man's Meat Is Another Man's Poison: A Revisionist View of the Seagull 'Miracle.'" *Nevada Historical Society Quarterly* 30 (fall 1987).

Martin, Russell. *A Story that Stands like a Dam: Glen Canyon and the Struggle for the Soul of the West.* New York: Henry Holt & Co., Owl Books, 1989.

McCune, Alice P. *History of Juab County.* Springville, Utah: Art City Publishing, in association with the Juab County Daughters of the Utah Pioneers, 1947.

McPherson, Robert S. "The Influenza Epidemic of 1918: A Cultural Response." *Utah Historical Quarterly* 58, no. 2 (spring 1990).

Medley, Florence B. "Colonization of Holladay, Salt Lake County, Utah." Manuscript, 1936. Daughters of the Utah Pioneers Library, Salt Lake City.

Miller, David E. *Hole-in-the-Rock: An Epic in the Colonization of the Great American West.* 2d ed. Salt Lake City: University of Utah Press, 1966.

Morgan, Dale L. *Jedediah Smith and the Opening of the West.* Lincoln: University of Nebraska Press, 1953.

Morgan Fine Arts Study Group, comp. *Mountains Conquered: The Story of Morgan with Biographies.* Morgan, Utah: Morgan County News Publishers, 1959.

Murphy, Miriam, ed. "Utah's Counties." *Beehive History* 14 (1988).

National Register of Historic Places. "Tampico Restaurant/165 Regent Street/169 Regent Street, Salt Lake City." Pamphlet. Utah State Historical Society, Salt Lake City.

Parson, Robert E. *A History of Rich County*. Utah Centennial County History Series. Salt Lake City: Utah State Historical Society, 1996.

Perkins, Cornelia Adams, Marian Gardner Nielson, and Lenora Butt Jones. *Saga of San Juan*. N.p.: privately printed by the San Juan County Daughters of the Utah Pioneers, 1957.

Peterson, Charles S. *Utah: A Bicentennial History*. New York: W. W. Norton & Co., 1977.

Poll, Richard D., et al., eds. *Utah's History*. Logan, Utah: Utah State University Press, 1989.

Poore, Janet J. "History of Community of Taylorsville." Manuscript, 1980. Daughters of the Utah Pioneers Library, Salt Lake City.

Powell, Allan Kent, ed. *Emery County: Reflections on Its Past and Future*. Salt Lake City: Utah State Historical Society, 1979.

———. *San Juan County, Utah: People, Resources, and History*. Salt Lake City: Utah State Historical Society, 1983.

———. *Utah History Encyclopedia*. Salt Lake City: University of Utah Press, 1994.

Pratt, Parley P. *Autobiography of Parley P. Pratt*. 1938. Reprint, Salt Lake City: Deseret Book Co., 1985.

Quaife, Milo M. *Kit Carson's Autobiography*. Lincoln: University of Nebraska Press, 1966.

Ramsey, H. H. "Utah State Training School." *Relief Society Magazine* 20, no. 1 (January 1933).

Reynolds, Thursey Jessen. *Centennial Echoes from Carbon County*. N.p.: privately printed by the Carbon County Daughters of the Utah Pioneers, 1948.

Richardson, Eunice H., et al. "History of Benjamin." Manuscript, 1939. Daughters of the Utah Pioneers Library, Salt Lake City.

Richfield Centennial Committee. *Golden Sheaves from a Rich Field, 1864–1964: A Centennial History of Richfield, Utah*. Ed. Pearl F. Jacobson. Richfield, Utah: Richfield Reaper Publishing, 1964.

Robertson, Frank C., and Beth Kay Harris. *Boom Towns of the Great Basin*. Denver: Sage Books, 1962.

Roland, Charles P. *Albert Sidney Johnston: Soldier of Three Republics*. Austin: University of Texas Press, 1964.

Roylance, Ward. *Utah: A Guide to the State*. Salt Lake City: Utah, a Guide to the State Foundation, 1982.

Russell, Osborne. *Journal of a Trapper, 1834–1843*. Ed. Aubrey Haines. 1914. Reprint, Lincoln: University of Nebraska Press, 1964.

Sessions, Colleen, ed. *Flood Fighters, 1983–84*. Bountiful, Utah: Carr Printing, 1984.

Sevier County Centennial Committee and Daughters of the Utah Pioneers, Sevier County. *Thru the Years: A Centennial History of Sevier County*. Ed. Irvin L. Warnock. Springville, Utah: Art City Publishing, 1947.

Stone, Irving. *Men to Match My Mountains: The Opening of the Far West, 1840–1900.* New York: Doubleday & Co., 1956.

Stott, Clifford L. *Search for Sanctuary: Brigham Young and the White Mountain Expedition.* Salt Lake City: University of Utah Press, 1984.

Stout, Hosea. *On the Mormon Frontier: The Diary of Hosea Stout, 1844–1861.* Ed. Juanita Brooks. Salt Lake City: University of Utah Press, 1964.

Tanner, Faun McConkie. *The Far Country: A Regional History of Moab and La Sal, Utah.* Salt Lake City: Olympus Publishing, 1976.

Thomson, Mildred Hatch. *Rich Memories, A History of Rich County: Some of the Happenings in Rich County from 1863 to 1960.* Springville, Utah: Art City Publishing, 1962.

Twain, Mark. *Roughing It.* New York: Harper & Row Publishers, 1959.

U. S. Department of the Interior Water and Power Resources Service. *Water and Power Resources Services.* Pamphlet. Washington, D.C., May 1981.

Utah Travel Council. *Utah! A Guide to the State.* Salt Lake City: Utah Travel Council, 1994.

Van Cott, John W. *Utah Place Names.* Salt Lake City: University of Utah Press, 1990.

Vestal, Stanley. *Jim Bridger: Mountain Man.* Lincoln: University of Nebraska Press, 1946.

———. *Joe Meek: The Merry Mountain Man.* Lincoln: University of Nebraska Press, 1952.

Warrum, Noble. *History of Utah.* Vol. 1. Chicago: S. J. Clarke Publishing, 1919.

Watson, Kaye C. *Life under the Horseshoe: A History of Spring City.* Salt Lake City: Publishers Press, 1987.

Winkler, Albert. "The Ute Mode of War in the Conflict of 1865–68." *Utah State Historical Quarterly* 60, no. 4 (fall 1992).

Newspapers

Deseret News

Garfield County News

Logan Herald Journal

Magna Times

Ogden Standard Examiner

Provo Daily Herald

Richfield Reaper

St. George Daily Spectrum

Salt Lake Tribune

Tooele Bulletin

Websites

www.celebsite.com/people/robertredford/index.html

www.osmond.com

Index

—CRAIG DIMONO

Cynthia Larsen Bennett was born in Utah to descendants of Mormon pioneers. She spent her school years in Michigan and Washington and earned her B.A. in humanities from Brigham Young University in 1981. That same year she married and settled in the Salt Lake area. Since then, Bennett and her husband, Keith, have "explored just about every square mile" of the state, and her love of the land, history, and people of Utah grew with each trip.

Ms. Bennett lives in Layton in the home she built with her architect husband. In addition to parenting her three children and helping run her husband's business, Bennett enjoys gardening, quilting, and cross-country skiing. *Roadside History of Utah*, her first book, "is the result of a lifetime of stories passed down from parents and grandparents . . . and seventeen years of in-depth exploration in this magnificent state."

We encourage you to patronize your local bookstore. Most stores will order any title they do not stock. You may also order directly from Mountain Press using the order form provided below or by calling our toll-free number and using your MasterCard or VISA. We will gladly send you a complete catalog upon request.

Other Roadside History titles:

_____Roadside History of Arizona	paper/$18.00	
_____Roadside History of Arkansas	paper/$18.00	cloth/$30.00
_____Roadside History of California	paper/$18.00	cloth/$30.00
_____Roadside History of Florida	paper/$18.00	cloth/$30.00
_____Roadside History of Idaho	paper/$18.00	cloth/$30.00
_____Roadside History of Montana	paper/$20.00	cloth/$32.00
_____Roadside History of Nebraska	paper/$18.00	cloth/$30.00
_____Roadside History of New Mexico	paper/$18.00	
_____Roadside History of Oklahoma	paper/$20.00	
_____Roadside History of Oregon	paper/$18.00	
_____Roadside History of South Dakota	paper/$18.00	cloth/$25.00
_____Roadside History of Texas	paper/$18.00	cloth/$30.00
_____Roadside History of Utah	paper/$18.00	cloth/$30.00
_____Roadside History of Vermont	paper/$15.00	
_____Roadside History of Wyoming	paper/$18.00	cloth/$30.00
_____Roadside History of Yellowstone Park	paper/$10.00	

Please include $3.00 per order to cover shipping and handling.

Send the books marked above. I enclose $ _____

Name _____

Address _____

City/State/Zip _____

☐ Payment enclosed (check or money order in U.S. funds)

Bill my: ☐ VISA   ☐ MasterCard   Expiration Date: _____

Card No. _____

Signature _____

MOUNTAIN PRESS PUBLISHING COMPANY
P.O. Box 2399 • Missoula, MT 59806
Order Toll Free 1-800-234-5308 • *Have your VISA or MasterCard ready.*
e-mail: mtnpress@montana.com • website: www.mtnpress.com